The Nazi Study of India and Indian
Anti-Colonialism

The Nazi Study of India and Indian Anti-Colonialism

Knowledge Providers and Propagandists in the 'Third Reich'

BAIJAYANTI ROY

OXFORD
UNIVERSITY PRESS

OXFORD
UNIVERSITY PRESS

Great Clarendon Street, Oxford, OX2 6DP,
United Kingdom

Oxford University Press is a department of the University of Oxford.
It furthers the University's objective of excellence in research, scholarship,
and education by publishing worldwide. Oxford is a registered trade mark of
Oxford University Press in the UK and in certain other countries

© Baijayanti Roy 2024

The moral rights of the author have been asserted

All rights reserved. No part of this publication may be reproduced, stored in
a retrieval system, or transmitted, in any form or by any means, without the
prior permission in writing of Oxford University Press, or as expressly permitted
by law, by licence or under terms agreed with the appropriate reprographics
rights organization. Enquiries concerning reproduction outside the scope of the
above should be sent to the Rights Department, Oxford University Press, at the
address above

You must not circulate this work in any other form
and you must impose this same condition on any acquirer

Published in the United States of America by Oxford University Press
198 Madison Avenue, New York, NY 10016, United States of America

British Library Cataloguing in Publication Data
Data available

Library of Congress Control Number: 2024936108

ISBN 9780192887542

DOI: 10.1093/9780191981951.001.0001

Printed and bound by
CPI Group (UK) Ltd, Croydon, CR0 4YY

Links to third party websites are provided by Oxford in good faith and
for information only. Oxford disclaims any responsibility for the materials
contained in any third party website referenced in this work.

MIX
Paper | Supporting
responsible forestry
FSC® C013604

Acknowledgements

This book took a decade in making. The reasons for this long gestation period are myriad, not the least among them being the outsider status of this writer in German academia and the controversies surrounding the subject of 'Indology in National Socialist Germany', the research project from which this study originated.

That the monograph could be written and published at all is due to the kindness and support of many individuals and organizations across several countries. Among them, my gratitude goes first and foremost to Professor Moritz Epple from the University of Frankfurt (*AG-Wissenschaftsgeschichte* or Working Group History of Science), for his interest in this contentious subject and for his invaluable guidance in writing a successful research grant proposal. Professor Epple has also helped by hosting a workshop related to the project which resulted in a publication as well as by giving me important feedback on my work. I also thank Professor Eli Franco (University of Leipzig) for his role as a cooperation partner in this project.

Of course, I am immensely thankful to the German Research Foundation (DFG) for approving the research project and providing us with a generous financial grant for three years.

It took me a fairly long time to reach Moritz. As I was despairing of the chances of pursuing this research due to the unresponsiveness that I received from different quarters, I had a rare stroke of luck. I chanced to meet Professor Patrick Olivelle, the famous scholar of ancient India. He has earned my lifelong gratitude for encouraging me and activating a network that included Dr Douglas McGetchin (Florida Atlantic University). I offer my heartiest thanks to Doug for his appreciation of my ideas, his constant kindness, expressed in various ways including reading and commenting on the most convoluted draft chapter of this book. Doug sent my research proposal to Professor Eric Kurlander (Stetson University). I am beholden to Eric for valuing my research proposal and referring me to Dr Fabian Link, who introduced me to Moritz. I cannot thank Fabian enough for this, as well as for critically reading one of the draft chapters of this book.

A primary impulse for this study is derived from the pioneering essay (1993) by the renowned scholar of Sanskrit, Sheldon Pollock. I am much obliged to Professor Pollock for reading the introduction to my book and offering his comments as well as reassurance.

I owe a large debt of gratitude to Professor Horst Junginger, who shared with me his unpublished talk on Indology in Nazi Germany which inspired this work to a great extent, as well as other archival resources from his collection. He also read my draft chapter on the Indian Legion which owes its origin to his suggestion.

My special thanks are extended to Professor Amar Farooqui of Delhi University for reading another draft chapter and for boosting my morale. Maria Framke, who has often been my academic pathfinder, kindly read a chapter and gave me useful insights. Jan Kuhlmann, whose book on Subhas Chandra Bose has been a treasured reference point for this monograph, readily shared his archival records on the Indian Legion with me.

I offer my heartfelt thanks to a number of other academics for their acts of kindness like supplying me with materials and inviting me to talk and write on my research. Among them are Professor Hermann Kulke, Dr Heiko Frese, Professor Hans Harder, Professor Heike Oberlin, Professor Carmen Brandt, Dr Heike Liebau, Dr Anandita Bajpai, Dr Serge Reubi, Dr Michael Fahlbusch, Dr Urvi Mukhopadhyay, and Kaushik Saha.

It is impossible to overstate the importance of having helpful colleagues. I am grateful to the late Dr Linda Richter, who drew my attention to an important archive in Berlin before her untimely death. Different kinds of collegial support and assistance were provided by Dr Falk Müller, Frederike Odenwald, Judith Delombre, and Nelli Kisser, as well as Professor Annette Warner (Imhausen) and Dr Dahlia Bawanypeck, all from the *AG Wissenschaftsgeschichte* at the University of Frankfurt. I also thank Dr Andrea Luithle-Hardenberg from the department of Ethnology for providing information on aspects of Jainism.

The academic peers from other universities who I would like to thank for their camaraderie include Dr Isabella Schwaderer, Dr Gerdien Jonker, Dr Cornelia Haas, Professor Julian Strube, Professor Christian Spang, and Divyaraj Amiya. I am particularly thankful to Dr Margrit Pernau for her encouragement, sympathy, and help.

My special gratitude is extended to Matthew Cotton of Oxford University Press for his faith in my book proposal, as well as to the unknown reviewers for their overwhelmingly positive reaction to the proposal and the manuscript. Imogene Haslam, my editor, has been a patient guide in this journey. I am very thankful to her. Manimegalai Devi has earned my profound thankfulness for her competence in managing the production process. I also thank Fathima R.F., Aalia Shaikh, and Mohammad Irfan for translating Urdu texts for me.

Assistance, often unsolicited and going beyond mere professional necessities, came from various colleagues at the different archives and libraries spanning Germany, England, India, and Poland. Among them, the colleagues from the archive of the Institute of Contemporary History and the Bavarian Main State Archives in Munich as well as those at the Federal Archives of Berlin deserve special mention. Dr Eleonore Schmitt facilitated my access to the library of the South Asia Institute at the University of Heidelberg, for which I am especially grateful to her. I also thank Dr Bert Pampel, director of the Document Center Dresden, who was very kind in providing me detailed answers about the life of an Indologist. My gratitude is extended to Leszek Krawiec from the archives of the University of Wroclaw and Dr Wojciech Płosa from The State Museum Auschwitz-Birkenau in Oświęcim for their prompt and kind replies to my queries.

A number of family members have provided me a home during my periods of research. I would not have been able to work so extensively at the British Library without the generosity of my sister-in-law Dr Nilanjana Sengupta and her husband, Dr Samrat Sengupta. My aunt Shubha Chaudhuri hosted me for a long time in Delhi, relinquishing her bedroom to me. She, her mother (and my grand aunt) Ira Chaudhuri, and the late Gautam Hemmady gave me a home full of warmth and fun for those weeks.

Some of my good friends have been, as such friends tend to be, inestimable sources of support. Professor Lorenz Rumpf from the University of Frankfurt has been a pillar of strength from the time when I was working on my PhD. He has continued to provide me precious academic and emotional assistance during my work on this book. Professor Suchetana Chattopadhyay (Jadavpur University) Kolkata, one of my oldest and closest friends, has helped and motivated me in every possible way.

The extended circle of friends and family members who afforded me comfort and hospitality during various research trips include Urmila De Banerjee and Professor Anindya Banerjee in Oxford, Dr Tapti Roy and Animesh Basu in Cambridge, and Dr Ramita Dey, also in Cambridge. My cousins Professor Maitreesh Ghatak, Dr Manishita Dass, and Tinni Mukherjee arranged for wonderful evenings with great food in London to refresh me after my long hours at the British Library. My old friends, Dr Sharmi Chakraborty, Shohini Majumdar, Madhuparna Banerjee, and Indrani Chatterjee gave me vital doses of succour while I was researching in Kolkata. Professor Suranjan Das, my former professor at the University of Calcutta who has always encouraged me to take up research, reassured me during this research trip to Kolkata.

Nearer home, Dr Subir Mitra and Sharmila Ghosh of Mainz have been steady sources of encouragement. In fact, without their persuasion, I would never have dared to step out of my role as an immigrant wife and mother at a relatively late stage of my life. Dr Madhusree Mukherjee offered me books, solidarity, and great lunches during her visits to Frankfurt from New York.

Virtual support from friends and family have enriched me and enabled me to cope with the solitary vocation of research and writing. Brother-in-law Supriyo Sen sent me relevant books and encouragement from Toronto. Brother-in-law Sumit Roy from New York took an active interest in my work and endorsed some of the political convictions which inform my work. Professor Anustup Basu

(University of Illinois, Urbana-Champaign) bolstered my confidence through his appreciation of my publications and ideas.

I have derived the greatest incentive for working on this book from the memory of my late parents, Professor Aniruddha Ray and Dr Indrani Ray, both famous historians. I have not inherited their acumen, but I consider myself fortunate to have received a share of their intellectual curiosity.

It is, however, my immediate family, comprising my husband Anup Roy and our children Ishani and Anish, to whom I am most in debt. They had to deal with my long and frequent physical absences as well as my emotional unavailability at times when I was too immersed in the entanglements between knowledge of India and Nazi politics. Anup has not only shouldered extra responsibilities, both domestic and financial, without complaining. He has also contributed to my work by translating many Hindi texts. Though I could not always provide them with necessary guidance during their formative years, Ishani and Anish have evolved into intellectually vibrant and humane adults, for which I am grateful to them.

The three of them reacted to the vicissitudes of my moods, which reflected my progress and occasional stumbling in this long and winding road, with understanding and good humour. I dedicate this book to them.

Baijayanti Roy

Frankfurt am Main

Contents

List of Figures

List of Abbreviations

AF	*Auslandswissenschaftliches Institut*/Institute for the Study of Foreign Countries
AH	*Ausland Hochschule*/Academy for the Study of Foreign Countries
AHU	Archive of the Humboldt University
ALMW Halle	Franckesche Stiftungen zu Halle (Francke Foundations in Halle)
AMU	Aligarh Muslim University
APMA-B	Archives of the Auschwitz-Birkenau State Museum in Oświęcim (*Archiwum Państwowego Muzeum Auschwitz-Birkenau w Oświęcimiu*)
AUW	Archive of the University of Wroclaw
BA	*Bundesarchiv*/Federal Archives
BA MA	*Bundesarchiv Militärarchiv*/Federal Military Archives
BayHstA	*Bayerisches Hauptstaatsarchiv*/Bavarian Main State Archive
DA	*Deutsche Akademie*/German Academy
DAWI	*Deutsche Auslandswissenschaftliches Institut*/German Institute for the Study of Foreign Countries
DKLV	*Deutsche Kultur im Leben der Völker – Mitteilungen der Akademie zur Wissenschaftlichen Erforschung und zur Pflege des Deutschtums – Deutsche Akademie*
DMG	*Deutsche Morgenländische Gesellschaft*
DOV	*Deutsche Orient Verein*
EKIR	Archives of the Evangelical Church of Rhineland (*Archiv der Evangelischen Kirche, Rheinland*)
FIC	Free India Centre
FMSS	*Förderndes Mitglied der SS*/Patron member of the SS
GstAPK	*Geheimesstaatsarchiv Preußischer Kulturbesitz* (Secret State Archives Prussian Cultural Heritage Foundation)
HfP	*Hochschule für Politik*/Academy for Politics
IIC	India Independence Committee
INC	Indian National Congress
IOR	India Office Records
NAI	National Archives of India
NAUK	National Archives, UK
NfO	Nachrichtenstelle für den Orient
NKVD	*Narodny Komissariat Vnutrennikh Del*/People's Commissariat of Internal Affairs
NRW	North Rhine Westphalia
NS	National Socialist
NSDAP	*Nationalsozialistische Deutsche Arbeiterpartei*/Nazi Party

NSDB	*Nationalsozialister Dozentenbund*/National Socialist Lecturers' Association
NSKK	*Nationalsozialistische Kraftfahrerkorps*/National Socialist motorized section
NSLB	*Nationalsozialister Lehrerbund*/National Socialist Teachers' Association
NSV	*Nationalsozialistische Volkswohlfahrt*/Nazi Party's welfare organisation
NWFP	North West Frontier Province
OKH	*Oberkommando des Heeres*/High Command of the Army
OKW	*Oberkommando Wehrmacht*/the High Command of the German Armed Forces
PA-AA	*Politisches Archiv Auswärtigen Amtes*/Political Archive of the Foreign Ministry
PK	*Propaganda Kompanie*/Propaganda Unit
RfD	*Reichsfachschaft für das Dolmetscherwesen*/Council for professional interpreters
RLB	*Reichsluftschutzbund*/National Air Raid Protection League
RSHA	*Reichssicherheitshauptamt*/Reich Security Main Office
SA	*Sturmabteilung*
SaHStA	*Sächsisches Hauptstaatsarchiv* (The Main State Archives of Saxony)
SD	*Sicherheitsdienst*
SPD	*Sozialdemokratische Partei Deutschlands*/Social Democratic Party of Germany
SRI	*Sonderreferat Indien*/Special Department India
SS	*Schutzstaffel*
StSG-*DokStSl*	*Stiftung Sächsische Gedenkstätten, Dokumentationsstelle Dresden* (Saxony Memorial Foundation, Document Center, Dresden)
UAB	University Archive, Bonn
UAHW	University Archive, Halle-Wittemberg
UAM	University Archive Münster
VDA	*Verein für das deutschtum ins Ausland*/Association for the Conservation of German Culture Abroad
WBSA	West Bengal State Archives
ZfP	*Zeitschrift für Politik*/Journal for Politics

Introduction

satyaṃ brūyāt priyaṃ brūyān na brūyāt satyam apriyam

He shall say what is true; and he shall say what is agreeable; he shall not say what is true but disagreeable.

Manusmriti. Verse 4.138.[1]

Fools rush in where angels fear to tread. This proverb is a perfect description of this Indian-origin woman's ambition to research the contentious subject of the trajectory of Indian Studies, particularly of its purveyors, in Nazi Germany. I will spare the readers the saga of my lonely and arduous battle to secure the resources necessary for conducting this research project in an academic space that is not yet ready to have a non-normative woman intellectually engaging with the darkest chapter of German history, not to mention critically examining the concealed or forgotten connections of German scholars of India with Nazi politics. A long search followed by an extraordinary amount of good fortune led to the German Research Foundation's decision that this project was worth funding. Do I dare to hope that times have begun to change? That more scholars of non-European origin will write on European history, overturning centuries of Orientalist tradition?

Research on the history of the natural sciences, as they were studied in various German universities and institutions under National Socialist rule, has gathered momentum from the 1990s, though a pioneering survey by Herbert Mehrtens was published as early as in 1980.[2] However, academic studies of subjects belonging to the 'humanities' under Nazi rule have accelerated only in this millennium. Most scholarly works on the humanities in Nazi Germany have focused on 'major' disciplines such as history, literary studies, or philosophy and their practitioners in universities.[3] This body of research has noted that certain discourses prevalent in these academic fields had an essential theoretical affinity with some of the dominant ideological precepts of the Nazi state. This intersection of ideas and influences was brought to the fore by some prominent academics.

Relatively little scholarly attention has been provided to those disciplinary areas which are either considered niche subjects, or whose methods and contents were used simultaneously by several academic disciplines. Indology in Germany is such a subject, whose trajectory under National Socialism has not yet been analysed in detail. The present monograph, a product of the project titled 'Indology in National Socialist Germany', supported by the German Research

Foundation (DFG) and conducted under Professor Moritz Epple at the Working Group, History of Science (*AG Wissenschaftsgeschichte*) at the Goethe University, Frankfurt am Main from 2018 to 2021, is the first systematic attempt to address this lacuna.

Despite the title of the research project from which it originated, the focus of this book is not narrowed down to the discipline of Indology as it is understood in the German academic tradition, in which the term is generally used to represent a broad category encompassing a number of fields concerned with the study of literary cultures, primarily of ancient India. Although some German-speaking universities had established professorships exclusively for Sanskrit/Indology from the early nineteenth century onwards, different kinds of ancient Indian literatures (religious, philosophical, historical, cultural) were studied as part of the syllabi in various disciplines including comparative linguistics (*Vergleichende Sprachwissenschaft*), ancient history and archaeology (*Altertumskunde*), religious studies (*Religionswissenschaft*) as well as disciplines that assumed political significance in the Nazi era, like *Rassenkunde* and *Völkerkunde*.

This book presents four organizations as case studies to examine the ways in which knowledge pertaining to India's modern history and contemporary politics were used by a number of Indologists and other scholars, non-academic 'India experts' and some Indian anti-colonial intellectuals to fulfil certain political goals of Nazi Germany. Hence, this study desists from using the term Indology except in specific cases. It employs the more generic 'knowledge of India' instead. Similarly, the term Indologist has been applied solely to scholars who specialized (in their doctoral dissertation and *Habilitation*, the second thesis required by German Universities for professorships) on subjects related exclusively to India (Vedic Sanskrit, Indian religions and scripts, and so on).

Strand of Research

It is well known that in his semantic work 'Orientalism', Edward Said had claimed that by 1830, German scholarship on the 'Orient' was pre-eminent in Europe, despite the absence of a 'national interest in the Orient'. According to Said, the German orientalists claimed to possess 'intellectual authority' over the Orient, much like their colleagues in England and France. However, unlike the British and French Orientalists who validated the imperialist ventures, the 'German Orient was almost exclusively a scholarly, or at least, a classical, Orient'.[4] It is also well known that Said's 'Orientalism' was concerned predominantly with the 'Islamic Orient' in the Middle East and North Africa. India played a relatively peripheral role in this classic work.

In the last few decades, several studies focusing exclusively on the history of German scholarly interest in India have emerged. These studies point out that

German academic engagement with Sanskrit and ancient India was not always motivated by a scholarly quest for disinterested knowledge. In the early nineteenth century, acquiring knowledge of the Sanskrit Orient was linked to a search for self-discovery, inspired by German Romanticism. Mastering Sanskrit also carried connotations of a difficult intellectual accomplishment. Thus, the devil invoked by the foremost poet of German Romanticism, Heinrich Heine, in his 'Book of Songs' (*Buch der Lieder*) from 1827 looked pale from his efforts to learn Sanskrit and read Hegel at the same time.[5] Studying the abstractions presented by the pre-eminent German philosopher and learning the Devanagari alphabets were thus complementary aspects of the intellectual profile of an ideal German *gelehrte* (erudite).

During the latter half of nineteenth century, this intellectual exercise often became a part of the burgeoning German nationalism and the search for a politicized German identity.[6] Sanskrit, which was by then established as a part of 'Indo-Germanic' linguistics, could 'be used effectively at the university to strengthen the hegemonic claims of German'.[7] The nationalist venture to discover, or rather fashion, a German identity began to entail establishing the superiority of the German language and a concomitant attempt to trace German ancestry to the Vedic/Indo-German/Indo-Aryan civilization, which was older than both the Judeo-Christian and the Greco-Roman ones in which the Germans felt marginalized.

The role of Sanskrit and Vedic India in forming a racialized cultural past for contemporary Germans has been recounted by various scholars and does not need to be elaborated upon here.[8] What concerns us is the contribution of some nineteenth-century German scholars to the Aryan discourse by appropriating India's ancient past and excluding Indians from it. This discourse propagated the racialized myth about an 'Aryan invasion and conquest' of India and equated the 'victorious Aryans' with blond and blue-eyed Europeans who were identified as 'racial ancestors' of modern Germans. These 'heroic Aryans' supposedly subjugated the dark-skinned aboriginals and established a primordial Aryan/Vedic civilization in the Indian subcontinent. The purported hallmark of this civilization was the 'pure Aryan' Sanskrit language which was devoid of any trace of 'Semitic' (and aboriginal) influence.[9]

Philology, including Sanskrit, thus had a significant role to play in the evolution of this racialized Aryan discourse. Though by the early twentieth century the emergent discipline of anthropology and 'race science' constructed the 'Aryans' as a biological and ethnological entity, the racialized philological discourse did not lose its relevance completely.[10] The notion of 'Aryan India' continued to be invoked after the disaster of the First World War, particularly by some young German scholars engaging in the study of ancient India, which seemed to provide them a refuge from the alienation that they felt from their dispirited social ambience permeated by what they considered to be a tired Protestant Christian tradition. These scholars projected their longings for a rejuvenated Germany on to an imagined 'Aryan India' which they construed as a vigorous, 'racially pure', intellectually and spiritually brilliant utopia. Such scholars included Jakob Wilhelm Hauer (1881–1962), who specialized in ancient Indian religion and yoga and Walther Wüst (1901–1993), an expert on Vedic linguistics. Both of them would later see in the Nazi ideology and politics the possibility of the fulfilment of their dreams of a resuscitated German nation. Wüst as well as Hauer thus went on to use their 'expertise in Aryan philology and religion in order to authenticate and even substantiate the ideology of National Socialism'.[11]

It is pertinent here to remind ourselves of the spurious nature of such imaginings and interpretations of 'Aryan India'. Recent research conducted on the earliest Veda or the Rig Veda as well as in the former sites of 'Aryan settlement' negates the idea of an 'Aryan invasion', suggesting instead a gradual transmigration of pastoral groups from central Asia in the northern areas of the Indian subcontinent and Iran, between 1500 and 1200 BCE. It has also been established by scholars that Rig Veda, a liturgical composition, contains non Indo-Aryan linguistic forms, denoting a commingling of the migrants with the indigenous population from the earliest times. Moreover, from the early centuries of the Common Era, the popularity of Puranic Hinduism, which included rituals and beliefs from various non-Vedic sources, exceeded that of the Vedic texts.[12] This interdisciplinary research confirms that the 'primordial and pure Aryan past' of India is simply a product of cultural and political wistfulness.

Another aspect that we should remember is that even prior to 1933, the humanities in Germany were dominated by professors with conservative nationalist leanings who disapproved of the democratic values symbolized by the Weimar Republic.[13] Anti-Semitic prejudices and 'angry nationalism' were also a part of this 'anti-Weimar' ambience at many universities. After 1933, sundry professors accepted and supported measures like the purge of Jewish and leftist academics and readily sacrificed their academic ideals for the sake of the 'political university' that was meant to support Nazi ideology and goals.[14] Many university-educated 'India experts' belonged to this political–ideological milieu.

Sheldon Pollock and the Politics of Indology's Past

This background knowledge is essential, since the issue of German Indology's deployment of the knowledge of 'Aryan India' to validate Nazi racial politics is central to most of the extant scholarly works which address the connections between Indian studies and Nazi politics. The most comprehensive analysis of the subject has been made by Sheldon Pollock in an article published in 1993. Pollock claimed that 'Sanskritists in the NS [National Socialist] state' functioned as 'experts in legitimation' by 'extrapolating and deepening' the existing myth of

Aryan origin as well as other aspects of 'philological and historical Indology' to answer the regime's search for authenticity.[15] 'The search for German identity and NS self-legitimation in the Aryan past' was provided, according to Pollock, through Indological texts written by the aforementioned Wüst and Hauer as well as others like Paul Thieme (1905–2001) and Erich Frauwallner (1898–1974).[16] Apart from singling out a number of texts which used the knowledge of 'Aryan India' to validate Nazi ideology, Pollock offered examples of 'academic-political discursive formations' by adding empirical research on the political affiliations of the writers.

Pollock's essay raised a vehement controversy in the German academia that is yet to be resolved. Notably, it took almost a decade for a German adaptation of the part of the essay that dealt with German Indology and Nazism, to appear. The German text, published in 2002, was suitably titled *Ex Oriente Nox* to highlight India-centred Orientalism's contribution to the most tenebrous years in German history.[17] Among Pollock's detractors, the most vociferous is Reinhold Grünendahl, who has repeatedly excoriated not only Pollock but also other 'post-Orientalists' like Suzanne Marchand and Douglas McGetchin for their critical studies of German Orientalism and Indology.[18] Grünendahl provides the following critiques against what he terms 'an American discourse': (i) German Indology was (and still is) an objective science, impervious to all ideological influences, (ii) Pollock misrepresented and manipulated the available data in the service of his predetermined theories, which include Michel Foucault's critique of authority/domination (*Herrschaft*) as well as Edward Said's use of the knowledge/power discourse from his 'Orientalism',[19] (iii) contrary to Pollock's integrated approach, one should distinguish between a scholar's 'Indological/academic' writings and their 'popular' and 'official' writings (memos, reports, and propaganda) and separate their 'personal politics' from their scholarly personae.[20]

Over the years, this controversy has become a multi-frontal and constantly mutating academic debate involving interventions in Pollock's support (e.g. by Vishwa Adluri in an essay published in 2011).[21] However, subsequently Adluri, together with Joydeep Bagchee protested against Pollock's acceptance of the Friedrich Weller prize, named after the occupant of the chair for Indology at the University of Leipzig from 1938 to 1958 due to Weller's involvement in Nazi politics.[22] Meanwhile, Indian proponents of Hindu nationalism, a majoritarian ideology that presents its own set of ahistorical claims about ancient India, have accused Pollock of having an 'anti-Hindu' stance as well as of maligning Sanskrit by linking this *devabhasha* or language of the gods with Nazism. An example of such views is a volume of essays, the contributors to which are a motley group of Sanskrit scholars and technologists.[23] This edited volume is financed by Rajiv Malhotra, a US-based Indian-origin entrepreneur of Information Technology turned public intellectual championing Hindu nationalism. The book is a manifestation of global Hindutva powered by Big Tech and Big Finance, or 'Hindutva 2.0', a phenomenon which Anustup Basu aptly defines as 'a diagram of informational power that brings together a Hindu sense of being and a neo-liberal credo of development.'[24]

Apart from the obvious question of the academic eligibility of technocrats and self-styled experts on Hinduism to criticize the work of a venerable Sanskrit scholar, it is notable that the contributors to this volume have either forgotten or are ignorant of the fact that the ideological progenitors of Hindu nationalism made no secret of their open admiration for Hitler and his racial politics, as a number of historians have established.[25] Also, it is well known that European Orientalist discourse on the Aryans from the nineteenth and early twentieth centuries supplied the nascent Hindu nationalist movement with its own ideologically tinted view of India's past.[26]

It is probably less surprising that Grünendahl, the (now retired) librarian at the University of Göttingen, has received support from influential academics like Jürgen Hannedar, professor of Indology at the University of Marburg who gave Pollock the epithet of a 'post-colonial inquisitor'.[27] Even the recently deceased, pre-eminent scholar of modern India, Dieter Rothermund, had exasperatedly commented to this author that he had resented Pollock's assertions. The Indologists, he had claimed, had 'arranged' or 'adjusted' with the totalitarian regime and not collaborated with it. A more nuanced, if cursory, repudiation of Pollock's claims has been recently made by Axel Michaels, retired professor of Heidelberg University, who has stated that 'German Indologists' were, 'with some extreme and repellent exceptions, tacit collaborators' in the sense of not offering any resistance to the Nazis and also for becoming members of the Nazi party and its affiliates even though this did not mean that they subscribed to Nazi ideology.[28]

Such disavowals indicate the grey zones that continue to prevail as far as *Vergangenheitsbewältigung* or coping with the (Nazi) past of German Indology is concerned. Such disclaimers are, of course, not limited to the subject of Indology, as some recently published works on different disciplines belonging to the corpus of humanities demonstrate.[29] In case of the history of Indian studies, the unwillingness of the academic establishment to engage with its difficult past is sometimes related to the *guru-shishya parampara* (literally: the continuity of a tradition involving the guru and his disciples) which prevailed in the *gurukul* or 'guru's domain', a form of schooling in ancient India. This tradition entailed an unquestioning reverence for one's guru and his academic forebears in the Brahmin-dominated, patriarchal, and authoritarian educational system of ancient India. Is it possible that learning ancient Indian languages in modern Germany has become synchronous with imbibing the obsequiousness and devotion to one's academic predecessors, which makes any critical examination of their work as well as politics a near sacrilege? It was probably not entirely in jest that several Indologists addressed their doctoral guides as 'guru' in their letters, as we will encounter in several instances in the course of this book.

Post-Pollock Interventions

Nevertheless, from the 1990s, a handful of younger scholars have conducted critical studies of some Indologists and their relationship with Nazi politics. Such studies have primarily examined the enmeshing of academic careers and political involvements of the three prominent scholars who specialized in ancient India—Walther Wüst, Jakob Wilhelm Hauer, and Erich Frauwallner. Works on Walther Wüst include the studies by Horst Junginger analysing the intricate links between Wüst's career, scholarship, and Nazi politics.[30] Another aspect of Wüst's multifarious role in the Nazi state, as the rector of the University of Munich, has been studied by Maximilian Schreiber.[31]

The similarly multidimensional career of Jakob Wilhelm Hauer, leader of the German Faith Movement from 1933 to 1936, professor of Religious studies and Indology at the University of Tübingen and director of the *Arische Seminar* (an institute whose main duty was to ensure the anchoring of an 'Aryan world view' in various fields like the academic curriculum) has also been studied, among others by Ulrich Hufnagel and Horst Junginger.[32] Erich Frauwallner from the University of Vienna is the third of the unholy Trinity of 'Nazi Indologists' (i.e. Indologists who combined their investment in Nazi ideology and politics with their scholarship and career). The 'Aryan approach' in his scholarship and politics has been the subject of a monograph written by Jakob Stuchlik.[33] This work has prompted an indignant response from Walter Slaje, (now retired) professor of Indology at the University of Halle who tried to 'whitewash' Frauwallner, prompting a rejoinder by Stuchlik.[34]

For fear of controversy, a critical paper presented by Horst Junginger at a conference in 2008 on the history of Indology during the National Socialist rule, aptly named 'Terra Incognita' has remained unpublished. This paper raised crucial questions about the connections of some Indologists (apart from the ubiquitous Wüst and Hauer) and their knowledge discourses, including but not restricted to the malleable concept of the Aryan race, with the Nazi political establishment. This paper forms an important inspiration for this book.

Notably, most of the above-mentioned interventions have come from scholars of Indology and/or *Religionswissenschaften* (Study of Religion). The first study of Indology during the National Socialist years by a historian was Maria Framke's relatively short discussion of Indological studies and the scholars involved at Berlin's Friedrich Wilhelms University (now Humboldt University), published in 2014.[35] My own handbook entry on *Völkisch* Indology (2017), a survey of the porous relationship between certain ideologemes of Indological scholarship and *völkisch* ideas in Germany both before and during the period 1933–45, is a continuation of this trend.[36]

The special issue of the journal *NTM*, titled 'Indology and Aryanism: Knowledge of India in Nazi Germany', published in September 2023, is the next significant step in the journey of conducting critical historical research on the subject. This issue features an introduction written by a number of scholars who participated in a workshop organized at Goethe University, Frankfurt am Main, on 31 January 2020, another collective essay on the state of research on the 'Nazi past' of Indology, as well as the four individual papers presented at the workshop.[37] My article on the Indologist Ludwig Alsdorf (1904–1978) as well as the one by Maria Framke on the Indian adventurer and intellectual Devendra Nath Bannerjea (1888–1954), explored a number of themes with which this monograph engages. Both Alsdorf and Bannerjea provided the Nazi regime with 'politically useful' knowledge pertaining to modern, colonial India, for which they received increased professional opportunities or, in case of Bannerjea, a non-white foreigner, the means to survive in the hostile and racist ambience of Berlin under Nazi rule. Eli Franco's paper in the same workshop and the resulting publication took up the debate on Erich Frauwallner, furnishing evidence of Frauwallner's complicity in Nazi ideology and politics as well as his continuing belief in Aryan supremacy and anti-Semitism even after 1945.[38]

This book continues this long deferred voyage of critical historical scholarship. It is written from the point of view of a historian of Nazi Germany and modern India. This is an empirical work drawing heavily on archival research, conducted in archives in Germany, England, and India, as well as on primary published literature. Among the German archives, I have consulted relevant materials held by the 'major' archives like the Federal Archives (*Bundesarchiv*) at Berlin and Koblenz, the Secret State Archives Prussian Cultural Heritage Foundation (*Geheimes Staatsarchiv Preußischer Kulturbesitz*) in Berlin, the main archives of the Bavarian state (*Bayerisches Hauptstaatsarchiv*) in Munich as well as the archives of a number of universities which provided me with records of the political and academic careers of some of the protagonists of this book, both during and after Nazi rule.

Colonial surveillance records in possession of the India Office Records in the British Library, London, the National Archives of India, New Delhi as well as the West Bengal State Archives in Kolkata form an important primary source for this book. It is, of course, well known that surveillance records collected by unscrupulous agents, often through underhand means and seeking to profit from the British Empire's persistent anxiety, are to be accepted with a substantial dose of scepticism. Therefore, attempts have been made as far as possible to corroborate the surveillance records with primary and secondary literature. In the former category, available texts written by the different protagonists have been studied, since these writings reflect the political engagements of the knowledge providers with a certain level of authenticity. However, in cases where such voices are muted or absent and relevant secondary literature is lacking, the historian must rely on circumstantial evidence to tell her story and accept the fact that her narrative must occasionally remain a simulacrum of the past.

The present monograph follows Pollock's thesis to claim that, by deploying their knowledge of modern India for the Nazi state, 'India experts' concurred with the 'basic ideological precondition for the intersection of scholarship with state power'.[39] By extension, this work contradicts Reinhold Grünendahl's claim that 'official' or popular knowledge discourses were distinct from the politically innocuous 'academic knowledge' cultivated by the same set of scholars, implying that their 'political personae', despite their Nazi involvements, were unconnected to their scholarly profile. The case studies presented here make it clear that, in most cases, the scholars in question could credibly project themselves as providers of useful knowledge to various arms of the Nazi government not only because most of them had 'live' experiences of India, but also due to their academic credentials as specialists on India. By contrast, the 'non-academics' who lent their practical knowledge of India to various organizations were assigned lesser positions in the hierarchy of prestige and power.

This is not to deny that the Nazis generally held non-utilitarian, 'Orchid subjects' (Orchideenfächer) like oriental languages as well as 'classical studies' in contempt.[40] The Nazi world view was indeed characterized by a strong anti-intellectualism.[41] My contention is that despite their contempt for academia which they derided as an ivory tower, various centres of power in the Nazi state did repose a certain amount of trust in the scholars who had doctoral titles and Habilitation or were trying to obtain them. Such an attitude can be attributed to the residual prestige associated with the university as a signifier of cultural capital in German society. This vestigial esteem for academia motivated Heinrich Himmler to place scholars in high positions in his pseudo-scientific research organization, the Ahnenerbe, or Alfred Rosenberg, the chief ideologue of the Nazi party, to court academics for his different projects. The case studies presented in this book also demonstrate that in the variegated entanglements of state power and discursive knowledge, a scholarly profile rather than actual scholarship played a key role.

This monograph does not engage explicitly with the knowledge of 'Aryan India' which is the central concern of Pollock's essay. The knowledge of India that was produced and deployed in the four organizations under review was meant primarily to disseminate Nazi ideology and political influence in India and to incite the Indians to rise in armed rebellion against the British. Only one among the four organizations explicitly invoked a 'common Aryan connection' between Indians and Germans for the purpose of conducting Nazi propaganda. Beyond this particular aspect, the Aryan discourse is marginal for this study, which engages with 'strategic' knowledge of modern India.

The Scope and Theoretical Underpinnings of This Book

Most of the existing works on the history of German Indology have largely disregarded the fact that from the time of the Wilhelmine Reich, there was a demand for knowledge of modern India and its 'living' languages in the Foreign Ministry, in the Army, and in the secret services. During the First World War, this demand was fulfilled by some scholars who saw this as a way of advertising their utility.[42] The most prominent example of such 'service' provided by a scholar of India was Helmuth von Glasenapp's involvement in the India Independence Committee or Berlin Committee, formed in 1914 under the aegis of the German Foreign Ministry and comprising a number of Indian anti-colonialists in Berlin.[43] While the Berlin-based India Independence Committee, which aimed to carry on anti-colonial (anti-British) propaganda and activities, has attracted the attention of historians, the role of Helmuth von Glasenapp (1891–1963) in this organization remains relatively unknown.[44] He is primarily remembered today as a famous scholar of Jainism and Buddhism.[45]

The Berlin Committee signified the institutional beginning of Germany's utilization of Indian anti-colonialism to fulfil its own political goals, for which Glasenapp played the roles of knowledge provider and cultural mediator. This study establishes that the main elements of this configuration, namely, the knowledge of contemporary India, especially, its anti-colonial movement and German cultural policy or politics, were adopted by the Nazi regime which added its own particular demands and characteristics to it.

In the initial years of Nazi rule, official interest in India was limited. There were, however, 'semi-official' attempts to propagate the virtues of Nazism among Indians. From 1938, as war with the British Empire seemed inevitable, India began to figure in 'official' German propaganda as well. The Foreign Ministry under Joachim von Ribbentrop embarked on a propaganda policy in which Germany strategically started to encourage the Indian anti-colonial movement. The aim was to destabilize the British Empire's most profitable colony, as various scholars have pointed out.[46]

Nazi Germany's concern about using the Indian anti-colonial movement as an instrument for anti-British propaganda increased significantly after the Indian anti-colonialist activist Subhas Chandra Bose (1897–1945) arrived in Germany in April 1941 as a political fugitive. Bose sought military support from the Axis powers with the aim of freeing India from British control. The Nazi government, however, saw in Bose a living mascot for Germany's anti-British publicity venture in India.[47] Scholars of India were called upon at this juncture of politics and propaganda by the different centres of power like the Foreign Ministry, the SS and the Wehrmacht (the armed forces) which controlled the organizations under review, to promote the image of Nazi Germany as a sympathizer of Indian nationalism and to generate the kind of knowledge discourses that were required to further this image.

Borrowing the concept of sharing of resources between *Wissenschaft* and the political spheres, as presented by Mitchel Ash, this monograph will look at the different dimensions of the exchange of resources between knowledge production related to India and Nazi politics.[48] The case studies make it clear that a number of scholars of India, as well as non-academics who were known to possess knowledge of 'living' India, offered their linguistic and cultural expertise, or intellectual/cultural resources to various power centres, for which they received access to symbolic (titles and honours), financial (grants, employments), and social (useful contacts) resources. This exchange, as this work aims to demonstrate, was marked not only by collusions; there were occasional instances of intense competition among the different individual and institutional stakeholders to secure the available resources.

It has been noted by Herbert Mehrtens in the context of natural sciences that academics generally had two ways to appear important to the Nazi ruling elite. One way was to pursue research that was compatible with different facets of National Socialist *Weltanschauung* or world view. The second course was to present research as a 'national duty' in the service of the entire German people (*Volk*). This path proved to be more popular in the first few years after 1933, since most academics preferred to offer their expert knowledge to different instruments of Nazi politics (the four-year plans, armament research, etc.) as long as a certain degree of professional autonomy was granted to them and the semblance of scholarly objectivity could be retained. In practice, this development led to patterns of collaborative relationship (*Kollaborationsverhältnisse*) between academics in the fields of the natural sciences (and technology) and the Nazi government.[49] This monograph makes use of this analytical tool to examine to what extent such a pattern of providing 'practical service' to the Nazi government, with its attendant phenomena of collaboration and self-mobilization, can also be located in the case of Indian studies in the four organizations.

Though it is misleading to speak of a coherent 'Nazi academic policy', historians have discerned a number of traits that characterized the regime's attitude towards academia. The first was the negation of the idea of *Wissenschaft* propagated by Wilhelm von Humboldt, which entailed 'the free pursuit of irrelevant truths' at the state-run universities.[50] This did not mean that 'non-utilitarian' scholarship was forbidden by the Nazi regime, but different centres of power including the newly appointed rectors of various universities called for the removal of the separation of *Wissenschaft* and 'life'.[51] This ideal of 'scholarship in the service of life' appeared particularly attractive to many scholars of the humanities as a way to exert an influence on politics or society, or simply to flaunt their utility and hopefully stem the tide of increasing marginalization that steadily befell the humanities.[52] The question of relevance was particularly poignant for 'those who specialize in the study of cultures and people distant in time (as most German orientalists in this era focussed on the ancient world) and in space'.[53]

An example of how the German Orientalists answered the expectations of the Nazi regime is a telegram sent to Adolf Hitler by the members of the *Deutsche Morgenländische Gesellschaft* (DMG), a prestigious association of orientalist scholars, during the opening of their conference on 3 September 1936. In this telegram, after greeting the 'Führer' with obeisance and gratitude, the scholars pledged to deploy their strength to extract 'the valuables' from foreign cultures and to make them useful for 'our people'.[54]

As far as the Indologists were concerned, Walther Wüst set the tone through an article published in 1939, titled *Die Deutsche Aufgabe der Indologie* ('The German Tasks of Indology'). In this essay, Wüst claimed that the German tax payers had the right to expect from the *luxusprofessoren* ('luxurious professors') of Indology, a subject without any 'practical use', that they should strive for achieving in their academic works a close connection with the prevalent German *Kulturpolitik* (cultural politics) through their scholarly works, which should also relate to the lives of the German *Volk*.[55]

It is pertinent to mention that here and throughout this work, I have used the term 'cultural politics' for *Kulturpolitik* instead of the more conventionally acceptable 'cultural policy', since 'policy' does not connote the full extent of the dynamics and scope of the Nazi *Kulturpolitik* which played out in the organizations under review. Though, in its initial years, the Nazi regime did not have any coherent cultural politics, it was not unaware of the importance of such politics as part of its approach to foreign countries. Thus, the department of Culture at the Foreign Ministry was renamed the Cultural Political Department (*Kulturpolitische Abteilung*) in 1933. The factor that became common to most organizations conducting cultural politics after 1933 was the influence of Nazi ideology, which they tried to propagate in different countries.[56] Cultural politics under Nazi rule was also not restricted to the dissemination of the 'cultural assets' of Germany, like language, art, the purported glory of the 'Reich' and its Führer, as well as scientific advancements in foreign countries, but was extended to collect 'politically relevant' information about these countries as well, as a few of our case studies will make manifest.

Wüst's vision of an 'ideal scholar' in the above-mentioned article reflected the views of the increasingly powerful SD (*Sicherheitsdienst* or 'Security Service'), the secret service of the SS. From 1936, this sinister but little known organization began to systematically infiltrate the universities. For this purpose, it recruited young academics, primarily from the humanities, as its informants.[57] It is not a coincidence that both Wüst and Hauer acted as informants for the SD.[58] The latter tried to influence appointments, research projects, and government funding in universities and academic institutions.[59] This monograph aims to evaluate the

'India experts' in the light of this ideal of scholarship espoused by the SD, which casts its dark shadow on some of the organizations to be discussed.

This book thus examines the 'Nazi connections' of the protagonists in terms of their engagements with the *Nationalsozialistische Deutsche Arbeiterpartei* (NSDAP or Nazi Party) and its affiliates. The aim is to ascertain whether such political engagements were actually more rewarding for the scholars than their so-called 'practical services' to the state, rendered through tactical deployment of their knowledge of India. In reviewing the trajectories of the purveyors of knowledge, the study follows Pierre Bourdieu's notion of viewing the individual not as a 'subject', but as a part of the matrix of an objective relationship between different fields.[60]

The knowledge providers discussed in this book, as already indicated, include certain German non-academics as well as some Indian intellectuals. Studying the role of these men sheds light on virtually unknown aspects of Nazi politics; for example, that the Nazi authorities displayed unexpected pragmatism in using the services of 'India experts' who sometimes had records of belonging to the leftist political spectrum. All shades of leftist politics, as is well known, were anathema to the Nazi world view. Also, the organizations sometimes ignored Nazi racial politics by according Indians different resources if they could prove their usefulness as knowledge providers.

The inclusion of non-scholarly Germans as well as Indian intellectuals in the purview of this work also signifies an attempt to look beyond the elite, conservative, and white male-dominated world of academic Indology. Though by the early twentieth century the academic scope of the discipline had widened considerably beyond Sanskrit studies, what the various strands of Indology seemed to have in common was a refusal to acknowledge Indians as capable of representing their own past cultures, thus lending weight to Edward Said's claim that the Orientalists 'represented the Orient and spoke on its behalf'.[61] This study aims to recover the hidden voices of Indians in this hegemonic constellation of knowledge and politics.

This work does not claim to belong to the currently fashionable genre of transnational history, despite incorporating several dimensions of the 'transnational turn', including the existence of individuals who lead 'transboundary lives', to borrow a phrase from Madeleine Herren, and examining some instances of 'transfers between countries and nations, cross-border exchanges and circulation of people and ideas', to quote Angel Alcade.[62] The transnational aspect of this study is reinforced by the pervasive presence of a third entity apart from Nazi Germany and colonial India—the ominously watchful British Empire.

However, regardless of the entangled presence of multiple spatial, personal, ideological, and political aspects, this study, barring some infrequent digressions, is anchored in the history of Nazi Germany since its focal point remains the deployment of the knowledge of India for Nazi politics.

The Four Case Studies as Chapters

The first case study or the first chapter pertains to the India Institute of the *Deutsche Akademie* (DA or German Academy). The latter was a private cultural organization founded in 1925 in Munich by a group of conservative nationalist academics affiliated to the university there. The purported aim of the DA was to disseminate German language and culture in the world, but it actually sought to spread German political clout in the guise of cultural contacts and exchanges. The India Institute, established in 1928, was the first of a number of committees within the DA that were formed for specific nations. The Institute came into being through the efforts of Taraknath Das (1884–1958), an Indian nationalist living in Europe and Karl Haushofer (1869–1946), professor of Geography at the University of Munich, who had visited India and developed sympathy for the colonized Indians.

Therefore, Indian nationalist aspirations and the intention of spreading German influence in India were the two dominant impulses behind the formation of the India Institute, which provided scholarships and stipends to Indians to study and train in German universities, laboratories, and companies. Knowledge of India was required to mediate between these German institutions and the Indian students and trainees, who were expected to further German interests after returning to India. A number of Indologists including Walther Wüst and Jakob Wilhelm Hauer, as well as some Indian intellectuals, performed this task almost from the beginning.

This chapter shows that both *Deutsche Akademie* and India Institute identified with various political concerns of successive German governments. After 1933, the Nazi regime started to take advantage of the India Institute's non-political façade to conduct Nazi propaganda as well as espionage in India, using different Indian religious sects, particularly certain Hindu revivalist groups and individuals, as conduits. This chapter traces the interface of National Socialist politics, Indian nationalist aspirations, and Hindu revivalism, with focus on certain German Indologists, Indian nationalists, and Nazi agents who acted as go-betweens.

The second case study involves an organization that came into existence during the war to answer specific wartime requirements of German politics, especially after the arrival of the Indian anti-colonial activist and political fugitive Subhas Chandra Bose in 1941. In response to Bose's request for assistance to militarily combat the British in India, the Foreign Ministry formed a *Sonderreferat Indien* (SRI) or 'Special Department India' in May 1941 to formulate and conduct German policy regarding India.

This chapter examines the epistemology of 'politically effective' knowledge-making regarding India, produced through the intersection of Nazi external politics and Indian anti-colonialism at the SRI, as expressed through two ventures that it undertook. One was a series of fortnightly reports on the current developments in India. The other was a series of German books on modern India. Both projects were meant to provide usable information to German policymakers concerned with India. These projects were conducted mainly under two functionaries of the SRI: the Indologist Ludwig Alsdorf and the former Social Democrat and trade unionist Franz Josef Furtwängler (1894–1965). A few Indians occasionally contributed to such knowledge as well.

The third chapter or case study relates to the pursuit of 'living' knowledge of India, as a part of the 'practical knowledge' of foreign countries that began to be cultivated from the days of the Wilhelmine Empire. This 'study of the foreign countries' (*Auslandswissenschaften*) was conducted in organizations like the Oriental Seminar of Berlin, which was established in 1887 in response to the German Empire's colonial ambitions. The 'practical/political knowledge' of other countries, including India, which was imparted at the Oriental Seminar, encompassed contemporary languages as well as the knowledge of the extant 'realities' (*Realien*) of politics, society, history, geography, and economics.

This chapter examines the study of the 'practical aspects' of modern India at the Oriental Seminar of Berlin and its successors, the *Ausland Hochschule* or Academy for the Study of Foreign Countries (established in 1936) and the faculty for the 'Study of Foreign Countries' (*Auslandswissenschaftlichen Fakultät*) at the University of Berlin formed in 1940. The aforementioned SD exerted considerable control on this faculty, as well as a corresponding research organisation for the study of foreign countries, DAWI (Deutsches Auslandswissenschaftliches Institut) which came into being in 1940.

Teachers of Indian subjects (various Indian languages and *Realien*) at the Oriental Seminar and its successors included German academics as well as a few Indian intellectuals. By examining their profiles and activities, this chapter establishes that right from the days of the Oriental Seminar, the teachers were expected to offer their knowledge and expertise about India not just in the classroom but beyond it, to serve certain commercial and political agendas of the German state. This chapter posits that, after 1933, teaching posts for India-related subjects, which attracted very few students, were increasingly offered as sinecures and 'rewards' for those who offered politically useful knowledge relating to India and Indians to different arms of the government.

The fourth and the last case study deals with the 'India experts' who functioned as interpreters in the 'Indian Legion', also known as Tiger Legion, which was set up jointly by Subhas Chandra Bose and the Wehrmacht (the German Armed Forces). The Legion comprised about 3,500 volunteers from the Indian prisoners of war (POWs) who had fought Rommel in Africa as part of the British Indian Army. In order to integrate the Legion into the Wehrmacht, the Indian soldiers needed to be trained by the German military. This 'training' comprised not only military aspects but also ideological indoctrination in the Nazi world view. 'India experts' were called on to mediate between the Wehrmacht and the

Indian soldiers, not only as interpreters of languages but also as propagandists of Nazi ideology.

This chapter focuses primarily on the Legion's pamphlet, called *Bhaiband* ('Brotherhood'), titled *Kamerad* or Comrade in German, which was edited by a number of German scholars. Written initially by hand in Hindustani and Nastaliq scripts, and from 1944 in Latin script, the pamphlet was published almost daily from 1943 until March 1945. The chapter not only examines the contents of *Bhaiband*, but contextualizes it within the nexus of Subhas Bose's anti-colonial agenda and Germany's political–military goals by reviewing the profiles of the 'editors' of the pamphlet.

Each of the chapters has an epilogue, dealing briefly with the trajectories of some of the protagonists in the aftermath of the war, especially in the context of the West German debates on *Vergangenheitsbewältigung* or coping with the (Nazi) past. The conclusion sums up the key outcomes of the study and points to some possibilities of future research.

This book begins with a quote from *Manusmriti*, an ancient document known for prescribing authoritarian patriarchal treatises. This quotation has been used with a conscious irony since this work, written by a woman of Indian origin, attempts to articulate some rather unpleasant truths about a number of protagonists in the (white) male-dominated networks of politics and knowledge. For the same reason, this writer remains, so to speak, the only woman in this narrative.

Notes

1. Jha, Ganganath, 1920 (1999 edition).
2. Mehrtens, Herbert, 1980, 15–87.
3. Some notable interventions are Schöttler, Peter (ed.), 1997; Dainat, Holgar and Danneberg, Lutz (eds), 2003; Bialas, Wolfgang and Rabinbach, Anson (eds), 2007; Levinson, Bernard M. and Erickson, Robert, P. (eds), 2022.
4. Said, Edward, 1978 (2019 edition), 19.
5. *Ich rief den Teufel und er kam Und ich sah ihn mit Verwund'rung an........Blaß ist er etwas, doch ist es kein Wunder, Sanskritt und Hegel studiert er jetzunder.* Heine, Heinrich, *Buch der Lieder*, 1827, XXXV, 211. https://de.wikisource.org/wiki/Ich_rief_den_Teufel_und_er_kam.
6. Roy, Baijayanti, 2016b, 218.
7. Sengupta, Indra, 2005, 160.
8. For example, Figueira, Dorothy M., 1994, 201–34; 2002; McGetchin, Douglas T., 2009; Marchand, Suzanne, 2009; Roy, Baijayanti, 2016b, 217–28.
9. Figueira, Dorothy M., 2002, 33–5; Roy, Baijayanti, 2016b, 218.
10. Roy, Baijayanti, 2016b, 224.
11. Junginger, Horst, 2008, 111.
12. Thapar, Romila, 2019, 72, 77.
13. Levinson, Bernard M. and Erickson, Robert, P., 2022, 21–2.
14. Ibid., 31–2.
15. Pollock, Sheldon, 1993, 86.
16. Ibid., 1993, 89–91.
17. Ibid., 2002, 335–71.
18. Grünendahl, Reinhold, 2006, 209–36; 2008, 457–78; 2012a; 2012b, 189–257; 2019.
19. Ibid., 2019, 158–60.

20. Ibid., 2012b, 228.
21. Adluri, Vishwa, 2011, 253–92.
22. The Banality of Indology: Franco, Pollock and the Friedrich Weller Prize. Adluri, Vishwa and Bagchee, Joydeep, 2019. https://www.academia.edu/41372157/The_Banality_of_Indology_Franco_Pollock_and_the_Friedrich_Weller_Prize.
23. Kannan, K.S. (ed.), 2017.
24. Basu, Anustup, 2020, 179.
25. For example, Casolari, Marzia, 2000, 222–25; Bhatt, Chetan, 2001, 106–8.
26. Roy, Baijayanti, 2016b, 218–22.
27. Hannedar, Jürgen, 2013, 162.
28. Michaels, Axel, 2022, 90–1.
29. For example, Bialas, Wolfgang and Rabinbach, Anson (eds), 2007; Levinson, Bernard M. and Erickson, Robert, P. (eds), 2022.
30. Junginger, Horst, 2008, 105–77; 2017a, 274–9; 2017b, 925–33.
31. Schreiber, Maximillian, 2008.
32. Hufnagel, Ulrich, 2003, 145–74; Junginger, Horst, 2003, 177–207; 2017, 230–4.
33. Stuchlik, Jakob, 2009.
34. Slaje, Walter, 2010, 447–63; Stuchlik, Jakob, 2011, 287–308.
35. Framke, Maria, 2014, 89–128.
36. Roy, Baijayanti, 2017a, 1190–7.
37. Epple, Moritz, Framke, Maria, Franco, Eli, Junginger, Horst, and Roy, Baijayanti, 2023, 219–31.
38. Roy, Baijayanti, 2023b, 275–306; Framke, Maria, 2023, 307–32; Franco, Eli, 2023, 245–74.
39. Pollock, Sheldon, 1993, 85.
40. Marchand, Suzanne, 2007, 292.
41. Tenorth, Elmar, H, 1993, 240.
42. Marchand, Suzanne, 2009, 484.
43. McGetchin, Douglas T., 2010, 98.
44. "Unternehmungen und Aufwiegelungen": Das Berliner Indische Unabhängigkeitskomitee in den Akten des Politischen Archivs des Auswärtigen Amts (1914–1920). Liebau, Heike, 2019. https://www.projekt-mida.de/reflexicon/unternehmungen-und-aufwiegelungen-das-berliner-indische-unabhaengigkeitskomitee-in-den-akten-des-politischen-archivs-des-auswaertigen-amts-1914-1920/.
45. Hoffmann, Helmut, 1964. Deutsche Biographie. https://www.deutsche-biographie.de/gnd118695215.html#ndbcontent.
46. Kuhlmann, Jan, 2003, 69–70.
47. Roy, Baijayanti, 2022a, 1–2.
48. Ash, Mitchell G., 2002, 32–51.
49. Mehrtens, Herbert, 1994, 13–32.
50. Marchand, Suzanne, 2007, 270.
51. Stuchlik, Jakob, 2009, 59.
52. Bialas, Wolfgang and Rabinbach, Anson, 2007, xii.
53. Marchand, Suzanne, 2022, 64.
54. Stuchlik, Jakob, 2009, 39.
55. Wüst, Walter, 1939, 339–48.
56. Gesche, Katja, 2006, 73–8.
57. Wildt, Michael, 2016, 20.
58. On Hauer's SD activities, see Junginger, Horst, 1999, 128–44; on Wüst, see Junginger, Horst, 2017b, 927.
59. Wildt, Michael, 2016, 21.
60. Bourdieu, Pierre, 1990, 75–81.
61. Said, Edward, 1978 (2019 edition), 20.
62. Herren, Madeleine, 2013, 100–24; Alcade, Angel, 2020, 243.

The Nazi Study of India and Indian Anti-Colonialism: Knowledge Providers and Propagandists in the 'Third Reich'.
Baijayanti Roy, Oxford University Press. © Baijayanti Roy 2024. DOI: 10.1093/9780191981951.003.0001

1

India Institute of the *Deutsche Akademie*

Background: Foundation of the DA

The *Deutsche Akademie* (German Academy) or DA was founded as a private cultural organization in 1925 by a group of conservative–nationalist academics affiliated to the University of Munich. Several scholarly studies have critically examined the DA's past.[1] However, the trajectory of the India Institute of the DA remains virtually uncharted, except for the well-researched but relatively short study by Maria Framke and an even shorter archival note published by me in 2021.[2] The Institute has been discussed by Kris Manjapra in his narrative of Germany–India entanglement, but unfortunately, not only are most facts relating to the Institute's foundation erroneous, but the complex nexus between the Institute as part of the DA and Nazi cultural politics regarding India has been glossed over in favour of a feel-good story about an 'exchange of gifts of enchantment'.[3] Benjamin Zachariah has very briefly touched on the institute and its connections with Nazism in some of his articles.[4]

This chapter deviates from the aforementioned works in attempting to provide an in-depth study of the different ways in which the Institute attempted to be of service to the Nazi regime. The foundational aim of the DA was to disseminate the 'cultural achievements' of Germany, particularly the German language, in the world.[5] The founders of the DA saw such cultural politics as a way to resurrect the national honour that was lost through the disastrous defeat in the First World War.[6] The cultural politics conducted by the DA echoed that of the Weimar Republic, which tried to compensate its lack of political clout in the international arena in the aftermath of the First World War with the 'soft power' of spreading German language and culture. This quest was presented as a non-political pursuit since the German Foreign Ministry in Berlin and the leading functionaries of the DA in Munich were conscious of the fact that German influence could be best disseminated in foreign countries if the political aspect remained latent.[7] In reality, the separation of political and cultural spheres was often only cosmetic.[8] The 'purely cultural' image of the DA rendered it an aura of political innocuousness and credibility which made it a perfect channel for conducting propaganda.

The DA was beset by financial problems from the beginning. Things looked up somewhat in 1927/8, as it came under the influence of the young and dynamic press agent Franz Thierfelder (1896–1963). He began to wield the real administrative and decision-making power in the DA, though the official president was the physician Friedrich von Müller (1858–1941).[9]

Thierfelder realized the importance of streamlining the focus of the DA on those countries which appeared predisposed to be susceptible to German influence.[10] The DA was to act as a cultural intermediary between Germany and these countries through committees set up for particular nations (*Länderausschüsse*).[11] It is significant that the *Indische Ausschuss* or India Institute (henceforth the Institute) was the first of such committees.[12] It came into existence in 1928, through the efforts of Taraknath Das, an Indian anti-colonialist living in Europe, and Karl Haushofer, professor of Geography at the University of Munich who was involved with the DA from its beginning. Their correspondence, held by the German Federal Archives in Koblenz, indicates that their shared interest in Indian anti-colonialism and their common resentment towards the British Empire were the foundational impulses of the Institute.[13]

Formally, the Institute claimed to promote cultural cooperation between India and Germany, as a brochure, composed by Thierfelder and published in 1937, declared. According to the brochure, such 'cooperation' included providing scholarships to deserving Indian students to study in German universities; helping Indian students in finding an opportunity for practical training in factories and to carry on research in hospitals and laboratories in Germany; promotion of the study of India at German universities by inviting Indian professors on lecture tours and arranging lectures on India in various cultural centres of Germany; welcoming distinguished Indian guests in Germany and helping them to come in contact with German cultural leaders; and spreading German culture in India through the co-operation of Indian universities and cultural bodies.[14] In its focus on providing scholarships, the DA was following the German state's traditional cultural policy of attracting international students. It was a way to achieve *Weltgeltung* (world renown) since these students were likely to return home and propagate the superiority of German *Wissenschaft* (lit. science but generally academic disciplines) and culture.[15]

Indian Anti-Colonialism, German Nationalism, and Hindu Revivalism: 1928–1933

In the following section, we will identify a few salient features relating to the Institute from its initial years, before looking at the process of its Nazification and the different kinds of knowledge production involved.

Taraknath Das, a brilliant student from a modest background in Bengal, found his calling in militantly opposing British colonial rule. As the colonial state tried to clamp down on him, Das left India, embarking on a journey which first took him to Japan and then to the United States in 1906.[16] He spent the next years organizing Indians in the USA to conduct diasporic nationalist politics.[17] His political activities brought him to Berlin in 1915, along with a dozen other Indians. Their journey was sponsored by the German government, which sought to encourage Indian nationalists to destabilize the British Empire through propaganda and combative acts. An 'India Independence Committee' or 'Berlin Committee' was set up in the German capital in 1914 for the purpose of steering anti-British propaganda and activities in and outside the 'Reich'.[18]

Such activities were, however, doomed to be unsuccessful. Das returned to the USA in 1917 and was immediately imprisoned in the so-called 'Hindu–German conspiracy case', in which he and a group of other Indians were accused of con-spiring against Great Britain, an ally of America, with German help. After his release in 1919, Das moved away from armed struggle for fear of reprisal from American authorities, though British surveillance reports indicate that at least until 1921, Das was in contact with various members of the former India Independence Committee, writing to them on the need to form 'a central committee of tried revolutionaries outside India'.[19]

By the mid-1920s, Das and his American wife, Mary Keating had to forfeit their American citizenship due to a law passed in the USA against naturalized Asians and their spouses. For the next 10 years, the couple spent long spans of time in Europe, particularly in Germany and Italy. Das began to correspond regularly with Karl Haushofer from August 1925.[20]

Karl Haushofer came from an elite academic family (*Bildungsbürger*) in Munich. After joining the military, he undertook a prolonged tour of Japan from 1908 to 1910 as a military envoy of the German government. During this time, he also visited parts of India and developed a sympathetic interest in the British colony. Haushofer, who served in the First World War, came to develop a deep hostility towards the British Empire as well. After the First World War, he joined the University of Munich as an honorary professor of geography. Haushofer pro-pounded geopolitical theories that opposed the territorial arrangements dictated by the Treaty of Versailles and contained ethnocentric dimensions like Germans being *Volk ohne Raum* (people without space) who needed living space or *leben-sraum*. These ideas appealed to right-wing German politicians, including the National Socialists. It is possible that Haushofer's geopolitical ideas reached Hitler through Haushofer's student and friend, Rudolf Heß, an early convert to Nazism who would later become Hitler's deputy. However, despite his ideological concurrence with certain notions propagated by the Nazis, Haushofer never joined the NSDAP.[21]

After the First World War, Haushofer began to believe that turning a blind eye to Asian nationalism and pan-nationalism had cost Germany the war. He was particularly enthusiastic about all that appeared progressive in the 'national movement in India'.[22] The geo-politician came to believe that India's struggle for freedom was 'connected through secret threads' with Germany which was striv-ing to be free of the constraints placed on it through the Treaty of Versailles.[23] These views appealed to Das, who also felt that Germany, like India, was a victim of British propaganda. The two countries were thus 'natural allies' against Britain, as he wrote to Haushofer in 1925.[24] This was the basis of the establishment of the India Institute, which aimed to bypass the British colonial state in furthering cooperation between India and Germany.[25]

Indian anti-colonialism and German resentment of the British Empire were sentiments that also appealed to the German Foreign Ministry in Berlin at the time. Nevertheless, the Foreign Ministry was initially indifferent towards the DA, offering it only a modest subsidy. However, Thierfelder managed to persuade leading representatives of German industrial concerns like Siemens, and Allianz and Stuttgarter, to cooperate with it by providing stipends and traineeships to Indians. Through his efforts, various state-level ministries, universities, and technical academies also offered scholarships to Indians.[26]

By 1930, the Foreign Ministry began to value Thierfelder's managerial qualities and became more inclined to encourage the DA's agenda.[27] The Ministry collaborated directly with the Institute in awarding of scholarships from the Alexander von Humboldt Foundation to Indians. The Humboldt Foundation, ostensibly an independent organization, was in reality a front for the scholarship programme of the Foreign Ministry.[28] Occasionally, the Institute and the Foundation jointly provided scholarships to Indians with the aim of attracting sympathy for Germany. Between 1928 and 1933, 24 scholarships offered by the Institute were in collaboration with Humboldt Foundation.[29]

An examination of the advertisements for scholarships makes it clear that they were, in effect, subsidies. They did not cover the costs of residing in Germany. Stipend holders were required to have a good grasp of German before coming to Germany. They were requested to arrive a few months before beginning their studies in order to acclimatize. It is evident that, under these conditions, only members of the Indian elite could make use of the stipends. This situation was not only due to the straitened finances of the DA; the implicit goal was to influence elite Indians from opinion-making classes who could promote German interests in India. This aspect, as we will see, would get increasingly politicized after the Nazis came to power. The culmination of this process was Thierfelder's statement, found among materials seized by colonial authorities from Horst Pohle, the DA's German lector in Calcutta in 1939, that ideal scholarship holders should be first and foremost 'trusted agents in various towns in years to come'.[30]

Another way to expand Germany's cultural influence in India that the Institute undertook was to invite Indian public figures to Munich and give receptions for them. It favoured those who were not only famous in their respective fields but who also tried to inculcate self-awareness among Indians. In 1930–1, the guests of the Institute included two Nobel Laureates—the poet Rabindranath Tagore and the scientist C.V. Raman.[31] Politicians from the Indian National Congress (INC) were preferred, following a conscious decision of the Institute, as a letter from Das to Haushofer indicates.[32]

The Institute was particularly well-disposed towards the nationalist-minded polymath intellectual and 'Germanophil' Benoy Kumar Sarkar (1887–1949), professor of Economics at the University of Calcutta. Sarkar, like Das, belonged to the Western-educated nationalist elite from Bengal, but Sarkar's nationalism stopped short of active politics.[33] Sarkar was also much more invested than Das in an 'overdetermined identification' of Bengal and Germany which had its roots in nineteenth-century British intellectual discourses.[34]

Sarkar's connection with the Institute was through Haushofer, whom he came to know in the early 1920s, when the Indian academic was touring Europe.[35] Through Haushofer's mediation, the Institute invited Sarkar to be a guest professor at the Technical University in Munich in 1930–1.[36] Sarkar would evolve into a consistent champion of both the DA and what he considered to be a rejuvenated Germany under Hitler. His most remarkable contribution integrating these two elements was the establishment of a Bengali Society of German Culture in 1933. This Society regularly arranged lectures on different aspects of German life. Erstwhile stipend-holders of the Institute and the Humboldt Foundation were involved in the Society as speakers and advisors. Lectures on subjects associated with National Socialism—like national community, militarization, and genetic selection—were preferred.[37] The Institute recognized Sarkar's contributions early on and elected him as one of its honorary life members in 1933.[38]

A significant contribution of Benoy Kumar Sarkar as well as Taraknath Das was to introduce Hindu revivalism as a cultural bridge between the Institute and India. Hindu revivalist movements had started in different parts of India in the nineteenth century. A common goal shared by these disparate movements was to revitalize Hinduism by taking it back to its supposedly glorious Vedic Aryan roots.[39]

Hindu revivalism, while not directly connected with either the mainstream Indian anti-colonial movement or the politicized Hinduism or Hindutva which emerged in the 1920s, had ideological intersections with both. Invoking the lost glory of the Hindus was often a surrogate way to express political nationalism for the colonial subjects, particularly the more educated and ambitious upper caste and upper-class Hindus, who were denied all democratic expressions of political will by the colonial rulers.[40]

Both Das and Sarkar deeply admired a revivalist Hindu sect based in Bengal that had formed around the mystic Ramkrishna (1836–1886) and his internationally famous disciple Swami Vivekananda (1863–1902). The English-educated monk Vivekananda sought to revitalize Hinduism by calling for a return to the golden age of Vedic Aryans when Hinduism was a pure, primordial religion, without any 'non-Aryan' elements.[41] In 1933, Sarkar introduced Haushofer to this strand of Hindu spirituality through *Prabuddha Bharata* ('Awakened India') the journal of the Ram Krishna Mission, the religious order founded by Vivekananda, by instructing the editor of this journal to send a copy of each issue to Haushofer.[42] The journal already enjoyed a high reputation among some German Indologists, who wrote articles for it. In an issue of *Prabuddha Bharata*, published in December 1932, for example, Walther Wüst wrote on Buddhism and Christianity in ancient western India while Taraknath Das wrote on the Asian origin of Mayan civilization.[43]

Hindu revivalist movements also appealed to some of the German scholars of India who were members of the DA. One such scholar was Jakob Wilhelm Hauer, whose name appears in a list of the members of the Institute in 1932.[44] Hauer's life and works, particularly before 1945, have received quite a lot of scholarly attention, as I have already indicated in the Introduction.[45] We will focus on his engagements with the India Institute, which have in contrast received little scholarly attention.

Hauer had trained as a protestant missionary in his youth. He had spent a number of years in India as a representative of the Basel Mission (Figure 1). In India, Hauer was deeply influenced by Hinduism or rather what he considered to be its Indo-Aryan component. As he would write in a memorial text in 1935, 'I did not find Christ in India, however, but Indo-Aryan wisdom found me.'[46]

After returning to Germany, Hauer followed an academic career, completing his doctorate in 1918 and his *Habilitation* in 1921. The turbulent days of the First

Figure 1 Jakob Wilhelm Hauer, 24 February 1935.
Source: Bundesarchiv 183-2004-0413-501/photographer unknown/CC-BY-SA 3.0.

World War and its despondent aftermath left him disenchanted with the Protestant Church since he felt that it was incapable of bringing about a much needed regeneration of Germany's spiritual life.[47] In his search for spiritual solace, Hauer turned towards the study of Aryanism on which he could project all his visions and aspirations for Germany. He 'constructed' a history of the Aryan/ Indo-German race which he identified as 'Nordic Aryans' of India who were supposedly the ancestors of modern Germans. In Hauer's view, the Aryan/Indo-Germans in India followed a spiritually and physically invigorating religion, devoid of all traces of Semitism which had 'contaminated' Christianity. Such thoughts resulted in Hauer's total repudiation of Christianity in favour of a revivalist Indo-German religious cult called the German Faith Movement (*Deutsche Glaubensbewegung*).

In July 1933, Hauer became the president of a group representing the German Faith Movement. The leaders of the movement tried in vain to make this 'religion' the official religion of the 'Third Reich'. Despite the futility of this effort, Hauer spent much of the 1930s and 1940s trying to historicize the Indo-Germans as 'Nordic Aryans' by reinterpreting ancient Indian texts like the Vedas and the Mahabharata through the prism of a racialized discourse on Aryanism.[48]

The groundwork for the spurious scholarly pursuit of co-opting Vedic Aryanism for constructing a Nordic/German past had been laid by influential Indologists like Christian Lassen (1800–1876), who had claimed that fair-skinned Nordic Aryans had invaded the Indian subcontinent and subjugated the dark skinned non-Aryan aboriginal inhabitants. This theory eliminated the Indians from their own history by claiming that all cultural achievements of the Aryan civilization, like the Vedas for instance, were created by the Nordic Aryans.[49]

However, unlike Lassen and some other purveyors of Indian Studies in Germany, Hauer claimed that the 'Aryan spirit' had remained more potent in present-day India than one generally presupposes. Though modern Hinduism was, to Hauer (as to Indologists like Lassen), the result of miscegenation of Aryan and non-Aryan blood, he saw the occasional manifestation of Aryan spirit in 'great personalities' like Tukarama, the seventeenth-century Hindu mystic and poet venerated as a saint in Maharashtra, as well as Vivekananda.[50]

Hauer's admiration of Hindu revivalists was not limited to the theoretical. In 1931, with the support of Taraknath Das, Hauer considered visiting India and residing at the ashram of the Ram Krishna Mission at the foot of the Himalayas.[51] It is not clear whether this visit ever took place. A monk belonging to this Mission, Swami Jyotiswarananda, was invited by the Institute in Munich, though the date of his visit remains unknown.[52] The Mission on its part had other contacts with Nazi Germany. In March 1934, the Mission requested the German Foreign Ministry to send its mouthpiece, the *Prabuddha Bharata* to different German universities.[53] The monks of the Mission in Calcutta were occasionally invited by the Bengali Society of German Culture to chair propagandistic lectures. A case in point is a lecture supporting the notorious law passed in Germany in July 1933 'for the prevention of hereditary defective progeny'. The President of the programme featuring this lecture was the monk Swami Sharvadananda from the Ramkrishna Mission. The audience included monks from the Ram Krishna Mission as well as members of the German diaspora in Calcutta who were reputed to be Nazi propagandists, including the German consul, Eduard von Selzam.[54]

Another distinctive—and perhaps inevitable—feature of the Institute was the involvement of German Indologists. The Institute needed discursive knowledge of India for its dealings with the country as well as to familiarize German opinion-making classes with India, in order to reinforce its own status as a mediator of Indo-German cultural relations and to facilitate stipends and training places for Indians. These expectations were fulfilled by a number of scholars engaged in studying India. Several well-known 'India experts' from various German universities became members of the Institute almost from the beginning. They included, apart from Hauer, Wilhelm Geiger (1856–1943), erstwhile professor of 'Aryan Studies' at the University of Munich, his student Walther Wüst, Hanns Oertel (1868–1952), who succeeded Geiger as professor of Indology at the University of Munich, Helmuth von Glasenapp, then professor at the University of Königsburg, Lucien Schermann (1864–1946), professor at the University of Munich and director of the Ethnological Museum there, and Otto Strauß (1881–1940), professor at the University of Breslau.[55]

In 1932, the Institute financed the publication of a number of books on modern India. These books were based on a lecture series, titled 'India in Modern World Economy and World Politics', held at the Technical University (*Technische Hochschule*), Stuttgart in the same year. The speakers included scholars and non-scholarly (and often self-styled) experts on India.[56] Franz Thierfelder, who belonged to the latter category, delivered a lecture on 'The Freedom Struggle of the Indians' (*Das Freiheitsringen der Inder*), in keeping with the Institute's interest in Indian anti-colonialism.[57] The lecture series and the book foreshadowed several trends that assumed great significance in the years following 1933: the strategic importance of India's anti-colonialist movement in Germany's cultural politics, the self-designed or state-ordained role of some Indologists, as well as non-academic 'experts' as providers of 'politically useful' knowledge of India and the self-image of the Institute as being the negotiator of India–Germany relations on behalf of the German state.

In winter 1932–3, the Indologists connected to the India Institute, along with some other scholars and experts, planned to hold a series of lectures on contemporary India at the University of Munich. These lectures were meant to form the groundwork for creating an 'oriental institute' for studying modern India, in collaboration with the University of Munich.[58] The Institute, however, did not materialize, probably due to the failure of the professors to cooperate among themselves.[59] From the titles of the proposed lectures, we can identify certain impulses that would prevail in the India Institute after 1933 (e.g. interest in Indian nationalist consciousness, Hindu revivalism, and 'practical' knowledge of contemporary India).

Nazi Politics and the Institute: 1933–1937

The Nazi government realized the importance of cultural politics early on, though it took some time to develop a coherent policy in this regard. As mentioned in the Introduction, already in 1933 the Department of Culture at the Foreign Ministry was renamed the Cultural Political Department (*Kulturpolitische Abteilung*). The factor that became common to most organizations conducting cultural politics after 1933 was the influence of Nazi world view, which they were expected to propagate in different countries. This entailed emphasizing the 'achievements' of Hitler and the new 'Reich'.[60] The DA, and with it, the India Institute became fully attuned to the requirements of such politics.

The Nazi government was welcomed by the DA, which was in essence a conservative nationalist and anti-democratic bastion.[61] The transformations in the DA after 1933 were basically measures of self-mobilization to 'coordinate' with Nazi ideology and politics (*gleichschaltung*). Such measures were driven by ideological as well as practical considerations since the DA hoped to receive increased financial assistance from the new government.[62] In the spring and summer of 1933, the DA 'purged' its senate and the *Kleinen Rat* (lit. 'little council'), the committee steering the DA, of 'politically and racially undesirable' members like Konrad Adenauer, Thomas Mann, and Max Liebermann. Ludwig Siebert, the Nazi chief minister of Bavaria was now welcomed into the *Kleinen Rat*, as was Rudolf Heß.

In 1934, Thierfelder, together with Richard Fehn, another 'manager' at the DA, persuaded the ageing president, von Müller, to give way to Karl Haushofer who became president of both the DA and the India Institute. Since Haushofer was not an official member of the Nazi party, the non-political façade of the DA could be maintained. It was hoped that through Haushofer's personal connection with Rudolf Heß, now the powerful deputy to the 'Führer', the DA would be able to gain some much needed funds from the government.[63]

As far as the India Institute was concerned, the most significant transformation after 1933 was the expulsion of the two 'Jewish' scholars, Lucian Scherman and Otto Strauß, from its executive committee. The journal of the DA, which now officially called itself 'Academy for Scientific Research and Fostering of Germanness' (*Akademie zur Wissenschaftliche Erforschung und Pflege des Deutschtums*), thereby stressing its importance for the German *Volksgemeinschaft* or national community that the Nazi regime claimed to have formed, reported in March 1936 that 'both the scholars have left the India Institute out of their own free will after their retirement.'[64]

This is a disingenuous statement. The Vedic scholar and ethnographer Lucian Scherman was forced into retirement in October 1933, a circumstance from which Walther Wüst tried to profit by recommending himself as Scherman's replacement to the concerned authorities. He did not let his conscience trouble him with the memory that Scherman, as the dean of the Philosophical Faculty had supported his, Wüst's, *Habilitation* with a positive assessment in 1926.[65] The aged scholar had to leave Germany for the USA in 1939, where he passed away in 1946.[66] Otto Strauß, the well-known expert on the Vedas and Mahabharata, was dismissed from his position in 1935, though not before suggesting his own successor—a particularly tragic episode to which we will revert in a later chapter. In the next few years, he tried unsuccessfully to eke out an existence in Berlin before immigrating to the Netherlands in 1939. He died of heart failure while trying to flee the Nazi invasion of Holland in 1940.[67]

The most prominent measure of self-mobilization that the Institute undertook after 1933 pertained to defending the Nazi regime against indictments of rising racism towards Indians. Hitler admired the British Empire and believed that Indians were incapable of ever ruling themselves. Hitler, as well as the Nazi ideologue Alfred Rosenberg, derided the Indians as a 'fallen race', the product of the miscegenation between the racially superior, white Aryan invaders and the racially inferior dark-skinned original inhabitants.[68] This theory, as we noted, corresponded to the views propounded by one strand of German Indology.

The openly derogatory attitude of the Nazi elite against Indians allegedly led to increased assaults on Indians in Germany as well as anti-Indian propaganda in the German media. One episode became particularly infamous. On 20 February 1933, the Sturmabteilung (SA), the Nazi party's paramilitary organization and its symbol of terror, imprisoned A.C.N. Nambiar, a journalist based in Berlin and the brother-in-law of the Berlin-based radical anti-colonialist, 'Chatto' or Virendranath Chattopadhyaya (1860–1937). J.S. Naidu, Chatto's nephew and a medicine student in Berlin, was also arrested. Both men were suspected of harbouring Communist sympathies and kept in custody without trial. Naidu was freed after eight days. Nambiar, who by his own admission was inclined towards Marxism, was kept in solitary confinement for more than three weeks.[69] He was released only through interventions of the British Embassy. Soon thereafter, he left for Prague. These events were reported in the Indian press and gave rise to vehement criticism.[70]

The result of such negative publicity was a decrease in the number of Indians applying to pursue academic studies or professional training in Germany. On behalf of the Institute, Thierfelder and Das embarked on a counter propaganda drive which insisted that beneficiaries of the Institute were 'safe' in Germany if they desisted from 'political activities', which was a euphemism for left-wing politics, including radical anti-colonialism. Though stipends continued to be provided to candidates from a wide range of academic and professional fields, it was now expected that the stipend holders were to acquire 'the best of German culture', which evidently stood for the National Socialist world view.[71] After their return, the erstwhile stipend holders were expected to keep in touch with the Institute and, through it, to 'the cultural life of Germany'.[72] It is, however, difficult to ascertain how many of the scholarship holders actually fulfilled this expectation. One of those who definitely did was the philologist Bata Krishna Ghosh, one of the first scholarship holders of the Institute who taught German at the University of Calcutta. He became the head of the student section of the German Society which Benoy Kumar Sarkar managed to start at this university and which became known to colonial surveillance as a pro-Nazi group.[73]

After 1933, the Institute also became concerned about the 'political activities' of the Indian students' club in Munich. Such 'activities' mainly comprised protesting against the mistreatment of Indians in Germany. The protest actions increased after the arrival of Subhas Chandra Bose in Germany in 1934.[74] Bose objected vigorously but unsuccessfully to the German Foreign Ministry in Berlin about the racist attacks on Indians in the German press and society.[75] He also urged the Indian students who formed a Hindustan Club in Munich to draw up a petition, which was submitted to the 'appropriate authorities' in Berlin but without any concrete result.[76]

Bose came to know Thierfelder personally when the Indian nationalist leader was 'honoured' by the Institute in 1934 and Thierfelder tried unsuccessfully to intervene with the Foreign Ministry on behalf of Bose.[77] Meanwhile, the 'politicization' of Indian students led to a deterioration of their earlier cordial relationship with the DA, as Thierfelder pointed out at a meeting of the Institute in 1934.[78] The executive committee of the Institute was relieved when 'certain people' instigating 'disturbances' among Indian students in Berlin and Munich (implying Bose) left Europe, as the protocol of a meeting held on 1 February 1937 demonstrates.[79]

The British diplomatic representatives and surveillance agents in Germany also noticed the DA's de-emphasizing of the anti-colonial agenda in favour of promoting pro-Nazi views. A letter sent to the India Office from the British consulate in Munich in December 1936 claimed that the tone of the *Deutsche Akademie* had changed 'somewhat for the better', implying that it was less anti-British. The letter attributed this change to the departure of Taraknath Das from Germany for the USA in 1934 as well as to the fact that Nazi authorities were now more tactful in their utterances about India due to Germany's falling export rate which resulted from the boycott of German goods by influential Indians as a reaction to press reports of anti-Indian racism in Germany.[80]

The changing cultural politics of both the Nazi state and the DA was summed up in a surveillance report from March 1937. The report claimed that as a result of the Nazi 'racial ideas', the Institute's earlier encouragement of Indian anti-colonialism gave way to the propagation of German *Kultur* to Indians. There was still an anti-British tinge and expressions of friendliness to Indians, but the latter were now made to feel that it would be good for India to be ruled by the white race.[81] Prominent but relatively moderate members of the INC, like Dr Bidhan Chandra Ray who visited Munich in 1937, continued to be felicitated by the Institute.[82]

On some occasions, Indian nationalism and anti-British sentiments continued to be invoked together for Nazi propaganda. In October 1936, for example, Karl Haushofer, as president of the India, stated in an address to newly arrived Indian scholarship holders that India was now home of 'an energetic modern movement' that had much in common with the 'contemporary German movement'. He also appealed to the Indian claims to Aryanism by announcing that Indians and Germans understood each other so well because of their 'common race origins'.[83] While Indian nationalism (re)emerged as a useful propaganda instrument for the Institute during the war, Aryanism came to be to be used by the Institute in different ways to generate support for the Nazi world view among Indians in the mid-1930s, as we will see soon.

The India Institute and the Nazi Network in India

By the mid-1930s, under the guise of its political neutrality, the India Institute emerged as the most important organization conducting Nazi cultural politics in India. It became a nodal point of a Nazi network that had begun to take shape in India from 1932, when an offshoot of the Nazi party (*Stützpunkt*) was established in Bombay, with 'branches' in different cities. Most members of the party unit belonged to the commercial firm Havero, which was officially a Dutch concern but actually a disguised subsidiary of the German conglomerate and chemical giant IG Farben. Havero had its head office in Bombay and branch offices in different urban centres of India.[84]

Following the *gleichschaltung* (synchronization) of the German state and the Nazi party, the official representatives of the German state (i.e. the diplomatic missions) were increasingly filled with Nazi party loyalists. The diplomatic personnel were also expected to make sure that every expatriate German belonged to the Nazi party's external branch (*Auslandsorganisation*) though they did not succeed in fulfilling this expectation.[85] The Institute maintained contacts with the Nazi network in India, which began to include German diplomats as well as functionaries of other German commercial concerns like Siemens and the insurance company Allianz and Stuttgarter.

Though not all stipends offered by the Institute together with German commercial firms were necessarily related to the Nazi network, some, like the one sponsored jointly by the Allianz and Stuttgarter and the Institute from 1933, did manifest such a connection.[86] Allianz and Stuttgarter was suspected by colonial surveillance of financing various Nazi ventures in India, including an organization called the Indo-German News Exchange which engaged in Nazi propaganda and espionage.[87] Notably, Allianz and Stuttgarter offered a scholarship to one Krishna Prasanna Mukherjee to write his PhD at the Political and Social Institute of the University of Heidelberg in 1934. He returned to India in 1936 and joined a college in Bogura (now in Bangladesh). He was appointed head of the Indo-German News Exchange in Delhi shortly before the war.[88]

Aryanism and Hindu Revivalism: Jakob Wilhelm Hauer and Walther Wüst

After 1933, the Institute began to display a certain interest in inviting scholars and mystics associated with Hindu revivalist sects other than the Ram Krishna Mission. The Aryan discourse was the most important trope shared between Nazi world view and Hindu revivalism. The Institute hoped that analogies based on Aryanism could be deployed to induce admiration for Nazism among the Hindus, who formed the majority community in India. This was also considered to be an effective way to counter the bad press that the Nazi regime was receiving in India.[89]

Two members of the Institute tried to link it with Nazi politics through the conduit of Hindu revivalism: the aforementioned Jakob Wilhelm Hauer and Walther Wüst. After 1933, Hauer not only provided theoretical support for Nazism through his scholarly writings, but he also engaged directly in politics espoused by the Nazis, for example by joining the Nazi Teachers' Association (*Nationalsozialistischer Lehrerbund* or NSLB) and the Nazi Lecturers' Association (*Nationalsozialistischer Dozentenbund* or NSDB) as well as the Nazi party in 1937.[90] Hauer was already officially admitted to the increasingly powerful—and infamous—paramilitary organization, the SS, as well as its secret service, the *Sicherheitsdienst* (SD) in 1934.[91]

Involvement with National Socialism brought Hauer material dividends. In 1940, he was made the director of an institute created especially for him at the University of Tübingen, called the *Arischen Seminar* 'Aryan Seminar' which was extended in 1942 to become an *Arischen Institut* 'Aryan Institute.'[92] The two main assignments of the Institute were: (i) to provide academic legitimacy to the concept of a religious foundation purportedly undergirding the Aryan world view and (ii) to ensure the anchoring of an Aryan world view (i.e. supremacy of the Aryan race) in various fields like the academic curriculum, the ideological indoctrination of Nazi party workers, the Gestapo, the SS, and the Army.[93]

Towards the end of the 1944, Hauer also became a part of the foreign intelligence service of the SS. He was made the director of an 'India Institute', also known as 'Working Group India', established by the 'Reich Security Main Office' (*Reichssicherheitshauptamt* or RSHA), an organization formed by Heinrich Himmler in September 1939 by combining the heads of the police or the 'Sipo' (which incorporated both the Gestapo and the criminal police) and the secret service (SD) of the SS. The RSHA formed the nucleus of a police force indoctrinated with Nazi ideology. It played a crucial role in developing and implementing the Nazi politics of terror and extermination.[94] An objective of this India Institute was to provide information on the political situation of India to the RSHA.[95]

Walther Wüst deployed, to a greater extent than Hauer, various aspects of the Aryan discourse to serve the cultural political goals of the Nazi regime through the Institute. As mentioned, Wüst studied under Wilhelm Geiger at the University of Munich, where he completed his PhD on a linguistic aspect of the Rig Veda in 1923. This was followed by *Habilitation* in 1925, on the stylistic history of ancient Indian (primarily Rig Vedic) poetry. The examiners of the second thesis commented that in future Wüst should engage more in working on the cultural aspects of Indian Studies, in ways that would be of relevance to the post-First World War German state. This was probably one of the reasons that led Wüst to turn to the study of 'Aryan-Nordic' primeval culture (*Urkultur*).

Though like Hauer, Wüst began to project his post-First World War frustrations and longings on to an 'Aryan past', unlike Hauer, he retained close ties with the Protestant Church in the 1920s. By the early 1930s, however, Wüst began to feel alienated from Christianity as he identified with the cultural criticism of scholars like Hermann Wirth (1885–1981) who claimed that the German spirit had lost its connection with its Nordic Aryan religious roots. A revitalization of the German nation could only be achieved through a spiritual rebirth, by rekindling the nation's connection to its 'pure' Nordic roots untainted by Semitism.[96]

Both Wüst and Hauer felt motivated to provide academic justification for Nazi racial politics through their dubious scholarship on Aryanism. However, while Hauer was ideologically invested in the Aryan/Indo-German religion, Wüst's religiosity remained ambivalent and his scholarship after 1933 was dictated primarily by opportunism.[97]

In essence, the Aryan discourse propagated by both Hauer and Wüst were influenced by the *völkisch* movement of the late nineteenth to early twentieth centuries, which celebrated a mystical notion of the German *volk* on the basis of language, race, and religion. An innate anti-Semitism as well as a racialized interpretation of India's 'Aryan past' made some German Indologists susceptible to the *Völkisch* agenda which also had close ties with the National Socialist movement.[98]

Wüst's connection to the DA was through Haushofer, whose lecturers he attended as a student at the University of Munich. The young ambitious scholar soon ingratiated himself with the senior academic, demonstrating an early talent for inveigling those in power.[99] After the Nazis came to power, Wüst busied himself trying to establish his credentials as a loyal National Socialist (Figure 2).

Figure 2 Walther Wüst giving a lecture on 'The Führer's Book "Mein Kampf"' as a Reflection of the Aryan Worldview' at the Hackerkeller, Munich, Germany, 10 March 1937.
Source: Bundesarchiv 146-1999-007-36/Bauer, Friedrich/CC-BY-SA 3.0.

He joined the Nazi party in May 1933 and the NSLB in December of the same year. He also began delivering lectures extolling Hitler and Nazi ideology to various affiliations of the Nazi party.[100]

The advancement of Wüst's academic career was proportional to his political pursuits. In 1932, he became a non-tenured professor (*außerordentlicher Professor* or *Extraordinarius*) at the University of Munich. In 1935, he succeeded the Indologist Hannes Oertel as a tenured professor for Aryan Philology (which was now renamed Aryan Culture and Philology to accommodate Wüst's politicized scholarly interests). Also in 1935, Wüst became the dean of the Faculty of Philosophy, a position which helped him to function as an agent of the SD as well as of the NSDB at the University of Munich. On 26 January 1937, he officially joined the SS and soon thereafter was given the rank of *Haupsturmführer* (akin to a captain) and inducted into the prestigious and powerful personal staff of Himmler (*Persönlicher Stab Reichsführer SS*). He made steady progress through the ranks of the SS, becoming an *Oberführer*, which was a fairly senior rank, in 1942.[101]

In 1941, Wüst became the rector of the University of Munich.[102] In his introductory lecture as the rector, Wüst proclaimed that the main purpose of German *Wissenschaft* and its carrier, the University, was to uphold the goals of the National

Socialist 'Reich'.[103] A particularly infamous act of Wüst was to deliver the siblings Hans and Sophie Scholl, leaders of the anti-Nazi group 'White Rose' and students of the University of Munich, to the Gestapo on 18 February 1943, for the crime of distributing anti-Nazi flyers. The Scholl siblings were guillotined on 22 February.[104]

After 1933, the Institute started to promote the works of Wüst and Hauer since they openly championed the ideological-political agenda of the Nazi state. In 1927, through the mediation of Haushofer, the DA, together with the *Notgemeinschaft der deutschen Wissenschaft* (precursor of today's German Research Foundation or the DFG) had awarded Wüst an allowance of 200 Marks for a year to work on an etymological dictionary of Indo-Aryan language.[105]

In 1935, the DA provided Wüst financial assistance to publish the first and eventually the only volume of this dictionary. At the time of its publication, Wüst boasted to the Bavarian Ministry of Culture that his plan was to publish several volumes comprising 3,000–3,500 pages and that this work would bring out the essence of the world view of the 'oldest and purest *Indogerman* language'.[106] The published work had an introduction and a bibliography which together spanned 197 pages, but the 'actual' work consisted of 11 pages with three lexemes with 'a'.[107]

In the same year, the DA offered Hauer an opportunity for self-promotion by advertising in its journal a booklet written by him, titled, 'Indo-Aryan Metaphysics in Combat and Deed: The *Bhagavad-Gita* in New Light' (1934).[108] In the tract, Hauer claimed that the ancient Hindu text actually celebrated Nordic Aryan ideals like the duty of the warrior to fight for honour and for the 'Reich', echoing the combative ethos of the SS. Himmler supposedly relied on this book for quoting from the *Bhagavadgita* with which he hoped to inspire the SS in pursuing its murderous goals.[109]

Hauer was instrumental in inviting the Hindu revivalist guru, Swami B.H. (Bhakti Hriday) Bon, to deliver a lecture at the Institute in 1934.[110] Bon, born a Bengali called Narendra Nath Mukherjee (1901–1982) belonged to the revivalist *Gaudiya* order, a neo-Hindu sect that tried to 'Aryanize' and 'modernize', which in this case implies infusing a kind of spirituality that would also speak to a Western audience, a medieval strand of non-Vedic popular cult of Krishna worship.[111] Bon had undertaken a lecture tour of Germany in December 1933, before he became involved in establishing a mission of the *Gaudiya* order in London in 1934. During his tour of Germany, he had secured a faithful disciple, a young German man called Ernst Georg Schulze (1908–1977), then a PhD student of Comparative Religion at the University of Leipzig.[112] Schulze followed his guru to London, taking up the position of Bon's private secretary. On 23 May and 21 June 1934, respectively, Schulze sent two letters to Hauer, asking for the latter's opinion about a German translation of *Bhagavadgita*, written in English by Bon from the perspective of *Gaudiya* order. Schulze wrote that he had chosen to write to Hauer since the latter was 'working with great enthusiasm for the renewal of the German faith'.

Schulze was clearly interested in the kind of 'renewal' that Hauer envisioned. In June 1934, he wrote again to Hauer that he, Schulze, searched for the primordial Aryan religion that Aryan Indians and the Aryans of the West had in common, adding that he was convinced that Swami Bon was bringing to the West a religion that is 'closer to the Aryan sensitivity than Jewish theology and groundless asphalt-Atheism'. Apart from this glimpse of anti-Semitism, another indication of Schulze's political inclination is his statement in the letter that he regularly received the *Völkischer Beobachter* ('The Peoples' Observer'), the mouthpiece of the Nazi party, as well as the Nazified weekly *Der Reichswart*, in London.

Schulze's guru seemed to have shared his disciple's political orientation. As Schulze wrote in one of his letters to Hauer, Bon had formed a positive impression of the 'new Germany of Adolf Hitler' during his tour of Berlin and he was convinced that 'the German people were the most suited of all western peoples for understanding the Indo-Aryan religion'. Hauer answered on 28 June 1934. He wrote that he could invite Swami Bon for talks since he had some influence over the DA through the India Institute. This, claimed Hauer, was to be a further step in inculcating an understanding between Aryan India and the new Germany.[113]

This invitation probably suited Bon's plans, since he, along with Schulze, travelled to Berlin in October 1934 to set up a branch of the *Gaudiya* Mission in the German capital. From this base, Bon began to hold regular talks, which he composed in English and let Schulze translate in German for Bon to read out. He also travelled widely in Germany, met various German scholars and theologians, and delivered talks in different universities on Indian religion and spirituality and their connections to Aryanism.[114] The Hindu mendicant was personally welcomed by Haushofer at the India Institute in Munich on 26 December 1934. Bon spoke in English on 'The Aryan Indian's Path to God'. The lecture was supposedly very well attended and enthusiastically applauded.[115]

The Nazi authorities in Berlin were, however, not particularly enthusiastic about Bon's growing popularity which, in the paranoid totalitarian mind-set of the ruling elite, seemed to threaten the messianic appeal of the 'Führer'. A similar attitude towards Hauer's powerful position in the German Faith Movement had led to his denunciation by the Nazi party's unit in Munich, which castigated the Indologist as a self-styled prophet who was not required by the NSDAP.[116] The 'official' stance of the regime was that Bon's world view contradicted the racial politics of the Nazis. In 1936, an article titled 'From Asian Cultures' by the German scholar Theodor Steche, published in the *Völkischer Beobachter*, claimed that the *Gaudiya* order's universalist and spiritualist creed lacked the racial perspective which was important for Nazi Germany.[117] This difference in attitude between the authorities in Berlin and the Institute in Munich indicates that the Nazi regime did not yet have a coordinated approach to propaganda as far as India was concerned.

Nevertheless, the connections between Nazi Germany and the *Gaudiya* order continued through the person of Schulze, who converted to Hinduism, assuming the name Sadananda Brahmachari, and followed his guru to India 1935. Colonial surveillance in India suspected Schulze, with good reason, for propagating Nazism among educated Indians under cover of his religious engagements. Schulze also used the *Gaudiya* mission temples in India as 'contact zones' for the Indians and Germans belonging to the Nazi network.[118]

Also in 1934, through Hauer's mediation, the Institute invited Mahendranath Sircar, professor of Philosophy at the University of Calcutta.[119] Hauer appreciated the religious ideas of Sircar, who was a devotee of Ramkrishna and Vivekananda, as his various essays in the *Prabuddha Bharata* demonstrate. Sircar's academic works revolved around Hindu philosophy as well as various mystical and revivalist concepts.[120]

During his trip of Germany, Sircar gave lectures on 'The Social Background of Indian Life' and 'A Synthetic View of Indian Mysticism' at the universities of Hamburg, Marburg, and Tübingen.[121] The journal of the DA published a predominantly positive review of Sarkar's book *Eastern Lights* (1935) which tried to highlight the so-called revival of Hindu enlightenment from the nineteenth century to the present.[122] There is, however, no evidence that Sircar expressed any interest in Nazism.

Through Wüst's intervention, *Arya Samaj*, an influential Hindu revivalist sect, became an important participant in the Institute's cultural political praxis after 1933. We will examine this particular aspect in detail in order to understand the dynamics of the collusion between religious revivalism and Nazi politics through the mediation of Wüst and the Institute.

The *Arya Samaj* ('Society of Aryans') was founded by the philosopher and social reformer Dayanand Saraswati (1824–1883) in Bombay in 1875 and in Lahore in 1877. Dayanand believed in the supremacy of the Vedic Aryans and considered modern-day Hindus to be their degenerate successors. Under his leadership, the *Arya Samaj* envisioned bringing the Hindus back to the 'true and pure faith' of Vedic monotheism. Though unlike European scholars, Dayanand did not formulate an Aryan discourse through racialized and Eurocentric tenets, he adapted the European image of the Aryans as noble, virtuous, and knowledgeable.[123] The 'Aryan connection' worked both ways, as the admiration for the *Arya Samaj* expressed by the Indologist Paul Deussen (1845–1919) during his travels in India (1892–3), demonstrates.[124] The *Arya Samaj* movement, with its emphasis on authoritarianism, majoritarianism, and the racially charged 'Aryan content', including a eugenicist dimension, concurred with some aspects of Nazism.[125]

Another factor that contributed to the Institute's preference for the *Arya Samaj* was the latter's influence on the emergent English-educated, middle-class and upper-caste Indians. This was at least partially due to the *Samaj*'s emphasis on patriotism without expressing direct opposition to British rule.[126] The *Arya Samaj* catered to the educational needs and aspirations of upper-caste middle-class Indians through its own educational system comprising the 'Dayanand Anglo Vedic' (DAV) schools and colleges. As the name suggests, these educational institutions aimed to combine 'modern knowledge' with Vedic traditions, which appealed to the tastes and ambitions of the burgeoning middle classes.[127] The kind of young men trained in the DAV institutions were possibly of interest to the Institute, since it was not difficult to foresee that many of them would be suscepti-ble to propaganda combining Aryanism, subtle anti-British sentiments, and the merits of Nazism.

Wüst used his position as professor of 'Aryan Studies' to link the Institute and the *Arya Samaj*. In 1936, he established a position of a lector of Indian languages at his department, reserved only for a scholarship holder of the India Institute. The two known occupants of this position were Dhirendra Kumar Mehta and Aryendra Sharma, respectively. Both had received scholarships provided jointly by India Institute and the Humboldt Foundation to write their dissertations under Wüst. Dhirendra Kumar Mehta was from Gurukul University, which had been founded in 1902 by the monk Shraddhanand, a member of the *Arya Samaj*. Through his thesis, Mehta tried to provide academic legitimacy to the religious education provided by the *Arya Samaj* in the schools that it controlled.[128] The dissertation, completed in 1935, was titled 'Methods and Directions of Contemporary Religious Psychological Research and Its Significance for India's Education System'. It was published as a monograph by the prestigious German publisher Springer in 1936.[129]

Aryendra Sharma completed his PhD in 1940 on 'Contributions to Vedic Lexicography: New Words in Bloomfield's Vedic Concordance' (referring to the monumental work by the Austrian–American Sanskrit scholar Maurice Bloomfield, 1855–1928). In the same year, he published a laudatory article on 'The *Arya Samaj* and Its Founder' in the journal of the DA, which was now called *Deutsche Kultur im Leben der Völker* (German Culture in the Lives of the People or DKLV).[130] In this way, the University of the Munich and the Institute collabo-rated to generate knowledge that symbolized Nazi Germany's espousal of this Hindu revivalist organization. British surveillance noted in 1939 that Aryendra Sharma was the president of the Indian Students Association in Munich. The report claimed that most Indian students in Munich were 'favourably impressed by Nazi principles' and could be expected to publicize them upon their return.[131]

A manifestation of the collaboration between the *Arya Samaj*, the India Institute, and the Nazi network in India was a scholarship, funded jointly by the Institute and the firm Allianz and Stuttgarter for the year 1934. It was awarded to Satanketu Vidyalankar, a professor of History from Gurukul University.[132] A sur-veillance report from September 1939 claimed that the German consulate in Calcutta worked closely with the DA in collecting nominations for a scholarship in Philology in Germany. Candidates who were members of the *Arya Samaj* or approved of its 'Aryan world view' were preferred. Horst Pohle, the German lector sent to Calcutta by the DA, seemed to have functioned as the link between the *Arya Samaj*, the German consulate in Calcutta, and the DA in spreading the word about these scholarships.[133]

The perception that belonging to the *Arya Samaj* provided an applicant an advantage seemed to have been quite widespread, at least in Calcutta. As a letter dated 25 August 1939 from Anil Bhusan Nandy Majumdar, a researcher in Chemistry, to the DA makes clear. In his letter, Nandy Majumdar claimed that he, a bona fide member of the *Arya Samaj*, had been notified by the latter about the scholarships, based on information supplied by Pohle. The young scholar also attached a certificate from the general secretary of the *Arya Samaj* in Calcutta to prove his *Samajist* credentials.[134] He could not receive the scholarship since such exchanges were halted due to the onset of the war.

The leaders of the *Arya Samaj* were receptive to the DA as well as to Nazism. Colonial surveillance noted repeated instances of the preachers (*pracharak*) of the *Arya Samaj* praising Hitler and Nazism in their addresses.[135] In 1939, Satya Deva, a preacher from the *Samaj*, visited Berlin and was greeted well by the Foreign Ministry which expressed satisfaction at the monk's promotion of 'the new Germany for years'. Bernhard Breloer (1894–1947) professor of Indology at the University of Berlin, a fanatic Nazi, and senior SS officer, was asked to arrange for lectures on Aryan religion that the monk offered to deliver.[136] Though it is not known whether Satya Deva actually gave such talks, it is evident that the regime now felt secure enough to welcome Hindu mendicants who were considered useful emissaries for propagating Nazism. The Nazi approaches to the Hindus, the majority community in India, were primarily through the *Arya Samaj*, as a surveillance record noted.[137] It is undeniable that the Institute contributed significantly to the interface between Nazi Germany and the *Arya Samaj*.

The Nazi network in India, as is well known, had connections with the incipient political Hinduism represented by the Hindu *Mahasabha*.[138] The latter was an organization of conservative Hindu upper castes, which stood for anti-Muslim, Hindu supremacist views. However, the Institute in Munich, under the influence of Indologists like Wüst and Hauer, displayed a preference for the established revivalist sects like the *Arya Samaj*. This bias was due to these scholars' personal interests in a revivalist agenda based on Aryanism as well as the far reach of *Arya Samaj*'s influence among the educated middle-class Hindus, which the Hindu *Mahasabha* was yet to achieve. The *Arya Samaj*'s revivalist objectives had an anti-colonial dimension, which rendered it attractive to the Institute's propaganda strategy of combining the rhetoric of Aryanist spiritual regeneration of the Hindus with a subtle disregard for the British. Though some *Arya Samaj* activists were involved in the *Hindu Mahasabha*, unlike the *Arya Samaj*, the Mahasabha generally embraced orthodox Hinduism and remained steadfastly loyal to the British.[139]

India Institute and the Muslims

It is evident from this discussion that the India Institute was intent on connecting primarily with the upper-caste Hindu elite of India. Due to a number of complex circumstances, including the policies of the British Raj, members of the Hindu upper castes had much more access to financial and cultural resources than the majority of Muslims or lower-caste Hindus. The influence of some German Indologists, whose anti-Semitic prejudices often extended to Indian Muslims, could have also been partially responsible for an overwhelmingly Hindu profile of the Institute's scholarship holders.

Nevertheless, Thierfelder personally assisted a Muslim student of engineering called Niaz Ahmed Khan in getting a PhD from TU Munich in 1933. Thierfelder claimed to Karl Kapp, then German Consul General in Bombay that, after receiving this assistance, Khan would have a good impression of Germany. He would also be a useful intermediary between the DA and the Indian Muslims who generally preferred to send their sons to England.[140] Niaz Ahmed Khan became a lecturer at the Aligarh Muslim University (AMU) in north India and was known to be a Nazi propagandist. He belonged to the 'German Society' of the AMU which responded very favourably to Nazism.[141]

The German Society was founded in 1932 by Otto Spies (1901–1981), a German scholar of 'Islamic' (Arabic, Turkish, and Persian) languages and a self-proclaimed follower of the Nazi 'movement' who joined the Arabic department of the AMU in October 1932 and Sattar Kheiri (1885–1945), the German lector at this university who, along with his brother Jabber, had lived in Germany for a long time.[142] This Society propagated Islamic nationalism in the form of supporting the idea of a separate state for Indian Muslims. It also displayed an unbridled admiration for Nazi Germany. The 'New Germany' was to serve as an inspiration for Indian Muslims to achieve their own independent homeland. The Society soon attracted the ire of the colonial government for its propagation of Hitler and Nazism, particularly through its journals which began to appear from 1934 and were replete with Nazi propaganda conveyed through various articles, some of which favourably compared Islam with Nazism and the Islamic prophet with the 'Führer'.[143] According to colonial surveillance records, Horst Pohle, the lector of the DA in Calcutta, drew attention to this journal in a letter written to the DA in 1935. Otto Spies also sent copies of this journal to the DA, which replied that the India Institute was in touch with Kheiri.[144] The journal of the DA advertised the German Society's journals, claiming euphemistically that they aimed to enlighten the members of the Society about German spiritual and intellectual life (*Geistesleben*).[145]

Kheiri's correspondence, examined by the colonial authorities after he was arrested as an ally of the Germans in 1940, revealed that in 1939 he requested the Institute to create a post, to be occupied by a Muslim candidate chosen by himself, for studying and teaching Philosophy at the University of Munich with scholarships from the Institute. The latter agreed and requested Kheiri to send his recommendations. The scheme had to be abandoned due to the war.[146]

Aryanism and 'Race Science'

If the Institute courted Hindu revivalists as a means to reach the souls and spirits of the Hindus, it cultivated academics specializing in racialized anthropology and ethnology after 1933 for appealing to 'scientific-minded' Indians. With the backing of the Institute, such ethnologists and anthropologists were to generate and disseminate 'scientific views' of Indian society using methods of racial classification that aligned with the kind of 'new anthropology' favoured by the Nazi regime. Such dissemination of racialized anthropology/ethnology represented the much vaunted *Weltgeltung* or world renown of German *Wissenschaft*.

One such guest of the Institute was Biraja Sankar Guha (1894–1964), professor of Anthropology at the University of Calcutta, who visited Munich in 1935. Guha had received his PhD in Anthropology from the University of Harvard in 1924 for his thesis on 'The Racial Basis of the Caste System in India'.[147] The subject traditionally enjoyed a shared interest among colonial officials in India who became hobby ethnographers, as well as European scholars propounding racialized views of India's history and society.[148]

Some of these scholars projected the different caste groups as perfectly endogamous, which, according to recent scholarship, was 'a fiction of colonial ethnology'.[149] The colonial scholars, following the European ethnological views, also juxtaposed the categories of race and caste by detecting an 'Aryan element' among light-skinned Brahmins in contrast to the supposedly non-Aryan, primarily dark-skinned Dravidians found predominantly in the south. Guha, a pioneer among Indian anthropologists, not only borrowed from such racialized works but also incorporated elements of 'biometrical nationalism' in his scholarship. Caste, in Indian biometric nationalism, became an allegory of racial distinction to determine an elite group, which could in future lay claims to being the natural successors of the colonial rulers.[150]

Guha's postulations fitted in well with German Racial Science (*Rassenkunde* or *Rassenlehre*), which was construed as a physical-anthropological discipline that sought to provide scientific validity to the biopolitical concept of race and racial differences. 'Racial Science' and its affiliate, the more clinically oriented 'Racial Hygiene' including its eugenicist component were established academic disciplines in German universities and research organizations by the mid-1920s. These disciplines attained a special political significance after 1933, as the Nazi regime started using these 'scientific' subjects to justify its racial politics. Many 'racial scientists' readily cooperated with the Nazi regime by providing scientific legitimacy to schemes like forced sterilization and euthanasia.[151]

The political relevance of Guha's scholarship in Nazi Germany is evident from the fact that the institute organized, in cooperation with the Anthropological Society and the German Society for Racial Hygiene, two lectures by him, on 'The Racial Composition of India' and 'The Racial Foundation of the Indo-Aryans and Racial Miscegenation in India', respectively. The second lecture was probably considered more significant, since it was published in the journal of the DA in 1935.[152] In this paper, Guha conformed to the racialized 'Aryan' tropes shared by some German ethnographers and Indologists. The article attempted to prove, through biometric analysis, that 'heroic' Vedic Aryans were ancestors of upper-caste Hindus from north India as well as of the tribes from the north-western border. It also claimed that these Aryan descendants had managed to retain some of the Indo-Aryan traits. The article concluded that artistic and philosophical expressions of Nordic Aryan thoughts that started with the Rig Veda had continued to live on in India through the literary works of Rabindranath Tagore, whom Alfred Rosenberg, the chief ideologue of the Nazis, had derided in his Magnum Opus, *Der Mythus des 20.Jahrhunderts* or, The Myth of the 20th Century, published originally in 1930. To Rosenberg, Tagore's support of non-violent nationalism was supposedly the result of the degeneration of the martial Aryan spirit.[153]

Guha's claim regarding the continuity of the Aryan spirit of the Rig Veda is eerily reminiscent of the view of the *völkisch*-oriented Indologist Leopold von Schroeder (1851–1920), who postulated that the 'Aryan spirit', manifested in the Rig Veda which was composed by the Nordic Aryans, found its fullest expression in the operas of Richard Wagner.[154] This claim was also made by Wüst in his aforementioned introductory address as the rector of the University of Munich in 1941, indicating that this racialized thought continued to have traction in certain branches of Indology and it sometimes intersected with ethnological scholarship.

Guha's student, Achyut Kumar Mitra (b. 1903) who had studied at a college established by the *Gaudiya* sect, was given a scholarship by the Institute jointly with the Humboldt Foundation in 1934–35, to write a dissertation at the University of Munich.[155] Mitra completed his PhD on 'A Contribution to the Racial Studies of the Bengalis (India)' in 1938. His research guide was Professor Theodor Mollison (1874–1952), director of the Institute of Anthropology at the University of Munich. Mollison was one of the leading 'race hygienists' of Nazi Germany, who provided the patina of 'science' to the eugenicist policies of the Nazi regime like the 'elimination of unworthy lives' from the German national community.[156] Not coincidentally, Mollison was also one of the two supervisors of the notorious physician Josef Mengele, who conducted inhuman medical experiments on the prisoners of Auschwitz.[157]

In February 1938, Mollison wrote a letter to the German Research Foundation, requesting a subvention for publishing Mitra's PhD. In this letter Mollison praised both Guha and Mitra for bringing the Indian anthropology in sync with contemporary German methods of examination, with racial categories like Aryans, primitives, Dravids, and so on.[158] In making this claim, Mollison refused to take note of the ethnological and eugenicist ideas prevalent among Indian anthropologists which were independent of contemporary German discourses.[159] Mollison's statement exuded the hubris of German *Wissenschaft*, that it was teaching the Indians to study their own society scientifically. It is not known whether the dissertation was published as a monograph, but the Institute could once again demonstrate to the Nazi regime that it had promoted a certain kind of scientific knowledge of India 'for extra-scientific purposes, wherein science is a mere vehicle of politics by other means'.[160]

Walther Wüst and Nazification

In 1933, the Institute and the University of Munich arranged a lecture course on India, comprising a 12-hour series. It was attended by 500 persons, an impressive number for a niche scholarly event.[161] Some of the subjects had political connotations, like Haushofer's talk on 'The Geopolitical Significance of India'. Hauer's paper on 'The Significance of Yoga in the Present Spiritual and Religious Situation' was an element of his venture to project Yoga as part of a purportedly glorious spiritual history of Nordic Indo-Aryans. Wilhelm Geiger, an expert on Ceylon (Sri Lanka), spoke on 'Buddhism in Ceylon'.[162] Geiger is considered a pioneer in establishing Sinhala as an Indo-Aryan language, for which he stands accused of 'Aryanizing' Sinhala and contributing to the development of Sinhalese Buddhist nationalism, with all its accompanying problems.[163]

In 1934, Karl Haushofer provided a glimpse of the Institute's role as provider of strategically important knowledge to the regime. As the president of the Institute, he gave a speech to the Nazi party unit in Berlin on 'Political Science and the Politics of the Far East'. He defined the role of the DA as a 'sounding board' for politics and economics of the 'Far East' for assisting in making political decisions.[164]

However, by 1936, despite Haushofer's efforts, the DA's economic situation became precarious. In order to attract funds, the DA increasingly turned towards the government, which on its part started to use it more intensively for spreading Nazi propaganda. The amount of influence that the regime was to exercise in the DA became a contentious issue. Unlike Haushofer, Thierfelder was against the DA's overt identification with the regime since he opined that propaganda was most effective when it was conducted covertly. As a result of the increasing differences of opinion regarding this issue, both Thierfelder and Haushofer resigned in 1937.[165] This did not signify Thiefelder's opposition to the Nazi regime, as he would claim after 1945. He continued to offer his knowledge to the

Nazi regime by writing two anti-British books and at least two articles promoting Subhas Chandra Bose which were published in the *Völkische Beobachter* during the war.[166]

Haushofer had to cede his post as president to Leopold Kölbl, who was a prominent leader in the notorious SA. Kölbl was also the rector of the University of Munich at the time. Nevertheless, Haushofer remained in the DA's executive council and succeeded in making his protégé Walther Wüst the president of the Institute in 1937.[167] Wüst had become Haushofer's trusted henchman after the latter became president of the DA. He had tried, albeit unsuccessfully, to fulfil Haushofer's wish of granting an honorary doctorate to Benoy Kumar Sarkar in 1935.[168] After becoming president of the Institute, Wüst thanked Haushofer profusely in a letter for the latter's 'parental trust' in him.[169]

Meanwhile, Wüst had successfully ingratiated himself with Heinrich Himmler who formally included the Indologist in the *Ahnenerbe* ('ancestral heritage'), a pseudo-scientific think tank under his control and staffed mostly with SS members. The *Ahnenerbe*'s main task was to conduct specious research about the purported Aryan legacy of the German people. Wüst's academic credentials were to lend the *Ahnenerbe* an aura of intellectual credibility. For the same reason, Wüst was made the president of the *Ahnenerbe* on 1 February 1937.[170]

One of Wüst's first plans as president of the Institute was to set up a branch of the Institute, named after his teacher Wilhelm Geiger, at the University of Munich. This signified Wüst's attempt to include Ceylon (now Sri Lanka) into DA's scope, since Geiger was considered to be an expert on Sri Lanka. This was to be a joint venture of the DA and department of Aryan Culture and Philology of the University of Munich, which Wüst headed. The president of this branch was to be none other than Wüst. The Institute would include Julius de Lanerolle (1896–1964), a linguist from Sri Lanka who studied at the University of Munich with assistance from the DA. A corresponding institute was to be set up in Colombo, where a German lector was to be sent. These ambitious plans did not come to fruition due to the onset of the war.[171]

Wüst tried to integrate the Institute into the network of *Ahnenerbe* and the SS in different ways. He suggested at a meeting of the Institute in 1937, that the aforementioned Bernhard Breloer should be invited to become a member of the Institute. The proposal was approved but it is not clear whether Breloer accepted.[172] Wüst also aimed to generate a knowledge discourse about India that would be congruent with the *Ahnenerbe*'s pseudo-academic projects that sought to establish the supremacy of the Aryan race and to render scientific respectability to the search for spurious Nordic Germanic rituals and cultic symbols. Himmler wanted to use the findings of such quests to design a 'neo Germanic ideology', an alternative religious cult for the SS.[173]

In 1938, under Wüst's aegis, the *Ahnenerbe* collaborated with the Institute in organizing an essay competition for postgraduates of Indian universities on

'Symbols and Signs in India: Meaning, Development and Life'. The choice of the subject came from the *Ahnenerbe*, which offered a sum of 5,000 *Reichsmarks* for the winner. The second prize was a scholarship for one year of study in Germany, without the costs of journey covered. The third prize was half a year of studying opportunity in Germany without travel costs. The Institute also held the right to publish the essays, which were to appear either in the journal of the DA or in one of the publications of the *Ahnenerbe*. The winning essays were to be selected by a committee of the Institute. The submission date was 1 April 1940.[174]

Wüst announced at a meeting of the India Institute in 1938 that this subject was chosen, after much deliberation, 'to take the Indians back to their roots and to demonstrate that German science (*Wissenschaft*) was ready to incorporate the suggestions and insights of Indian academics'. Since this was the first essay competition of its kind, the subject needed to sound politically innocuous. For the next competition, claimed Wüst, a more explicitly political subject could be chosen.[175] Indeed, in March 1939, another essay competition was advertised in Indian newspapers, on the unambiguously propagandistic subject of 'Aryan Origin of the Swastika and Its Common Usage in India and Germany'.[176] The fates of these essay competitions remain unknown.

Meanwhile, ever since Joachim von Ribbentrop (1893–1946) became the foreign minister in February 1938, the Foreign Ministry started taking increasing interest in the DA. In June 1938 the DA was brought under the responsibility of the 'cultural political section' of the Foreign Ministry. This section was responsible for conducting propaganda in India.[177] In 1939, Leopold Kölbl, the president of the DA, was imprisoned on charges of homosexuality. This crisis propelled the DA further into the control of the Foreign Ministry which led to its further Nazification. Ludwig Siebert, a committed Nazi and the chief minister of the state of Bavaria, replaced Kölbl as the president of the DA in 1939. This change at the top ushered in a process of increasing financial and administrative stability for the DA. Walther Wüst now became both vice-president and head of the 'research and publications' section of the DA.[178] With Siebert and Wüst at the helm, the last remnants of the veneer of the DA's political neutrality were dispensed with. By the time the DA officially became an organ of the National Socialist state through a decree by Hitler in 1941, its Nazification had long been complete.

After Siebert's death in November 1942, Wüst became the working head of DA in addition to being the head of the India Institute. He continued in this role until Arthur Seyß-Inquart (1892–1946), *Reichsminister* and Commissioner for the occupied Netherlands, became the president of DA on 10 February 1944.[179] The appointment of a member of the Nazi ruling elite as the president of the DA symbolized the prestige that the DA now enjoyed as the most important organization representing Nazi cultural politics.

The convergence of interests of DA, the Nazi state, and a strand of German Indology was manifest in a speech given by Wüst on 27 April 1939 at the 'Society of Berlin Friends of the *Deutsche Akademie*.[180] The speech, titled 'The German Tasks of Indology' was published in the journal of the DA in August 1939 and has been briefly mentioned in the Introduction.[181] Here, Wüst stated that the intellectual capability of an Indologist was dependent on his racial affiliation. Jewish Indologists, he claimed, had always been concerned with barters and trade-offs since they saw themselves as teachers, while the 'Aryan Indologists' were concerned with the noble task of determining the hereditary kinship between the Aryans and the Germans. As we noted, he also claimed that the task of *luxusprofessoren* of Indology was to support the cultural politics of the 'Third Reich' through their scholarly works, which should also relate to the lives of the German *Volk*. Wüst himself fulfilled this patriotic duty by writing a book, titled *Dawn of Germany and Spiritual History of the Aryans* which was published by the DA in 1939.[182]

Wüst sought to make the DA a mouthpiece for the venture of deploying 'the full and ponderous apparatus of philological and historical Indology' to establish the superiority of the Aryans of ancient India and construing a racial kinship between them and the Germans.[183]

While such attempts had already gained currency through the works of earlier scholars like Max Müller, what set Wüst's speeches and papers apart were his attempts to anchor them in National Socialist ideology, through the invocation of concepts such as 'the sense of race and the conscious desire for racial protection' and 'popular (*volksnahe*) kingship' as he did through a speech, delivered to the DA on 6 December 1939, on 'German Antiquity and the History of Aryan Thought'.[184]

An article by Wüst, titled 'Heredity as the Source of Power for the People: Science in the Life Struggles of the German People' appeared in a special publication to commemorate 15 years of the DA's existence in 1940. It tried to 'scientifically' prove that German people's inner strength was determined by their Aryan heredity.[185]

'Pandit' Bhatta: From Scholarship Holder to Nazi Publicist

In 1939, Wüst appealed personally to the '*Reichsführer*' Heinrich Himmler to provide the necessary financial assistance to send an erstwhile scholarship holder of the DA to India as an agent of Nazi Germany. This agent was to conduct 'cultural politics', which denoted, in this context, both propaganda and espionage. Along with this appeal, Wüst submitted a positive 'evaluation' (*Beurteilung*) of the Indian man, based on the files of the DA and Wüst's own personal observations. The SD also sent a favourable report of this prospective agent to Himmler who now agreed to Wüst's proposal. However, the scheme was stalled due to the war.[186]

The agent in question was Koodavuru Anantrama Bhatta (b. 1908), who represented like no other Indian living in Nazi Germany the convergence between the India Institute, knowledge of India, and Nazi politics. Bhatta's trajectory merits detailed attention, also because we will encounter him again in this book. 'Pandit' Bhatta, as he was known, studied Sanskrit and Pali in India and Sri Lanka. From 1929 to 1932, he taught Sanskrit at Vidyalankar College near Colombo in Sri Lanka.[187] Bhatta arrived in Germany in 1932 with a scholarship provided jointly by the DA and the Humboldt Foundation and started a dissertation on Shaivism in Sanskrit dramas under Hauer at the University of Tübingen. It is not clear whether he ever completed it.[188] Hauer considered Bhatta to be his 'most capable student', while Bhatta referred to him as 'my dear, revered Guru' in their correspondence.[189] As we will soon see, Bhatta would emerge as a successful Nazi publicist. He gained access to information on contemporary India, which he passed on to Hauer. The latter used it to compose secret reports for the 'India Institute' that he headed.[190]

Bhatta, who mastered German well, regularly delivered public lectures on behalf of the Nazi organization, 'Strength through Joy' (*Kraft durch Freude*) which sought to make ordinary Germans appreciate National Socialist ideals. Bhatta also lectured at meetings organized by the Wehrmacht for boosting the morale of the soldiers.[191] He was considered an 'exceptionally reliable' Indian by Alfred Rosenberg's department, which watched over the spiritual and ideological indoctrination and education of the Nazi party members. This department gave its permission to deploy Bhatta occasionally for the German *Volksbildungswerk*, which was another important organization for spreading Nazi world views through public lectures.[192]

During the war, probably through Haushofer's mediation, Bhatta published three articles in the *Journal for Geopolitics* (*Zeitschrift für Geopolitik*) which Haushofer edited. After 1933, this prestigious journal had become increasingly responsive to the demands and interests of Nazi politics. The three articles by Bhatta dealt with aspects of contemporary India that were evidently considered strategically important by the Nazi regime. The essays are (i) 'Internal Problems of India' (July–December, 1939); (ii) 'British Defence Politics in India' (January–June, 1940); and (iii) 'Political Scopes of Different Parties in India' (July–December, 1940).

Bhatta occasionally published texts on India in German newspapers including the *Völkischer Beobachter*, a rare feat for an Indian.[193] A similar 'achievement' of Bhatta was to publish an article in 1942 on 'The Youth Movement in India' in the magazine *Will and Power* (*Wille und Macht*), the propaganda organ for Nazi youth edited by the 'Reich Youth leader' Baldur von Schirach.[194] He also propagated the virtues of Nazism in India from Germany, as evidenced in his essay published in a south Indian journal, the date of publication of which is unfortunately lost. The long article in Kannada language was on 'Youth and Young Women's Movement in Today's Germany' (Figure 3). Basically, this article lionized the Hitler Youth Movement and the role of the Nazi state in conducting it.[195]

Due to his reputation as a publicist approved by the Nazi regime, Bhatta was named the editor of the bilingual (English/German) *Azad Hind* magazine, which

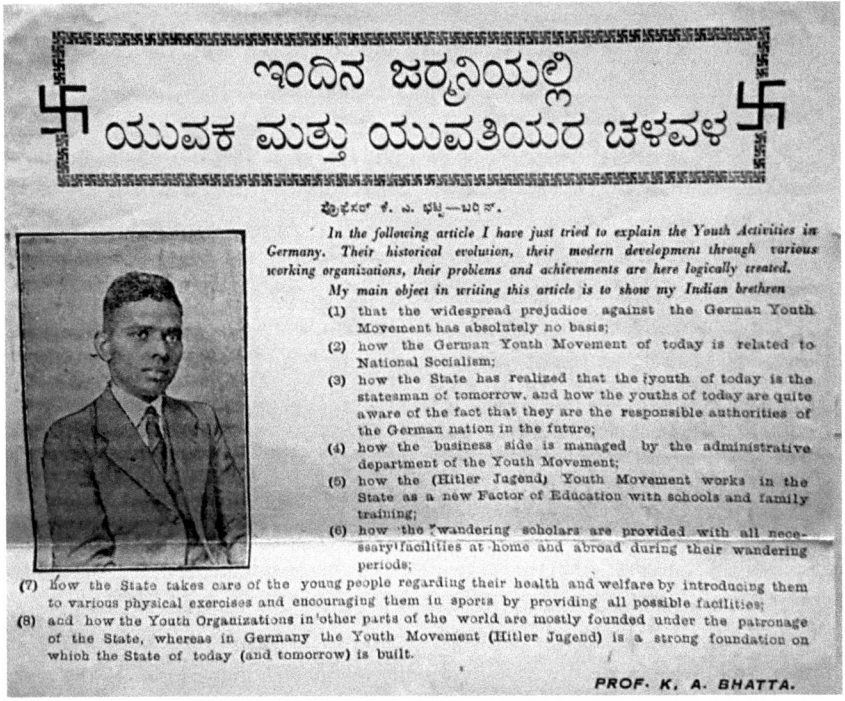

Figure 3 K.A. Bhatta and his article 'Youth and Young Women's Movement in Today's Germany', in Kannada.

was published in Berlin from 1942 to 1944. It was the mouthpiece of the Free India Centre (FIC), established in Berlin jointly by the German Foreign Ministry and Subhas Chandra Bose, who had landed in Berlin in April 1941. Bhatta's role as an editor of *Azad Hind* was largely representational, as the actual editing was done by other anti-colonial Indians from the FIC.[196] More politically significant were Bhatta's articles advocating Bose and his politics in the Nazified press. In May 1942, for example, he wrote an article titled 'Fighter for India: Subhas Chandra Bose's Path' for the *Pariser Zeitung*, an organ of the Nazi occupying authorities in France.[197]

Bhatta also reported about the 'events' organized by the FIC, as his article on the celebration of Gandhi's birthday by Bose and the FIC, published in the *Völkischer Beobachter* in October 1942, demonstrates.[198] Both this celebratory event and the article reflected the change in Germany's propaganda policy towards India, following a conscious decision of Foreign Minister Joachim von Ribbentrop. Under his influence, German propaganda began to express its strategic support for the Indian anti-colonial movement led by Gandhi and the Indian National Congress (INC). The aim was to destabilize the British Empire by stirring up political disturbances in its most profitable colony (Figure 4).[199]

Figure 4 K.A. Bhatta speaking at the Second International Congress of the Union of National Journalists in Vienna at Palais Schoenborn, 1943.
Source: Ullstein Bild/Getty Images.

Return of Indian Anti-Colonialism: 1939–1945

With the start of the war, 'cultural ties' with India became impossible to maintain. The Institute now openly participated in the politically expedient venture to present Nazi Germany as a sympathizer of India's anti-colonial movement by publicising in the DA's journal reviews of books that were strongly anti-British/anti-colonial.

Until about 1939, books on India which were reviewed in the DA's journal were mostly orientalist works depicting India as an exotic land steeped in mysticism, spirituality, and religiosity. An indication of a change in the journal's orientation is provided by a review written by Wüst, of a German book published in 1941. It was a translation from an English work, titled *The Indian War of Independence*.[200] The author of the virulently anti-British book, which was banned by the government in India, was simply called 'an Indian nationalist'. This book in question was actually written by the Indian politician Vinayak Damodar Savarkar (1883–1966) and published in 1909. Savarkar had written the polemicist tract as a young and radical anti-colonial activist. By the time of the publication of the book's German translation, Savarkar had metamorphosed into a champion of politicized Hinduism which kept away from anti-colonial politics but ardently admired Nazism.[201]

In his review, Wüst wrote that the book arrived 'to us through an unusual route', hinting at a secret German–Indian alliance. He paid glowing tributes to the work, claiming that it 'provided a fiery, dazzling chronicle of the history of India's passionate resistance to oppressive British rule'. The book was actually a hate-filled populist treatise, calling for unrestrained and indiscriminate violence against the British, not only for being colonial rulers but also because they were Christians.[202]

The German translation and publication of this tract was carried out by the Foreign Ministry as a propaganda venture, as the preface, written by the head of the press section of the Foreign Ministry, demonstrates. Interestingly, as part of his review, Wüst referred to a work written by the aforementioned Bhatta on the same subject, titled 'India Bleeding: The Rebellion of the Sepoy', published in 1940.[203] Remembering the tragic failure of the First War of Independence in India of 1857 was a part of Subhas Chandra Bose's anti-colonial agenda. He referred to it as the 'great revolution of 1857'.[204] The publication of Savarkar's work constituted another part of this commemorative venture.

The journal also promoted a book series titled 'India in Individual Portraits' (1943), which were written and published under the aegis of the German Foreign Ministry. These books dealt with various aspects of India's history, culture, economy, society, and politics. They were written for the benefit of the officials concerned with Nazi Germany's policy towards India and also to signify to the world Germany's sympathy for Indians chafing under British rule. These books will be examined in detail in the next chapter.

The role of DA was to propagate, in the guise of book reviews, these commissioned works. In 1942, the imminent publication of the Indologist Ludwig Alsdorf's book *The Spiritual Relationship between Germany and India* was announced by the journal with great pomp, claiming that the book would discuss the influence of Indian thought on German thinkers and scholars so that India would emerge not as a mere colony but as having its own cultural heritage.[205] Another book, published under Bhatta's name was advertised in the journal in 1943. Titled *India in British Empire*, the book claimed to analyse the nature of England's rule in India and discuss the conditions under which this colonial domination could be done away with.[206]

Three of the books were reviewed in the DA's journal in1942 by the young scholar, Raghunath Paranjpe (b. 1914). He had come to Germany from Pune in 1938 with a scholarship from the Humboldt Foundation to write his dissertation on German literature under Professor Herbert Cysarz at the University of Munich. Paranjpe completed his dissertation on 'The Historical Dramas of Gerhart Hauptmann' in 1942.[207] Cysarz was a member of the NSDAP, who tried to legitimize various aspects of the Nazi world view through his scholarly works.[208] He was a member of the academic department (*Wissenschaftliche Abteilung*) of the DA, which probably explains Paranjpe's selection as reviewer.[209]

Paranjpe praised the books for providing the information necessary to understand India, which was supposedly at the centre of the world's interest at the time. He lauded the author Hermann Lufft for exposing the capitalist exploitation of India's rich reservoirs of raw materials, mines, and human resources by the British colonialists in his book *The Economy of India*.[210] Another book, *Men and Powers in India*, published under the name of Mukund Rai Vyas, a young Indian anti-colonialist in Berlin, was declared to be a suitable work for understanding the history of the anti-colonial movement in India. Tamil expert Hermann Beythan's book *What Is India?* was acclaimed as an exemplary attempt by a German writer to represent the sober reality of India, in contrast to the 'imperialist school of Kipling' which projected India as an exotic, sensational land of tigers, snakes, maharajas, and so on.[211]

A British surveillance record from 1939 described Paranjpe as 'a keen nationalist but not a Nazi'.[212] Paranjpe's role in advocating the above-mentioned books proves that Indians did not always have to be indoctrinated in National Socialism to contribute to Nazi Germany's cultural politics concerning India through the DA.

Cultural Political Reports

Meanwhile, another very different and non-scholarly form of knowledge of India was being generated under the patronage of the DA by the German lectors stationed in India. By the beginning of 1930s, Thierfelder succeeded in forming a network of lectors who were sent to different parts of the world to teach German on behalf of the DA. In keeping with the objectives of the DA, these men were expected not just to teach the language but also to spread German influence through cultural mediation. However, as Nazi politics began to turn aggressive, 'cultural political activities' of the German lectors began to incorporate another aspect—gathering 'politically important' information about the host country. This implied that the lectors themselves had to be politically reliable. In the early days of Nazi rule, membership of the Nazi party was not officially required but it was nevertheless expected that these young men should be sympathetic towards the ruling ideology.[213] By 1937, Thierfelder insisted on membership of the National Socialist Teachers' Association for the lectors.[214]

The first lector sent to India was Dr Heinz Nitzschke, who arrived in Calcutta in November 1933.[215] Nitzschke was a member of the Nazi Party, who seemed to have utilized his stay in Calcutta for propagating the virtues of the 'Third Reich' rather than collecting information.[216] Nitzschke returned to Germany in 1934. His successor was Horst Pohle, also a member of the Nazi Party, whom a colonial surveillance record described as 'a silent and active worker who mixes with students and young profs quite intimately and carries on Nazi propaganda.'[217]

The surviving correspondence between Pohle and Joachim Schulz, head of the department of lectors in foreign countries at the DA from January 1938, demonstrates that Pohle was expected to provide 'politically relevant' information about India regularly in the form of 'cultural political reports'.[218] The lector was not particularly keen on providing such reports. He complained in July 1939 that he was being watched by the police in Calcutta.[219]

The few available letters from Pohle reveal that he was an active part of the Nazi network in India. He paid a personal visit to 'party comrade' Dr Oswald Urchs, head of the Nazi party unit in India, in Bombay where Urchs was based, and promised to spare no efforts to work as closely as possible with 'the party'.[220]

'Politically relevant' information sent by Pohle included occupational and personal details of the victims of Nazi persecution in Europe who had found refuge in Calcutta, as well as of those Germans and Indians whom the DA regarded as inimical or as competitors. Pohle supplied the names of nine 'Jewish physicians' who practised in Calcutta, as well as those of the exiles who offered German courses, challenging Pohle's monopoly. One such person was a Mrs Sorge, a German (meaning 'non-Jewish') woman who had a romantic relationship with a Bengali physician called Dr D.N. Moitra, an erstwhile scholarship holder of the DA who nevertheless 'refused to visit the DA during his recent trip to Munich'.[221]

Pohle also reported on the efforts of Jawaharlal Nehru to provide employment to highly qualified Austrian and German Jews in India. Nehru, claimed Pohle, had already appointed Jewish experts in the governments of Bihar and Orissa.[222] The Congress politician visited Europe in the summer of 1938 and openly articulated his disapproval of the rising anti-Semitism in Germany after his return.[223] 'The general mood here is not exactly German-friendly, though the effect is not as strong in Calcutta as it is in Bombay,' Pohle wrote, adding that both he and Würfel, the lector at Banaras, thought that the prospects (of increasing German cultural influence) did not appear rosy at that time.

Information about other nations seeking to establish their cultural influence in India was also provided by Pohle, who claimed France was getting ahead of Germany by offering more lucrative stipends that attracted streams of Indian students.[224] According to a surveillance report, the German lector had a network of Indian assistants and agents who toured India to collect information for him.[225]

The other lector of the DA in India, Alfred Würfel (1911–2011) had trained as a community school teacher at the Technical Academy in Dresden, where he studied languages (especially English) and pedagogy (Figure 5). After teaching stints in different schools in Dresden, Würfel became a lector of the DA and was sent to Calcutta in September 1935. He moved to Banaras in October, ostensibly to learn Sanskrit at the Banaras Hindu University (BHU). Würfel had joined the NSLB in 1934.[226] The available correspondence between Würfel and Schulz shows that the latter regularly demanded extensive reports on the range and organization of Würfel's activities in India. Würfel's few letters to Schulz contain various details of his propagandistic activities among the students and faculty of the BHU.[227]

Figure 5 Alfred Würfel (approximately 1935).
Source: Bundesarchiv Berlin R51/10128.

Würfel distributed propagandistic journals in English and German which were sent to him from Germany, among his friends and pupils. *Germany and You* was one such propaganda journal.[228] He also publicized news of the essay competition for Indian students on 'Symbols and Signs in India', a subject which he appreciated.[229] Around the end of 1938, Würfel began to write secret reports to Fochler-Hauke, Thierfelder's successor at the DA, as he informed Nitzschke in a letter from February 1939.[230] These reports are not traceable.

Both the lectors were interned along with all other Germans and Austrian males (initially including Jewish refugees as well) in the Indian subcontinent as 'enemy subjects' on 3 September 1939. The internees were sent first to a camp at the foothills of the Himalayas and afterwards to Ahmednagar in western India, where they spent the rest of the war.[231]

The End and Resurrection of the Institute

The end of the India Institute was heralded by the occupying American forces, which categorized the DA as a Nazi organization and banned it in 1945. The DA's association with the 'war criminal' Arthur Seyß-Inquart, who was executed in 1946 following the verdict of the Nuremberg Trial, added to its stigma.

The DA was partially resurrected in November 1961 as the Goethe Institute. The driving force behind this resuscitation was none other than Thierfelder, who had managed to present himself as an opponent of the Nazi regime.[232] He had already revived the India Institute as a separate entity in the 1950s. The Institute now focused on organizing lecture tours for visiting Indian dignitaries and offering a Hindi course in Munich.[233] In an article which he wrote in 1958 to commemorate 30 years of the Institute's existence, Thierfelder offered a highly manipulated account of the Institute's past by portraying it as a fundamentally non-political organization which kept its distance from the Indian anti-colonial movement under Subhas Chandra Bose, as well as Nazi politics.[234] The current website of the Institute presents a similarly 'corrected' version of its past from which all associations with the National Socialist regime have been elided.

Among the other functionaries, Walther Wüst was dismissed from the University of Munich in 1946. Initially, de-Nazification authorities declared him to be 'encumbered' (belastet) and he served a three-year prison sentence. In 1950 he was declared minderbelastet (moderately encumbered) as a result of his appeal for a revision and the testimonies of his acquaintances and friends who claimed falsely that he had not known about the crimes of the Nazi regime and had tried to help persecuted colleagues.[235] Hauer was interned by the French from May 1945 to August 1947. In the de-Nazification process, he was categorized as a Mitläufer (fellow traveller) and made to retire from his post at the university.[236] Karl Haushofer, together with his wife, committed suicide in 1946. The depression caused by the execution of his son Albrecht in 1945 by the Gestapo due to his alleged connections with the attempt on Hitler's life on 20 July drove the couple to this tragic end.[237]

Notes

1. Harvolk, Edgar, 1990; Kathe, Steffen, R., 2005; Michels, Eckard, 2005.
2. Framke, Maria, 2013, 66–79; Roy, Baijayanti, 2021. https://www.projekt-mida.de/wp-content/uploads/2021/02/Roy-Baijayanti-India-Institute-of-the-Deutsche-Akademie-1928–45.pdf.
3. Manjapra, Kris, 2014, 204–6.
4. For example, Zachariah, Benjamin, 2014, 145; 2022, 111–14.
5. Roy, Baijayanti, 2021. https://www.projekt-mida.de/wp-content/uploads/2021/02/Roy-Baijayanti-India-Institute-of-the-Deutsche-Akademie-1928–45.pdf.
6. Michels, Eckard, 2005, 16, 18.
7. Ibid., 27.
8. Scholten, Dirk, 2000, 41–2.
9. Michels, Eckard, 2005, 34.
10. Ibid., 47.
11. Ibid., 53.
12. Thierfelder, Franz, 1937, 92.
13. Bundesarchiv (BA; Federal Archives) Koblenz: NL1122/6.

14. Institut für Zeitgeschichte (IfZ) Munich: Haushofer collection, 932 b: India Institute of the Deutsche Akademie, 1937, 9–10.
15. Paletschek, Sylvia, 2010, 29–54.
16. On biographical details of Taraknath Das, see Günther, Lothar, 1996. See also Mukherjee, Tapan, 1998; Framke, Maria, 2016, 55–81; Bose, Neilesh, 2020a, 157–77.
17. For details of this period, see Bose, Neilesh, 2020b, 67–88.
18. On India Independence Committee, see Barooah, Nirode Kumar, 2004; Liebau, Heike, 2019; 2022; Jenkens, Jennifer et al., 2020.
19. India Office Records (IOR), Public and Judicial (PJ). British Library, London, IOR/L/PJ/12/166. Report dated 8.3.1923.
20. BA Koblenz: Nachlass Haushofer NL 1122/6. Das to Haushofer, 10.8.1925.
21. Among recent works on the subject, see Koops, Tilman, 2017, 281–2.
22. Sebastian, Luna, 2018, 233.
23. Spang, Christian, 2013, 336.
24. BA Koblenz: NL 1122/6. Das to Haushofer, 10.8.1925.
25. Ibid. Das to Haushofer, 31.7.1928.
26. Ibid. Franz Thierfelder: Jahresbericht, October 1930.
27. Michels, Eckard, 2005, 68.
28. Impekoven, Holger, 2013, 20.
29. Ibid., 222.
30. IOR/L/PJ/12/506. Survey number 20, September 1939, 2.
31. BayHstA, Munich: MK 40444, Vol. 2 (1930–3).
32. BA Koblenz: NL 1122/6. Das to Haushofer, 8.2.1931.
33. For biographical information on Sarkar, see Mukherjee, Haridas, 1953; Flora, Giuseppe, 1994; Sen, Satadru, 2015; Zachariah, Benjamin, 2015; 2022.
34. Sartori, Andrew, 2010, 68–84.
35. Kuhlmann, Jan, 2003, 39.
36. IfZ Munich: Haushofer collection, 932 b: India Institute, 19.
37. Roy, Baijayanti, 2023a.
38. The journal of the DA: *Mittelungen*, December 1933, 533.
39. Roy, Baijayanti, 2021.
40. Aijaz, Ahmed, 2016.
41. On Vivekananda and Hindu nationalism, see Sharma, Jyotirmaya, 2013.
42. BA Koblenz: NL 1133. Sarkar to Haushofer, 28.2.1933.
43. BayHtstA, Munich: MK 40446.
44. BayHstA, Munich: MK 40443. List of members, November 1932.
45. Notable biographies of Hauer are Dierks, Margarete, 1986; Bautz, Friedrich Wilhelm, 1990, 593–4; Baumann, Schaul, 2005; Junginger, Horst, 2008; 2017., 274-279. On Hauer's political activities and works, see Junginger, Horst, 2003, 177–207; Hufnagel, Ulrich, 2003, 145–74; Poewe, Karla, O., 2005, 195–215.
46. Poewe, Karla, O., 2006, 80–1.
47. Junginger, Horst, 2017a, 274.
48. Junginger, Horst, 2003, 178.
49. Roy, Baijayanti, 2016b, 217–28.
50. Hauer, Jakob Wilhelm, 1937, viii–ix. I am grateful to Professor Hermann Kulke and Dr Heiko Frese for providing me with a copy of this book.
51. BA Koblenz: N 1131. Das to Hauer, 18.8.1931.
52. IfZ Munich: Haushofer collection, 932 b: India Institute, 19.
53. Politisches Archiv Auswärtigen Amtes (Political Archive of the German Foreign Ministry): PA-AA Berlin: R122626.
54. BA Berlin: R57/10712. The programme was on 14 May 1936.
55. BayHstA, Munich: MK 40443. List of members, November 1932.
56. BayHstA, Munich: MK 40443. *Mitteilungen*, December 1932. Indien in der modernen Weltwirtschaft und Weltpolitik (Auslandskundliche Vorträge der TH Stuttgart, Band 5).
57. BayHstA: MK 40443. Franz Thierfelder: Das Freiheitsringen der Inder.
58. IfZ Munich: MA 1190.
59. Ibid. Letter from Das to Haushofer, 15.7.1933.
60. Gesche, Katja, 2006, 73–8.
61. Michels, Eckard, 2005, 102.
62. Roy, Baijayanti, 2021.

63. Michels, Eckard, 2005, 105–6.
64. *Mitteilungen*, March 1936, 165.
65. Junginer, Horst, 2017b, 928.
66. See https://www.deutsche-biographie.de/sfz111765.html.
67. See https://www.deutsche-biographie.de/pnd117312312.html.
68. For details, see Voigt, Johannes H., 1971, 33–6; Kuhlmann, Jan, 2003, 37–46; Framke, Maria, 2013, 118–20.
69. NAUK: KV2/3904/2. 6. For more details, see Kuhlmann, Jan, 2003, 48–50; Barooah, Nirode Kumar, 2018, 89–92, among others.
70. Framke, Maria, 2013, 69.
71. Franz Thierfelder, India Institute of the Deutsche Akademie, *Calcutta Review*, June 1933, 403; Taraknath Das, 'Position of Indian Students in National Socialist Germany', *Modern Review*, 1933, 184. For a good summary of the events, see Framke, Maria, 2013, 69–74.
72. IfZ Munich: MA1190. Meeting of the India Institute, 27.10.1938.
73. West Bengal State Archives (WBSA) Calcutta: IB File No. 355–41.Sl.183.
74. *Mitteilungen*, April 1934, 104.
75. Zöllner, Hans-Bernd, 1999, 25–6.
76. IOR/L/PJ/12/214; Voigt, Johannes H., 1971, 41–2.
77. Zöllner, Hans-Bernd, 2000, 26–8; Kuhlmann, Jan, 2003, 24–7.
78. IfZ Munich: MA1190, Protocol of the meeting of Institute, 23.10.1934.
79. IfZ Munich: MA241, Protocol of the meeting of the India Institute, 1.2.1937.
80. IOR/L/PJ/12/410, letter dated 31.12.1936, addressed to a 'Sir John'.
81. Ibid., letter dated 22.3.37.
82. *Mitteilungen*, October 1937, 436.
83. IOR/L/PJ/12/410, Report of British Consul General, Munich, 22.10.1936.
84. Schnabel, Reimund, 1968, 14–15; Roy, Baijayanti, 2024.
85. Koop, Volker, 2009, 39.
86. *Mitteilungen,* July 1933, 248.
87. IOR/L/PJ/12/505, survey of the activities of Germans, 18.2.1939, 2.
88. WBSA, Kolkata, 1941: Notes 355–41.
89. Roy, Baijayanti, 2024, 256. https://link.springer.com/chapter/10.1007/978-3-031-40375-0_11
90. See https://www.leo-bw.de/detail/-/Detail/details/PERSON/kgl_biographien/118773429/Hauer+Wilhelm+Jakob.
91. Junginger, Horst, 2017a, 275.
92. Ibid., 2017a, 274–76.
93. Ibid., 2003, 198.
94. Wildt, Michael, 2019, 7.
95. Junginger, Horst, 2003, 203–4.
96. Ibid., 2008, 6.
97. Ibid., 2017b, 924–6.
98. Roy, Baijayanti, 2017a, 1190–1.
99. Schreiber, Maximillian, 2008, 32–3.
100. Junginger, Horst, 2017b, 926–7.
101. Ibid., 927.
102. Schreiber, Maximillian, 2008, 217.
103. Wüst, Walter, 1941, 28.
104. Junginger, Horst, 2017b, 930.
105. BA Koblenz: Nachlass Haushofer NL 1122/23, note dated 2.4.1927.
106. BayHStA Munich: MK 40443, Vol. 1, Wüst to Bayerisches Staatsministerium für Unterricht und Kultur, 20.7.1935.
107. Schreiber, Maximillian, 2008, 34.
108. *Mitteilungen*, March 1935, 158; J.W. Hauer, *Eine Indo-Arische Metaphysik des Kampfes und der Tat. Die Bhagavadgita in neuer Sicht*. Stuttgart, 1934.
109. Poewe, Karla O., 2006, 115.
110. *Mitteilungen*, March 1935, first issue, 157.
111. On the Gaudiya order, see Sardella, Ferdinando, 2013.
112. Ibid., 160.
113. Poewe, Karla, O., 2006, 73–4.
114. Sardella, Ferdinando, 2013, 161–2.
115. *Mitteilungen*, March 1935, first issue, 157.

116. Rennstich, Karl, 1992, 17.
117. Sardella, Ferdinando, 2019, 81.
118. Roy, Baijayanti, 2024.
119. Poewe, Karla, O., 2006, 73–4.
120. See https://worldcat.org/identities/lccn-n89202217/.
121. *Mitteilungen*, July 1934, 255.
122. *Mitteilungen*, November 1936, 448–9.
123. Bhatt, Chetan, 2001, 16–17.
124. Deussen, Paul, 1922, 87.
125. Roy, Baijayanti, 2021.
126. Bhatt, Chetan, 2001, 20.
127. Fischer-Tiné, Harald, 2013, 290–1.
128. *Mitteilungen*, July 1936, 330.
129. The title of Mehta's dissertation is 'Methorden und Richtungen der religionspsychologischen Forschung der Gegenwart und ihre Bedeutung für das indische Bildungswesen'. I am grateful to Dr Claudius Stein from the Archive of the University of Munich for this information.
130. DKLV, April 1940, 147. The title of his dissertation is 'Beiträge zur vedischen Lexikographie: Neue Wörter in Bloomfield Vedic concordance'.
131. IOR/L/PJ/12/410, 30.1.1939.
132. *Mitteilungen*, July 1934, 254.
133. IOR/L/PJ/12/506, survey number 7 of 1939.
134. WBSA: Sl.350. IB File 583/39.
135. Gould, William, 2009, 158.
136. IOR/L/PJ/12/506, survey number 9, 1939, 6. On Breloer's Nazi affiliations, see Framke, Maria, 2014, 89–128.
137. IOR/L/PJ/12/506, survey for the week ending 9 September 1939.
138. D'Souza, Eugene, 2000; Casolari, Marzia, 2000.
139. Bhatt, Chetan, 2001, 57.
140. BA Berlin: R51/16. Notice on Niaz Ahmed Khan's PhD, 16.8.1933. Thierfelder's letter to Kapp, 19.8.1933.
141. National Archives of India (NAI) New Delhi: Home Political, NA-F-111–40, 94.
142. For details on the Kheiri brothers, see Liebau, Heike, 2019, 341–361.
143. Roy, Baijayanti, 2024.
144. NAI: Home Political, NA-F-111–40, 55.
145. *Mitteilungen*, March 1935, 158.
146. NAI: Home Political, EW-1939-NA-F-93-KW, 55.
147. Sinha, D.P. and Coon, Carleton S., 1963.
148. Roy, Baijayanti, 2016b, 218. For more details on the subject, see Bates, Crispin, 1995; Trautmann, Thomas, 1997 and, more recently, Ghoshal, Sayori, 2021.
149. Mukharji, Projit Bihari, 2022, 82.
150. Ibid., 50–1.
151. Hoßfeld, Uwe and Simunek, Michal V., 2017, 1114–22.
152. BayHStA, Z236; *Mitteilung*, 1935, 488–96.
153. Rosenberg, Alfred, 1934, 661.
154. Roy, Baijayanti, 2017b, 740.
155. BA Berlin: R73/13179.
156. See https://www.deutsche-biographie.de/sfz64945.html; Klee, Ernst, 2005, 415.
157. Schmul, Hans-Walter, 2005, 362.
158. BA Berlin: R73/13179, letter dated 26.2.1938.
159. Ghoshal, Sayori, 2021, 6–7.
160. Raina, Dhruv, 2022, 65.
161. BayHtstA: MK 40443 Deutsche Akademie/1581, July 1933, 9.
162. IfZ Munich: Haushofer collection, 932 b: India Institute, 19.
163. Wijeyeratne, Roshan de Silva, 2014, 90.
164. *Mitteilungen*, November 1934, 408.
165. Michels, Eckard, 2005, 102.
166. Thierfelder, Franz, 1940a; 1940b; 'Begegnung mit Subhas Chandra Bose', *Völkischer Beobachter*, 27.3.1942; 'Inder in Ausland', *Völkischer Beobachter*, 11.4.1942.
167. Michels, Eckard, 2005, 119–21.
168. IfZ Munich: MA241, Wüst to Haushofer, 11.8.1935.

169. Ibid., Wüst to Haushofer, 14.2.1937.
170. Junginger, Horst, 2017b, 926–7.
171. IfZ Munich: MA241, meeting of the India Institute, 1.2.1937.
172. Ibid.
173. Kater, Michael H., 2006, 56.
174. BA Berlin: NS21/297.
175. IfZ Munich: MA1190, meeting of the India Institute, 27.10.1938.
176. Framke, Maria, 2013, 74.
177. Kathe, Steffen R., 2005, 75.
178. Michels, Eckard, 2005, 122–3.
179. Schreiber, Maximillian, 2008, 200.
180. Ibid., 199.
181. DKLV, August 1939, Walther Wüst, *Deutsche Aufgaben der Indologie*, 339–48.
182. DKLV, September 1941, Walther Wüst, *Deutsche Frühzeit und arische Geistesgeschichte*, Munich, 1939.
183. Pollock, Sheldon, 1993, 89.
184. Ibid.
185. Wüst, Walter, 1940, 13–30.
186. BA Berlin: NS19/1086, correspondence between Wüst, Himmler's personal staff, and the SD, 9.5.1939–9.9.1939.
187. IOR/L/PJ/12–659, list of disloyal Indians in Germany, 1944, 42.
188. Archive of the University of Tübingen, *Bhatta Lebenslauf*, 578/150.
189. BA Koblenz: NL 1131/117, correspondence between Hauer and Bhatta, 1944.
190. Junginger, Horst, 2003, 204.
191. BA Berlin: NS15/260, letter from *Kulturpolitisches Archiv* to *Außenpolitisches Amt der NSDAP*, Berlin, 4.7.1940.
192. BA Berlin: NS15/31. Bl.142.
193. National Archives of UK (NAUK), Kew: KV3904-3, statement of A.C.N. Nambiar, 58.
194. K.A. Bhatta, *Die Jugendbewegung Indiens*. In *Wille und Macht*, Heft 8, August 1942, 14–17.
195. K.A. Bhatta, 'Youth and Young Women's Movement in Germany' ('Indina Germanyalli Yuvaka mattu Yuvatiyara chalavala'). I am grateful to R.F. Fathima for the translation and Professor Horst Junginger for providing me with the original text.
196. Roy, Baijayanti, 2022a.
197. K.A. Bhatta, *Kämpfer für Indien: Subhas Chandra Bose's Weg, Pariser Zeitung*, 19.5.1942.
198. Hauner, Milan, 1981, 546.
199. Kuhlmann, Jan, 2003, 69–70.
200. DKLV, December 1941, 122. *Indien im Aufruhr*: the Indian War of Independence by an Indian Nationalist. *Verlag für volkstum, Wehr und Wirtschaft*, Berlin, 1940.
201. For details on Savarkar's admiration of Nazism, see Casolari, Marzia, 2000, 218–28; D'Souza, Eugene, 2000, 77–90; Delf, Tobias, 2008, 55–92; Framke, Maria, 2013, 170–4, 297–9.
202. Sharma, Jyotirmaya, 2007, 1717–19.
203. DKLV, December 1941, 122.
204. *Azad Hind*, 9/10, 1942; Subhas Chandra Bose, 'Free India and Her Problems', 2.
205. DKLV, first issue, 1942.
206. DKLV, first issue, 1943.
207. Archive of the University of Munich (UAM), Stud-Kart II.
208. Kaider, Gerhard, 2006, 104.
209. DKLV, 1943, 89.
210. DKLV, 1942, 319.
211. DKLV, 1942, 320.
212. IOR/L/PJ/629, list of Indians in Germany, 1939, 12.
213. Michels, Eckard, 2005, 95–6.
214. Scholten, Dirk, 2001, 98.
215. IfZ Munich: Haushofer collection, 932 b: India Institute, 18.
216. Framke, Maria, 2013, 75.
217. WBSA: File 234/39(I), hostile foreigners, who are objects of particular suspicions.
218. BA Berlin: R51/5, Schulz to Pohle, June 1938.
219. BA Berlin: R51/144, Pohle to Schulz, 19.7.1938.
220. BA Berlin: R51/5, Pohle to Schulz, 15.8.1938.
221. BA Berlin: R51/144, Pohle to Schulz, 3.10.1938.

222. BA Berlin: R51/144, Pohle to Schulz, 3.10.1938.
223. For details, see Sareen, Tilak Raj, 1999, 55–63; Egorova, Yulia, 2006, 45; Framke, Maria, 2013, 148–60.
224. BA Berlin: R51/5, Pohle to Schulz, 15.8.1938.
225. WBSA: IB File 355–41, Sl.183.
226. BA Berlin: R51/10128, biographical note, 19.2.1939.
227. BA Berlin: R51/10128, correspondence between Schulz and Würfel, 1938.
228. BA Berlin R51/10128, Würfel to Schulz, 22.2.1938.
229. BA Berlin: R51/10128, Würfel to Schulz, 14.12.1938.
230. BA Berlin: R51/10128, Würfel to Nitzschke, 16.2.1939.
231. Oesterheld, Joachim, 2005, 29.
232. Michels, Eckard, 2005, 1, 3.
233. Thierfelder, Franz, 1959, 98–9.
234. Ibid., 92–102.
235. Junginger, Horst, 2017b, 931.
236. Junginger, Horst, 2017a, 278.
237. Koops, Tilman et al. (eds), 2017, 283.

The Nazi Study of India and Indian Anti-Colonialism: Knowledge Providers and Propagandists in the 'Third Reich'.
Baijayanti Roy, Oxford University Press. © Baijayanti Roy 2024. DOI: 10.1093/9780191981951.003.0002

2

Special Department India (*Sonderreferat Indien*) of the German Foreign Ministry

Background: Indian Anti-Colonialism and Nazi Politics in Berlin

In the first chapter, we noted the presence of contemporary India as a subject of interest among scholars and quasi-scholars who were politically and intellectually invested in the 'living' India. We also witnessed the increasing urgency rendered to this category of knowledge through the transformations in Germany's cultural policy towards India after Joachim von Ribbentrop became Foreign Minister in February 1938. This chapter examines the different categories of 'useful' knowledge about modern India, produced through the interface of Nazi politics and Indian anti-colonialism, under the auspices of a Special Department India or *Sonderreferat Indien* (SRI) of the German Foreign Ministry. This special office was set up in 1941 in response to the demands of Subhas Chandra Bose, who landed up in Berlin on 2 April 1941 as a political fugitive seeking Germany's help to free India from British rule.[1]

The SRI has been treated as a backdrop to Bose's operations in Germany by most historians who have spared only a few lines on it.[2] Among the exceptions are Milan Hauner and, more recently, Willy Bushak, who have provided brief histories of the SRI's foundation and functions. To my knowledge, Jan Kuhlmann is the only historian to examine the activities of the SRI in some detail and irrespective of Bose.[3] This chapter will not focus on the foundation of the SRI or its workings. It will concentrate on how the SRI integrated Bose's anti-colonial agenda with Germany's foreign policy objectives. The primary aim of the chapter is to examine the production and uses of the knowledge of modern India under the SRI and the links of such knowledge production to Nazi politics.

The idea of setting up a department for directing Germany's policy towards India had a precedent from the First World War, when an Information Centre for the Orient (*Nachrichtenstelle für den Orient*; NfO) conducted pro-German propaganda in the 'Orient' and functioned as a news and espionage agency for Germany.[4] The activities of the NfO also entailed assisting the different Independence Committees which were formed in Berlin, comprising anti-colonialists from various countries of the 'Orient' including India.[5] A number of German scholars were involved in the NfO, including the Indologist Helmuth von Glasenapp who was concerned with the propaganda related to India, as we noted in the Introduction.[6] Glasenapp was also involved with the India Institute, as we have seen.

The SRI was a direct successor to the *Arbeitskreis Indien* (Working Group India), set up in August 1939 under the Information department of the Foreign Ministry. The aim of this department was to conduct political propaganda in foreign countries.[7] The head of the Working Group India was Adam von Trott zu Solz (1909–1944), an aristocrat who had studied at Oxford as a Rhodes Scholar. Trott zu Solz secretly opposed the National Socialist regime and tried to use his connections in the Anglo-Saxon world to garner support for overthrowing it. This was probably his reason for joining the Foreign Ministry.[8] He was involved in the conspiracy leading to the failed coup of 20 July 1944 and was subsequently executed.[9] Trott belonged to the anti-Nazi Kreisau circle from where he recruited the trade unionist and Social Democrat Franz Josef Furtwängler (1894–1965), who was to be one of the important producers of knowledge at the SRI. Furtwängler started working at the Working Group India from August 1940.[10]

According to Trott's secretary Marie 'Missie' Wassiltschikow, by the end of 1940, Trott had a programme titled *Freies Indien* ('Free India') already in place.[11] The arrival of Subhas Chandra Bose in Berlin in 1941 injected a new vigour in this enterprise. Bose's spectacular life and death have been recounted by generations of historians across different continents.[12] Only a few of the multiple dimensions of Bose's trajectory are important for this discussion. One such aspect is the radical nationalist's political differences with Gandhi. The young leader from Bengal believed that the Mahatma's non-violent methods were not effective enough against the brutal colonial rule.[13] In 1938, Bose was elected president of the INC at the annual meeting of the party at Haripura. He called for full independence of India and did not rule out the use of force to achieve this end. At the annual meeting of the INC in 1939 at Tripuri, Bose was re-elected president against the wishes of Gandhi. Subsequently, he had to resign under pressure from the faction loyal to Gandhi. This prompted him to form his own party, the Forward Bloc, which he defined as the 'socialist wing' of the INC.[14] In 1940, Bose was imprisoned by the colonial authorities for the umpteenth time. He managed to escape house arrest in Calcutta and arrived in Berlin on 2 April 1941 after an adventurous sojourn through Afghanistan and Moscow.[15] This was not Bose's first trip to the German capital, as we have already seen. Between 1933 and 1936 and in 1937 Bose had visited Germany and Italy (along with Austria, England, and Czechoslovakia). He first visited Berlin in July 1933 and made it his base until August 1934.[16]

Since the second decade of the twentieth century, the German capital had provided a space for different kinds of diasporic politics including left-wing activism combined with anti-colonialism as well as right-wing activities.[17] Surveillance records in the British archives provide the impression that in the 1920s, a number of anti-colonial Indians who had belonged to the India Independence Committee

(IIC), as well as radical communists and 'mainstream' nationalists fleeing colonial repression, apart from conventional students and professionals from India, formed an informal group in Berlin.[18] The centre of this anti-colonialist and leftist clique was 'Chatto' or Virendranath Chattopadhyaya, the anti-colonialist turned Marxist revolutionary who had taken a leading role in the IIC. He left permanently for the Soviet Union in August 1931 as the German state turned increasingly to the right.[19]

Indian anti-colonialism in Berlin, which had become subdued after the advent of the Nazis, was rejuvenated by Bose who established an 'Indian Students' Association' in 1934.[20] The politically innoxious name of the association was a cover for anti-colonial activities involving Indians living in and around Berlin, some of whom had been followers of 'Chatto'. The association formed by Bose took the wind out of the sails of an earlier organization of Indians in Berlin—an 'Indo-German Association' which had been set up around 1931 with encouragement from the Foreign Ministry in order to keep the Indians in Berlin under control. The Indian intellectual Devendra Nath Bannerjea, who was in charge of this Association, was another knowledge provider (in different senses) to the Nazi regime. We will discuss him in detail in the next chapter.[21]

Mukund Rai Vyas (1919–), one of the leading members of this Association and a loyalist of Bose, stated in his post-war statement to the British authorities in Germany that the Indian Students' Association organized special functions on 26 January (commemorated as 'India's Independence Day'), Jallianwala Bagh Day on 13 April (in remembrance of the merciless firing on an unarmed crowd of civilians by the British Brigadier General Reginald Dyer at the Jallianwala Bagh in Amritsar, Punjab, on the same date in 1919) and, despite Bose's reservations about Gandhi, a symbolic celebration of the Mahatma's birthday on 2 October. Vyas also claimed that the Nazi government was not unsympathetic towards these celebrations.[22] With time, ritualistic observation of these occasions would become an integral component of the joint anti-British propaganda conducted by Bose and the Nazi government.

According to a British surveillance report from September 1939, the Indian Students' Association maintained cordial relations with the Nazified organization, Deutsche Orient Verein (Orient Association of Germany; DOV).[23] The DOV officially focused on maintaining commercial ties between Germany and India, but unofficially it had the political function of trying to disseminate a positive image of National Socialist Germany in the 'Orient' including India.[24] The link between the DOV, the Nazi regime, and Bose was personified by Habibur Rahman (1901–), an Indian journalist who had, in 1931, allegedly joined an 'Indian Independence Union' started by Chatto, before offering his services to the Nazi Propaganda Ministry. He was also active in the Indian Students' Association.[25]

Interestingly, Heinrich Lüders (1869–1943), professor of Indology at the University of Berlin until 1935, became a member of the committee for Arts and Sciences of the DOV in 1934.[26] On 21 January 1935, he delivered a lecture titled

Indien (India) as a part of DOV's programme to acquaint Germans with the 'Orient'.[27] The lecture regurgitated the age-old discourse of Aryan supremacy and the latter's degeneration into Hinduism which as we have seen, conformed to National Socialist *Weltanschauung*, as expressed by Alfred Rosenberg in his book, to which we have referred earlier.

The ties between the Indian Students' Association and the DOV demonstrate that long before he landed up in Berlin as a political exile in 1941, Bose collaborated with the Indian anti-colonialists of Berlin as well as some organs of the Nazi government, for carrying out anti-British propaganda. For the Indian diaspora in Berlin, the 'global authoritarian moment' of the 'anti-colonial nationalists' started not in 1941 but in 1934.[28]

Bose's official agenda, presented to the Foreign Ministry soon after his arrival in Berlin in 1941, included establishing a 'government of Free India in exile' and raising an Indian Army, which would in time march into India under his own command. He also wanted to conduct propaganda in India, urging fellow Indians to rise in armed rebellion against the British.[29]

It is well-known that Bose's demands for the establishment of a provisional Indian government in Berlin fell on deaf ears, mainly due to Hitler's apathy towards anti-colonial movements and his latent wish to come to an understanding with England.[30] The Indian politician had to remain content with participating in the Foreign Ministry's propaganda towards India. However, Ribbentrop made it clear to Bose in course of their first meeting on 29 April 1941 that Gandhi, who had already been legitimized as the face of the Indian nationalism by the British colonial authority, was never to be criticized directly in German propaganda.[31] Public endorsement of Gandhi co-existed with promotion of Bose's brand of belligerent politics in German propaganda throughout the war years, conveniently ironing out their fundamental differences.

Nevertheless, Bose was allowed to set up a Free India Centre (FIC) in Berlin in May 1941 with the help of the German Foreign Ministry to conduct his brand of anti-colonial propaganda. The SRI, following a directive from the Foreign Minister, monitored the activities of the FIC. The latter included not only members of the Indian Students' Association but also Indian communists and anti-colonialists including Nambiar, who were hiding from the Nazis in France and were now invited to work for Bose.[32]

The SRI was placed under Wilhelm Keppler, Secretary of State for Special Duties, in June 1941.[33] Keppler, a member of the Nazi party from 1927 and of the SS from 1933, had the privilege of enjoying the trust of three Nazi top bosses—Hitler, Himmler, and Ribbentrop. He had functioned as an intermediary between the Austrian Nazis operating underground and the Nazi regime in Germany before Austria joined the German 'Reich' in March 1938.[34]

It is unknown whether Bose had met Keppler in Vienna during one of his visits in the 1930s, but the possibility cannot be ruled out. Bose had formed an

'Indian Central European Society' in Vienna in 1934 with the help of Otto Faltis, a businessman and a member of the NSDAP.[35] By September 1938, Karl Pesta, a well-known National Socialist was listed as the chairman of this organization, which Bose purportedly tried to support from India through his position as the president of the INC.[36]

The SRI: Aims and Objectives

The work plan of the SRI, defined in an undated and secret memorandum of the Foreign Ministry, entailed various categories like information and news of India, supporting different groups of activists in India, and supervision of the FIC. The category of 'information' is particularly important as far as knowledge of India was concerned. This category included publication of a series of books about India, to explain India to the Germans through the prism of Nazi political expediency and to provide the German press a strategic direction for covering India. 'Information' also included promotion of propagandistic writings in German on India and periodic publication of reports on political and economic developments in India, as well as generating materials for radio programmes on India.[37] The main objective of the 'news' section was to control all the India-related publications in the German press through an official regulation (*Sprachregelung*).[38]

Specialized knowledge on modern India was urgently required for carrying out these objectives. Ludwig Alsdorf, a young Indologist, was appointed as an 'academic associate' of the SRI in May 1941 to fulfil these goals. He soon emerged as the most influential 'knowledge provider' of the SRI. Alsdorf's career in Nazi Germany exemplifies the complex nexus between the demands of Nazi politics and knowledge of contemporary India.[39]

Enter Ludwig Alsdorf

Alsdorf (1904–1978) is remembered primarily as a leading scholar of the ancient monastic religion, Jainism. He wrote a much acclaimed PhD thesis on a medieval Jain text, *Kumarapalapratibodha*, in 1928 from the University of Hamburg. In the autumn of 1930, Alsdorf went on a study tour to India. He taught German and French at the University of Allahabad and used this opportunity to visit different areas of the Indian subcontinent. This 'lived experience' of India would later equip Alsdorf to lay claims to being an expert on contemporary India as well. In July 1932, Alsdorf returned to Germany. The young ambitious scholar soon oriented himself to the prevailing political wind and joined the Nazi party from 1 August, 1933 (membership number 2697931), as his membership card notes (Figures 6a, 6b).[40]

(a)

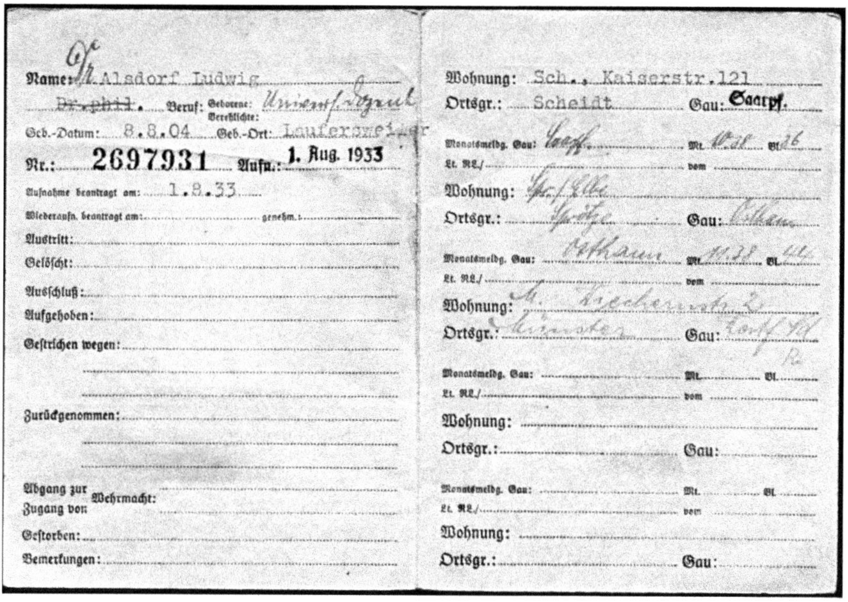

(b)

Figures 6a, 6b Alsdorf's Nazi Party (NSDAP) membership card.
Source: BA Berlin: R9361-VIII Kartei/40368.

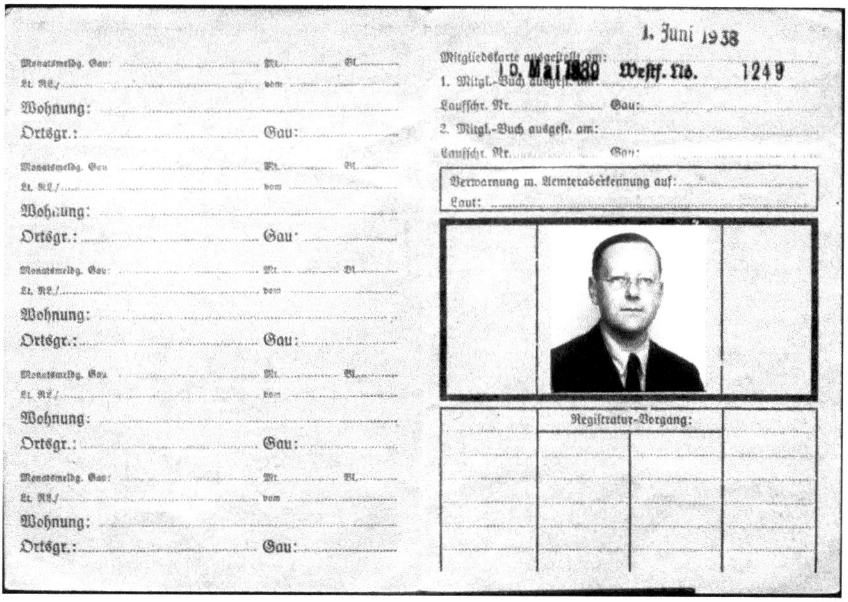

Alsdorf underwent compulsory labour service (*Arbeitsdienst*) in Bredtstadt from 17 January to 31 March 1934.[41] This was followed by a three-week course at the Prussian Lecturers' Academy (*Dozentenakademie)* attached to the University of Kiel. Lecturers' Academy was a training camp for those aspiring to be university professors. In such training institutes, scholars underwent physical drill as well as ideological indoctrination so that they could fulfil the National Socialist ideal of a 'scholar-soldier'. A list of suggested books which were made compulsory reading material at this camp included—besides *Mein Kampf* and Hitler's published speeches—works by Houston Stewart Chamberlain and Alfred Rosenberg championing Aryan supremacy, as well as writings of Nazi party leaders like Robert Ley and Fritz Sauckel. The 'candidates' were assessed on criteria like 'National Socialist thinking' and 'National Socialist disposition' besides physical fitness and service mentality.[42]

The Lecturers' Academy that Alsdorf visited had the reputation of being the model centre for indoctrination in Nazism (Figure 7).[43] A questionnaire that Alsdorf had to fill in here shows that his 'special cultural political interests' were *Rassenkunde* ('Race Science') and *Auslandsdeutschtum* ('Germandom outside Germany'), subjects which enjoyed considerable political currency under the Nazi regime.[44]

Figure 7 Ludwig Alsdorf at the Lecturers' Academy.
Source: Geheimes Staatsarchiv Preußischer Kulturbesitz, Berlin, IHA Rep76.

Unfortunately for Alsdorf, the 'Lecturers' Academy' gave him an unequivocally negative verdict, stating that he was 'politically opaque' and that his attitude could hardly be characterized as National Socialist, not even in the academic sense.[45] Nevertheless, Alsdorf was allowed to pursue his second thesis or *Habilitation* which is still required to qualify for professorial posts in German universities. Intervention from a fellow Indologist in the form of an undated secret report to the Ministry of Education in Berlin helped Alsdorf to receive his *Venia Legendi* or teaching licence after his *Habilitation*. The secret report, signed with the initials 'HZ', indicating that the writer was most probably the Indologist Heinrich Zimmer from the University of Heidelberg, stated that Alsdorf should be given his *Venia Legendi* since he could still be trained to become a true Nazi. His *Venia Legendi* could be revoked later if he did not develop enough commitment.[46] Ironically, it was Zimmer whose teaching licence was revoked in 1938 because of his wife's purported Jewish ancestry, leading him to lose his teaching position at the University of Heidelberg, despite his efforts to collaborate with the Nazi regime. Collusion with Nazi authorities did not always protect scholars from the harrowing repercussions of the regime's politics.[47]

The ambivalences regarding Alsdorf's commitment to Nazism highlights the importance of being perceived as a genuine National Socialist as opposed to simply being enrolled in the Nazi party. The letter from 'HZ' also points to the Byzantine academic politics of the Nazi regime which impelled this internationally known scholar to spy on a junior academic for ensuring his own survival.

Alsdorf's *Habilitation* was a critical translation of *Harivamshapurana*, a tenth-century Jain narrative text. He completed this work in June 1935 from the University of Berlin.[48] The thesis (published in 1936), received high praise not only from his academic peers but also from Wolfgang Erxleben, who 'evaluated' scholars and their works on behalf of the Nazi Party's Department of Science (*Hauptamt Wissenschaft*) under Alfred Rosenberg.[49]

Along with his academic pursuits, Alsdorf began to engage in different organizations affiliated to the Nazi party. He was involved in the Foreign Affairs section of the *Deutsche Dozentenschaft*, a Nazified association of non-tenured teaching staff of German universities, indicating that he was building up his credentials as a specialist in external affairs.[50]

In December 1936 Alsdorf joined the NSKK (*Nationalsozialistische Kraftfahrerkorps*), the motorized section of the Nazi party.[51] The NSKK operated closely with the more visible and more notorious SA and SS, but unlike these two paramilitary organizations, the NSKK was not declared a criminal organization by the Allies after the war, because of its relatively inconspicuous existence. Hence, after 1945, many former members of the NSKK, including Alsdorf, could present their membership of this organization as the 'lesser evil'.[52]

Alsdorf took an active part in this organization, as he wrote in a letter to the University of Münster on 18 February 1938, justifying his candidature for a teaching post. In the letter, Alsdorf proclaimed that he 'indeed' belonged to the motor boat section (*Kraftbootsturm 4/Kb*) as Second Lieutenant (*Sturmmann*) of the NSKK.[53] By 1936, he had also joined the National Socialist Lecturers' Association (*Nationalsozialistische Deutsche Dozentenbund* or NSDB).[54]

Despite his affiliations to these Nazi associations, Alsdorf's dedication to National Socialism continued to be suspected by various Nazi agencies, including the aforementioned NSDB and the secret service, the SD. The latter spied on scholars and read their works to make sure whether, despite providing lip service to Nazism, they exhibited any hidden subversive tendencies. Every appointment of a high-ranking government official (including professors) required an appropriate report (*Gutachten*) from the SD.[55]

Reservations from the SD came to the fore when Alsdorf tried unsuccessfully to obtain a professorial position at the University of Leipzig in 1937. Negative reports on Alsdorf from the SD to the Ministry of Education in Saxony led to his failure in securing the position.[56] However, Alsdorf managed to receive the post of a non-tenured lecturer at the University of Münster in 1938. He succeeded the retired professor of Indology, Richard Schmidt, an expert on Sanskrit who is remembered today primarily for translating the Kamasutra in German and Latin.[57]

The documents related to Alsdorf's appointment suggest that the university authorities did not place too much emphasis on Alsdorf's loyalty to Nazism. This was probably due to the particular political path chosen by the University of Münster, where academic staff responded to Nazi politics primarily by making the courses they offered 'politically relevant' rather than taking part in political activities.[58] As records from this university show, Alsdorf's academic accomplishments as well as the purported 'political utility' of Indology, particularly its focus on ancient India and Aryanism that supposedly facilitated a friendship between Germans and Indians and contributed to the *Weltgeltung* (worldwide recognition) of the Germans, were factors in his favour.[59]

However, Alsdorf's membership of the Nazi Party was not wholly irrelevant: it made him more likely to conform to the academic and political ambience of the University of Münster, where 90 per cent of the professors were members of the NSDAP, though relatively few engaged in active politics.[60] In this respect, Alsdorf made a suitable successor to the Indologist Richard Schmidt who had joined the NSDAP in 1933.

Indien

The year 1938 was a turning point in Alsdorf's career. Apart from his shift to Münster, it was in 1938, according to Alsdorf's post-war statement, that the historian Egmont Zechlin requested him to write a book about India for a series titled *Weltpolitische Bücherei* (Library of World Politics).[61] Zechlin, together with another academic, Georg Leibbrandt, were entrusted by Alfred Rosenberg to co-edit the series in question. The books were to be 'political' and written by scholars to impart 'world political education to Germans' so that the German *Volk* could be prepared for their 'historic mission', as an article in the Nazi Party's monthly magazine claimed in 1941.[62]

No doubt Alsdorf was chosen for this series because he had already acquired a reputation as an expert on contemporary India. In 1939, as war with Britain seemed inevitable, the University of Münster entrusted him to lecture on colonial India as part of a course on 'Knowledge of Foreign Countries and Colonies'.[63] In 1940, Alsdorf was lecturing on 'English Rule and Nationalist Movement in India'.[64]

The book written by Alsdorf for this series, titled *Indien* (India) and published in 1940, ran to at least four editions (Figure 8). This work, dealing primarily though not exclusively on the history and effects of colonization, established Alsdorf as an unquestioned authority on modern India in Nazi Germany. One reason for this was due to the fact that *Indien* won praise from the 'Führer' himself, who supposedly directed all high functionaries of 'the party' to peruse it, as the head of the National Socialist Lecturers' Association (*Reichsdozentenführer*) wrote to the party office of the NSDAP in February 1942.[65] This seal of approval by Hitler also laid to rest all previous doubts and questions relating to Alsdorf's allegiance to Nazism. At the same time, Alsdorf's academic credentials rendered the book an aura of authenticity. No wonder that his professional rank as 'Lecturer of Indology at the University of Münster' appeared just under his name on the front page.

It must be noted that *Indien* was the not the first work on modern India in German written by an academic specializing on India. During the 1920s, two scholars who were involved in the aforementioned NfO, published books on India under British rule. One of them was Josef Horovitz (1874–1931), professor of Islamic Studies at the University of Frankfurt and the other was Helmuth von Glasenapp, whose academic profile as well as political activities within the NfO foreshadowed those of Alsdorf.[66]

The success of *Indien* lay primarily in the fact that it reflected certain tropes that had started to dominate Nazi Germany's propaganda policy towards India from 1938. In the book, Alsdorf dutifully gave the nod to 'Aryan race theory' as it was applied to India by anthropologists and ethnologists who found favour with the Nazi political establishment, like Hans F.K. Günther and Egon Freiherr von Eickstedt. However, unlike Günther, Alsdorf refrained from glorifying the Indian caste system as a form of racial hygiene programme designed to prevent the racially superior Nordic Aryans from commingling with the dark-skinned aboriginals.[67] Racially denigrating Indians in public was not politically advantageous at the time.

Without being overtly polemical, the book portrayed the British as ruthless exploiters of India's economic potentials. The book also unequivocally expressed sympathy for India's anti-colonial movement. Significantly, Alsdorf justified Nazi racial politics while castigating the British colonialists as racist. He claimed that

Figure 8 *Indien*: the book that changed the Nazi regime's perception of Alsdorf.

though it was correct to maintain a separation of Indian and British 'races', it was not fair to deny even upper-class Indians entry into exclusive British establishments, since, unlike the Jews of Germany who did not belong to the country, Indians were natives of India. Alsdorf also accused the British of propagating a 'distorted view of National Socialist racial thinking' to generate anti-German feelings.[68]

Alsdorf's book presented Gandhi as the undisputed leader of Indian nationalism. It also 'orientalized' Gandhi by explaining him from the standpoint of a strand of German Indology that glorified Vedic Aryan civilization. Thus, Gandhi's propagation of the ethics of *satyagraha* (affirmation for truth) symbolized to Alsdorf a return to the 'original Indian spirit' found in the oldest religion of the Indo-Iranian Aryan peoples.[69] At the same time, the book expressed veiled doubts about the efficacy of Gandhi's non-violent methods and subtly suggested that Indians should utilize the turmoil caused by the war to forcefully end colonial rule. Alsdorf also made indirect overtures to the Indians to approve of the Nazi dictatorship by claiming that parliamentary democracy was unsuitable for India.[70] Alsdorf's perspective on Gandhi faintly echoes the claim of Alfred Rosenberg, that the meagre residue of the superior racial essence of the Nordic Aryans in India has produced 'only the tired Gandhi and not a commander personifying reinvigoration (of the lost racial traits)'.[71]

It is difficult to overstate the significance of *Indien* for Alsdorf's career. The book secured Alsdorf professional opportunities and fame in ways that his excellent academic record could not since, to the Nazi political establishment, the value of a scholar was commensurate with his (it was rarely hers) willingness and ability in deploying his knowledge to address various 'practical' issues faced by the regime. The extent to which *Indien* validated Alsdorf as an authority on modern India, particularly with regard to British colonization, is evident from the fact that soon after its publication two competing political authorities enlisted his service. Alsdorf wrote a memorandum on India which Alfred Rosenberg, then 'Minister for the Occupied Eastern Territories' presented to Hitler in autumn of 1941. Hitler supposedly described the memorandum, titled 'On the Exercise of British Domination on India', as 'very interesting'.[72] This prompted Rosenberg's rival Ribbentrop to submit a 'counter report' titled 'Foundation, Development and Methods of British Domination in India', which was composed primarily by Alsdorf.[73]

Indien was undoubtedly the main reason that prompted Alsdorf's appointment at the SRI, for which he was given a lien from the University of Münster and exempted from war duties.[74] Alsdorf seems to have enjoyed substantial influence in the SRI since he was in a position to render a stamp of scholarly authority to the knowledge that he produced and moulded.

In their post-war statements, the two important functionaries of the FIC, A.C.N. Nambiar (1896–1986) and Mukund Rai Vyas concurred that Alsdorf became the de facto chief of SRI and Keppler's right-hand man after Trott zu Solz was executed in 1944.[75] This was one of the few points on which these two loyalists of Bose could actually agree, indicating that it might have corresponded to the truth.

Alsdorf took a predominant role in two projects of the SRI which entailed the production and circulation of 'politically significant' knowledge. These ventures included writing fortnightly reports on the current situation in India and publishing a book series on India comprising eight titles, which we came across in the last chapter. In the following sections, we will examine both these enterprises.

Fortnightly Reports on India

Between 1941 and at least till the end of 1944, the SRI provided the German Foreign Minister, Joachim von Ribbentrop, with fortnightly reports on the political and economic developments in India. Alsdorf seems to have written most of these reports, as his signature or initials on them suggest. A number of reports bear the signature of Furtwängler or of both, suggesting a close collaboration between the two.

Glimpses into these memoranda provide an idea of which aspects of contemporary India were considered usable by Alsdorf and Furtwängler as the representatives of the Nazi state. A memorandum that evidently belonged to this category was 'A Few Prominent Personalities of Contemporary Indian politics' (1941). This unsigned text, probably compiled by Alsdorf and Furtwängler together, contains details about the leading Indian politicians from every political party.[76] In another report in October 1941, Alsdorf reinforced Nazi Germany's policy of acknowledging Gandhi as the leader of the masses in India. As justification, he invoked the opinion expressed in *Indien*, that the Mahatma was uniquely Indian, embodying the 'best and oldest Indian ideals'.[77]

A pressing issue facing Nazi Germany's propaganda concerning India was the question of how to react to the growing tension between Hindus and Muslims in the Indian sub-continent. By the early 1940s, the 'Pakistan movement' (i.e. the demands for a separate 'Muslim state' by a section of Indian Muslims) became increasingly loud. Alsdorf helped the Foreign Ministry to respond to this issue by writing a number of relevant memoranda. The INC, led by Gandhi and Jawaharlal Nehru, who advocated a secular and pluralist India, was against the idea of Pakistan, while the separatist All India Muslim League formally demanded it. Bose, who was against both Hindu and Muslim religious fundamentalism, was also opposed to the Pakistan movement since he considered Muslims to be an integral part of India. Following his secular ethos, the Indian leader insisted that German propaganda in India should desist from using religion based rhetoric or imageries. It should also refrain from attaching any importance to the Pakistan movement.[78]

This posed a problem for the Foreign Ministry, which had already embarked on a wartime strategy of courting Muslim support in different areas of the world, for which Islamist rhetoric was often employed.[79] The participation of Orientalists in deciding on the German state's outreach to Indian Muslims had a precedent during the First World War. In 1915, the aforementioned Joseph Horovitz, the scholar of Islam who had spent some years teaching at the Aligarh Muslim University in India before joining the University of Frankfurt, had recommended that the Foreign Ministry should influence the Muslims in north India with references to the pan-Islamic movement and the Ottoman Caliphate.[80]

However, Keppler, the official head of the SRI, supported Bose's standpoint and opposed the Foreign Ministry's line of Islam-based propaganda in India.[81] Presumably under instructions from Keppler, Alsdorf prepared a number of memoranda on this issue. An important memorandum among them was 'The Indian Muslims, the Pakistan Plan and the German Politics of the Orient', dated 2 December 1941. In this memo, Alsdorf stressed the importance of cultivating the support of India's 90 million Muslims who, due to their sheer number, were important for the entire central Asian and Near Eastern strategy of Germany. Alsdorf suggested that the subject be considered an internal matter of India, which was not to be commented on.[82] This memo was in some ways a continuation of an earlier report dated 10 October 1941, in which Alsdorf criticized Mohammad Ali Jinnah, the Western-educated leader of the separatist Muslim League, as an ambitious opportunist who became a stooge of the British.[83] These memoranda possibly contributed to Ribbentrop's directive from February 1942 that propaganda for India should not contain Islamic religious rhetoric.[84]

Alsdorf returned to this subject in May 1943. By that time, Bose had left Germany for East Asia. As is well known, he was allowed to form a Provisional Government of Free India in Singapore in October 1943. Meanwhile, some functionaries of the Foreign Office, like Wilhelm Melchers of the 'Orient Office' who was responsible for 'Orient propaganda', started to claim that keeping silent on the Pakistan movement would alienate the Arab countries which sympathized with the religion-based separatist aspirations of Indian Muslims.[85] In a memorandum dated 15 May 1943, Alsdorf once more foregrounded the necessity of opposing the Pakistan Plan. He claimed that most Muslims and practically all Hindus of India were against Pakistan and they would remain grateful to Germany for being on their side on this issue.[86] Presumably around the same time, Alsdorf wrote an undated tract titled 'Pakistan, the Indian Ulster', in which he traced the rise of Muslim separatism in India under British political machinations of *divide et impera* and compared the Indian situation to that of Ireland and Palestine.[87]

Interestingly, these comparisons had been expressed by Bose in an article titled 'Free India and Its Problems', which was published simultaneously in English in *Azad Hind*, the bilingual (German/English) mouthpiece of the FIC and in German in the magazine for the Nazi youth, *Wille und Macht* (*Will and Power*) in

1942. Both Alsdorf's report and Bose's article are remarkable for combining an essential element of Nazi propaganda aimed at Arabs (i.e. Muslim victimhood), with Bose's ideal of Hindu-Muslim unity.[88]

The SRI and the 'Orient Office' of the Foreign Ministry needed to establish a coordinated guideline for the German propaganda directed towards Egypt, Afghanistan, Saudi Arabia, Palestine, Syria, Turkey, India, Iran, Sudan, and Ceylon (Sri Lanka).[89] To achieve a common platform, a special meeting of an 'India Committee', possibly comprising representatives of both the SRI and the German Foreign Ministry, was convened on 20 May 1943. In this meeting it was decided that Muslim League and Pakistan would not be directly criticized to avert hurting Islamic sentiments. At the same time, no separatist- and religion-based politics would be supported by German propaganda since such movements only strengthened the hands of British colonialism.[90] Alsdorf was thus instrumental in synchronizing Nazi propaganda with Bose's secular visions on this sensitive issue.

However, unlike Bose who was ideologically invested in Hindu Muslim unity in the subcontinent, Alsdorf's attitude was guided primarily by the demands of German politics. Personally, he seemed to have inherited an anti-Islam bias that prevailed in the strand of German Indology which engaged with Vedic Aryanism, as well as British colonial historiography, which Alsdorf drew on in *Indien*.[91] Alsdorf's prejudices were reflected in his occasional references in *Indien* to 'Mohammedan fanaticism' and 'Turkish brutality' of the Indian Muslims, to whom he attributed 'low intellectual capacity' as well.[92]

According to Nambiar's post-war testimony, Alsdorf acted as the liaison between the SRI and Jamil Ahmad Khan, an Indian soldier turned Axis ally who was responsible for Italian propaganda concerning India.[93] Italian propaganda was more inclined to employ Islamic religious rhetoric and to support the Pakistan movement, as a memorandum written by Alsdorf, dated 8 March 1943 and presented by Keppler to Megerle, pointed out.[94] In the memorandum, Alsdorf noted with equanimity that Italian propaganda was sympathetic towards the Pakistan movement. Italian propaganda continued to be so despite protests from Bose.[95]

Alsdorf's cynicism about the subject is reflected in a report written in October 1944, in which he commented that it was beneficial for German propaganda that Gandhi continued to oppose the Pakistan Plan, which was encouraged by the British. If an agreement on this subject had been reached, there would have possibly been a compromise between the INC and the British, which was detrimental to Germany's interest.[96]

Geopolitics occasionally featured in the memoranda. For example, in February 1942, Alsdorf wrote a report on, 'The Possibility and the Probable Outcome of the Construction of a Road between Assam in India to China, as Replacement for the Old Burma Road'.[97] The 'old Burma Road' stretching 700 miles from Kunming in China to Lashio in Burma had been built by the Chinese during the Second

World War to receive supplies from the British. As Burma fell to the Japanese in 1942, this road became off-limits to the Allies. Subsequently, British and American forces stationed in India constructed an alternate road, named 'Stilwell Road' after the American general Josef Stilwell, who supervised the venture.[98] Alsdorf correctly foresaw the strategic significance of this alternative road.

Cultural affairs figured rarely in these reports. A notable exception was the death of the Indian poet laureate Rabindranath Tagore on 7 August 1941. In his note written soon thereafter, Alsdorf claimed that since Tagore had visited Germany several times, his death should be used as an opportunity for the German press to express its sympathy for this deep loss suffered by Indians and to convince the latter of the Germans' interest in India's culture. Alsdorf remarked that Tagore's nationalist feelings and his regard for Germany should be high-lighted, while omitting his reserve about National Socialism. He also maintained that German propaganda should make use of this opportunity to underscore the fact that Tagore had rejected his knighthood in protest against the bloodbath at Jallianwala Bagh.[99] The traumatic 'Jallianwala Bagh incident' which was com-memorated by the Indian Students' Association, thus entered the register of Nazi propaganda themes concerning India.

Alsdorf commented once in a while on the economic effects of colonial poli-cies in India, with an eye to the opportunities for German propaganda. In a report in October 1942, for example, Alsdorf discussed the failure of the British government to control inflation and check the rapid spread of malaria, a situation that, according to him, opened up a chance to sell two German-manufactured anti-malaria drugs: Atebrin and Plasmochin.[100]

Political developments in India and the effects of the ongoing war formed the dominant themes of the memoranda. In a memorandum dated 13 April 1942, Alsdorf predicted the failure of the so-called 'Cripps Mission'—the attempt of the British politician Sir Stafford Cripps to negotiate between the British Empire and the Indian nationalists in 1942, which, he noted, provided increased possibilities for German propaganda in India.[101] As the INC embarked on the so-called 'Quit India' movement under Gandhi's leadership, Alsdorf examined the effects of the nationwide agitation on the Indian Army and Police as well as on war-related production.[102]

A significant intervention by Alsdorf was to highlight the meeting between Hitler and Bose on 29 May 1942. Though it turned out to be damp squib for the Indian nationalist, Alsdorf wrote that 'The reception of Subhas Chandra Bose by the *Führer* has signalled for the entire world Germany's sympathy for India's struggle for freedom.... The present lack of echo of this incident in the interna-tional press can be traced to the conscious tactic of silence, which has to be coun-tered from our side.'[103]

Apart from the 'mainstream' anti-colonial movement, Alsdorf also kept watch on the emerging right-wing Hindu nationalist politics in India. Both Alsdorf and

Furtwängler appeared to be favourably disposed towards the Hindu Mahasabha, the party representing the nascent Hindu nationalist movement. An unsigned report, possibly written jointly by Alsdorf and Furtwängler in March 1942, offered the misguided view that the Mahasabha had played a substantial but not clear-cut role in Indian politics since the beginning of the war.[104]

Another report, dated 4 September 1942 and bearing the signatures of both, was titled, 'What Is Hindu Mahasabha?'. In this note, Furtwängler exaggerated the anti-British sentiment espoused by this organization of conservative Hindus, claiming that it took a leading role in the 'Quit India' movement after the leaders of the INC were imprisoned by the British.[105] Alsdorf continued the report, claiming that the Mahasabha joining the INC in demanding full freedom for India was a 'difficult blow' for the British.[106] The misinformed views expressed in this note on Hindu Mahasabha were taken up in an article published in the newspaper *Frankfurter Zeitung*, which greeted this 'progress'.[107] In reality, between 1942 and 1945, though certain strands of the Mahasabha showed pro-INC sympathies, there was no demand for full independence. The influence of the Mahasabha in determining the course of colonial politics also remained limited.[108]

One can only speculate on the possible reasons for this misreading of the situation by Alsdorf and Furtwängler. Alsdorf, as we noted, seemed to have imbibed a long-sustained anti-Islamic prejudice that prevailed in a branch of German Indology. Such a predisposition could have made Alsdorf sympathetic towards the Mahasabha, which had also incorporated certain tenets of European Orientalism in its world view (e.g. the glorification of Vedic Aryans and the contention that the latter were the progenitors of modern Hindus, as well as intolerance towards Muslims who could stake no claims to an Aryan legacy).[109] Despite his leftist leanings, Furtwängler was also influenced by the racialized Aryan discourse as they were applied to India by scholars of Indology and popular writers. Furtwängler's writings at the time contained glorification of Brahmins as true Aryans and denigration of the indigenous tribes of India as 'primitive'.[110] Such racialized perspectives had evidently circulated beyond political and class barriers within German society.

It is also possible that the source of this inaccurate report was the information collected by the officials of the German Legation in Kabul, Hans Pilger and Karl Rassmus. These 'reports' were sent in the form of telegrams to the Foreign Ministry in Berlin.[111] Alsdorf occasionally participated directly in the transfer of information between the German Legation of Kabul and the Foreign Ministry at Berlin. In 1944 (if not earlier) Alsdorf sent telegrams with coded messages to the Legation of Kabul. Sometimes, the Indologist acted as a conduit between Bose, who was then in East Asia, and the latter's associate Bhagat Ram Talwar (code-named Rahmat Khan or R.K.) a Communist belonging to the Kirti Kisan Party of northern India, which had links to Soviet Union. Talwar acted as a liaison between Bose and the German consulate in Kabul as well as between Bose and his party, the Forward Bloc. Talwar soon became a multiple agent, providing information to the British, Russians, Italians, and Germans. He began to turn against the Germans after the Soviet Union joined the Allies and began to supply deliberately inaccurate or exaggerated accounts to the Germans.[112] Alsdorf sent as well as received coded messages from Talwar through the consulate in Kabul, as his signatures, encrypted by the British surveillance, reveal.[113] Thus, Alsdorf went beyond the theoretical provider of knowledge to the SRI to being an active political mediator.

Alsdorf probably became aware of Talwar's conflicting loyalties towards the end of the war. In a report dated 26 August 1944, he claimed, 'R.K.'s pressing insistence to be given the wireless plan might arouse the suspicion that the real reason was his intention to hand it over to the Russians before leaving Kabul.'[114]

Alsdorf himself seems to have occasionally embellished his reports in order to present an amplified impression of the success of German propaganda in India. In a report from September 1942, he wrote that a 'National revolutionary Committee', filled with Bose's followers, instigated widespread protests among farmers and factory workers. He attributed to German radio propaganda 'a significant role' in these protests and accompanying sabotage actions.[115] German broadcasts, particularly those by Bose and his cohorts at the FIC were popular among Indians but it is doubtful whether their effects went beyond soaring Bose's personal popularity and reinforcing prevalent nationalist sentiments.[116] In any case, the nationwide protests and actions of the 'Quit India' movement, which began from August 1942, had died down by March 1943 due to the ruthless suppression methods employed by the colonial authorities.[117] Moreover, most Indians had rallied behind the INC which had officially declared its opposition to imperialism and fascism alike in March 1939, a stance which remained consistent throughout the war.[118]

Some of the reports by Alsdorf and Furtwängler repeatedly referred to the same incidents, like the defection of 40 soldiers and their Sikh officer from the British Army to the Germans in late summer 1942 and an even more dubious account of 4,500 deserters from the Indian Army joining Bose's Forward Bloc. It is not known whether the functionaries of the Foreign Ministry were credulous about such questionable reports, but the officials of the Wehrmacht remained sceptical and let the SRI know that there were no discernible ramifications of the German 'India Propaganda'.[119]

Nevertheless, the reports contributed substantially to the German Foreign Ministry's wartime propaganda concerning India. The press section of the Foreign Ministry had two officials whose task was to 'launch' information on India: Hans-Georg von Studnitz and Hilmar Baßler. According to Nambiar's post-war statement, Baßler acted under Alsdorf's influence.[120] From the same statement, it appears that Alsdorf also acted as the link between the SRI and the FIC.[121] Alsdorf himself admitted after the war that he was regularly sent to the FIC's headquarters which had shifted from Berlin to Hilversum in Holland between 1943 and 1944.[122]

Alsdorf apparently followed the Nazi regime's exhortation to fight until the bitter end. According to Mukund Rai Vyas, as late as in February 1945, Alsdorf arrived in Helmstadt in Bavaria where most of the activities of the FIC were being carried out since August 1944 to avoid Allied bombing. The Indologist brought with him samples of propagandistic pamphlets prepared by Jamil Ahmed Khan. Alsdorf supposedly urged the FIC to produce similar leaflets which were to be air dropped among the Indian soldiers in the Allied Front, urging them to desert.[123]

During his stint at the SRI, Alsdorf sometimes wrote polemical articles in German newspapers. An example of such propaganda is the article titled 'India Fights' that appeared in the *Berliner Börsen Zeitung* on 25 August 1942.[124] He also authored at least one pamphlet under the pseudonym Botho Ludwig. Titled 'India's Way to Freedom', this text was full of anti-British vitriol. The book, published in 1942, praised Bose without directly criticizing Gandhi and ended by prophesying the victory of the Indian anti-colonial movement. It proclaimed, somewhat ironically for someone working for the Nazi government, 'no one can sit on bayonets, especially when the bayonets are required all over the world'.[125]

Franz Joseph Furtwängler

Furtwängler was the second most important producer of knowledge after Alsdorf at the SRI. Unlike the latter, however, Furtwängler was not in a position to render scholarly authority to the knowledge of India that he helped to produce. The fact that he still played a fairly important role in the SRI's knowledge production process was due to his 'lived experience' of India. Furtwängler's role in the SRI is a case study of political pragmatism, displayed both by him as well as the Nazi regime.

Furtwängler, who was born into a working-class family, was primarily an autodidact with commendable linguistic and organizational skills. He joined the German Social Democratic Party (SPD), in 1919. After a brief stint as a student at the Academy of Labour in Frankfurt am Main, he was appointed Secretary for Foreign Affairs in the General German Trade Union Federation in 1923.[126] He toured India extensively in 1926–7 as part of a delegation of the Textile Workers Union.[127] In the years following this trip, he wrote a number of books and articles on contemporary India which established him an authority of the 'living' India. Among these works, the book *Working India* (Das *werktätige Indien*) which Furtwängler co-authored with his fellow trade unionist and travelling companion to India, Karl Schrader, was particularly influential.[128] The book was impressive in connecting its analysis of India's labour conditions with a critique of British colonialism.[129] Furtwängler was held to be the main author this work, which res-onated with readers spanning a large political spectrum including conservatives like Karl Haushofer and Nazi intellectuals like Ernst Graf von Reventlow.[130]

In his post-war reminiscences, Furtwängler recounted that during his trip to India, he met Gandhi twice at the Sabarmati Ashram. He also met Rabindranath Tagore at the latter's home in Shantiniketan. But he could not meet Subhas Bose since the firebrand Indian activist was in prison in Burma at the time. Bose was released from this prison in 1928, by which time Furtwängler had left India.[131] Here, it is pertinent to point out that Kris Manjapra's contention that Furtwängler met Bose during this visit and he 'encountered Gandhi at a distance' appears to be yet another example of the many inaccuracies masked up as facts in his book.[132]

Furtwängler met Subhas' brother and fellow nationalist politician, Sarat Bose, in Calcutta who recounted the details of his more militant brother's revolution-ary ideals and struggles.[133] What he heard from Sarat Bose and others about Subhas Bose impressed Furtwängler so much that he wrote an article on Subhas in the *Vorwärts*, the mouthpiece of the SPD.[134] Furtwängler also claimed that he wrote a few more articles 'honouring Bose's personality' in the German press, which were translated and published in USA. Subhas Bose came to know of them and wrote to him conveying his gratitude.[135]

Apart from his expertise on India and his admiration for Subhas Bose, what made Furtwängler a suitable candidate for providing useful knowledge for the SRI was his political flexibility, which he demonstrated by trying to ingratiate himself with the Nazi party soon after it came to power. However, his efforts remained fruitless as he, along with other trade union leaders, were imprisoned by the SA in May 1933. From May to October 1933, Furtwängler was intermit-tently imprisoned. He also became unemployed and, after living in fear of his life for some months, he could leave the country in 1934. He managed to return to Germany in 1938. In April 1939, he succeeded in securing an employment at the Institute for Conjuncture Research (*Institut für Konjunkturforschung*) in Berlin. This was possible because of the important connections within the Nazi Party which he managed to secure, underscoring his dynamism. To convince the Nazi state of his loyalty, Furtwängler joined the NSV (*Nationalsozialistische Volkswohlfahrt*), the Nazi welfare organization, as well as the DAF (*Deutsche Arbeitsfront* or German Labour Front), the Nazi trade union.[136]

Unlike Alsdorf, however, Furtwängler was ideologically invested in Indian nationalism. Furtwängler's meetings with Gandhi left him in complete awe of the Mahatma. The trade unionist would claim in his memorial work, titled 'Men Whom I Saw and Knew' (1951) that the Indian icon was also favourably impressed by him, sending him the handwritten draft (in Gujarati) of his book *Hind Swaraj* as a memento. This book was allegedly taken away by the Gestapo during a search of Furtwängler's house in 1933. For the Gestapo, the book was a proof of Furtwängler's 'treacherous relationship with foreign countries'.[137] However, these post-1945 claims could have been Furtwängler's retrospective attempts to distance himself from the Nazi regime and ennoble himself through claims of the Mahatma's approval.

Furtwängler published at least one article, 'The King of Coolis' (*Der König der Kuli*), in the *Frankfurter Zeitung* on 6 April 1930, explaining Gandhi to the German leaders. He also tried to subsume the Mahatma, not known to be the greatest friend of the industrial proletariat, into his Social Democratic political agenda by claiming that Gandhi's passive resistance was in reality the same fight against injustice that the European proletariat had been conducting for several decades.[138] Nevertheless, Furtwängler's view of Gandhi also remained steeped in Orientalist stereotyping, as various references to the Mahatma's 'ancient Indian wisdom and piety', 'the empathy of a Fakir', 'the lack of material want of a *kuli*' (an Indian porter) demonstrate.[139]

In his memorial work, Furtwängler wrote that he was outraged by what he considered to be Bose's expressed wish to agitate against the Mahatma from Germany. He supposedly told Bose that from the latter's shelter under Hitler, he should not think, even in his dreams, of contesting the old, revered Mahatma to whom India owned everything. Bose did not take this admonition kindly and never met Furtwängler again.[140] While Furtwängler's regard for Gandhi seemed to have been genuine and consistent, this post-war version of his meeting with Bose, who had become controversial due to his collaboration with the Nazis, needs to be viewed with some scepticism.

Furtwängler's memoranda for the SRI in 1942 were sometimes unreservedly optimistic. In a memorandum stamped secret (*Geheim*), dated 30 June 1942, he exaggerated the difficulties faced by the colonial defence apparatus in India and hinted that the Stilwell Road from Assam to China could not be built since the coolies constantly abandoned their work.[141] Another memorandum, dated 26 September 1942, claimed that the 'Quit India' movement engulfing the country gave reasons for the Axis powers to hope that Gandhi and the INC would be henceforth more receptive to their agenda.[142]

Despite his sympathy for India's distress, Furtwängler was not swayed by emotions as he looked for Germany's strategic interests. In a report dated 5 May 1942 on the recently concluded convention of the INC at Allahabad, he wrote that the task (of the Germans) was to keep the enmity between the INC and the British alive, thus following Alsdorf's pragmatic approach. This statement was made in the context of the possibility of the INC entering into a compromise with England.[143]

Furtwängler's most significant contribution to the knowledge of India produced at the behest of the SRI was a report on the catastrophic 'Bengal famine' of 1943. This terrible episode in the history of late colonial India was cynically deployed by the German Foreign Ministry for anti-British propaganda, as a note from the Information section of the Ministry to the SRI, demanding evaluations of the British reactions to the famine, indicate.[144]

In an undated report, Alsdorf had noted the threat of the famine resulting from the policy of the colonial government as well as by unscrupulous Indian business interests.[145] Writing under the pseudonym Indicus, Furtwängler provided an in-depth analysis of the causes of the famine. He correctly identified the British strategy of diverting all available food grains from civilians to soldiers at the front as one of the factors that led to the disastrous famine which claimed the lives of a few million people.[146] The report admirably served the cause of German propaganda through a combination of empirical data and polemical tone, describing India as a 'hungry Reich' and ridiculing the British war-time slogan of 'freeing the humanity'.

Nambiar, who stated in his post-war statement that Furtwängler used the pseudonym Indicus, maintained that the latter left the SRI in 1944.[147] The cause of his departure is not known. Furtwängler, however, continued to contribute to Nazi propaganda concerning India by writing newspaper articles as Indicus. Such articles include one championing the provisional government of Free India formed by Subhas Bose in Singapore.[148] This 'event' was celebrated with great fanfare in Berlin by the members of the Free India Centre, with the support of the SRI (Figure 9).

Furtwängler also published a well-received pamphlet containing information on India for the use of German armed forces in October 1942 under the pseudonym F.J. Vöhrenbach (Figure 10).[149]

Bundesarchiv, Bild 146-1985-130-38
Foto: Hoffmann | 1943

Figure 9 Wilhelm Keppler speaking at a function of the Free India Center in Berlin celebrating the foundation of the Provisional Government of Free India by Subhas Bose in Singapore, November 1943.

Source: Bundesarchiv, 183-J08486/Hoffmann/CC-BY-SA 3.0.

Figure 10 The book *Indien* by F.J. Vöhrenbach, alias Franz Josef Furtwängler.

Jogendra Kumar Banerji

The 'Bengal famine' of 1943 not only provided German propaganda with a unique instrument of publicity against the British, it also generated a rare opportunity for an Indian to write a memorandum for the SRI. Jogendra Kumar Banerji (b. 1907), an Indian working for Bose at the FIC, contributed a report for the SRI on the 'causes and background' of the famine. Before discussing Banerji's view of the famine, we should note his background, particularly his pragmatic change of orientation from an itinerant Communist revolutionary to a participant in Nazi Germany's propaganda venture. His was by no means an exceptional case.

Banerji's involvement in the Indian Communist movement began in his youth, in the north Indian city of Lucknow. He managed to escape incarceration by the increasingly repressive colonial authorities by leaving India in 1931. After travelling through underground Communist networks in Europe, South America, and Cuba, Banerji landed in Paris where he eked out a living writing for Indian newspapers.[150]

According to British surveillance records, around 1939, Banerji became receptive to the idea of seeking Germany's help to free India, a goal which came to overshadow his earlier commitment to Communism. He also enrolled at the University of Sorbonne, from where he obtained a doctorate degree in Economics in May 1940.[151] During his time in Paris, Banerji associated with other Indian left-wing activists living there, like A.C.N. Nambiar and Promode Sengupta, who would all join the FIC.[152] These 'British Indian' leftist activists fled to the south of France after the German occupation of Paris in June 1940. Nevertheless, they were interned by the Germans in October 1940. In March 1941, the Indians were set free again, presumably because they promised to cooperate with the Nazis.[153] Bose had got in touch with these Indians through the SRI and had offered them to join his venture. Banerji joined the FIC in Berlin in May 1942.[154] According to the post-war statement of Mukund Rai Vyas, Banerji occasionally wrote articles for the German press on the economic condition of India.[155] His degree from Sorbonne, an elite European academic institution, probably bestowed on him an aura of intellectual authority that elicited some respect from the representatives of the Nazi state.

In his report on the famine, Banerji tended towards a Marxist critique of the feudal and colonial economy of India. He opined that the only way to prevent such famines was to reform the 'parasitic' agricultural structure in order to abolish the systematic rural poverty which turned the entire Indian economy into a 'deficit economy'. This could not be achieved without destroying British rule in India since the feudal system was perpetuated through colonial arrangement of landholding.[156] Banerji, as well as his colleague at the FIC, Promode Sengupta, reiterated such views in the *Azad Hind.*[157]

The memoranda produced at the SRI on the famine contained critical insights which have still not lost their relevance. The irony that the National Socialist regime, which thrived on colonialist exploitation of the human and natural resources of the lands that it occupied, allowed a Marxist Indian to offer a leftist critique of a colonial policy that led to the disastrous famine, highlights once again the malleability of Nazi politics.

Presumably in the same year, Banerji wrote a detailed 'report' on the provisional government of Free India, formed by Bose in October 1943 in Singapore, then under Japanese occupation. Through his undated and blatantly overhyped essay, Banerji tried to claim that the significance of the newly established government was not purely symbolic.[158] The tone of this text suggests that it was meant to be directly circulated in the German press.

Abdul Rauf Malik

Another member of the FIC, Dr Abdul Rauf Malik, was entrusted to write a report on behalf of the SRI on 'Indian Muslims and Turkey' in June 1942.[159] Malik's trajectory was quite different from that of Banerji. Born in 1902 in Rawalpindi, Punjab (now in Pakistan), Malik completed his graduation from the Aligarh Muslim University. It is not clear when he came to Germany. British surveillance mentions that he studied History and Philosophy at the University of Berlin and earned a doctorate in 1931. Around that time, he was allegedly a follower of Chatto. After a short stint as a journalist at the newspaper Eastern Times of Lahore from 1931 to 1934, Malik returned to Berlin via Palestine, where he was received by Amin Al Husayini, the Grand Mufti of Jerusalem.[160] The Mufti would, like Bose, land up in Berlin in 1941 as an ally of the Nazi regime and be used as a symbol of Nazi support for the Arabs as Bose was projected as a manifestation of Nazi sympathy for Indian anti-colonialism.[161]

It is not known whether Malik was in touch with Bose during the latter's visits to Europe in the 1930s. The Indian journalist returned to his native country in 1935, this time as the special correspondent of the German newspaper *Berliner Tageblatt*. He remained with this Berlin-based newspaper until 1938, when he accompanied Jawaharlal Nehru to Europe indicating his link to the mainstream Indian nationalist movement. From 1939, Malik started working for the German Ministry of Propaganda, writing virulently anti-British texts for both German and Indian publications. By the beginning of 1940, Malik was an indispensable part of the German radio propaganda aimed at India.[162] Radio programmes in English and Hindustani targeting India had begun under the supervision of the Ministry of Propaganda from January 1939.[163] The post-war statement of Nambiar indicates that like K.A. Bhatta, Malik was also invited to give public lectures, presumably on propagandistic subjects, by various arms of the National Socialist state like the Labour Front.[164] Mukund Rai Vyas claimed that Malik was one of the first to join Bose's 'Azad Hind Sangh'

(Free India Association) as the Indian leader informally styled his group of Indian followers in 1941 in Berlin.[165] Though Bose was not supportive of the Mufti's attempts at propagating pan-Islamism to the Muslims of India, Malik was in contact with the Islamic leader in Berlin.[166] This biographical note makes it clear that Malik managed to integrate in his political oeuvre the secular Indian anticolonialism as expounded by Bose as well as the pan-Islamist politics of Amin al-Husayini. Malik readily deployed both these political elements in the service of the Nazi state.

Given his trajectory, it is hardly a surprise that Malik viewed the relationship between the Indian Muslims and Turkey through the prism of Islamism. In his report for the SRI, he echoed the views expressed by the Orientalist Joseph Horowitz in 1915 that Turkey was still considered to be the leading Muslim nation of the world and the protector of Islam by the Muslims in India. Hence, it would be opportune to influence the Indian Muslims through Islamic propaganda involving Turkey. This was not an accurate analysis. Not only did a substantial number of Indian Muslims endorse the secular anti-colonialism of the INC during this time, Turkey had become a secular state after the First World War and did not respond positively to German propaganda based on Islamic religiosity.[167] In any case, the SRI, following Bose's secularist rationale, was not receptive to Malik's views which, however, found some resonance in the Propaganda Ministry's broadcasts.[168]

Another report (*Bericht*) written by Malik on 26 June 1942, on 'Free India Conference' was probably meant to be a radio broadcast, as its belligerent tone suggests.[169] This 'report' celebrated a conference held in Bangkok in which the aged Indian nationalist Rash Behari Bose, who had been living in exile in Japan for a long time, urged the assembled members of the Indian community to take up arms against the British. The political significance of the event was the symbolic support of the Axis powers which sent their representatives to this assemblage.

Production of such texts were part of the 'India action' (*Indien Aktion*) that Ribbentrop called for in February 1942. The 'action' was to intensify the propaganda concerning India by emphasizing certain themes, like the exploitative, iniquitous character of British rule which had ruined the wealthy and internationally esteemed land that was India, the imminent arrival of the hour of freedom for Indians which was synonymous with the victory of the Axis powers, and so on.[170]

In their role as knowledge providers and propagandists, Banerji and Malik remained the exceptions among the Indian collaborators of the Nazi regime as far as the SRI was concerned. The explanation lies probably in ability of these two itinerant Indians to convince the influential members of the SRI like Alsdorf and Furtwängler, of 'scientific expertise' (Banerji) or of political trustworthiness (Malik). No other Indians involved with the SRI could achieve this feat, as we will see in the next section.

Book Series on India

Publication of a series of books on India, both as propaganda venture and to provide utilizable knowledge to German policymakers and press representatives, figured at the top of the SRI's work plan, as we have noted. The plan for publishing a series of books on India was developed by the German Foreign Ministry before the arrival of Bose, as the post-war statement of Mukund Rai Vyas indicates.[171]

Vyas, an Indian born in Mombasa, Kenya, which was a part of the British Empire like India, had arrived in London at the age of 18 with a scholarship to study law.[172] According to his own memoirs as well as British surveillance records, the young student soon became involved with Indian nationalist politics. He was particularly in thrall to the self-styled socialists among the INC like Nehru and Bose, whose speeches he chanced to hear in London.[173]

In 1939, Vyas came to Bonn to study German and was allegedly prevented by the onset of war from returning to England. In 1940, he moved to Berlin to start on his dissertation on Lord Cornwallis (1738–1805), a powerful British colonial governor of India. His supervisor was Bernhard Breloer, professor of Indology at the University of Berlin whom we have come across already. Breloer was, to quote Vyas, 'a fanatic Nazi' who, however, 'never mixed his politics with teaching.'[174]

In his post-war statement, Vyas claimed that he was introduced to the 'Orient propaganda section' of the Foreign Ministry in March 1941 by Habibur Rahman and Devendra Nath Bannerjea. Subsequently Vyas was asked to write a book on India for a planned book series in German. The book was to be on 'Men and Powers in India' (*Männer und Mächte in Indien*).[175]

As the SRI was formed in response to Bose's arrival, the book series on India was prioritised. Though Furtwängler was the official editor, it was Ludwig Alsdorf who dominated the publication process, commensurate with the authority that he commanded within the SRI. The series, titled 'India in Individual Portraits' (*Indien in Einzeldarstellungen*), was to be published by the Heidelberg-based Vowinckel Publishers, known for publishing conservative right-wing texts.

The series was to comprise the following titles: 1. *What Is India* (*Was ist Indien*) by Hermann Beythan; 2. *The Indian Economy* (*Die Wirtschaft Indiens*) by Hermann Lufft; 3. *India in the British Empire* (*Indien im Britischen Reich*) by Koodavuru Anantrama Bhatta; 4. *Men and Powers in Today's India* (*Männer und Mächte in heutigen Indien*) by Mukund Rai Vyas; 5. *Islam in India* (*Islam in Indien*) by Abid Hassan; 6. *The Social Question in India* (*Die soziale Frage in Indien*) by Abdul Quddus Faroqhi; 7. *The Spiritual Relationship between Germany and India* (*Deutsch-indische Geistesbeziehungen*) by Ludwig Alsdorf; and 8. *Monuments of Indian Art* (*Denkmäler Indischer Kunst*) by Wilhelm Kruse.[176]

That the book series was published during the war, when the resources of the Nazi state were concentrated on war efforts, indicates the importance of the 'Indian question' for German politics. The urgency to publish the series is further emphasized by the fact that Adam von Trott zu Solz wrote a letter on 23 January 1942 to the *Reichsschrifttumskammer* (Reich Chamber for Literary Assets), requesting a waiver on the compulsory censor that every publication in Nazi Germany was subjected to, so that the books could be published without delay.[177] The *Reichsschrifttumskammer* was an organ of the *Reichskulturkammer* (Reich Chamber of Culture) established under Joseph Goebbels in 1933 to control all aspects of cultural life in Germany and to bring all cultural productions in sync with the Nazi world view.[178] Evidently, this powerful organization agreed to Von Trott's request, denoting the political expediency of the publication.

However, the plan of having four Indian and four German authors to demonstrate the equal stakes of the partners in this project, ran into troubled waters very soon. A report from Furtwängler in April 1942 to the SRI makes it clear that he, 'acting on Alsdorf's advice' found the manuscripts of the Indian writers not worthy of publication. Abid Hassan's book had to be 'corrected to the smallest detail' while Bhatta's manuscript had to be completely rewritten although Bhatta was allowed to make some changes with the permission of Keppler.[179] The book by Abdul Quddus Faroqhi turned out to be a 'complete flop', while the manuscript of Vyas was 'unusable'.[180] The Indians in turn protested to Bose that 'corrections' to their manuscripts were undertaken without their knowledge and consent and the resulting works often did not reflect their thoughts and views.[181] Bose took up the matter with Keppler.[182] As a result of Bose's intervention, 'the fiction of the principle of parity', as Furtwängler claimed in an official response to Keppler dated 28 August 1942, was finally abandoned. Faroqhi's manuscript was returned unused and the book was published under the name of Hermann Beythan, who actually wrote it.[183]

Another note from Furtwängler to Keppler, dated 31 August 1942, makes it clear that Furtwängler rewrote Bhatta's manuscript, while Alsdorf acted as the 'selfless corrector' of Vyas' work. In the memo, Furtwängler gave the damning verdict that none of the Indians at the FIC was capable of delivering a competent literary work about issues pertaining to their own land.[184] Alsdorf, on his part, wrote an official note dated 17 September 1942, denouncing the authorial qualities of Indians in question. The brunt of Alsdorf's ire was directed at Abdul Quddus Faroqhi, whose book manuscript, according to Alsdorf, was excessively propagandistic. Other accusations included plagiarizing from the by then near-canonical *Indien* as well as Faroqhi's socialist leanings which allegedly found their expression in his criticisms of Gandhi.[185]

The rejection of the Indian authors' manuscripts by Alsdorf and, following him, Furtwängler, calls to mind Edward Said's contention that the orientalist 'makes the Orient speak' (i.e. depicts the Orient since the latter is not capable of representing itself).[186] The conjecture that this distrust of the Indians was largely due to Alsdorf's (and Furtwängler's) prejudices gains traction, considering that two of the four Indians in question had already established themselves as useful publicists in the Nazi state. Alsdorf's intellectual conceit was reinforced by the racialized arrogance that characterized some of the German functionaries of the SRI. Keppler, for example, while officially calling Bose His Excellency, referred to him as 'Bose the Indian' in his correspondence with Himmler.[187]

As we have observed, long before the arrival of Bose in Berlin in 1941, K.A. Bhatta had established himself as a Nazi propagandist. Nevertheless, Bhatta, for all his complaints, did not refrain from making political capital out of the book published in his name. He sent a copy of 'his book' to Franz Alfred Six (1909–1975), a high-ranking SS officer (*Oberführer*) and important functionary of the SD, who in 1943 became the head of the Cultural Political section of the Foreign Ministry (Figure 11).[188]

As we noted in the last chapter, the DA had become a part of the Cultural Political department. Notably, by early January 1944, Six also became the official head of the Information department, to which the SRI belonged. Through Six, the influence of the SS infiltrated both the Cultural Political department as well as the Information department.[189]

We will get to know Franz Alfred Six, whom Marie 'Missie' Wassiltschikow, secretary to Adam von Trott zu Solz, described inelegantly as a 'swine,' better in

Figure 11 *Franz Alfred Six, 1940/1941 (approximately). Photographer unknown. Wikimedia Commons.*

the next chapter.[190] What we need to note here is Bhatta's claim that he had met Six in 1939, through the mediation of Jakob Wilhelm Hauer, which demonstrates yet another channel of communication with the SS that Hauer initiated for Bhatta. In his answer to Bhatta, Six claimed that he would read the book as soon as he could find some time from his exhaustive work schedule and added that he had heard from his staff that 'your book represents an especially valuable contribution to German-Indian collaboration', thereby formally acknowledging the propagandistic worth of such production of politically useful knowledge.[191]

Among the other Indian writers, Abid Hassan or Zain-ul Abedin Hassan (b. 1911) was, like Habibur Rahman, a political bridge between Bose and the Nazi authorities. Hassan, an adherent of the nationalist movement conducted by Gandhi, had left India in 1931 after being imprisoned for six months by the colonial authorities. He landed up in Berlin, where he enrolled as a student at the Technical Academy (TH). During Bose's first visit to Berlin, Hassan became a follower of Bose and started taking an active part in the Indian Students' Association. By 1939, Hassan was allegedly 'receiving Nazi patronage' and contributing articles to the Indian press 'eulogizing the Nazis'.[192]

Abdul Quddus Faroqhi or Faruqi (b. 1901) came to Germany in 1921 to study engineering. Soon he became involved in a network of radical Communist activists spanning several European countries. Around 1925, Faroqhi was traced as a resident of Paris which at the time offered a relatively safe space for Asian and African political activists from the Third World to conduct radical politics.[193] He returned to Berlin in 1927 and engaged in leftist anti-colonial politics under the leadership of Chatto.[194] From 1929 to 1932, Faroqhi claimed to have studied national economy and philosophy at the University of Gießen, earning a doctorate in 1932.[195] However, his doctoral thesis, available at the library of the same university, is on 'Hindu Muslim Conflict' (*Der hindu-mohammedanische Konflikt*) which did not pertain directly to either economy or philosophy.

Not content with this degree, Faroqhi went on to study medicine in Berlin from 1934 to 1939.[196] By the time he completed his medical degree, he had successfully realigned his political loyalty in favour of the Nazi regime. From 1939, Faroqhi became an announcer in Urdu and English in the 'official' German radio programmes aimed at India.[197] In 1940, his photograph appeared in the medical magazine of 'Reichsgau Wartheland', an area of Poland which was newly occupied by Germany. In this propaganda photograph, Faroqhi was shown to be a part of a team of international doctors who supposedly investigated the alleged atrocities that the Poles had been committing on the German citizens there a spurious allegation.[198] Faroqhi's involvement with Nazi politics and his two doctorates speak of the Nazi regime's trust in him as well as his intellectual abilities.

Similarly, it can be assumed that Vyas possessed enough acumen to be accepted as a doctoral student by Bernhard Breloer, whose scholarly works on ancient India were both acclaimed and wide-ranging.[199] Moreover, if Vyas is to be believed, the Foreign Ministry invited him to write a book before the SRI was founded, indicating his academic reputation.

Another Indian, whose manuscript about Gandhi was rejected by the Furtwängler on Alsorf's advice, was Devendra Nath Bannerjea with whom we have already made a brief acquaintance. According to a British surveillance report, after Subhas Chandra Bose established the Indian Students' Association in Berlin, Bannerjea worked for a time as Bose's press agent. His services were terminated by Bose after Bannerjea tried to report several members of the Indian community in Berlin as communists to the Gestapo.[200] We will discuss this issue in more detail in the next chapter.

Bannerjea also had a relationship of mutual animosity with Alsdorf.[201] The Indologist did not pass up the opportunity to reject Bannerjea's manuscript in the autumn of 1942. He would later call it 'a ludicrous representation which was in essence a watered down version of Gandhi's own biography.'[202] In retaliation, Bannerjea not only set his lawyer to extract monetary compensation for his efforts, but also denunciated Furtwängler to the Foreign Ministry as the leader of 'an anti-Hitler clique' in the SRI.[203] This allegation was subsequently refuted through enquiries by the Foreign Ministry, as a letter from Keppler to Martin Luther, a functionary of the Ministry, shows.[204] Alsdorf not only defended Furtwängler but also tried to incite Vowinckel, the publisher, to demand that Bannerjea should repay the advances made to him for writing the book.[205] The controversy dragged on until 1944. In the end, Bannerjea did not have to return the money and the biography of Gandhi was never published.[206]

Another measure of Alsdorf's authority within the SRI was that he was instrumental in preventing the publication of a German translation of Subhas Bose's book, *The Indian Struggle*. Bose was eager to publish the book, for which he had secured the approval of the Foreign Ministry. In an official note to Keppler dated 29 September 1942, Alsdorf claimed that the exhaustive political details of the book would tire German readers. Moreover, claimed Alsdorf, 'politically the book was a continuous apologetic-polemical debate with Gandhi, whose mistakes at every step were reviewed.' The publication of such criticisms, claimed Alsdorf, would go against Germany's policy of not directly criticizing Gandhi.[207]

Portrayals of India

An examination of the books in the series shows Alsdorf's 'correcting hand' in most of them, his book *Indien* serving as a template. The author of *What Is India?*, the first book of the series, was Hermann Beythan (1875–1945), a former missionary and an expert on Tamil who served the NS regime in different ways, as we will see in the next chapter. Alsdorf's intervention is apparent in the introduction, which stated that one needed to understand the relationship between India and

British colonial rule, since the British obsession to hold on to India had dictated the Empire's decisions on war and peace for the last one and half centuries. This passage was almost a verbatim reproduction from *Indien*.

Beythan's experience as a colonial scholar of South India is reflected in the book through his attempts to invert the traditional discourse propagated by some German Indologists who denigrated Dravidian culture which was widely prevalent in South India, while extolling the Sanskrit-based north Indian culture which they associated with Nordic Aryans. However, in his efforts, Beythan borrowed from the same arsenal of racialized ethnological tropes, possibly due to his connection to the influential ethnologist Eugen von Eickstedt, whom Beythan helped to write one of his books. Beythan made this claim in a letter to his friend Carl Ihmels, the director of the Evangelical Mission in Leipzig.[208]

Beythan tried to posit Dravidian language and culture as symbols of a highly developed pre-Aryan civilization. To him, the upper castes in Tamil Nadu were members of a pre-Aryan aristocracy, which learnt to keep their ranks 'pure' through endogamy and by distancing themselves from 'impure' lower castes.[209] Though Beythan's book criticized the idealization of Brahmins in the *Manusmriti*, which was purportedly praised by Nietzsche for advocating social hierarchy, it glorified the Bhagavad-Gita as a masterpiece of Aryan heroic ideals.[210] In this context, one can recall Jakob Wilhelm Hauer's attempts to establish the Bhagavad-Gita as a precursor of the cult of duty and death advocated by the SS. Evidently, the Gita had become a scholarly instrument in the hands of certain Indologists to celebrate aspects of Nazi world view. *What is India?* ended with a call for Hindu–Muslim unity as promulgated by Bose and adapted by German propaganda. Despite following Bose's secular agenda, the book was not free from anti-Islamic prejudices.[211]

In *soziale Frage in Indien* (*The Social Question in India*), the other book that he wrote for the series, Beythan used materials (photographs, statistics, reports) from the Evangelical mission in Leipzig which were provided to him by Carl Heinrich Ihmels. Beythan seemed to repay this service by lavishing praise in the book on the 'exemplary' social and educational work done by the missionaries, particularly German Protestants, in India.

The book is a dense, statistics-filled treatise on different aspects of social life in India—especially in the villages. This work aimed to highlight the oppression and exploitation inflicted on the Indians by the British colonialists. Unlike his earlier book, theories of caste and race are absent in this one. But the influence of German Indology is manifested through Beythan's contention that ancient India had achieved a remarkable level of material and cultural advancement, as demonstrated through the ancient treatises of *Arthasastra* and the Vedas. Like the Vedas, the *Arthasastra* was used by some German scholars as a template to construct an idealized ancient Indian past. Such scholars included Bernhard Breloer, the first volume of whose 'Kautilya Studies' was consulted by Beythan for this book.[212]

Recent research suggests that the *Arthasastra* was a text written over several centuries, espousing different ideals of statecraft and society, rather than describing an actual situation.[213]

In conclusion, the book embarked on a tirade against the 'overseas power' that forced India to be the 'blood donors' for Britain's wars. The author called for an invocation of the 'power of the spirit' which would lead to the awakening of 'the Will', a metaphysical concept that ran through German philosophy and was particularly valued by Nietzsche, who enjoyed a cult-like status among some Nazis, including Hitler.[214]

It is noteworthy that in a letter to Ihmels, Beythan emphasized this book's propagandistic nature, claiming that it was a 'combat organ' which was influenced by 'political considerations'. He also stated that the editor of the series substituted some of Beythan's moderate statements for more aggressive ones.[215]

The political economist and publicist Hermann Lufft, who wrote the second book of the series, was not a specialist on India but a writer who had published on Latin America and the British Empire before 1933. Lufft wrote, apart from the book in this series, two other books on British imperialism for propagandistic uses by the Nazi regime.[216] He also published at least two anti-British articles on India in the newspaper *Berliner Lokal Anzeiger* in 1942.[217]

Lufft's book, titled *India's Economy* (*Die Wirtschaft Indiens*) began with a survey of the economic importance of different regions of India. It then proceeded to discuss different aspects of Indian economy: agriculture as the dominant mode of economic activity, village economy organized around caste and joint families, as well as the traditional relationship between environment and food production. This was followed by an analysis of the changes brought about by colonial policies, which increased rural poverty due to excessive taxation on agriculture and farming, on the one hand, and the emergence of factory-based labour due to the introduction of a capitalist economy, on the other. The book used comprehensive data to highlight the exploitation of India's natural and human assets by the 'Anglo-Saxon–Jewish world imperialism'.[218] This phrase makes it clear that this book was primarily meant to be a vehicle of Nazi propaganda.

Similarly suggestive is the statement, expressed early on in the book that a new India, full of 'strength of life' (*lebenskraft*) can only emerge under an Indian 'Führer' who will render unsuccessful the colonial politics of destroying the sociological basis of Hinduism and of dividing the Indians.[219] Interestingly, parts of Lufft's book, particularly the passages on Indian labour, showed a suspiciously close resemblance with *Working India* (*Das werktätige Indien*), written by Furtwängler and Schrader, though this work is not mentioned in the bibliography.[220]

The book *India in British Empire* (*Indien im Britischen Reich*), ascribed to K.A. Bhatta and published in 1942 provided a detailed description of how the interests of commercial profit always guided British politics in India. The book repeated many of the statements and arguments from *Indien* as well as several tropes of German Indology. Thus, it claimed that Indian history starts from Aryan invasion, sparing only half a sentence on the Indus valley civilization that preceded the Vedic one. The presence of a highly developed urban, pre-Vedic indigenous civilization was an inconvenient obstacle for those German Indologists who presented the Aryans as the civilizing force conquering an Indian subcontinent inhabited by primitives. This book glorified a purportedly primordial Aryan civilization in which the purity of Aryan blood was preserved. It combined this ideological construct with a discourse shared by European orientalists and imperialists; that in this Aryan utopia, women did not know 'oriental enslavement'.[221] Another 'classic' orientalist view reproduced in the book was that Indians lacked a 'sense of history'.[222] The medieval period, when India was ruled by the Mughal dynasty, was almost glossed over, reflecting an anti-Islamic prejudice. Nevertheless, it followed the guidelines of German (and Bose's) policy by criticizing British politics for engendering communal antagonism.

The book *Men and Powers in India* (*Männer und Mächte in Indien*) published under the name of Mukund Rai Vyas in 1942, traced the course of Indian nationalism from the Hindu reformist movements and an attendant religious nationalism in the nineteenth century, to the emergence of secular Indian nationalism in the first decade of the twentieth century.

The book dealt primarily with the history of the Indian National Congress, which it equated with the evolution of the entire anti-colonial movement. The Communist movement, conducted largely underground, was barely mentioned. The Muslim League was presented as a reactionary, pro-British party that did not really care for the interests of Indian Muslims. Hindu religious nationalism was also disparaged as reactionary, presumably in accordance with Bose's imperative to reject religion-based politics.

This book stands out for its mention of the participation of women in the anti-colonial movement which was a welcome departure from the Orientalist trope of 'enslavement' of women. It presented Sarojini Naidu, INC leader and poet, as an example of the 'modernization of the Indian woman and the strength of her soul'.[223]

The book did not refrain from insidiously criticizing Gandhi, whom it described through a racialized prism as 'rather short, rather dark and almost ugly'.[224] Much like Alsdorf's *Indien*, this book also orientalized Gandhi, warmly praising his 'saintly' qualities that won him the epithet of Mahatma.[225] Unlike Alsdorf's book, however, this work accused Gandhi of refusing to radicalize the anti-colonial movement in order to cater to the interests of Indian industrialists and financiers.[226] Such left-wing critique of Gandhi was also expressed by a number of Marxist anti-colonialists including the aforementioned Jogendra K. Banerji in the magazine *Azad Hind*. Despite its ideological opposition to all forms of leftist politics, such rhetoric was tolerated in the case of India by the Foreign Ministry since it had found out that a large number of Indians were inclined towards socialism.[227]

The book supposedly written by Abid Hassan, *Islam in India: India in World Islam* (*Der Islam in Indien. Indien im Weltislam*), began with the rote mention of the conquest of India by the 'Nordic Indogermanic race'.[228] Subsequently, however, it deviated from the narrative of 'Islamic invasion' and Muslim despotism by tracing the rise of a composite culture in India which resulted from willing conversions of (mainly lower-caste) Hindus to Islam and different forms of intermingling of Hindus and Muslims. The book stated that the linguistic and cultural differences between Hindus and Muslims in India were so indistinct that it is 'absurd to speak of a Mohammedan nation in India'.[229] Remarkably, various articles in the *Azad Hind* magazine expressed very similar views, indicating that Alsdorf and Furtwängler had to concur with Bose's agenda.[230]

This book spelt out the political importance of India in the Islamic world, as already articulated by Alsdorf in his memoranda for the SRI. Reading of this book was made mandatory by the Wehrmacht, which had to engage with Muslims in parts of Europe and Africa.[231]

Ludwig Alsdorf's book, *The Spiritual Relationship between Germany and India* (*Deutsch-indische Geistesbeziehungen*) published in 1942, supposedly had a 'unique propagandistic value' in Nazi Germany, as reviews presented by the 'Office of Science' (*Amt Wissenschaft*) of the NSDAP claimed.[232]

The book's introduction shows why it was considered valuable for the Nazi state's propaganda towards India. It started with the claim that there existed an 'essential kinship' between the European nation of 'poets and thinkers' and the classical 'land of religion and contemplative mediation' in Asia, a stereotype used by generations of Orientalists to describe India. The political undertone of the book becomes clear as Alsdorf proceeded to claim that this 'essential kinship' was reinforced through a sense of solidarity shared by the colonized Indians and the Germans chafing under the unjust treaty of Versailles.[233]

The rationale of the book was a view expressed by an earlier generation of German Indologists who claimed that while the British colonized India and siphoned off its material wealth, Germans were interested only in the intellectual treasures of India, particularly the knowledge of Aryan India which they had helped, with great success, to unearth and preserve. The Indologist Hermann Oldenberg had expressed this opinion in his book *Indian and Classical Philology* (*Indische und klassische Philologie*) published in 1906, claiming: '...we who do not have to participate in the administration of India but who seek to interpret the documents of the Indian tradition concerning the problems of human history... We know the Hindu less well than our colleagues who live in his country and breathe his air. But to us is given, I hold, the possibility of knowing the Aryan of old India better...'[234]

While Oldenberg's attempt to establish the superiority of German Indology was aimed at the British, Alsdorf addressed the Indians, claiming that the latter knew what their 'Fatherland' had given to 'the great Germans' as well as what

German Indology had achieved for India.[235] He then proceeded to make the hegemonic claim that 'just as the people from other nations need to learn German to enjoy the fruits of German research on medicine, science and technology, Indians need to learn German in order to fully participate in researching their own history and culture, religion, philosophy, literature and language.'[236] The book was essentially a paean to German Indological scholarship, the evolution of which was lucidly traced by Alsdorf. Indians were mentioned only in the margins and through British colonial stereotypes. This book was primarily meant to make the Nazi state aware of the importance of the contribution of German Indologists to the nationalist project of enhancing the prestige of German academia in the world.

Another book of the series, *Monuments of Indian Art*, was written by Wilhelm Kruse, who was presumably identical to the Berlin-based sculptor of the same name. The book is a slim volume with 48 photographs of the major works of Indian art, comprising mostly sculptures. The book begins with the apparently mandatory assertion that the 'Indogerman Aryans' who invaded India and conquered the native inhabitants were the true bearers of Indian culture, though it devoted a line to the 'high culture' that reigned in the Indus valley before the Aryan invasion.[237] Kruse, however, admitted that South India, which could boast of spectacular Hindu temples from the ancient and medieval period, was practically 'devoid of Aryan blood'. The book did not attempt to reconcile these conflicting statements. It gave a perfunctory nod to the racialized view that art was generally 'a product of the race' and concluded with the propagandistic claim that Indian art, which had degenerated due to 'European colonizing capitalism', would have scope for regeneration with the emergence of the Indian anti-colonial movement.[238]

Some of the books went into a second edition. Publisher Kurt Vowinckel tried to induce Trott to continue the series. But Ribbentrop was not interested in providing the required subvention after the debacle of Stalingrad in 1943, after which the chances of the Axis powers having any real influence on India seemed remote.[239]

End and New Beginnings

From the winter of 1943, many functionaries of the Foreign Ministry including Alsdorf shifted to Krummhübel (in present day Czech Republic) in order to avoid Allied bombing. Presumably, the activities of the SRI were conducted from there until the end of the 'Reich'.[240] We will discuss Alsdorf's post-1945 fate in the next chapter. Among the other knowledge providers, Furtwängler, who was a co-conspirator of von Trott in the planning of the attempt on Hitler's life on 20 July 1944, could save his life due to a combination of sheer luck and his impressive talent for survival. He managed to endure the end of war in the relative safety of obscurity.[241] Furtwängler resurfaced in 1946 and after a short stint as the head of the Academy of Labour in Frankfurt, devoted himself to a successful career as a publicist.[242] Much like the Indian anti-colonialists who worked for Bose, Furtwängler's collaboration with the Nazi regime in the form of providing utilizable knowledge has been largely excised from historical narratives as he is remembered primarily as a 'life-long friend of India' and an admirer of Gandhi.[243]

As passport holders of 'British-India', the Indians came under the jurisdiction of the British authorities after 1945. Among them, Vyas returned to independent India at the request of Jawaharlal Nehru, the first prime minister of independent India. He became an educationalist and was subsequently nominated as a member of the Rajya Sabha, the upper house of the Indian parliament, commensurate with his reputation as a 'freedom fighter'.[244] Such prestige was denied to Bhatta, whose last archival trace is an undated letter that he wrote from a farm in the French zone of occupation in Württemberg (possibly near Tübingen) to Nehru in 1947. In this letter, Bhatta requested 'Your Excellency the prime minister' to include him in the Indian Embassy that was soon to open in Switzerland. In the letter, Bhatta presented a highly manipulated version of his time in Germany. He claimed that he consistently defended India in the German press, for which he was imprisoned by the Nazi authorities for two weeks in 1939. Only the threat of a hunger strike could induce the SS to release him. Bhatta not only highlighted his work with Subhas Bose but also with Haushofer, who had committed suicide in 1946, which imparted to him a posthumous reputation as an opponent of the Nazis. Bhatta's letter makes it clear that the British knew about his collusion with various Nazi organizations and were searching for him. The Indian External Affairs Department replied tersely in a letter dated 1 April 1947 that there was no vacancy in the Indian Embassy in Zurich.[245]

Among the other Indians, Faroqhi's post-war trajectory can be traced. He went to India for some years after the war, returning to Germany in 1958. Soon thereafter, he began a successful career as a surgeon in Hamburg. He is remembered mainly as the father of the filmmaker Harun Farocki (1944–2014).[246] Abdul Quddus Faroqhi's role as a publicist for the Nazi regime has been completely erased from public memory.

Notes

1. Kuhlmann, Jan, 2003, 131.
2. See, for example, Werth, Alexander, 1971, 129; Zöllner, Hans-Bernd, 1999, 31; Bose, Sugata, 2011, 207.
3. Hauner, Milan, 1981, 358–9; Kuhlmann, Jan, 2003, 158–65; Bushak, Willy, 2010, 183–5.
4. Liebau, Heike, 2014b, 110. On the NfO, see Krug, Samuel, 2020.
5. Liebau, Heike, 2022; Jenkins, Jennifer, Liebau, Heike, and Schmid, Larissa, 2020, 61–79.
6. McGetchin, Douglas, 2010, 105; Liebau, Heike, 2014a, 43; Brückenhaus, Daniel, 2017, 55–7.
7. Kuhlmann, Jan, 2003, 129.
8. Barooah, Elizabeth and Barooah, Nirode Kumar, 2015, 86–8.
9. Conze, Eckart et al., 2010, 303.

10. Ibid., 298, 301.
11. Wassiltschikow, Marie 'Missie', 1991, 57.
12. Notable among such biographies are Werth, Alexander, 1971; Bose, Mihir, 1982; Gordon, Leonard A., 1990; Toye, Hugh, 1991; Bose, Sugata, 2011.
13. Bose, Sugata, 2011, 136.
14. Hayes, Romain, 2011.
15. Kuhlmann, Jan, 2003, 115–25.
16. Zöllner, Hans-Bernd, 1999, 24; Kuhlmann, Jan, 2003, 23–7.
17. Brückenhaus, Daniel, 2017, 115.
18. IOR/L/PJ/12/629, list of disloyal Indians in Europe.
19. Barooah, Nirode Kumar, 2004, 283.
20. IOR/L/PJ/12/214.3.
21. IOR/L/PJ/12/659.74.
22. NAUK: KV23-907, statement of Mukund Rai Vyas, 1945. Appendix E1.
23. IOR/L/PJ/12/410, Indian Societies and Associations in Germany, 2.
24. Ellinger, Ekkehard, 2006, 107.
25. IOR/L/PJ/12/659.80; IOR/L/PJ/12/214.3.
26. Ellinger, Ekkehard, 2006, 107.
27. Lüders, Heinrich, 1935 (republished 2020), 68–92.
28. Motadel, David, 2019, 843.
29. Kuhlmann, Jan, 2003, 131–3.
30. Hayes, Romain, 2011, 36.
31. Ibid., 43.
32. Kuhlmann, Jan, 2003, 166.
33. Ibid., 160.
34. Padfield, Peter, 1991, 115, 119, 219.
35. IOR/L/PJ12/506, survey number 10, 1939, 26.
36. PA-AA: R10477, memo dated 1.9.1938.
37. PA-AA: RZ501/60671: Arbeitsprogram für die Indienpropaganda, E303552–3.
38. Ibid., E303554.
39. For a detailed study of Alsdorf's career, see Roy, Baijayanti, 2023b.
40. BA Berlin: R9361-VIII, Kartei 40368.
41. Geheimesstaatsarchiv Preußischer Kulturbesitz or GstAPK (Secret State Archives Prussian Cultural Heritage Foundation) Berlin: 1 HA Rep.76 Kultusministerium. Bl.189.
42. GstAPK: 1 HA Rep.76 Kultusministerium. Bl.303–4, Bl.423.
43. Göllnitz, Martin, 2016, 54.
44. GstAPK: IHA Rep.76 Sek.11. Nr.7a.
45. BA Berlin: R4901/24118, P.0619.
46. Ibid., P.0624.
47. Roy, Baijayanti, 2022b, 11–29.
48. UAM: Bestand 63, Nummer 7, Bd.1.
49. IfZ Munich, 116–1.
50. AHU: UK Personalia, Alsdorf, A051 Fragebogen.
51. UAM: Bestand 63, Nummer 7, Bd.1.
52. On NSKK, see Hochstretter, Dorothee, 2005.
53. BA Berlin: R9361/II 10407, 54.
54. BA Berlin: R4901/24118, 0594.
55. Schreiber, Carsten, 2019, 42–3.
56. Sächsisches Staatsarchiv Hauptstaatsarchiv (SaHStA), Dresden: Ministerium für Volksbildung, 10230. Abtlg: 1b.L8.VIII.No.73.Bd.3 Heft2, letters dated 6.2.1937 and 23.3.1937.
57. UAM: Bestand 63, Bd.2, letter from the Education Ministry to Alsdorf, dated 31.8.1938; Schmidt, Richard, *Das Kamasutram. Die indische Ars Amatoria*, Leipzig, 1900.
58. Thamer, Hans-Ulrich, Droste, Daniel, and Happ, Sabine (eds), 2012.
59. For details on the uses of Indology in the context of Alsdorf's appointment, see Roy, Baijayanti, 2023b, 280–1.
60. Benz, Wolfgang, 2013.
61. BayHstA Munich: MK 69695, Alsdorf's statement, 2.
62. Rudiger, Karlheinz, 1941, 74–5.
63. UAM: Vorlesungsverzeichnis, SS 1939, 85.
64. UAM: Vorlesungsverzeichnis, Second Trimester, 1940, 69–70.

65. IfZ Munich: 116–1, letter dated 18.2.42.
66. Ahuja, Ravi, 2020, 9.
67. Roy, Baijayanti, 2017a, 1192.
68. Alsdorf, Ludwig, 1940, 64.
69. Ibid., 170–1.
70. Ibid., 220–1.
71. Rosenberg, Alfred, 1934, 662.
72. Voigt, Johannes, H. 1971, 50.
73. Kuhlmann, Jan, 2003, 165.
74. UAM: Bestand 63, Nummer 7, Bd.1.
75. NAUK: KV3904 (3), statement of Nambiar. Appendix B. P.35; KV23-907: statement of Mukund Rai Vyas, Appendix D1.
76. NAUK: Verzeichnis: Einiger prominenter Persönlichkeiten der gegenwärtigen indischen Politik, GFM33-564, Serial No.1314.
77. NAUK: GFM33/558, 10.10.1941, Serial No. 345788.
78. Roy, Baijayanti, 2022a, 6.
79. Among recent works on the subject, see Herf, Jeffrey, 2009; Motadel, David, 2014.
80. Liebau, Heike, 2022, 2.
81. Kuhlmann, Jan, 2003, 318.
82. NAUK: GFM33/565, Serial No.1313.350491, L. Alsdorf, Die indische Mohammedaner, der Pakistan plan und die Deutsche Orientpolitik, 2.12.1941.
83. NAUK: GFM33/558, Serial No. 345795.
84. PA-AA: RZ501-60670, 11.2.42.
85. BA Berlin: R901-60423, note by Melchers, dated 7.5.1943.
86. BA Berlin: R901-60423, 15.5.1943, Bl.180–4.
87. BA Berlin: R901-60423, L. Alsdorf, Pakistan, das indische Ulster, Bl.185–92.
88. Roy, Baijayanti, 2022a, 6.
89. Herf, Jeffrey, 2009, 39.
90. BA Berlin: R901/60423, Bl.196–8.
91. Roy, Baijayanti, 2016b, 219–20.
92. Alsdorf, Ludwig, 1940, 88.
93. NAUK: KV(2)/3904, statement of Nambiar, 46.
94. PA-AA: RZ501-67660, note titled Propagandistische Erfassung des indischen Muslims, 4.
95. Kuhlmann, Jan, 2003, 322.
96. NAUK: GFM33/565, Serial No. 1313, 349884, report dated 14.10.1944.
97. NAUK: GFM33/558, Serial No. 1313, 345780, 25.2.1942.
98. Bayley, Christopher and Harper, Tim, 2005, 270
99. NAUK: GFM33/2109, Indienbericht No. 4, 7.8.1941–19.8.1941, E233497–E233499.
100. BA Berlin: R901/60423, Indienbericht No. 30, 8.10.1942–22.10.42, Bl.224.
101. Hauner, Milan, 1981, 277.
102. NAUK: GFM33/558, Serial No. 1313, 350004, 8.9.1942.
103. NAI: Subhas Chandra Bose Private Archives, Indienbericht No. 22, 28.5.1942–9.6.1942, 240.
104. BA Berlin: R901/60423, 25.3.1942, 140.
105. BA Berlin: R901/60423, 156.
106. Ibid., 157.
107. BA Berlin: R4902/10466.
108. Gondhalekar, Nandini and Bhattacharya, Sanjoy, 1999, 48–74.
109. Roy, Baijayanti, 2016b, 222.
110. Ahuja, Ravi, 2020, 19–20.
111. Kuhlmann, Jan, 2003, 164–5.
112. For a full account of Talwar's activities, see Bose, Mihir, 2017.
113. NAUK: HW12/303, encrypted messages from Alsdorf: No. 134645 (9.8.1944), No. 135656 (18.8.1944), No. 135101 (20.8.1944), No. 135284 (26.8.1944).
114. NAUK: HW12/303, No.135284.
115. NAUK: FGM33/564, Serial No.1314, 8.9.1942.
116. Gupta, Diya, 2019, 10.
117. Bose, Sugata, 2011, 223.
118. Framke, Maria and Tschurenev, Jana, 2018, 74.
119. Buschak, Willy A., 2010, 201–2.
120. NAUK: KV2/3904/3, 58.

121. NAUK: KV2/3904/3.7 (63).
122. Archive of the University of Munich (AUM): Philosophische Fakultät, Bd.1, Bl.1625.
123. NAUK: KV23-907, Mukund Rai Vyas, 133.
124. NAI: Subhas Chandra Bose Private Archives, Serial No. 124.6.
125. Ludwig, Botho, 1942, 64.
126. Barooah, Elisabeth and Barooah, Nirode K., 2015, 11–12.
127. Ibid., 17.
128. Furtwängler, Franz Joseph and Schrader, Karl, 1928.
129. Ahuja, Ravi, 2020, 13.
130. Buschak, Willy A., 2010, 107.
131. Furtwängler, Franz Joseph, 1951, 197.
132. Manjapra, Kris, 2014, 186. Manjapra cites *Das Werktätige Indien* (1928, 157) as his source though none of the events are mentioned there.
133. Furtwängler, Franz Joseph, 1951, 171–85, 164–70.
134. Buschak, Willy A., 2010, 189.
135. Furtwängler, Franz Joseph, 1951, 197.
136. Buschak, Willy A., 2010, 180.
137. Furtwängler, Franz Joseph, 1951, 181–2.
138. Barooah, Elisabeth and Barooah, Nirode K., 2015, 72–3.
139. Furtwängler, Franz Joseph, 1951, 172–3.
140. Ibid., 199–200.
141. PA-AA: R270505.
142. NAUK: GFM33/565/1313, Sl, No. 350080.
143. PA-AA: R27505, 5.5.42, 3.
144. PA-AA: R27501, Handakten Keppler, undated, 350207.
145. NAUK: GFM33/565, Serial No. 1313, 349951–9.
146. NAUK: GFM33/565/1313, Sl, No. 349775–81, Indicus: England und die indische Hungerkatastrophe, 27.9.43.
147. NAUK: KV/3904/3, 2.
148. BA Berlin: R4902/8968.
149. Buschak, Willy A., 2010, 196–7.
150. Roy, Baijayanti, 2022a, 8–9.
151. IOR/L/PJ/12/659, 15.
152. NAUK: KV2/3904/2, 10.
153. IOR/L/PJ/12/514, 3.
154. NAUK: KV2/3904/2, 19.
155. NAUK: KV23-907, Appendix C3.
156. NAUK: GFM33/565/1313, Sl, No. 350343.
157. Roy, Baijayanti, 2022a, 9.
158. NAUK: GFM33/565/1313, Sl, No. 350344–9.
159. NAI: Subhas Chandra Bose Private Archives, Bericht No. 163, 16.6.1942, 23–6, Indische Muslimen und die Türkei.
160. IOR/L/PJ/12/659.
161. Herf, Jeffrey, 2009, 8.
162. IOR/L/PJ/12/659.
163. Kuhlmann, Jan, 2003, 76.
164. NAUK: KV/3902/2, 2 (58).
165. NAUK: KV/23-907, Appendix H1.
166. NAUK: KV/23-907, Appendix C2.
167. Motadel, David, 2014, 103.
168. NAUK: KV/3902/3, 2 (58).
169. PA-AA: RZ501-60673.
170. PA-AA: RZ501-60670.
171. NAUK: KV23-907, Appendix P9.
172. IOR/L/PJ/12/659.
173. Vyas, Mukund Rai, 1982, 67, 86; IOR/L/PJ/12/659.
174. Vyas, Mukund Rai, 1982, 196–7.
175. NAUK: KV23-907, Appendix P9.
176. NAUK: GFM33/564/1312, notice dated 15.4.1942.
177. PA-AA: RZ501/60670.

178. Stier, Antje, 2015.
179. PA-AA: R27504, Handakten Keppler, note from Keppler to Furtwängler, 3.12.1942.
180. NAUK: GFM/33/564/1312, 9.4.1942, Serial No. 349827.
181. NAUK: GFM/33/564/1312, undated letter by Bhatta, Serial No. 349823.
182. NAUK: GFM/33/564/1312, undated letter by Bose, signed as Orlando Mazzotta, Serial No. 349829.
183. NAUK: GFM/33/564/1312, Serial No. 349818.
184. PA-AA: R27504, Handakten Keppler.
185. NAUK: Kew GFM/33/565/1313, Serial No. 349809–11.
186. Said, Edward, 1978 (2003 edition), 20–1.
187. BA Berlin: NS 19/3769, letter dated 16.2.1943.
188. Hachmesiter, Lutz, 1998, 244.
189. Wassiltschikow, Marie, 1991, 165.
190. Ibid.
191. PA-AA: RZ501/60677, letter dated 20.5.1943.
192. IOR/L/PJ/12/629.
193. On Paris as a safe space for radical politics, see Goebbel, Michael, 2015.
194. IOR/L/PJ/12/612, 1940.
195. Parzer, Robert, 2015.
196. Ibid.
197. IOR/L/PJ/12/659, 72.
198. Parzer, Robert, 2015.
199. Vyas, Mukund Rai, 1982, 196; Losch, Hans, 1955, biography of Bernhard Breloer, http://www.deutsche-biographie.de/pnd127431799.html#ndbcontent.
200. IOR/L/PJ/12/659, 74.
201. Framke, Maria, 2023.
202. PA-AA: R27504, Handakten Keppler, Alsdorf's note, 7.4.1943.
203. NAUK: GFM/33/564/1312, No. 349782–5.
204. NAUK: GFM33/564/1312, 27.2.1943.
205. PA-AA: R27504, Handakten Keppler, Alsdorf's note, 7.4.1943.
206. Framke, Maria, 2023.
207. PA-AA: Handakten Keppler, R27504, Aufzeichnung: Über die geplante Ausgabe von S.C.Bose's "Indian Struggle".
208. Franckesche Stiftungen zu Halle, ALMW II, Beythan's letter, 13.4.1943.
209. Beythan, Hermann, 1942, 32.
210. Ibid., 48, 162.
211. Ibid., 151.
212. Breloer, Bernhard, 1927.
213. Olivelle, Patrick, 2013.
214. Beythan, Hermann, 1942, 166; Strehle, Stephen, 2011, 125.
215. Franckesche Stiftungen zu Halle, ALMW II, 10.4.42.
216. Lufft, Hermann, 1936; 1940.
217. NAI: Subhas Chandra Bose Private Archives, Serial No. 124, 6.
218. Lufft, Hermann, 1942, 156.
219. Ibid., 11.
220. Buschak, Willy A., 2010, 199.
221. Bhatta, K.A., 1943, 12.
222. Ibid., 10.
223. Vyas, Mukund Rai, 1942, 107.
224. Ibid., 111.
225. Ibid., 83.
226. Ibid., 116.
227. Roy, Baijayanti, 2022a, 12.
228. Hassan, Abid, 1943, 1.
229. Ibid., 15.
230. For example, Sengupta, Promode, Azad Hind, 1942, 7/8, 12–29; Hassan, A., Azad Hind, 1942, 9/10, 18–30; Shahbuddin, Pir, Azad Hind, 1944, 3/4, 38–45.
231. Kuhlmann, Jan, 2003, 169.
232. IfZ Munich: MA1190, 16.5.1942.
233. Alsdorf, Ludwig, 1942, 1.

234. Oldenberg, Hermann, 1906, 1518, quoted in Adluri, Vishwa, 2011, 270.
235. Alsdorf, Ludwig, 1942, 3.
236. Ibid., 11.
237. Kruse, Wilhelm, 1942, 1–2.
238. Ibid., 9, 22.
239. Buschak, Willy A., 2010, 201.
240. Roy, Baijayanti, 2023b, 296.
241. Buschak, Willy, 2010, 209–10.
242. Barooah, Elizabeth and Barooah, Nirode K., 2015, 103.
243. Ibid., xiv.
244. Vyas, Mukund Rai, 1982, 1.
245. NAI: EAD File No. 36 (36), Eur/47.
246. See https://www.tagesspiegel.de/kultur/harun-farocki-bilder-die-die-welt-zerlegen-6914563.html.

The Nazi Study of India and Indian Anti-Colonialism: Knowledge Providers and Propagandists in the 'Third Reich'.
Baijayanti Roy, Oxford University Press. © Baijayanti Roy 2024. DOI: 10.1093/9780191981951.003.0003

3

'Political Knowledge' of India in Berlin

Background: From *Eudaimonia* to *Auslandswissenschaft*

This chapter examines the pursuit of 'political' knowledge of India, as opposed to the academic discipline of Indology, at a series of organizations affiliated to the Friedrich Wilhelms University (now Humboldt University) of Berlin. This chapter focuses on the trajectories of a number of scholars engaged in the teaching and study of India at these organizations.

Traditionally, the concept of 'Politics' in German academic arena was oriented towards the idea of *Eudaimonia* or the pursuit of welfare for all, following Aristotle's political philosophy. However, by the time the German Reich came into being in 1871, politics came to be seen as a functionalist, practice-oriented study of state as well as the study of foreign lands in their relations to the German state.[1] As the German Reich turned increasingly imperialistic, obtaining knowledge of foreign countries acquired a colonialist dimension. The establishment of the Seminar for Oriental languages (henceforth the Seminar) in Berlin in 1887 was a manifestation of the Reich's colonialist tendencies. Founded at the initiative of Chancellor Otto von Bismarck (1815–1898) and affiliated to the Friedrich Wilhelm University of Berlin, the Seminar was financed partially by the Foreign Ministry, which reserved for itself a say in its administration in return. Professors from the University of Berlin were usually appointed directors of the Seminar. Eduard Sachau (1845–1930), the first director of the Seminar (from 1887 to 1918) was followed by Eugen Mittwoch (1876–1942), who remained in office until 1933. Both of them were not only full professors but also directors of the Institute of Semitic and Islamic Studies (*Semitistik* and *Islamkunde*) of the University.[2]

In contrast to the University with its 'pure academic/scientific' (*Wissenschaftlich*) profile and focus on historical and philological aspects of 'oriental' languages and cultures, the Seminar was dedicated to fulfilling 'the tasks arising out of Germany's entry into the group of colonial powers.'[3] Most important among such 'tasks' was to connect theoretical lessons in contemporary Oriental languages with practical knowledge which could be of use to soldiers and administrators in Germany's newly acquired colonial possessions. Thus, apart from languages, the Seminar imparted lessons on *Realien* which in this case meant knowledge relating to practicalities of colonial administration like tropical hygiene, colonial law, geography, history, and economics.

The languages initially taught at the Seminar included Swahili, Nama, Herero, and Ovambo which pertained to German colonial possessions. Thus, the knowledge imparted at the Seminar had a definite political undertone.

Over the years, commercial concerns were added to colonial ones as the Wilhelmine Empire increased its business dealings with certain Asian countries. Therefore, courses in Chinese, Japanese, Arabic, Persian, Turkish, and Hindustani were also introduced.[4] As far as knowledge of Indian languages was concerned, apart from Hindustani (the predominant north Indian language of the time), 'Guzerati' (Gujarati), a West Indian language, was also taught at the Seminar since it was widely spoken by Indians living in East Africa many of whom were prosperous business owners, in the sphere of influence of the German Reich.[5] The Seminar, which had become a de facto training centre for colonial administrators, changed its focus after Germany lost its colonies as a result of the Treaty of Versailles in 1919. It began to concentrate on furthering the burgeoning commercial concerns of the Weimar Republic. In the 1920s, the languages of the Near and Far East which were already taught at the Seminar assumed more importance than the African languages, due to Germany's increasing business activities in Asia.[6]

Following the First World War, the concept of 'political' study of foreign countries shifted from providing lessons in colonial administration to analysing the messages that the lost war taught the nation. The study of politics, even democratic politics, was to be used to recover Germany's purportedly lost greatness.[7] Such ideas influenced the establishment of an organization called the *Hochschule für Politik* (HfP) or Academy for Politics in 1920, with which the Seminar would eventually be merged. The end of the First World War also ushered in several changes at the Seminar. In 1918, it was brought under the aforementioned Eugen Mittwoch. He had offered his expert knowledge to the German Foreign Ministry by heading the *Nachrichtenstelle für den Orient* (NfO) which we have already come across, from 1916 to its dissolution in 1921.[8]

Study of India at the Seminar for Oriental Languages until 1933

During the Wilhelmine Empire, Germany's interest in India was defined primarily by trade and commerce to which a political dimension was added during the First World War as we have noted. Teaching of contemporary Indian languages and *Realien* at the Seminar was related to these commercial and political interests. Ardeshir Vacha, a Parsi from Bombay, taught Hindustani, Gujarati, and Persian at the Seminar for 40 years, until his retirement in 1934. The notice of Vacha's retirement in the bulletin of the Seminar states that during his decades of engagement, a notable achievement of 'Herr Vacha' was to teach 'Guzerati', the language of trade and civil administration in East Africa, to generations of German civil servants and traders, 'until it (German East Africa) was robbed from us through the peace treaty'. The notice also praised 'Herr Vacha' for trying to establish commercial relationships between 'India and Germany'.[9] This notification provides us the first intimation of the nature and significance of the 'extra-curricular activities' of the teachers of the Seminar.

These were also the justifications on the basis of which the Orientalist scholar Hans Heinrich Schaeder (1896–1957), who succeeded Mittwoch as director of the Seminar in 1933, requested the Education Ministry to provide additional financial assistance to Vacha after the latter's retirement. Schaeder also made the claim that due to Vacha's role in advising German firms about the Indian market, the German imperial government desisted from interning him, a British subject, during the First World War.[10] This claim indicates that a system of exchanging resources between the German state and the academics at the Seminar had already started during the First World War.

A similar association between Germany's external politics and the Seminar can be identified in the case of Devendra Nath Bannerjea, whom we came across in the last chapter. Bannerjea's role in the University of Berlin and Nazi Germany has been discussed in detail by Maria Framke in two different essays.[11] I intend to provide my own interpretation of Bannerjea's role by drawing on my own archival research and supplementing it with Framke's work where necessary.

Bannerjea's trajectory before coming to Berlin, as gleaned from a British surveillance record, shows him to be an itinerant and precarious adventurer who often exhibited charlatan-like tendencies.[12] Born to an educationist father in Lahore in Punjab (now in Pakistan) in 1890, Bannerjea came to England and enrolled at the University of Oxford in 1912. In 1916, he became a member of the Indian Volunteer Ambulance Corps and joined a hospital in Brighton as a sanitation worker. He was dismissed from the Ambulance Corps for supposedly trying to 'tamper with the loyalties of the *sepoy*' (Indian soldier) patients (i.e. trying to incite them against colonial rule). Subsequently Bannerjea held various odd jobs and wrote what the British surveillance records considered 'extremist articles' for newspapers including the *Manchester Guardian*. In 1919, he was appointed as a spokesperson for the Indian anti-colonial cause in England by the Indian nationalist leader, Bal Gangadhar Tilak.

By the time of Tilak's death in 1920, Bannerjea was claiming that he had a degree from Oxford. He was also writing articles urging improvement of labour conditions in India, indicating some left-wing sympathies. Around this time, Bannerjea married an English lady called Hilda Howsin, a radical left-wing activist who had been interned from 1917 to 1920 for allegedly acting as an intermediary between left-wing politicians in England and revolutionary Indians on the continent. British records claim that Hilda Howsin met Virendranath Chattopadhyaya in Switzerland to take part in a 'plot' to kill British politicians. This 'plot' was never executed.[13]

In 1922, the Bannejeas received a one year visa to visit the German health resort of Baden-Baden, supposedly because Hilda needed a change of air. British authorities next heard of him in 1925 as 'Professor Devendra Nath Bannerjea', who was a member of the Committee for Intellectual Co-operation at the League of Nations in Geneva. Bannerjea stated in a letter to the India Office, London that he received an offer to join the League of Nations while at Baden-Baden. The India Office noted that Bannerjea managed to get this position on the false claim that he had been a professor at the University of Calcutta. Following this, possibly due to the intervention of the British, Bannerjea was 'ejected with some difficulty from the Committee'. Meanwhile, Bannerjea had already succeeded in projecting himself as a sympathiser of the plights of post-First World War Germany, as an article by him titled *Das heutige Deutschland* (Germany Today) published in the German magazine *Die Woche* (*The Week*) in 1923 illustrates (Figure 12). The article, which portrays Germany as a victim of the tyranny and oppression of the victorious Allies after the First World War, introduces 'Prof. Bannerjea' as a member of the Commission for Intellectual Co-operation at the League of Nations.[14]

A note, submitted by Hermann Schumacher, professor of Political Science at the University of Berlin to the authorities of the University of Berlin, dated 2

Figure 12 Article 'Das heutige Deutschland' by Devendra Nath Bannerjea (1923), published in the magazine *Die Woche*.
Source: BA Berlin: R4901/24156.

November 1929, provides some indications of the next few years in Bannerjea's life.[15] This note indicates that not long after his ejection from the League of Nations, Bannerjea succeeded in finding a position at the International Institute of Agriculture in Rome, where he spent the next few years completing a monograph on 'Agriculture in India' supposedly for the Berlin-based Research Institute for Agriculture and Land Settlement. Bannerjea probably met Max Sering, the director of this institute and a renowned economist, at the World Economic Conference at Geneva in 1927.

In 1928, Bannerjea and his wife shifted to Berlin. Bannerjea's long and eventful association with the University of Berlin began in November 1929, when he received a contract to lecture on Indian *Realien*, which in this case encompassed the social, economic, and political aspects of contemporary India, at the Seminar.[16] An example of the support that Bannerjea received from influential Germans, as well as the way the Indian adventurer constantly embellished his own curriculum vita, is the aforementioned note written by Professor Schumacher. It claimed that Bannerjea was a representative of India at the Committee for Intellectual Co-operation in Geneva and he subsequently worked part time for Max Sering's institute. Schumacher certified Bannerjea to be a 'highly regarded academic' (*wissenschaftlich hochstehend*) since, apart from his intellectual engagements in Geneva and for Max Sering, he had worked 'for years as a post-graduate research scholar at the University of Oxford.' Schumacher was ready to believe this claim though it was apparently not backed by any proof.[17]

Another possible reason for Bannerjea receiving this post can be gleaned from an unsigned memorandum from 1936, which claimed that this teaching contract was given to Bannerjea because of his academic knowledge of modern India and his 'German-friendly writings' in the international press. The memo further stated that knowledge of modern India was a political necessity and no German lecturer could be found to teach the subject.[18] By the early 1930s, Bannerjea was contributing to the external cultural politics of the German state in several ways. He received a stipend from the Alexander von Humboldt Foundation. As a stipend holder, Bannerjea was expected to play a role in the international network and propaganda for Germany among foreign students.[19] Bannerjea fulfilled this expectation by giving at least one propagandistic lecture at a programme organized by the Humboldt Foundation. The lecture was on 'The spiritual relationship between Germany and India' and was later published in the journal *Hochschule und Ausland* which was financed by the Foreign Ministry.[20]

A report on four lectures delivered by 'Professor Bannerjea' on 'The foundations of the Indian culture' (*Grundlagen der indischen Kultur*), published in the newspaper *Deutsche Allgemeine Zeitung* on 28 February 1930, indicates that, by that time, Bannerjea had established himself as an India expert who 'corrected' the image of India prevalent in Germany through his lectures.[21] He was also a member of the Humboldt club which was used by the German state to propagate the virtues of the German nation. After 1933, it came to be used as a mouthpiece for National Socialist propaganda.[22]

Bannerjea's 'work' was rewarded by the German government by allowing him to preside over a German–Indian Association which the Foreign Ministry set up in 1931, as we saw in the last chapter. The aim of the Foreign Ministry was to keep the Indian community in Berlin under control and away from the kind of anti-British activities that were encouraged during the First World War. The association not only organized 'cultural' events like talks and 'German Indian evenings', but it also established contacts between Indian and German commercial firms. The association was short lived, as we noted. Bannerjea claimed later that this was because the Weimar government did not invest enough in it.[23] The reality, as indicated in the last chapter, was more complex.

Not long after joining the Seminar, Bannerjea asked for extra financial help from the then director of the Seminar, Eugen Mittwoch, complaining about his 'very low remuneration'. His request was granted by the Ministry of Education. Such payments, presumably a part of the reward for Bannerjea's perceived usefulness for the German state, would become a recurrent pattern in the following years.[24]

From 1928, Bengali, another Indian language, was introduced at the Seminar by a decree of the Education Ministry.[25] The lector was a teacher at a high school (Gymnasium), Reinhard Wagner (1881–1945).[26] The primary source of information on Wagner's academic and political trajectory is an undated curriculum vita which he submitted to the University of Berlin, presumably in the early 1940s.

Born in Thuringia in 1881, Wagner enrolled at the University of Berlin in 1902 to study German, English, French, Old Norse, and Sanskrit. He ended his studies at the same university with a PhD in English Philology in 1908.[27] In 1911, Wagner completed his training as a high school (Gymnasium) teacher and started teaching in a school at Schwetz, which later became a part of Poland. He was commissioned for serving in the German Army during the First World War. After a short stint in active duty, he was deployed as an 'enlightenment provider' for the Prussian Army Group XVII.[28] There are no records of the kind of 'enlightenment' that Wagner provided to soldiers, but from the available history of propaganda among soldiers of the German Army during and after the First World War, it appears likely that his talks focused on the glorification of German nation and on disparaging its opponents.[29]

After the war, Wagner became a member of the VDA (*Verein für das deutschtum ins Ausland* or an 'Association for the Conservation of German Culture Abroad'). In the 1920s, this nationalist conservative organization received financial assistance from the German Foreign Ministry to 'conserve the Germanic traits' of those Germans who became 'cut off' from the 'Reich' as a result of the Treaty of Versailles. As the VDA continued to expand, it developed strong anti-Semitic and xenophobic traits.[30]

In 1918, Wagner secured a post at a school in Tempelhof in Berlin. Being in the German capital probably rekindled his earlier interest in Indology, leading him to attend a series of lectures by Heinrich Lüders on Vedic Sanskrit, Pali, and Prakrit at the University of Berlin. However, as he would claim later in his undated curriculum vita, a wish to 'make inroads into the academic study of new Indian languages' led him to discover Bengali. Since there was no German academic who could help him master the language, he supposedly learnt it by communicating with Bengali students in Berlin and through an exchange of letters with Bengalis in India.[31]

Wagner remains well-known for his book *The Bengali Raconteur: The Victory of the Soul (Bengalische Erzähler: Der Sieg der Seele)* published in 1926. It was a collection of short stories and poems by contemporary Bengali authors, though the sub-title of the book claimed rather misguidedly that it was translated from '*Indisch*' (Indian) into German.[32] In his curriculum vita mentioned above, Wagner claimed that on 7 September 1928, he was offered an authorization (*Ermächtigung*) for teaching Bengali at the Seminar for Oriental Languages by the Minister for Education with the consent of the Foreign Ministry.[33] Wagner's reputation as a scholar of Bengali definitely facilitated this 'authorization'. It is not known whether his engagements with the VDA contributed to this appointment as well, but the possibility cannot be ruled out. Apart from the symbolic resource that this prestigious teaching contract denoted for Wagner, the Seminar published two textbooks written by him. The textbooks, published as part of the Seminar's own textbook series, were on Bengali script in original and transcript (1930) and on texts in spoken and colloquial Bengali (1933).[34] It is not clear whether Wagner drew a salary from the Seminar at this point.

The Seminar for Oriental Studies: 1933–1936

Several changes occurred at the Seminar after the Nazi assumption of power in January 1933. As a part of the Seminar's *gleichschaltung* (synchronization) with the Nazi regime's politics, the director Eugen Mittwoch was discharged from his duties due to his 'Jewish' origin. He was succeeded by Hans Heinrich Schaeder on 27 July 1933.[35] Schaeder was not a member of the Nazi party, but he belonged to several affiliated organizations including the NSV (*Nationalsozialistische Volkswohlfahrt* or National Socialist Welfare organization) and the NSLB (*Nationalsozialistischer Lehrerbund* or National Socialist Teachers Association).[36]

As far as the 'Indian subjects' were concerned, a significant change occurred after the retirement (and subsequent death) of Ardeshir Vacha in 1934. Gujarati was discontinued. Already in 1927, Abdullah Sebastian Beck, a scholar of Iranian studies had been given a contract to teach Persian along with Vacha.[37] Beck, who had served in the First World War, had worked for a time as an interpreter at the

German Consulate in Kabul.[38] According to Beck's curriculum vita from 1940, he began to work for the Foreign Ministry in Berlin from 1927 as the editor for Persian and Afghan press reports and as an expert for 'Muslim law as applied in Persia and Afghanistan'.[39] His appointment at the Seminar in the same year was presumably a reward for his services to the Foreign Ministry.

On 1 November 1932, Beck joined the Nazi party. He was one of the first Orientalists to do so.[40] This step probably had a bearing on the fact that on 18 December 1933 (retroactively from 1 October), he became a full professor for Persian at the Oriental Seminar even though he did not have a doctorate or any formal academic qualification to justify this appointment. On 8 January 1935, Beck took the formal oath of allegiance to 'the Führer and Reich Chancellor' Adolf Hitler.[41] Apart from his Nazi affiliation, Beck's supposed love for Persian and his extensive knowledge of the language, which, Schaeder claimed in a letter to the Minister for Education (*Wissenschaft, Kunst und Volksbildung*), did not weigh less than a doctoral degree, helped Beck in securing this position.[42] This appointment shows once more that 'practical expertise' together with perceived political loyalty and in case of professorships, racial membership of the German national community (*Volksgemeinschaft*) often weighed more than formal academic qualifications as far as the Seminar was concerned.

In 1934, another contemporary Indian language, Telugu, was added to the Seminar's repertoire. The lector of Telugu was Hugo Figulla, the librarian at the Seminar. This appointment was due to Schaeder's perception of Telugu as an important Indian language, which, as he wrote to the Education Ministry, was spoken by 22 million people. Figulla, who did not have a doctorate and moreover, was of partially Jewish origin, could receive the teaching contract primarily due to Schaeder's recommendation. As in the case of Beck, Schaeder justified this choice to the Education Ministry on the basis Figulla's purported expertise in Telugu.[43] This appointment indicates that despite his complicity with the Nazi regime, Schaeder sometimes separated his ideological inclinations or political pragmatism, whichever the case might have been, from considerations of professional competence. Little wonder that certain sections of the Nazi party considered Schaeder to be 'friendly to the Jews' and, like Alsdorf, he was suspected of being an opportunist and lacking enough commitment towards Nazi politics.[44] The circumstances of this appointment suggest that Nazi racial politics did not yet hold complete sway over the Seminar.

In 1934, another Indian, Tarachand Roy, joined the Seminar as the lector for Hindi and Hindustani. Born in Lahore in 1890, Roy had studied at the Arya-Samaj affiliated Dayanand Anglo Vedic College. He won a gold medal for his MA and came to Heidelberg in 1912 with a scholarship from the Indian government.[45] Subsequently, Roy shifted to the University of Leipzig where he enrolled as a student of Sanskrit, English, German, and Comparative Philosophy.[46] According to a questionnaire that Roy submitted to the Seminar in 1934, he was invited by the

German Foreign Ministry in 1915 for working under Eugen Mittwoch at the *Nachrichtenstelle für den Orient*.[47] Actually, Roy was one of the members of the Indian Independence Committee in Berlin, along with Virendranath Chattopadhyaya, Taraknath Das, and a host of other Indian anti-colonialists from Europe and the USA.[48] According to the post-war statement of Nambiar, Tarachand Roy worked along with Chattopadhyaya in the 'National Committee for Propaganda' within the Indian Independence Committee.[49] Roy was understandably not keen to inform the Nazi authorities that he once associated with the radical Marxist anti-colonialist, 'Chatto'.

After the First World War, Roy became the president of an organization called 'Hindustan Association of Central Europe', which became a meeting point for the Indian diaspora in Berlin in the 1920s. The Association was anti-colonial in tone and tried to make Germans aware of the history and political situation of India.[50] In 1923, Roy started studying for his Masters in Indology under Friedrich Otto Schrader at the University of Kiel.[51] In 1925, soon after completion of his Masters, Roy was appointed an assistant lecturer (*Außerplanmäßige Lektor*) at the 'Seminar for *Indogerman* Studies' at the University of Berlin.[52] He was to remain in this position until 1934 though he was not made a *Beamter* or a tenured government official.[53]

During the Weimar years, Tarachand Roy assisted the German Foreign Ministry in different ways (e.g. by taking part in organizing international cultural events like the official reception of Rabindranath Tagore in Berlin in 1926).[54] Roy also gave regular talks in fluent German in Germany and in Europe on subjects like German culture, German spirit (*Geist*), and Indo-German *Weltanschauung* (world view).[55] Between 1925 and 1933, he also wrote a number of articles in the German press glorifying Gandhi and explaining Indian politics. One such article was on 'Mahatma Gandhi and the party question in India' (*Mahatma Gandhi und die Parteifrage in Indien*) in the *Hamburger Fremdenblatt* on 25 July 1925.[56] In 1929, he gave a public lecture on 'the significance of Gandhi for India and the world' at the Anthroposophical Society, which earned him quite a lot of media attention.[57] Roy thus conducted 'cultural politics' with his knowledge of India long before such politics began to be deployed by the Nazi regime.

Roy was evidently aware of the political value of his activities as a cultural mediator. In 1932, he asked for an extension of his teaching contract at the University of Berlin, justifying his demand not only on the basis of his academic credentials but also for his 'contribution to the cause of German–Indian friendship', particularly in the form of public speeches.[58] He had evidently established himself as a gifted speaker who had mastered German perfectly, a rare feat for a foreigner, as several German newspapers claimed. Roy collected such praise from the press on a pamphlet, which he sent along with his letters demanding an extension.[59] Meanwhile, he had been made an honorary member of the *Deutsche Sprachverein* (German Language Association), a rare accomplishment for a non-German, which Roy made a point to mention in another letter sent to the Education Ministry in February 1933.[60]

From 1933, Roy became eager to present himself as a propagandist for Nazi Germany. In a series of letters to the Education Ministry, which he sent as part of his effort to extend his contract, he mentioned his 'Germany friendly engagements', claiming to be a correspondent of the newspapers *Vishal Bharat* in Calcutta and *The Tribune* in Lahore.[61] Roy also maintained that he had been a professor at Lahore, an assertion which the Foreign Ministry seems to have accepted without much investigation. The Foreign Ministry remained a source of constant support to Tarachand Roy. An internal note of the Ministry from July 1931 stated that Roy is well known in its Press section as a friend of Germany who tries to advance the country's cause in India. The note also praised Roy for campaigning for India's freedom in a 'mild, gentle tone', which corresponded to the attitude of the Weimar Republic towards Indian anti-colonialism.[62]

Unlike the Foreign Ministry, however, the police of Berlin, which evidently kept all foreigners in the city under observation, observed in 1931 in a complaint to the authorities of the University of Berlin that the two Indians, Bannerjea and Roy, used the title of 'professor' though they did not have a right to do so under the rules prevalent in Prussia.[63] The University in turn asked Professor Heinrich Lüders which academic title 'Herr Roy' had the right to use.[64] Lüders' answer remains unknown, but it can be assumed that it was not incriminating since Roy continued to use the title. This episode demonstrates the amount of solidarity and trust that Tarachand Roy received from the political and academic establishment in Berlin due to his 'services'. His contract at the *Indogermanischen Seminar* (which included Indology) at the University was extended and he was officially chosen to succeed Vacha as the 'lector for *Indisch*' (denoting Hindustani) at the Oriental Seminar from 1 April 1934.[65] The latter contract was extended in 1935.[66]

However, Schaeder, the director of the Oriental Seminar, was initially not willing to have Roy as a lecturer for Hindustani. Being a scholar of Iran and of Islamic Studies, Schaeder wanted the Seminar to focus on Urdu, a form of Hindustani with a strong Islamic influence. At the time, Urdu was more commonly spoken and written in north India whereas Hindi/Sanskrit-based Hindustani was limited to sections of educated and mostly Hindu elite. Schaeder had his own candidate for teaching Urdu—a Berlin-based young Indian called Mohammed Basharat Ali, who had taught as Vacha's substitute for one semester at the Seminar. Ali was also supported by the 'Urdu-speaking community' of the Indian Muslims in Berlin.[67] On behalf of the 'Urdu-speaking community of Berlin' the journalist Habibur Rahman, who was loyal to Subhas Bose as well as the Nazi regime, wrote to the Education Ministry in protest against the appointment of Roy as a lector for Hindustani, claiming that, as a Hindu, Roy's mastery over Urdu was doubtful.[68] The 'Indian Muslims in Berlin' could enlist support from Georg Kampffmeyer, the noted scholar of Islam and president of the German Society for Islamic

Studies, indicating the existence of networks between the Indian diaspora and different Orientalist scholars in Berlin.[69]

It is therefore surprising that Schaeder changed his mind in November 1933. He officially recommended Roy for the post of lector for Hindustani, praising the Indian lector's 'remarkable proficiency' in German as well as his mastery of Urdu, though there was to be no separate course offering Urdu.[70]

A number of factors contributed to this about turn. Roy had offered Schaeder proof of his command of Urdu and Persian in several letters.[71] In addition, Schaeder's earlier favourite Basharat Ali proved to be a disappointment, as Schaeder confessed in a letter to the Education Ministry.[72] However, the most important factor seemed to be Roy's 'extraordinary and effective ability to create cultural political understanding between *the new Germany* (italics: mine) and his Indian homeland', as Schaeder wrote to the Education Ministry.[73]

The change in Schaeder's attitude was also influenced by Curt Prüfer, who was then in charge of the 'Oriental' section of the Foreign Ministry. Prüfer, an expert on Arabic, had used his academic skills in the service of the German state in different ways during the First World War. His loyalty to the Nazis long predated his joining the NSDAP in 1937.[74] In his above-mentioned letter to the Education Ministry, Schaeder claimed that Prüfer had recommended Roy for the latter's 'political reliability', a quality, as we have seen, that had assumed special significance during the years of Nazi rule.[75] Roy himself had provided an example of his 'political reliability' in a letter that he wrote to Schaeder in September 1933, in which he claimed that he had written an article endorsing Hitler and his government in the Hindi weekly magazine *Jagaran*, published in Banaras.[76] British surveillance records also noted that Roy was 'pro-Nazi' and 'anti-communist'.[77] One report claimed that he was active in the Nazified organization, *Deutsche Orient Verein*.[78] This organization, we may recall, also included Heinrich Lüders, Roy's 'boss' at the department of *Indogerman* Studies.

On 1 October 1933, Tamil, a south Indian language, was added to the Seminar's repertoire. The lector for Tamil was Hermann Beythan, whom we encountered in the last chapter. Beythan was an ex-missionary of the Evangelical Lutheran Mission of Leipzig, which had a base in south India since the mid-nineteenth century.[79] Beythan's application for a teaching position was viewed positively by the association of the lecturers of the Seminar on the grounds that Tamil was a widely spoken language and more importantly, courses in Tamil were likely to benefit future missionaries of the Leipzig Mission.[80]

Beythan, born in 1875 to a family of farmers in Thuringia, had joined the Leipzig Mission in 1895. He went to south India in 1902 as a representative of this mission.[81] During his stint in south India which lasted till 1909, Beythan applied himself to learning both colloquial Tamil, which he needed for conducting missionary activities among the indigenous people, and literary Tamil.[82] Such scholarly interest in Tamil on the part of the German missionaries working in south

India had a long tradition. Whereas a strand of German Indologists devoted themselves to the study of Sanskrit which could be used to establish the superiority of ancient Aryan culture, the German scholar-missionaries in south India often tried to establish the primordial purity of Tamil, which was a non-Aryan Dravidian language.[83]

The German missionaries in south India often acted both as spiritual leaders and as temporal administrators who 'looked after' the natives in a 'fatherly fashion', requiring from their 'childlike' charges strict discipline and obedience.[84] Beythan's relationship with the indigenous people in India also had a similarly colonial dimension. In a curriculum vita that he submitted to the University of Berlin in 1928, probably as part of an unsuccessful attempt to secure a teaching contract at the Oriental Seminar, he claimed that during his stay in India, he had come into contact with all classes of indigenous people and was liked by them, as a result of which he was made a member of the municipal council of the 'Brahmin dominated town' of Kumbakonam.[85]

After leaving the mission and returning to Germany, Beythan, like Wagner, trained as a high school teacher. In 1916, he started teaching at a high school (Gymnasium) in Berlin. Beythan completed his PhD in English literature from the University of Münster in 1918. Unlike Wagner, Beythan was not qualified to fight in the First World War because of his frail health. However, he also joined the VDA like the scholar of Bengali and his future colleague. Beythan belonged to the Berlin-based coterie of leaders of the VDA called 'protectors', who took a dominant role in propagating aggressive and reactionary nationalist messages among Germans living in areas 'severed' from the Wilhelmine Reich. Beythan was one of the prominent 'protectors' who, by his own admission, drew on his colonial experiences for this purpose.[86]

Beythan's politics, combining elements of revisionist German nationalism and racist ethnological stereotypes associated with colonialism, blended well with National Socialism. In 1934, Beythan joined the National Socialist Teachers Association or NSLB. The former missionary now saw it as his mission to propagate the merits of the 'new Reich' and its leader in India. In order to counter the anti-Nazi attitude prevalent in India, Beythan wrote 'enlightening' articles in Tamil and English for newspapers in India and in South Africa where the Leipzig Mission had a presence as well.[87]

The high point of Beythan's propagandistic engagements for Nazi Germany was a book that he wrote in Tamil, under the title, *Who is Adolf Hitler?* with the subtitle *Victory of Strength*. The purported reason for writing such a book, as Beythan wrote to his friend Carl Ihmels, director of the Leipzig Mission, was to hinder the growing influence of Bolshevism in India, especially in Tamil Nadu where the lives of Marx and Lenin were available in Tamil, as a result of Soviet propaganda.[88] Beythan's book was published in 1936 in Madras (present-day Chennai) with financial assistance from the German Foreign Ministry and the

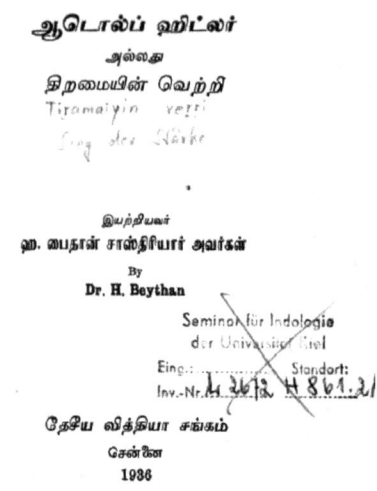

Figure 13 Hermann Beythan's book *Who is Adolf Hitler?* written in Tamil.

Ministry of Propaganda. Beythan submitted a copy of the Tamil book, together with a German translation, to the 'Führer's office' and received a signed photograph of the dictator in return (Figure 13).[89] Beythan was fully aware of the political implications of this book, which he wanted to be translated into Telugu and Bengali, as his correspondence with Werner Otto von Hentig, director of the Orient Section of the Foreign Ministry from 1937 to 1938, demonstrates.[90]

Who is Adolf Hitler? was a paean to the supposed genius and achievements of the German dictator. Beythan unabashedly referred to Hitler as Mahatma or 'the great soul', whom the German people rightly recognized as a leader who did not aspire to power or wealth but was dedicated solely to restoring Germany's lost independence and self-respect.[91] In a particularly bizarre move, Beythan tried to connect Nazi propaganda to Tamil cultural nationalism by interspersing descriptions of the 'achievements' of the 'Führer' with quotations from *Tirukkural*, an ancient Tamil book of aphoristic verses about virtue, wealth, and love, which enjoys a semi-divine status in Tamil Nadu. Such attempts reached its high point as Beythan stated that the words of Thiruvallar, the writer of *Tirukkural*, had found their true expression in Hitler.[92]

Beythan rendered Hitler a messianic aura by depicting him as a leader who established a new 'dharma' (religion/moral codex) with the aim of improving the lot of the downtrodden and returning to the country its lost autonomy. The quasi-Christian analogy was reinforced through a portrayal of the supposed victimization of Hitler's ever-increasing band of followers. Beythan claimed that loyalists of Hitler had to fight the police, set upon them by their enemies who controlled state power, with their bare hands. These supporters of Hitler who assisted him in serving the people formed, according to Beythan, the core of the SA and the SS.[93]

The eulogy ended with a chapter on Hitler's 'efforts to achieve world peace', in which the author contended that, contrary to widespread slander, Hitler was intent on maintaining international peace, albeit without compromising Germany's honour and independence.[94]

In a bid to associate anti-colonialism to Nazi propaganda, Beythan provided a fully distorted image of the National Socialist racial politics by claiming that the motto of the Nazi party was that every race should have the right to self-reliance, conveniently eliding the fact that the Nazi world view accorded this right only to the 'master race.'[95] This book thus brought together Beythan's scholarly knowledge of Tamil language and Tamil cultural nationalism, his awareness of India's anti-colonialist agenda, and several tenets of Nazi world view in a potent—if occasionally preposterous—demonstration of deploying knowledge of India for furthering Nazi cultural politics.

The surviving correspondence between Beythan and Carl Heinrich Ihmels, the director of the Leipzig Mission, makes it clear that the Mission in Tamil Nadu helped Beythan to find a local publisher, though after making him tone down or omit some of the hyperbole from the manuscript, since the colonial government in India disapproved of Nazi propaganda. The resulting book became, according to Beythan, an 'unsuspecting, neutral weapon for the Germans living in Tamil land' for propagating Hitler's achievements. Beythan assured Ihmels that the publication of the book would show the Nazi regime that an evangelical mission in a foreign country could be of use to the 'Fatherland'.[96] The Mission published a short review of the book in its journal, claiming that the book described the struggles of Adolf Hitler for the revitalization of Germany in order to counter the false impressions prevalent in India.[97]

Following his correspondence with von Hentig from the Foreign Ministry, Beythan prepared an English version of the book, which was to be published by the Press division of the Foreign Ministry, as Beythan proudly proclaimed in a letter to Ihmels. In another letter, he informed Ihmels that a Bengali translation of the book was also to be published under the aegis of the German Consul General in Calcutta. Beythan also boasted in this letter that other missions in India wanted to translate his book into different regional languages, and suggested that the book should be translated into Swahili for the Leipzig mission in Africa.[98]

However, the publication of the different translations of the book never materialized because the colonial authorities in India soon proscribed the Tamil book for its blatantly propagandistic content.[99] A translation in Swahili was considered 'unnecessary' by Ihmels since, 'the Niggers in our regions were not amenable to the propaganda of the British'.[100]

Devendra Nath Bannerjea, who had conformed well to the external cultural politics of the Weimar Republic, was also quick to collaborate with the new regime by dispensing with whatever left-leaning sympathies he might have cherished earlier. A significant manifestation of such collusion was Bannerjea's denunciation of Virendranath Chattopadhyaya (who lived in Moscow since 1932) as a communist in March 1933 to the Gestapo. This step reflected Bannerjea's efforts to adapt to the changed political ambience since one of the first victims of Nazi political persecution was the leftist anti-colonialist organization, the League against Imperialism (LAI) in which Chatto played a pre-eminent role.[101] This act of denunciation found approval from certain influential individuals in the Nazi political apparatus. As Emil Gansser, one of Bannerjea's benefactors, wrote to the newly appointed Education Minister, Bernhard Rust on 2 April 1933, through this act, Bannerjea had proved himself to be a 'true and as far as possible active friend of the new Germany', and as one 'whose attitude was steadfastly committed to the principle of nationalism, without any internationalist or communist influences'.[102]

Dr Emil Gansser was an employee of Siemens who specialised on pyrotechnic materials. An early convert to National Socialism who helped Hitler to raise funds from industrial concerns, Gansser at the time wielded some political influence.[103] It is not clear how Bannerjea came to know him but the fact that Gansser was willing to vouch for him indicates the Indian adventurer's networking skills as well as his ability to impress influential personalities in both academia and politics under different German regimes.

Bannerjea refashioned his personal narrative once again to suit the new political ambience by hinting that he had connections to the Nazi party before 1933. He wrote to Rust, the Education Minister, on 29 March 1933, that the Weimar government had denied him all possibilities of professional advancement because of his closeness with the 'national parties of Germany'.[104] Similarly, from 1933, Bannerjea customized his curriculum vita to suit the racial politics of the regime by claiming in at least two CVs that, as a Brahmin, he descended from a family of 'Indo-Aryans'.[105]

He also sought to improve his future prospects by completing a PhD (which he claimed was his second) under Ernst Schultze. The latter, a sociologist and economist, was the director of the Institute for World Economy at the reputed Business School (Handelshochschule) at Leipzig in Sachsen. It must be noted, however, that Bnnerjea's attempt at pursuing a PhD began before 1933. He was supported in his efforts by influential personalities including Fritz Grobba, the head of the Oriental Section of the Foreign Ministry until 1932.[106] By July 1933, Bannerjea had developed favourable connections with the External Affairs section of the Nazi Party in Berlin, which wrote to the Ministry of Education at Leipzig to facilitate his PhD.[107]

Bannerjea managed to complete the thesis in November 1933.[108] It was published as a monograph in 1934 under the title *Indian Farmers under British Domination* (*Das indische Bauerntum unter britischer Herrschaft*).[109] A glowing review of the book appeared in December 1934 in *Der Zeitspiegel*, a political journal oriented towards National Socialism.[110] The costs of the publication of the book as well as the fees for conducting his *Rigorosum* (viva voce) were covered by the Education Ministry, which also sent directives to its counterpart in Sachsen to make sure that Bannerjea's doctoral thesis was passed.[111] The directives were sent in the Minister's name by Theodor Vahlen, professor of Mathematics, an early National Socialist and influential functionary at the Education Ministry who was evidently favourably disposed towards Bannerjea.[112]

Much like Tarachand Roy, Bannerjea successfully demonstrated to the Nazi authorities that he was attempting to disseminate a positive image of Germany in India. In 1934, he submitted a memo titled 'Possibilities of propaganda in India' to the Education Ministry, suggesting, for example, distributing English language pamphlets in India 'explaining the fundamentals of National Socialism'.[113] Both he and his wife Hilda used their connections in England to publish propagandistic articles in the British press. While his wife wrote in praise of 'Personal Liberty under National Socialism', Bannerjea extolled Nazi Germany's 'Winter Help' programme.[114]

Along with his propagandistic activities, Bannerjea repeatedly embroiled himself in disputes and intrigues. In January 1934, as part of his course in Indian *Realien* at the Seminar, Bannerjea wished to lecture on Aryan philosophy and *Weltanschauung* as well as on Communism and India, subjects which were likely to find the regime's approval. But Schaeder, the director, forbade the course on the history and philosophy of the Aryans. The reason, as Schaeder wrote to the Education Minister, was that Bannerjea, whose academic specialization was modern Indian economy, was not competent to teach these subjects, which anyway did not belong to the curriculum of the Seminar, oriented as it was towards 'practical aspects'.[115] Bannerjea attempted to take revenge by raising doubts about Schaeder's commitment to National Socialism. He reported to the Nazi Students Association of the University of Berlin that Schaeder had claimed that the Nazis misused the word 'Aryan' by using it as a catchword.[116]

Schaeder, who could ultimately disprove Bannerjea's allegations, tried to end Bannerjea's teaching contract as an act of retribution. Due to Vahlen's intervention, Bannerjea came away with just an official admonition and his teaching contract was 'silently renewed', as Schaeder complained in his aforementioned letter to the Education Minister.[117] Bannerjea's connections to the Nazi political establishment thus proved stronger than his falsehoods and intrigues.

Bannerjea also attempted in vain to denounce Tarachand Roy since he coveted the latter's position of lector of Hindustani. Bannerjea wrote an undated and 'strictly confidential' note to the Seminar authorities in which he alleged that Roy lacked the necessary academic qualifications for this position. He also cast aspersions on Roy's moral character for supposedly seducing and later marrying the wife of his German host.[118]

In January 1934, Bannerjea tried to capitalize on the Nazi government's paranoia about Communism by reporting three Berlin-based Indians (A.C.N. Nambiar, J.S. Naidu and S.C. Guha) as communists to several Nazi authorities even though by then Nambiar and Naidu had already left Germany.[119] In March 1934, Bannerjea submitted a secret note to the Gestapo in which he dwelt on the close relationship of Virendranath Chattopadhyaya, Habibur Rahman, A.C.N. Nambiar, and S.C. Guha with the League against Imperialism. Much of Bannerjea's enmity was directed towards Habibur Rahman who worked for Ministry of Propaganda. Bannerjea insinuated that Rahman was an agent of Chatto and the aforementioned Indians used their anti-colonial activities as a smokescreen for conducting espionage for the Soviet Union.[120] However, accusations against Habibur Rahman were disregarded by the German authorities since Rahman had already established his usefulness for and loyalty towards the Nazi state.

The denunciations of Indians ended in an 'official' action of the Indian Students Association (formed by Subhas Bose) against Bannerjea, who was formally ousted from this organization at a meeting dated 28 February 1934.[121] Bannerjea's reaction to this ouster is not known, but he continued to use the ideological aversion of the Nazi regime to all forms of leftist politics. In 1934, he published an article titled 'Communism and the Indian Tradition' in the *Völkischer Beobachter*, in which he claimed that Communism in theory and practice was incompatible with Indian traditions.[122]

In September 1939, Bannerjea wrote a letter to the Indian newspaper *Bombay Chronicle* countering the allegations of M.S. Khanna, an erstwhile scholarship holder of the India Institute of the DA, who had published two articles in the same newspaper about the racist abuses faced by Indian students in Germany, as well as on the role of the DA as an instrument of Nazi propaganda.[123] Bannerjea wrote in his article that Indians who tarnished the image of Nazi Germany were 'undesirable political agents' (i.e. communists).[124]

Bannerjea also denounced another Indian who had a proven communist background: Nalini Bhushan Das Gupta, who owned a restaurant called "Hindustan Haus" in Berlin. The restaurant was a popular meeting point for the Indian community living in the German capital. Nalini Gupta, as he was known, had been convicted and jailed in India due to his 'Bolshevik activities' in December 1923 in the so-called 'Kanpur conspiracy case'. He was released on grounds of ill health in 1925.[125] After his release, Gupta became a part of the communist network that spanned several European cities including Berlin. Through this nexus, Gupta landed in Berlin in 1927 and opened his restaurant in 1928. Until 1933, Gupta was a Comintern agent, who changed his ways after Hitler came to power. He tried, albeit without success, to induce the Indian community to make peace with Bannerjea. Gupta was suspected of being in pay of the British.[126] Gupta did indeed find refuge in England 'just before the frontiers were closed', but the suspicions of spying were never confirmed.[127]

Bannerjea's accusation against Gupta seems particularly treacherous since the two were apparently on friendly terms. In April 1933, following a dispute outside the Hindustan House, a mob broke into it and abused and injured at least four

Indians. When Monindra Sen, a boarder of the Hindustan House, tried to organize a protest march of the Indians in response to such violence, Bannerjea prevailed upon Nalini Gupta to make Sen desist from it.[128] Moreover, Bannerjea denounced Sen to the Gestapo as an 'anti-German' Indian who had insulted Hitler and suggested that Sen should be expelled from Germany.[129] Sen was in fact extradited, despite objections from the Foreign Ministry, which was concerned about Germany's reputation abroad.[130] In the end the Foreign Ministry managed to revoke the decision of extradition.[131] In a report written around November 1933, the Gestapo quoted Bannerjea as claiming during a questioning session that he considered Nalini Gupta to be among those Indians who were capable of acting against the interests of Germany.[132]

It is not known when Bannerjea gave the above statement against Gupta to the Gestapo. By the end of 1933, however, he seems to have backtracked. In a letter to Gestapo, dated 19 December 1933, Bannerjea mentioned that he knew Gupta but he did not advance any further implicative claims against the restaurant owner. This caution was probably due to the fact that Gupta was in a position to know about Bannerjea's own past flirtations with left-wing politics.[133] The Gestapo was, however, not particularly well-disposed towards the troublesome Indian lecturer. In 1934, it reported to the Education Ministry that the Foreign Ministry had complained about Bannerjea and asked that the latter be expelled from Germany.[134] Nevertheless, the Gestapo could not have its way since Ernst Schultze, Bannerjea's research guide, wrote a letter defending Bannerjea to Eugen Mattiat, an important functionary of the Education Ministry. Mattiat was a theologian and an ethnologist, as well as an ardent Nazi who spied for the SD.[135] Schultze invoked Bannerjea's 'service' to Germany in the form of denunciation of the Indians 'who were in danger of becoming Bolshevists and Bolshevism was not be tolerated in the National Socialist state'.[136]

In January 1935, Schaeder finally managed to oust Bannerjea from the Seminar. Bannerjea's teaching contract was not renewed as his responsibilities were officially transferred to Tarachand Roy.[137] At this juncture, Bannerjea once again demonstrated his survival skills. In February 1935, he managed to secure a teaching contract at the *Staatswissenschaftliche Seminar* (Seminar for Public Policy) at the University of Berlin to teach subjects related to India.[138]

It is fairly certain that Bannerjea's clever exploitation of the Nazi regime's hatred and paranoia about communists, combined with his knowledge of India as well as of the Indians in Berlin, played an important role in this appointment. As Walter Lierau, the Consul at Reichenberg (in present day Chechnya), claimed in a letter to the Education Ministry, the main justification of Bannerjea's continued employment was his 'great service of providing reliable information about his communist countrymen'.[139] Lierau could exert some influence on Bannerjea's appointment since he was a *Sturmführer* (something akin to Lieutenant Colonel) belonging to an elite and powerful group of the SS—Himmler's personal staff.

Lierau also wrote to Eugen Mattiat in April 1935, vouching for Bannerjea's 'political reliability' and expressing the conviction that the Indian would carry on his duties at the University of Berlin 'in the spirit of the Third Reich'.[140] The Lecturers' Association of the University of Berlin also wrote to the university authorities in September 1935 that Bannerjea was an 'other-worldly' (*Weltfremd*) and frequently misunderstood figure whose financial remuneration did not match his great service of identifying Indian communists.[141]

This letter signified a transformation, since a report from April 1935, submitted by the Lecturers' Association to its 'Führer' Werner Knothe was unequivocally negative, both about Bannerjea's academic abilities and about his denunciation of an 'old party comrade' who had helped him.[142] It was Bannerjea's contribution towards the 'disbandment of the Indian communist cell in Berlin' and his German-friendly propaganda in the Indian press' as he himself reminded Mattiat in September 1935, which tipped the scales in his favour.[143]

The issue about Bannerjea defaming an 'old party comrade', denoting the Indian lector's volatile temperament, resurfaced in 1936. Bannerjea complained to Richard Meckelein, professor of Georgian Studies at the Oriental Seminar (which had become *Ausland Hochschule* or 'Academy for the study of Foreign Countries' from 1 January 1936) and Liaison Officer of the Nazi Lecturers' Association of the University of Berlin, about his erstwhile patron Emil Gansser, accusing the latter of influencing the Education Ministry against him. Meckelein considered the matter important enough to write directly to Hitler's adjutant Fritz Wiedermann.[144] In this letter, dated 11 December 1936, Meckelein reiterated Bannerjea's claim that Gansser knew well that it was through Bannerjea's intervention it came to light that Indian communists, together with Agnes Smedly (an American left-wing activist and Virendranath Chattopadhyaya's partner for a time) and Willi Münzenberg, an influential member of the KPD in the Reichstag and a media mogul who helped found the League against Imperialism, were damaging Germany's interests.

It is not known whether Gansser had to suffer any consequences but it is evident that Bannerjea could forge a lasting and helpful myth in political circles about his key role in ferreting out Indian communists, even though his denunciations did not carry much weight for the Gestapo. The latter claimed in a letter to the Education Ministry in 1937 that it knew about the presence of Indian communists in Berlin even before Bannerjea's report.[145]

Among the other lectors, Reinhard Wagner, who was inclined towards revisionist German nationalism which had points of intersections with National Socialism, was also not slow to adapt to the new regime. In his undated curriculum vita preserved at the archives of the Humboldt University which we have mentioned, Wagner provided some glimpses of his academic expertise and political engagements, which converged occasionally.[146] Wagner stated that he was a member of both the NSDAP and the NSLB. Documents from the Federal

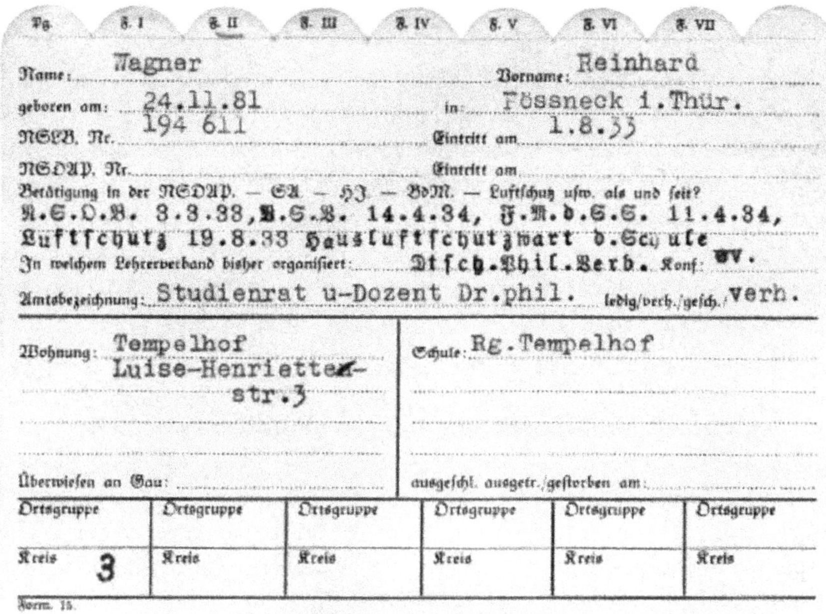
Pg. F. I F. II F. III F. IV F. V F. VI F. VII

Name: Wagner Vorname: Reinhard
geboren am: 24.11.81 in: Pössneck i.Thür.
NSLB. Nr. 194 611 Eintritt am 1.8.33
NSDAP. Nr. Eintritt am
Betätigung in der NSDAP. — SA — HJ — BdM. — Luftschutz usw. als und seit?
R.S.O.B. 3.3.33, B.S.B. 14.4.34, F.M.d.S.S. 11.4.34,
Luftschutz 19.8.33 Hausluftschutzwart d.Schule
In welchem Lehrerverband bisher organisiert: Dtsch.Phil.Verb. Konf: ev.
Amtsbezeichnung: Studienrat u-Dozent Dr.phil. ledig/verh./gesch.: verh.

Wohnung: Tempelhof Luise-Henrietten-str.3 Schule: Rg.Tempelhof

Überwiesen an Gau: ausgeschl. ausgetr./gestorben am:

Ortsgruppe	Ortsgruppe	Ortsgruppe	Ortsgruppe	Ortsgruppe	Ortsgruppe
Kreis 3	Kreis	Kreis	Kreis	Kreis	Kreis

Form. 15.

Figure 14 Reinhard Wagner's card showing his membership of various Nazi organizations.
Source: BA Berlin: Signature BDC.

Archives of Berlin confirm that Wagner enrolled in the NSLB on 1 August 1933 (membership number 194611) and in the NSDAP in 1937 (membership number 5381234) (Figure 14).[147]

Some ideas of Wagner's activities for the NSLB can be gleaned from secondary sources. His name appears as one of the lyricists of a book of songs for school children. The book, *Never Turn Back, Look Forward* (*Nimmer zurück. Vorwarts den Blick*) was published by a branch of the NSLB in 1935 and was replete with Nazi propaganda.[148] He was also a member of the editorial staff of the widely circulated school magazine *Hilf Mit* ('Help with') published by the NSLB.[149] It was not a magazine by the students for the students, but a carefully and professionally crafted tool designed by members of the NSLB to indoctrinate young minds with Nazi ideals like *Führer* cult, anti-Semitism, and militarism.[150] Wagner also joined the External Affairs department of the NSDAP. Here, he belonged to the group 'England' in the *Gau* or administrative unit of Berlin.[151]

Wagner's curriculum vita also lists a number of services that he provided to the Foreign Ministry. These included translating propagandistic articles from German to English to be sent out to the Anglophone world, as well as intercepting and translating letters written in English (and Bengali). Wagner also claimed that he proofread the manuscript of a book written in Bengali 'on the Führer, which is scheduled to be released in Calcutta'. Whether it was a Bengali transla-tion of Beythan's book on Hitler is not known.

The scholar of Bengali claimed to have joined a few other Nazi organizations as well. These included the RLB (*Reichsluftschutzbund* or the National Air Raid Protection League), the NSV, and the FMSS (*Förderndes Mitglied der SS*) or patron member of the SS. The patron members of the SS did not take part in active duty but contributed financially to it. The truth of these claims is corrobo-rated by documents from the Federal Archives in Berlin.[152] What Wagner omitted to mention in his bio-data was that he joined the NSDB or Nazi Lecturers' Association in March 1933.[153]

The *Ausland Hochschule* and Nazi Politics: 1937–1939

As already mentioned, from 1 January 1936, the Seminar was renamed *Ausland Hochschule* (AH) or the Academy for Study of Foreign Countries. Anton Palme, professor of Russian Studies from 1924 at the University of Berlin, became its director.[154] Palme had written in 1914 about the necessity to redefine the profes-sional duties of the German Foreign Ministry in the light of the increasing 'world-political significance' (*Weltpolitische Bedeutung*) of Germany. He claimed that it was necessary for future German diplomats to study foreign countries so that they could conduct tasks relating to the military, economic, and political ambi-tions of Germany. The AH was to take up this concept by training such diplomats under 'strict Nazi leadership'. They were to be imparted knowledge of foreign countries filtered through Nazi world view.[155]

With the nomination of Palme as the acting head of the AH and the exit of Schaeder, the last feeble hindrances to complete Nazification of this organization were gone. As far as the Indian studies were concerned, this resulted in certain changes. Hugo Figulla, the librarian of the Seminar and lector of Telugu, was dis-missed in October 1937 for being a 'half-Jew'.[156] Devendra Nath Bannerjea, who had to leave the Seminar earlier, now joined the AH with a contract to teach Indian *Realien* from the winter semester of 1938, in addition to teaching at the Seminar for Public Policy.[157] This was, however, not due to but despite Palme, who had provided a negative verdict about Bannerjea to the Nazi Lecturers' Association in 1934.[158]

There is no indication that Palme had changed his mind. Bannerjea's reappear-ance could have been the result of his contacts with Rudolf Heß, the deputy to Hitler as well as to von Hentig, then the director of the Oriental Section in the Foreign Ministry, as a British surveillance report claimed.[159] The veracity of this report cannot be proved. What is certain is that Clemens Scharschmidt, profes-sor for Japanese Studies and the then acting head of the AH, appealed to the

Education Ministry in October 1937 to reinstate Bannerjea, whom he considered to be more competent than Tarachand Roy.[160]

Bannerjea's lectures at the *Auslands Hochschule* as well as the seminar for Public Policy reflect the German state's intention of acquainting its citizens with aspects of contemporary India on the eve of a possible war with England. He lectured on the workings of the colonial government and the anti-colonial movement, as well as Indian economy, education, and defence. At the AH, Bannerjea lectured on the history and workings of the INC and on Gandhi. In the same semester, his lectures at the seminar for Public Policy included one on the state and the political parties in India and another on the interaction between British parliament and India from the eighteenth century onwards.[161] Since Bannerjea's dissertation was on the economic problems of modern India, he appeared to have a greater claim to provide usable knowledge of contemporary India than Tarachand Roy, whose academic specialization was philology.

Probably emboldened by his return to the AH, Bannerjea applied for a *Habilitation* in August 1938, on 'The economic and legal foundations of the Mughal Empire in India, 1526–1768' (*Die Volkswirtschaftlichen und Staatsrechtlichen Grundlagen des Moghulen Kaiserreichs in Indien*).[162] The fate of this *Habilitation*, however, remains unclear. In 1942, Bannerjea complained to the rector of the University of Berlin that he submitted his *Habilitation* thesis around September 1940 but received no response.[163] This claim is doubtful, since around 1942, the acting head of the AF, Karl Heinz Pfeffer informed Bannerjea that though the faculty would welcome his *Habilitation*, as a foreigner he would not be eligible to become a professor, indicating that Bannerjea had not yet submitted it.[164]

Franz Alfred Six, the dean of the AF and the DAWI, wrote to the Ministry of Education on 20 April 1942 that Bannerjea's *Habilitation* was first submitted to the Seminar of Public Policy but it was not accepted as its content supposedly did not match the faculty's academic focus. A second submission to the Philosophical Faculty of the University of Berlin was also declined for undisclosed reasons. Bannerjea submitted the *Habilitation* at the University of Munich in 1942 but most probably it was not accepted as there was no further mention of it.[165] The *Habilitation* episode illustrates the limits to which an Indian, even if considered 'politically useful', could aspire in the Nazified German academia.

Notwithstanding the *Habilitation* fiasco, Bannerjea continued to demonstrate his commitment to Nazi politics for which he reaped other kinds of rewards. By 1939, in addition to signing his letters with 'Heil Hitler!' he was allegedly decorating his house with 'a swastika flag'.[166] In the same year, he received a contract for teaching a course on 'England and India' for one semester at the *Wirtschafts-Hochschule* (Academy for Economics) in Berlin. Bannerjea convinced Edwin Fels, professor at this Academy and a German nationalist turned Nazi that this subject was important for 'the interests of German politics'.[167]

Among the other lectors, Hermann Beythan received a contract to teach at the AH. He was allowed by the Education Ministry to draw a salary from the AH from April 1937, after he retired from the school where he had been teaching. Anton Palme, then the head of the AH, pointed out to the Education Ministry in November 1936 that apart from being a good scholar, Beythan had provided an extraordinary service to the nation by writing a book in Tamil about 'the Führer', which is making waves in India and is being translated in other Indian languages. Since Beythan's request to be allowed to continue in the school for a few more years could not be granted, he was to be compensated through paid employment at the AH.[168] The Foreign Ministry also requested the Education Ministry to remunerate Beythan.[169]

The AH's log for the summer semester of 1937 reveals that Beythan's teaching hours were extended from two to four per week. His courses focused on Tamil grammar, phonetics, and reading contemporary Tamil texts, and were devoid of any connections to politics.[170] He continued to serve the regime outside the classroom by writing articles in English and Tamil for the Indian press promulgating the achievements of Hitler and his 'Reich'.[171]

Around the time of AH's formation, three different organs of the Nazi state began to strive towards controlling it. Apart from the Education Ministry which controlled the University of Berlin, the Foreign Ministry was keen to train diplomats following its own ideals at the AH. The third and the strongest contender was the SS, or rather its increasingly powerful secret service, the SD which saw the possibility of training spies and agents who would combine ideological fanaticism with ruthless methods.[172] The SD would ultimately win this power struggle.

In light of their political engagements, the question arises whether the teaching contracts given to the lectors at the AH were meant to serve as sinecures or fronts for their more important 'services' to Nazi Germany. The case for this assumption becomes stronger as one considers the case of Michael Achmeteli, who was appointed associate professor and head of the Russian institute of the AH in 1938 by the SD, which increased its hold on this institute around the time. Franz Alfred Six, who already wielded considerable influence on the AH, stated openly that Achmeteli's teaching position was to be 'a camouflage for his actual tasks'.[173]

In the late 1920s to early 1930s, some lectors (Wagner and Beythan, for example) were allowed to have prestige, a symbolic resource, in the form of teaching posts and publications without little or no financial remuneration, in return for conducting different forms of cultural politics. After 1936, as the Nazi regime consolidated its power, it attempted to intervene in the newly formed AH by implementing its racial politics as well as initiating a direct exchange of resources between the lectors and the state. Thus, Bannerjea was 'rewarded' through a resuscitation of his lost teaching contract while Beythan began to receive monetary compensation for his services.

Study of India at the AF (*Auslandswissenschaftliches Institut*) and the DAWI (*Deutsche Auslandswissenschaftliches Institut*): 1940–1944

The AF (Institute for the Study of Foreign Countries) and the DAWI, a corresponding research institute, were established in January 1940 as faculties affiliated to the University of Berlin. The AH was now incorporated in the AF. The AF and the DAWI claimed to have the following aims: 1. Training of specialists with expert knowledge of state, culture and economy of foreign countries, 2. Conducting and publishing research on peoples and states of the world, 3. Training of interpreters in multiple languages, 4. Propagating the world view of 'new Germany', 5. Training diplomats for maintaining Nazi Germany's relationships with other states. The AF focused on teaching while the DAWI was engaged in research and publications.[174]

It is significant that the foundation of the AF and the DAWI followed soon after the SD, along with the Gestapo and the criminal police, formed the RSHA (*Reichssicherheitshauptamt* or Reich Security Main Office) on 27 September 1939. The 'area studies' conducted by the AF and the DAWI corresponded to the SD's views of 'knowledge of foreign countries' on which Franz Alfred Six, who was made a full professor and the founding dean of both the AF and the DAWI, was supposed to be an expert. Six held the exposé *Rasse, Volk, Staat und Raum* (*Race, People, State and Space*) by the ethnologist Karl Christian von Loesch as an 'exemplary work' for studying different ethnic groups. Following this concept, the AF and the DAWI were similarly organized into a central administrative department, sections on different 'areas' (called *Volks und Landeskunde* or People and Land Studies) and an institute for 'the science of interpretation/translation'.[175]

Six was an ideal scholar-soldier envisaged by the SS. He joined the Nazi party and the SA while studying at the University of Heidelberg, where he completed his PhD under the guidance of Arnold Bergstrasser, a proponent of the politicized 'study of Foreign Countries' (*Auslandskunde*).[176] Six joined the SD in 1934 and rapidly rose to become the chief of the Office for Press in 1935.[177] In April 1937, Six was made director of the department for 'Ideological evaluation' (*Weltanschauliche Auswertung*) of the SD. This department was concerned with 'studying' (i.e. spying on) the ideological opponents to the Nazis.[178] Six professionalized this department through various measures.[179]

As a reward, he was initially made the director of *Gegnerforschung* (researching the opponents) in the department II of the RSHA. Reinhard Heydrich, the notoriously brutal cohort of Himmler and chief of the SD, made Six the head of the entire department VII of the RSHA, which researched ideological opponents of the Nazis, in 1941. After the death of Reinhard Heydrich in 1942, Six shifted to the Foreign Ministry, occupying the prestigious position as head of the cultural political department in April 1943, as we have noted.[180]

The heightened political importance of India contributed to increasing entanglements between the Nazi state and the teachers of Indian subjects after the onset of the Second World War. The lecturers of the AF were now expected to contribute not only to propaganda ventures but also to 'war efforts'. Though there was not yet a separate section on India in the section 'People and Land Studies', 'politically relevant' themes related to India were introduced through a course taught by Bannerjea. The course, titled 'India: Race, People and Space', emphasized politically loaded subjects like 'England and India: a comparative study of racial psychology' as well as the propagandistic topic that Bannerjea had not been allowed to teach at the Seminar: 'The basic features of the Indo-Aryan society'.[181] The reappointment of Bannerjea with increased academic freedom was due to Six's recommendation. Six justified this assignment on the basis of Bannerjea's teaching experiences as well as his 'confidential assignments' for the Foreign Ministry.[182]

From the second trimester of 1940, Reinhard Wagner was given a contract at the department of 'Languages and Interpretation' (*Sprachenkunde und Dolmetscherwesen*) of the AF to teach Bengali for six hours every week. He was also allotted a salary, signalling a new kind of recognition for his political engagements.[183] Beythan's teaching contract was renewed and he was placed in the same department as Wagner.[184] Tarachand Roy also received a contract for teaching Hindustani/Hindi, presumably at the same department.[185]

The fact that Reinhard Wagner started to draw a salary was presumably due to his contribution to the war efforts which included censoring the letters of the prisoners of war (POW) letters for the OKW (*Oberkommando Wehrmacht* or the High Command of the German Armed Forces) apart from supervising the English translations of propagandistic magazines and pamphlets that the German Foreign Ministry continued to send to different countries, including India.[186] Tarachand Roy allegedly began to provide reports on the situation in India to Wilhelm Melchers, who succeeded von Hentig as head of the Oriental Section in the Political Department of the Foreign Ministry in 1939.[187] Melchers, who had joined the diplomatic service in 1925, officially entered the Nazi party in 1939. He took a leading role in conducting anti-Jewish propaganda in Arab countries.[188]

In 1939, the office of Alfred Rosenberg, which had the responsibility of 'monitoring the entire spiritual and ideological education of the NSDAP' enquired to the Gestapo about the academic credentials and political reliability of Roy, who was to be engaged as a speaker for *Deutsches Volksbildungswerk*, which, we should recall, was an instrument of propaganda that aimed to inculcate the spirit of National Socialism among ordinary German citizens. The answer is unknown but it is unlikely to have been negative.[189]

Around this time, Roy started using his image of a cultural mediator between India and Germany to further Nazi Germany's propagandistic goals. A British secret report notes, for example, that at a tea party given by the Nazi-oriented

Deutsche Orient Verein in Berlin in 1940, Tarachand Roy spoke on the literary achievements and spirituality of the Indians and compared them to German philosophers. The secret report claimed that the main objective of the tea party was to stress that Germany 'not only maintains friendly relations with India, but also wishes to make them deeper and very cordial'.[190]

In his attempts to glorify Nazism, Roy invoked a dubious hypothesis found in a strand of German Indology that linked ancient India to 'Nordic ideals' which were often glorified by the Nazi regime. Leopold von Schroeder, professor of Indology at the University of Vienna, had set a precedent of providing scholarly legitimacy to the spurious idea of a connection between 'Nordic races' and Aryans in India as we noted in the first chapter.[191] On 29 January 1940, Roy spoke on 'India and the Nordic Spirit' at the *Nordische Gesellschaft* (Nordic Society) in Berlin.[192] Originally formed as an association to promote economic and cultural ties between Germany and the Scandinavian countries, the Nordic Society came under the influence of the External Affairs section of the Nazi Party after 1933. The extolling of the so-called 'Nordic traits' by the Nazis made it a valuable instrument of propaganda.[193]

In another talk on 'England as the adversary of the Nordic spirit in India' delivered in 1942, Roy tried to connect Nordic racial tropes with anti-British sentiments. The lecture was mentioned in the journal *Der Norden*, a mouthpiece of the Nordic Society.[194] In this address, Roy alleged that the British, through their oppressive rule in India, were proving themselves to be unworthy of belonging to the noble Nordic race.[195]

Simultaneously, Roy's mildly nationalistic tone gave way to polemic commensurate with Nazi propaganda concerning Indian anti-colonialism. He spoke at a programme organized by the Indian Students' Association at Berlin's hotel Kaiserhof in 1940, 'against the tyrannical British rule in India'.[196] The fact that this programme was held at this prestigious venue indicates that the association received support from the Nazi government, presaging the collusion between Bose and his coterie of diasporic Indian anti-colonialists and the Nazi regime.

Roy also conducted cultural politics by writing propagandistic articles. One such article, a diatribe against the exploitative nature of British rule in India, appeared in 1940 in 'News from Germany', an English-language pamphlet produced by the foreign press section of the NSDAP. The 'news' published here, as can be surmised, was Nazi propaganda in disguise. The article introduced Roy as a 'complete part of Germany`s culture'.[197] This pamphlet managed to evade wartime British surveillance to reach different parts of India.[198] The American Embassy in Berlin, where Roy applied for an extension of his British passport in 1941, sent another anti-British article written by Roy in the same year for the propagandistic journal *Germany and You* to the British Foreign Ministry.[199] This magazine was distributed among Indians by Alfred Würfel, the German lector of the DA in Banaras as we have seen in the first chapter.

Roy joined the Free India Centre that Subhas Chandra Bose was allowed to form in 1941. This appointment was presumably mediated by the SRI which helped Bose to recruit nationalist-minded Indians to this organization.[200] In January 1942, as part of his 'Azad Hind' (Free India) movement, Bose formed a 'Press and Letters Committee' in which he included Roy. The committee members were to propagate the cause of Indian nationalism through articles and lectures.[201] One such contribution of Roy was an article in German on Subhas Chandra Bose, highlighting the latter's radio address to Indians, delivered in February 1942.[202] Roy also employed German scholarly interest in India to serve the cause of Nazi propaganda in 1942, in the very first issue of the *Azad Hind*, the journal published by Bose's Free India Centre under the supervision of the Foreign Ministry. In an article titled 'Indian Influence on German Poets and Thinkers', Roy stated that the two nations shared 'spiritual and mental talents' as well as 'the same noble aims and ideals which they strive to realize'.[203] Though Roy left the Free India Centre on 31 May 1943, he continued to act as a mouthpiece for Germany.[204] For example, he urged India to cooperate with Japan in an interview which he gave to the newspaper *Deutsche Allgemeine Zeitung* on 8 March 1942.[205]

Mukund Rai Vyas mentioned in his post-war statement that Roy was being paid a handsome amount of money per month, first by Bose and later by his successor at the Free India Centre, Nambiar. Bose supposedly described this payment as a 'bribe'.[206] Roy's influence at the Foreign Ministry probably made the Indian nationalists in Berlin apprehensive about the possibility of denunciations by him. Vyas also claimed that both Tarachand Roy and Devendra Nath Bannerjea worked for the 'Special Services Seehaus', a secret monitoring service set up by the Foreign Ministry at the 'Villa Seehaus' in Wannsee, Berlin, to tap foreign radio stations.[207] The details of Roy's engagement at the Seehaus are not known.

According to Gerd Rühle, who was in charge of the 'Political Broadcasting Section' of the Foreign Ministry which aimed at influencing enemy states, from 1 May 1940, Bannerjea was given the task of supervising the Hindustani broadcasts. However, his commitments at the University prevented Bannerjea from performing this duty properly and he was transferred from 30 July 1940 to *Seehaus* for listening to the Hindustani programmes supervised by the British colonial administration from Delhi and London. He had to resign from this service for the same reason on 30 June 1941.[208] The courses taught by Bannerjea were evidently considered more useful by the Nazi authorities than his work at the *Seehaus*.

In the *Seehaus*, the transcripts of the tapped material were translated and sent to the key policy- and propaganda-making authorities—the Foreign Ministry, the Propaganda Ministry, and the OKW. By 1940, the monitoring service at the *Seehaus* was listening to radio stations in Madras as well.[209] Since Tamil was the main language of Madras, it is possible that Hermann Beythan was also involved in this 'listening in' service. From 1944, Beythan was engaged in broadcasting propaganda in Tamil as part of the German radio programmes aimed at India. Later in the same year, Tarachand Roy started broadcasting in Hindustani. Such programmes, conducted by the *Reichsrundfunk Gesellschaft* (Reich Broadcasting Society) under Goebbels, comprised both anti-British polemic and pro-National Socialist propaganda.[210]

Separate Section on India: Ludwig Alsdorf

India's symbolic value for the external cultural politics of Nazi Germany was manifested in the creation of a separate section of the AF, on 'People and Regional Studies of India' (*Volks und Landeskunde Indien*) in 1942. A corresponding section on research relating to India was also started at the DAWI. The justifications for the formation of this section on India can be found in a note written in January 1942 by Six to the Main Office for Science (*Wissenschaft*) of the Nazi party.[211] This note, titled 'Justifications for the creation of a chair for India', needs to be studied in some detail since it provides a window into the diverse uses of the knowledge of India for the Nazi state.

Six began by reiterating aspects of German Romantic interest in India, claiming that India could boast of an ancient and unique culture which was no less valuable than that of Europe. For Six, however, the real importance of India lay in its present and future: India occupied a large geographical area and had a huge population. The country was destined to assume an important place in world politics after its independence, which it was poised to achieve. Six claimed that an Indian section at the AF would be good propaganda for Germany in India. This department would also prepare Germany for forging political, economic, and cultural contacts with an independent India.

The most pressing reason for establishing this 'chair for India' was, however, the need to respond to the increasing demands for propaganda concerning India after the arrival of Subhas Bose in 1941. As Six wrote: 'The current increase and intensification of the functions of the Reich officials with regard to India make the absence of such a section particularly objectionable.' Six wanted, apart from a professor and lectors for teaching languages, the 'crucially important' courses by Bannerjea to be continued. He also aimed to introduce another south Indian language and Gujarati, as well as to employ an Indian lector for Bengali besides Wagner, since Bengali was 'an especially important language spoken by 60 million people'. Six's favourite candidate for the professorial position for India was Ludwig Alsdorf, whose trajectory until 1941 has been recounted in the last chapter.

Meanwhile, Alfred Rosenberg, the 'chief ideologue' of the Nazi Party who was interested in India's 'Aryan/*Indogerman* past', wanted Alsdorf to be a professor for Indo-Aryan studies at the *Hohe Schule*, a kind of political university that he wished to set up in Munich. In a letter to Martin Bormann, Hitler's secretary and the head of the Nazi Party chancellery, Rosenberg claimed that Alsdorf's strength lay in the academic study of ancient India which was ideologically important for the new German *Wissenschaft*, particularly at a time when 'we are trying to replace Palestinian tradition by Aryan ethics'.[212] Rosenberg received support from Dr Gustav Borger, the head of the Department of Science (*Amt Wissenschaft*) of the NSDB or Nazi Lecturers' Association, who considered the reasons offered by Rosenberg to be more substantial than the 'momentary need for knowledge of modern India'.[213]

The conflicting demands relating to scholarly expertise on ancient India and 'practical' knowledge of modern India symbolize the two divergent 'utilities' of Indian studies for the Nazi regime. Alsdorf was finally 'awarded' to the AF and DAWI as a result of the perceived importance of the knowledge of modern India for Nazi politics, the clout of the SS/SD that superseded Rosenberg's influence, and Alsdorf's reputation as an expert on 'living' India.

In March 1942, Alsdorf was instructed by the Education Ministry to lecture on 'People and Land' of India at the AF.[214] On 31 March 1942, he was made '*Außerplanmäßgen professor*' (somewhat akin to adjunct professor).[215] Alsdorf was also made the head of the section on India at DAWI, as Six stated in a report in 1942 in the *Zeitschrift für Politik* (*Journal of Politics*) which was then a publication of the DAWI, the twin organisation of the AF.[216]

Alsdorf started lecturing at the AF from the summer semester of 1942. He offered a course on 'The history of Indian freedom movement' while Bannerjea held courses on the cultural and economic relationship between Germany and India and on Indian culture.[217] With the appointment of Alsdorf, however, Bannerjea's position at the AF became precarious. By January 1943, Six was complaining to the Education Ministry that Bannerjea's courses were redundant.[218] In April 1943, Alsdorf became the sole lecturer of 'People and Land of India' as Bannerjea's contract was not renewed.[219]

There were a number of reasons for Six's volte face regarding Bannerjea's courses. In April 1942, Six wrote to the Education Ministry that Bannerjea was better suited to be a teacher in the Indology department, since due to the present tensions and problems engulfing India, it will be difficult for him to maintain the necessary emotional distance for teaching contemporary India.[220] This was, of course, a pretext. A secret report on Bannerjea submitted to Six by Reinhard Wagner in April 1942, disproving Bannerjea's claim to have doctorates from Lahore and Oxford, presumably influenced this decision.[221] Spying on a colleague for the SS must have been considered a valuable service rendered to the 'Reich'.

Bannerjea meanwhile was harbouring the delusion that he had been promised a professorial chair by Werner Otto von Hentig, the erstwhile director of the section 'Orient' in the Foreign Ministry.[222] Despite being categorically informed by the office of von Hentig that it was a misunderstanding on Bannerjea's part, the

Indian lector continued to demand a professorial chair, feeling emboldened enough to write to the Foreign Minister himself.[223] This 'audacity' in directly addressing the Minister, as the administration of the AF claimed, was not compatible with his position as a foreigner in Nazi Germany. Bannerjea had landed himself in a dangerous spot which the AF saw as unsustainable with its own political profile.[224] This episode thus signified once more the limits of the 'rewards' that an Indian could hope to receive from the Nazi authorities.

As we noted in the last chapter, the antagonism between Bannerjea and Alsdorf came to the fore in 1943 over Alsdorf's rejection of the biography of Gandhi that Bannerjea wrote for the book series of the SRI. An interesting fall-out of the controversy was that in a long note addressed to Trott zu Solz and Wilhelm Keppler, Alsdorf called for removing Bannerjea from the University and recommended threatening Bannerjea with the prospect of imprisonment at a concentration camp.[225] Alsdorf thus demonstrated that he was prepared to make use of the Nazi terror apparatus in intimidating his adversaries.

Bannerjea's conflict with the SRI led Keppler to send an official note to Six in 1943, in which Keppler urged Six to remove Bannerjea from the AF for falsely denouncing members of the SRI 'to a third party'. Retaining Bannerjea at the AF after this scandal, wrote Keppler, would damage the reputation of the AF.[226] Alsdorf's resentment and Keppler's complaint probably sealed Bannerjea's fate as far as the AF was concerned.

While Bannerjea's services were not enough to secure him certain professional prospects, other doors opened for him. The Education Ministry arranged for a teaching contract for Bannerjea at the department of *Indogerman* studies of the University of Berlin with an increased salary after his dismissal from the AF.[227] This decision was influenced by Bannerjea's repeated pleas to Johann Karl von Stechow, a high functionary of the political section of the Foreign Ministry who had been involved in the establishment of the AF and DAWI.[228] Von Stechow, who privately described Bannerjea as 'muddleheaded' to Herbert Scurla, an influential employee of the Education Ministry, felt some sympathy towards the Indian lector following the latter's description of his financial distress.[229] It is, however, unlikely that the authorities representing the Nazi state would have been similarly moved if Bannerjea had not provided some valuable 'services'. Notably, during this stint at the seminar for Indology (1943–5) Bannerjea taught Urdu and Hindustani, the history of Indian religion, philosophy, and the politically relevant subject of the relationship between India and England.[230]

AF in 1944–1945

Despite his pressing engagements at the SRI, Ludwig Alsdorf managed to hold regular lectures on Indian society, politics, religion, culture, and economics at the

AF until the summer semester of 1944, when he also held a colloquium on the current issues affecting India.[231] By the time Alsdorf was promoted to an *Außerordentlicher* professor (akin to a Reader) in May 1944, he had been transferred, along with a number of his colleagues at the Foreign Ministry, to Krummhübel, located in present day Czech Republic, to avoid Allied bombing.[232]

Hermann Beythan was given a contract to substitute Alsdorf when the latter shifted to Krummhübel.[233] The shift was probably somewhat unplanned, since several courses on topics like Indian art and economy were already announced under Alsdorf's name for the winter semester of 1944–5.[234] Beythan, as we saw in the last chapter, had contributed two books to the series published by the SRI. Expanding on the theme of one of the books, Beythan taught a course on 'the social question in India' at the AF in the winter semester of 1944–5. A more lasting and scholarly contribution of Beythan was a book on Tamil grammar in German (with an accompanying practice book) which was published by the DAWI in 1943 as a part of its series titled *Sprachenkundliche Lehr und Wörterbücher* (Linguistic Textbooks and Dictionaries).[235]

In the winter semester of 1944–5, the Department of Indian Studies (*Volks und Landeskunde Indien*) at the AF gave a teaching contract to a scholar called Albert Wissler (b. 1904) to teach India's economy. Ludwig Alsdorf, as the head of the section on India, approved this appointment.[236] Wissler seemed to be an ideal scholar for the AF, combining academic usefulness and political loyalty. According to his bio-data submitted at the AF, Wissler completed his doctorate from the University of Basel on the 'opium question' in 1931. His dissertation was published in the same year as part of a series on the problems of world economy, from the prestigious World Economic Institute in Kiel with which Bannerjea also had connections. Subsequently, Wissler worked for a time with the League of Nations in Geneva. In his bio-data, he claimed that his dissertation provided practical help to the UN's work of controlling the global production and consumption of opium.

After a stint at the foreign countries section of the 'Reich' Office of Statistics (*Statistischen Reichsamt*) in Berlin where he studied the economic problems of India, China, and Japan, Wissler joined the German Institute for Economic Research in Berlin in 1933. Here, he worked on the economic aspects of British Empire and colonialism. Also in 1933, Wissler joined the Nazi Party. Since then, claimed Wissler in his bio-data, his empirical, political, philosophical, and historical knowledge coalesced with his practical-political engagements, leading him to perform 'tasks important for war'. In 1944, Wissler applied to complete his *Habilitation* from the AF, on 'The Economic Foundations of India's Freedom'. This was, according to Wissler, a secret assignment given to him by the OKW, the head office of the Wehrmacht or the German Armed Forces.[237]

However, despite his initial enthusiasm for Wissler, Alsdorf and two other academics subsequently found Wissler's *Habilitation* thesis to be lacking in academic rigour and refused to pass it.[238] This incident underscores once again Alsdorf's role as an authority and a gatekeeper as far as the knowledge of modern India was concerned.

It is clear from the preceding discussion that there was a definite correlation between the different kinds of services provided by teachers of the Indian subjects and their teaching contracts at the Oriental Seminar and its successor organizations. The hopes of the Nazi regime, of a victorious German state having a diplomatic and strategic relationship with an independent India, probably played a role as well. Demand for studying Indian subjects could not have been a justification for the regime's expenditure on the Indian section. Between 1940 and 1944, only one student is recorded to have completed a diploma in Hindi translation.[239] The available number of students attending the courses in the section on India between 1942 and 1944 was also limited, as this list shows: WS (winter semester) 1942–3: eight students for Hindi, two for Hindustani, three for Bengali, three for Tamil. SS (summer semester) 1943: seven for Hindi, ten for Hindustani, three for Tamil. WS 1943–4: eleven for Hindi, eight for Hindustani, one for Tamil, one for Bengali.[240]

DAWI: Political Research of Foreign Countries

The research conducted at the DAWI (*Deutsche Auslandswissenschaftliches Institut*) aimed to help the AF by accumulating relevant knowledge and to contribute directly to the war, which, according to Karl Stuthoff, secretary of DAWI, was being fought at the level of *Weltanschauung* or world view as on the battlefield.[241] Karl Heinz Pfeffer, professor for the section on Great Britain at the AF, who became the acting dean of AF and president of DAWI as Six was involved in the invasion of Soviet Union and subsequently transferred to the Foreign Ministry, wrote a significant essay on the concept and methods of 'the study of foreign countries'. In this article published in 1942, in the DAWI's mouthpiece *Jahrbuch der Weltpolitik* (Yearbook of World Politics) which was officially edited by Six, Pfeffer claimed that the three main domains of the study of foreign countries as envisaged in Nazi Germany are space, race, and Volk. These three spheres need to be examined through the study of political histories, economic and legal situations, and the spiritual expressions of the different people. In this way, claimed Pfeffer, the study of foreign countries will combine the basic tenets of political science with the practical knowledge of spoken languages and contemporary situations of different countries.[242]

The publication program of the DAWI, which was based on the principles outlined by Pfeffer, was ambitious and could only be carried out partially. Publications on India appeared under different series. Ludwig Alsdorf, as the head of the section on India at the DAWI, contributed a book titled *Indien und*

Ceylon to the series *Kleine Auslandskunde* ('Short Studies of Foreign Countries') in 1943.[243] This series published slim books written in accessible style containing 'practical facts' about different countries. Each book had a blurb announcing that the series was written from the viewpoint that Germany's newly achieved position as a world power requires a deeper understanding of foreign countries, thereby indicating its role as an instrument of Nazified political education.

In this book, Alsdorf depicted the history of Ceylon (Sri Lanka) through the prism of Indology, claiming that the island was 'conquered' by the Aryans of north India.[244] Ceylon was described by Alsdorf as a more blatant example than India of being a 'tropical colony for exploitation'.[245] However, the focus of this book was on 'practical' aspects like geography, economy, administration, trade, commerce, and defence, with religion forming an essential background.

Alsdorf regularly wrote articles on India for the publications of DAWI, which included a monthly journal, a yearbook, and several specialized periodicals. In most of his articles, Alsdorf not only encouraged Indian nationalism but also analysed the implications of the war for India. In an article titled *Indien*, published in the aforementioned journal Yearbook of World Politics (*Jahrbuch der Weltpolitik*) in 1943, Alsdorf wrote glowingly about the reception of the 'radical Indian nationalist' and the 'leader of Bengali activists', S.C. Bose, by Hitler on 29 May 1942. Alsdorf portrayed this meeting, which was a disappointment for Bose, as a symbol of the 'joint struggle of Germany and India against England'.[246]

The report by Alsdorf for the year 1943 in the *Jahrbuch* (published in 1944) was a desperate attempt to draw attention away from the unfavourable war situation. Alsdorf thus exaggerated the effects of Japanese advances in Burma, the significance of Subhas Bose's formation of a provisional government of Free India at Singapore and the Free Indian Legion that fought under the Japanese at India's border, as well as the token recognition of the Free India government's authority over Andaman and Nicobar islands by Japan.[247]

Between 1940 and 1945, Alsdorf also reviewed a number of books on India in the prestigious Journal for Politics or *Zeitschrift für Politik* (ZfP) which conformed to various aspects of Nazi ideology after 1933.[248] In 1941, the ZfP was officially made a publication of the DAWI, with Six as its editor.[249] The book reviews in ZfP demonstrate Alsdorf's role as the arbitrator of how India was to be portrayed in 'official' publications. Alsdorf criticized, for example, the analysis of Hindu-Muslim conflict in the Italian author Virginia Vacca's book because it went against Nazi Germany's 'official' stance of not supporting the Pakistan movement.[250] He also reviewed, or rather propagated, four of the books from the series published by the SRI, where he had acted as de facto editor. In 1943, Alsdorf wrote a favourable review of the book *Indien ohne wunder* (*India without Wonders*), written by Hafiz Manzooruddin Ahmed, an Indian living in Berlin who was part of the Nazi propaganda enterprise in the Islamic world.[251]

The ZfP also published several writings on India by other authors. The focus was always determined by the principles of Nazi propaganda concerning India, along with certain tenets of German Indology: emphasis on the glorious Aryans, the failure of Hinduism to defend itself from invasions, establishment of British colonialism, oppression of British colonizers resulting in poverty and lack of progress of Indians, commiseration with the Indian anti-colonial movement.

Incidentally, Bannerjea claimed in an undated letter to Six that the publisher of Alsdorf's bestselling *Indien* had sent him a review of the book, urging him to lend his name as the reviewer, to be published in the ZfP. The review was laudatory and unabashedly propagandistic in tone. In the letter, Bannerjea stated that he refused to oblige and claimed that the review that he actually wrote (which was presumably not particularly benevolent) was denied publication by the ZfP.[252] If Bannerjea's version is to be believed, then this incident represented another use of an Indian scholar in Nazi Germany: the rendering of one's name to authenticate propagandistic writings concerning India.

India also figured in another book series of the DAWI, titled 'The British Empire in World Politics'. This series, comprising 35 individual books, was partially financed by the Foreign Ministry. The academic in charge of this series was Fritz Berber, who provided different political services to Joachim von Ribbentrop before and after the latter became Foreign Minister.[253] The book on India in the series, titled 'The Freedom Struggle of Indians' (*Das Freiheitsringen der Inder*), published in 1940, was written by Franz Thierfelder, whom we have known as the moving force behind the DA until 1937. It is evident that, contrary to his post-war assertion, Thierfelder was willing to contribute his knowledge to the Nazi regime's cultural politics even after resigning from the DA.

Thierfelder's book was an open polemic against British rule. It began with a condemnation of the 'Jallianwallahbag massacre' of 1919, which, as we noted, was commemorated by the Indian Students' Association.[254] Thierfelder also invoked another historical event that occupied a special position in the Indian anti-colonialist imagination: the 'First War of Independence' of Indians in 1857. For his portrayal of this anti-British uprising, Thierfelder relied on the book *The Indian War of Independence*, written by Vinayak Damodar Savarkar. As we saw in the first chapter, the book, proscribed in India, was translated into German and published anonymously during the war. Thierfelder interpreted Savarkar's agenda of Hindu religious-political awakening in this book as a call for 'independent culture and self-rule based on *völkisch* religiosity', thereby giving a National Socialist dimension to Hindu nationalist politics, which was in any case influenced by tenets of fascism and Nazism.[255]

Nazi propaganda using Indian anti-colonialism for the DAWI came also from an 'expert' on Great Britain, Heinz Lehmann, who was a lecturer at the 'England section' at the AH and a member of the Nazi Party from 1933. In 1944, Lehmann was recruited as a researcher for the RSHA.[256] Being a scholar favoured by the SS explains Lehmann's use of his knowledge of British colonial politics to write an article for the *Jahrbuch der Weltpolitik* in 1942 about the 'moving incidents' affecting India at the time and calling on Indians to resist their colonial masters.[257] He regularly wrote similar articles in other journals like the *Monatshelfte für Auswärtige Politik*, a monthly magazine on external politics published by the Foreign Ministry.[258] These articles contributed to the lasting reputation of Lehmann as an expert on modern India. The political context of his knowledge production on India was conveniently expunged after the war, when, as professor at the University of Tübingen, Lehmann wrote a book on Jawaharlal Nehru.[259]

A book on India that spoke directly to the geopolitical imperatives of the Nazi state was Herbert Hörhager's *Die Volkstumsgrundlagen der indischen Nordwest-Grenzprovinz* (*The Ethnological Foundations of Indian North West Frontier Province*), published in 1943 by the right-wing nationalist publisher Kurt Vowinckel. Hörhager's book was published in DAWI's 'Regional Studies Series' (*Länderkundliche Schriftenreihe*), which was academic in tone and had different specialists as editors. Ludwig Alsdorf edited this book, which was to be the only publication from this series. This book was based on Hörhager's dissertation at the University of Munich under Karl Haushofer. Thus, the work followed Haushofer's approach to 'Defence Studies' (*Wehrwissenschaft/Wehrkunde*), on which the Munich-based scholar had published a book in 1941.[260]

Hörhager was another ideal knowledge provider for the Nazi state. Born in Düsseldorf in 1913, he engaged in Nazi politics from his school life, actively participating in the Hitler Youth from 1931 and becoming a member of the National Socialist School Students Association (*NS Schülerbund*) in 1934 (Figure 15). Hörhager joined the NSDAP on 1 August 1935.[261] As part of his doctoral studies, he undertook a 'field trip' to the North West Frontier Province (NWFP) of India in 1938. Hörhager conducted research here by applying Haushofer's theories to examine the border security organization of the British colonial administration. One product of this research trip was Hörhager's politically observant article, 'The Attitude of the Indo-Afghan Border Tribes towards the Indian Crisis', published in 1940 in the *Journal of Geopolitics*, edited by Haushofer.[262] The political significance of this article becomes clear in the context of an unsuccessful attempt by Germany to incite an anti-British uprising in the NWFP in September 1941.[263]

In his dissertation turned monograph which was published by the DAWI, Hörhager provided reports on the security arrangements as well as the economic and social conditions of the area. The resulting book, which was meant to serve as a manual for German political involvement in this area, was published too late to be of any use to the Nazi regime.

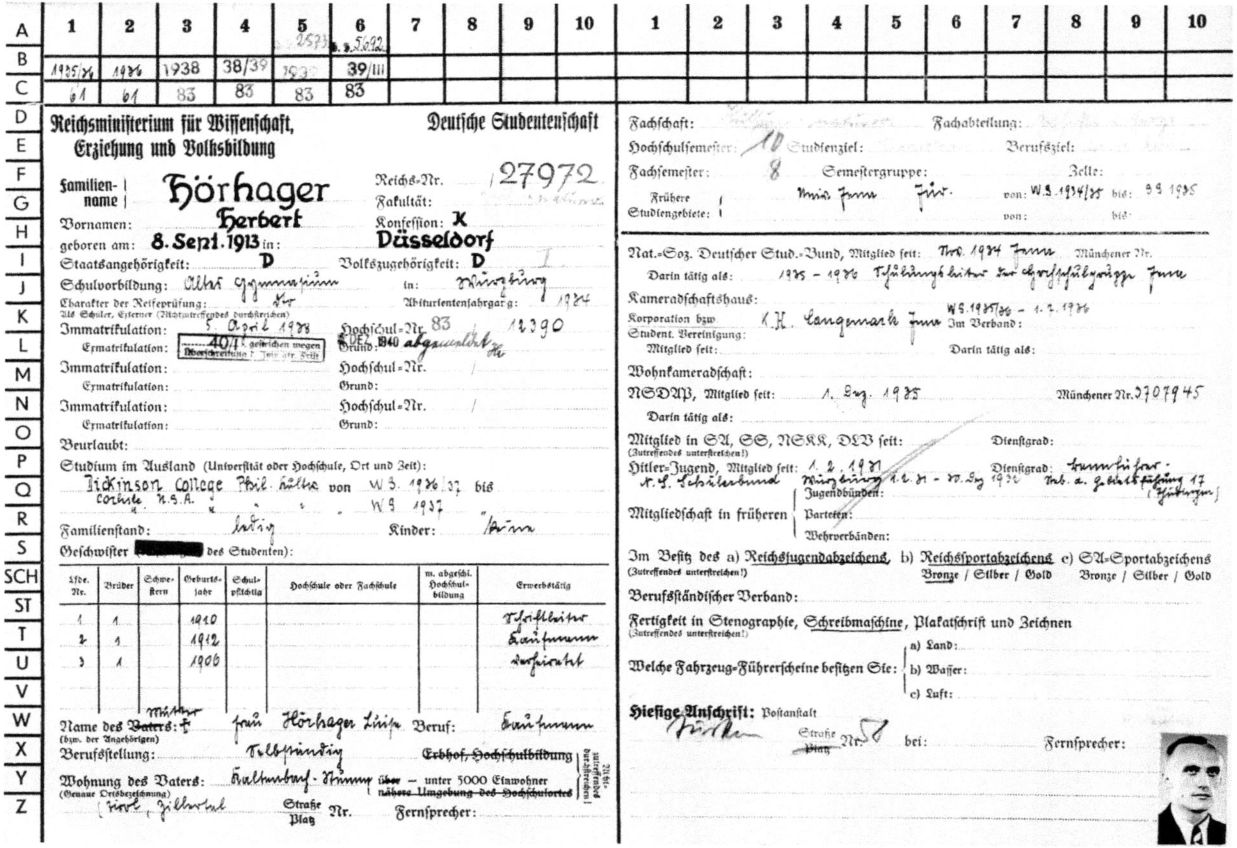
Reichsministerium für Wissenschaft, Erziehung und Volksbildung

Deutsche Studentenschaft

Familien-name: Hörhager

Reichs-Nr.: 27972

Fakultät:

Vornamen: Herbert

Konfession: K

geboren am: 8. Sept. 1913 in: Düsseldorf

Staatsangehörigkeit: D

Volkszugehörigkeit: D

Schulvorbildung: Altes Gymnasium in: Würzburg

Charakter der Reifeprüfung: (Als Schüler, Externer (Nichtzutreffendes durchstreichen))

Abiturientenjahrgang: 1934

Immatrikulation: 5. April 1938 Hochschul-Nr. 83 12390

Exmatrikulation: 40/1 gestrichen wegen Nichterneuerung 7 Jahre str. Frist

Grund: 1940 abgemeldet

Immatrikulation: Hochschul-Nr.

Exmatrikulation: Grund:

Immatrikulation: Hochschul-Nr.

Exmatrikulation: Grund:

Beurlaubt:

Studium im Ausland (Universität oder Hochschule, Ort und Zeit): Dickinson College Phil. Kultur von W.S. 1936/37 bis Carlisle U.S.A. W.S. 1937

Familienstand: ledig

Kinder: keine

Geschwister [redacted] des Studenten):

Lfde. Nr.	Brüder	Schwestern	Geburtsjahr	Schulpflichtig	Hochschule oder Fachschule	m. abgeschl. Hochschulbildung	Erwerbstätig
1	1		1910				Schriftleiter
2	1		1912				Kaufmann
3	1		1906				verheiratet

Name des ~~Vaters~~ Mutter: Frau Hörhager Luise

Beruf: Kaufmann

(bzw. der Angehörigen)

Berufsstellung: selbständig

~~Erbhof, Hochschulbildung~~

Wohnung des Vaters: (Genaue Ortsbezeichnung) ~~über~~ — unter 5000 Einwohner ~~nähere Umgebung des Hochschulortes~~ (Nichtzutreffendes durchstreichen!)

Tirol, Zillertal

Straße Platz Nr.

Fernsprecher:

Fachschaft:

Fachabteilung:

Hochschulsemester: 10

Studienziel:

Berufsziel:

Fachsemester: 8

Semestergruppe:

Zelle:

Frühere Studiengebiete:

von: W.S. 1934/35 bis: 9.9.1935

von: bis:

Nat.-Soz. Deutscher Stud.-Bund, Mitglied seit: Nov. 1934

Münchener Nr.

Darin tätig als: 1935 – 1936

Kameradschaftshaus:

Korporation bzw. Student. Vereinigung: K.H. Langemarck

W.S. 1935/36 – 1.7.1936

Im Verband:

Mitglied seit:

Darin tätig als:

Wohnkameradschaft:

NSDAP, Mitglied seit: 1. Aug. 1935

Münchener Nr. 3707945

Darin tätig als:

Mitglied in SA, SS, NSKK, DLV seit: (Zutreffendes unterstreichen!)

Dienstgrad:

Hitler-Jugend, Mitglied seit: 1.2.1931

Dienstgrad:

Mitgliedschaft in früheren Jugendbünden: Parteien: Wehrverbänden:

Im Besitz des a) Reichsjugendabzeichens, b) Reichssportabzeichens c) SA-Sportabzeichens (Zutreffendes unterstreichen!)

Bronze / Silber / Gold Bronze / Silber / Gold

Berufsständischer Verband:

Fertigkeit in Stenographie, Schreibmaschine, Plakatschrift und Zeichnen (Zutreffendes unterstreichen!)

Welche Fahrzeug-Führerscheine besitzen Sie: a) Land: b) Wasser: c) Luft:

Hiesige Anschrift: Postanstalt

Straße ~~Platz~~ Nr. 8

bei:

Fernsprecher:

Figure 15 Index card of Herbert Hörhager at the University of Munich, showing his membership of the Hitler Youth and the Nazi party.

Source: Archive of the University of Munich.

End of the AF and the DAWI

It is a sign of the deemed importance of AF and DAWI that most of their functions, particularly the teaching of Oriental languages, continued until the end of
the war. It was a few months after the surrender of the German Reich that the AF
and the DAWI were closed down due their evident proximity to the National
Socialist state.[264] Among the scholars of Indian Studies at the AF and DAWI who
now became unemployed, Ludwig Alsdorf spent the next few years with his
relatives in the countryside.[265] Alsdorf's membership of the NSDAP meant that
he had to go through the legalities of de-Nazification. He was classified as a
Mitläufer ('fellow traveller'), belonging to Category IV of political culpability by
the de-Nazification authorities. Though he was given permission to teach at the
University of Münster by the Military government in June 1947, the Ministry of
Culture of the state of North Rhine Westphalia (NRW) was reluctant to provide
the required directive. The University of Münster, however, was interested in
his return to the practically defunct department of Indology. To bypass the
impediments resulting from Alsdorf's proven complicity with the Nazi regime,
the University authorities, Alsdorf himself, and a number of Orientalist scholars
including Walther Schubring, Hans Heinrich Schaeder, and Helmuth von
Glasenapp, presented an exculpating narrative about Alsdorf to the Ministry. In
this retrospectively manipulated bio-data, Alsdorf's involvements with Nazi
politics were minimized and trivialized. A letter, written by Walther Schubring in
April 1948 to the Faculty of Philosophy at the University of Münster claimed that
Indology had contributed greatly to the prestige of German *Wissenschaft*.
Alsdorf's reappointment would enable him to bring in new honours for it.
Moreover, through Alsdorf's personal contacts with Indian scholars, Münster
could be a source of profitable academic relationships with India. Similar claims
of 'national prestige' and 'international connections' were often used by German
academics and institutions after 1945 to re-establish themselves.[266]

The scholars supporting this mendacious narrative had conformed in different
ways to Nazi politics. Walter Schubring, Alsdorf's research guide, was among the
scholars who had officially declared their allegiance to Adolf Hitler on 11 November
1933.[267] Glasenapp was invited to lecture on India by the *Volksbildungswerk*
which, as we have noted, aimed to spread Nazi ideology among ordinary
Germans through public lectures from 'politically reliable' academics.[268] Schaeder
was no opponent of the Nazi regime either, as we saw in this chapter. After 1945,
by attesting to Alsdorf's 'inner distance' from Nazi politics, these scholars were
also distancing themselves from their own pasts.

The 'politics of history' conducted by Alsdorf and his cohorts met with success
as the Ministry finally relented on 19 May 1948, giving Alsdorf permission to
become a guest lecturer at the University of Münster. Alsdorf continued in this
position until 1950, when he succeeded Schubring as professor of Indology at the

University of Hamburg. By the time of his death in 1978, Alsdorf had established himself as a renowned Indologist. Alsdorf's obituary mentions his early academic works related to Jainism and discusses his prolific academic writings after 1945. His wartime writings on modern India are acknowledged through a few exonerating lines, thus depoliticizing them.[269]

Among the others, Beythan and Wagner were much less fortunate. On 20 September 1945, Beythan was taken prisoner from his home at Treptow in Berlin and brought to the 'investigative custody' set up under the NKVD, the Soviet Union's secret police, a forerunner of the KGB. The NKVD had ordered the 'cleansing' of elements inimical to the Red Army, including writers who expressed anti-Soviet opinions.[270] Beythan was officially indicted by the Soviet administration of writing six articles inciting Indians to join the war against the Soviet Union. He was sentenced to 10 years of 'reformative labour' in November 1945. The septuagenarian scholar died a month later on 25 December 1945 in prison number seven at Frankfurt on the Oder in East Germany. The 'official' cause of his death was asphyxiation. Beythan was posthumously 'rehabilitated' as a victim of political oppression by the Military Prosecutor of Russian Federation on 18 November 2002 (Figure 16).[271]

A similar fate befell Reinhard Wagner in 1945. According to the historian Walter Leifer, Wagner was working on a translation of a Bengali classic novel, *Srikanto* and campaigning 'to persuade political and cultural circles in Bengal to adopt Latin alphabets for their language' when he was imprisoned by the 'Allies'. Most probably, Wagner, who lived in what would become West Berlin, was interned by the US Army. Wagner supposedly met his end at an Allied camp, the details of which are unavailable.[272] Unlike Alsdorf, who had a vast network of influential contacts who would exculpate him along with themselves, the two aged lectors had no resourceful associates who could come to their rescue.

The two Indian lectors, Tarachand Roy and Devendra Nath Bannerjea, were officially British subjects. Hence they were interned in a camp under British authority at Paderborn along with other Indian collaborators of the Nazis. In June 1946, the authorities decided to set them at liberty.[273] Roy could successfully establish that he was an insignificant lector at the University of Berlin who occasionally published philosophical and moderately nationalistic articles. In 1946, Roy managed to get a position as a lector for Indian languages at the University of Bonn.[274] In 1949, he was appointed a cultural attaché at the newly opened Indian consulate in Switzerland.[275] In 1952, Roy returned to the University of Bonn where he was welcomed back by Otto Spies, then head of the department of Oriental Studies. Spies had been involved in Nazi propaganda in India as well as in Germany, as we will see in the next chapter.[276]

When Roy applied for a German citizenship in 1957, Otto Spies as well as another Orientalist at the University of Bonn, Professor Paul Hacker, supported Roy's application, claiming that he had become a 'German in his soul'.[277] Paul

ГЕНЕРАЛЬНАЯ ПРОКУРАТУРА
РОССИЙСКОЙ ФЕДЕРАЦИИ

ГЛАВНАЯ ВОЕННАЯ ПРОКУРАТУРА

пер. Хользунова, 14,
Москва, Россия, К-160

18.11.02 № 7у/4-604302

СПРАВКА
(о реабилитации)

Гражданин: Байтан Герман
Год и место рождения: 1875 г.р., г. Тайхель (Тюрингия)
Гражданин какого государства: Германия
Национальность: немец
Место жительства до ареста: г. Берлин-Трейтов, Лайбельштрассе, 25
Место работы и должность (род занятий): писатель
Дата ареста: 20 сентября 1945 г.
Когда и каким органом осужден (репрессирован): 20 ноября 1945 г. военным трибуналом гарнизона г. Берлина
Квалификация содеянного и мера наказания (основная и дополнительная): ст. 58-2 УК РСФСР, десять лет лишения свободы в ИТЛ
Скончался в местах заключения: 25 декабря 1945 г.

На основании п. "б" ст. ст. 3 и 5 и ч. 2 ст. 8 Закона РФ от 18 октября 1991 г. "О реабилитации жертв политических репрессий" гражданин Байтан Герман реабилитирован.

П Р И М Е Ч А Н И Е: Решение о реабилитации не может служить основой для имущественных требований граждан Германии, идущих вразрез с действующим законодательством и международными обязательствами.

Заместитель начальника
управления реабилитации жертв политических репрессий
Главной военной прокуратуры   А.В. Чичуга

БА № 001123

Figure 16 Rehabilitation certificate for Hermann Beythan, issued by the Chief Military Prosecutor of the Russian Federation, dated 18.11.2002.

Source: Dokumentationsstelle Dresden/Stiftung Sächsische Gedenkstätten.

Hacker had been a member of both the Nazi Party and the SA and had served at the Eastern Front as a soldier.[278] Their support for Roy, who surely knew about their pasts as they did about his, is yet another example of collusion among professionals after 1945 to refashion their individual and collective pasts.

Devendra Nath Bannerjea taught at the Department of Indology of the University of Berlin till May 1945. His estrangement from the anti-colonial venture under Bose enabled him to erase all traces of his connections with the Nazi regime. He had, however, not given up his ambitions. In a letter to the University authorities written in December 1945, Bannerjea enquired whether the professorial post for 'Land and People of India' at the AF that had been intended for him, could be relocated in the Faculty of Philosophy in Berlin. He claimed that this post, originally designed for him, was given to Alsdorf due to intrigues of the SS with Subhas Chandra Bose, who favoured the German Indologist. Bannerjea then pointed out the different functions that Alsdorf had undertaken for the SS officer Keppler and the Foreign Ministry, without mentioning his own association with Nazi politics.[279]

In November 1946, the British surveillance in Germany wrote to the India Office in London that 'the Englishwoman Mrs Bannerjea' and her husband led a low-key existence in Germany. While they were careful not to offend the Nazis, there was no evidence that they held pro-Nazi views.[280] This lenience shown by the British authorities was probably part of a complex and problematic process of incomplete efforts at de-Nazification in the context of the Cold War since the British surveillance was thoroughly aware of Bannerjea's complicity with the Nazi regime as we saw in this chapter. Bannerjea could receive a teaching position at the University of Bamberg in Bavaria in 1946. He taught English literature there until 1950. He passed away in Bamberg in 1954.[281]

Notes

1. Bleek, Wilhelm, 2001, 192–4.
2. Ellinger, Ekkehard, 2006, 168.
3. Deutsches Kolonial Lexikon, Bd. III, 347.
4. Ibid.
5. Stoecker, Holger, 2002, 117.
6. Ibid., 120.
7. Bleek, Wilhelm, 2001, 198, 200, 203.
8. Krug, Samuel, 2020, 49.
9. Mitteilungen des Seminars für Orientalische Sprachen an der FW Uni zu Berlin (15.10.1933–15. 10.1934), 11.
10. GstAPK: IHA Rep.76 Nr.124 Bl.476, Schaeder to Reichsministerium für Wissenschaft, Erziehung und Volksbildung or Reich Education Ministry (REM), 13.4.1934.
11. Framke, Maria, 2014, 89–108; Framke, Maria, 2023, 307–32.
12. The details of Bannerjea's early life, unless otherwise stated, are from IOR/L/PJ/12/2.
13. Barooah, Nirode, 2004, 134, 230.
14. BA Berlin: R4901/24156.
15. GstAPK: IHA Rep.76 Nr.124 Bl. 637.

16. Mittheilungen des Seminar für Orientalische Sprachen an der Königliche Friedrich Wilhelms-Universität zu Berlin. Band 32, Ausgaben 2–33. 1929. VI.
17. GstAPK: IHA Rep.76 Nr.124 Bl.637.
18. BA Berlin: R4901/16260. Memorandum dated 11.12.1936.
19. Günther Lothar, Rehmer, 1990, 221.
20. Minerva Zeitschrift, Band 7–8, 1931, 122.
21. GstAPK: IHA Rep.76 Nr.124. Grundlagen der indischen Kultur. Vier Vorlesungen von Professor D.N. Bannerjea, 28.2.1930.
22. IOR/L/PJ/12–659. List of suspected Indians in Germany, 7.
23. NAUK: GFM33/565. No. 349697. Bannerjea's letter to Ernst von Weiszäcker, secretary of state of the Foreign Ministry, 29.5.43.
24. GstAPK: IHA Rep.208A Nr.3 Bl.228, Bannerjea's letter to Mittwoch, dated 5.10.1929; Bl.231, Mittwoch's letter to the Ministry of Education, 29.10.1929.
25. Mitteilungen des Seminar für Orientalischen Sprachen an der Friedrich Wilhelms Universität, Berlin. Winter Semester 1928/29, VI.
26. AHU: Rektor und Senat (R/S), 234. Auslandswissenschaftliche Fakultät. Lebenslauf Dr Reinhard Wagner.
27. Ibid.
28. Ibid.
29. On German propaganda in the First World War, see Bremm, Klaus-Jürgen, 2013.
30. On the VDA and its politics, see Krekeler, Norbert, 1973.
31. AHU: R/S 234, Lebenslauf.
32. Wagner, Reinhard, 1926, 4.
33. AHU: R/S 234, Lebenslauf.
34. Wagner, Reinhard, 1930, 1933.
35. Botsch, Gideon, 2006, 41.
36. Ellinger, Ekkehard, 2006, 39.
37. AHU: R/S 163, Personalakten Sebastian Beck. Letter from the Ministry of Education to Beck, 28.6.1927.
38. AHU: Beck's letter to the University of Berlin, 13.2.1929.
39. AHU: R/S 163, Personalakten Sebastian Beck. Dienstlaufbahn, 1940.
40. Ellinger, Ekkehard, 2006, 35.
41. AHU: R/S 163, Personalakten Sebastian Beck. Dienstlaufbahn, 1940.
42. BA Berlin: R58/7486, letter dated 22.10.1933.
43. GstAPK: IHA Rep.76 Nr.124 Bl.385. Schaeder to the Education Ministry, 4.4.1934.
44. Ellinger, Ekkehard, 2006, 182.
45. AHU: Oriental Seminar Band 245, Nr. III. Personalakten Tarachand Roy, 1934.
46. University Archive, Bonn (UAB): Tarachand Roy. Personalakt 7606.
47. AHU: Oriental Seminar Band 245, Nr. III. Personalakten Tarachand Roy, 1934.
48. Liebau, Heike, 2022.
49. NAUK: KV2/3904/3. Post-war statement of A.C.N. Nambiar, Appendix A.1.
50. Oesterheld, Joachim, 2010, 89.
51. AHU: Oriental Seminar Band 245, Nr. III. Personalakten Tarachand Roy.
52. AHU: Note of the Education Ministry, 7.5.1925.
53. AHU: note dated 28.2.1935.
54. Barooah, Nirode K., 2004, 213.
55. AHU: Oriental Seminar Band 245, Nr. III. Personalakten Tarachand Roy.
56. UAB: Tarachand Roy. Personalakt 7606. He published articles on the occasion of Gandhi's 60th birthday as well as on the Indian National Congress in different newspapers in the year 1931.
57. Das Goetheanum, 1929. Bände 8–10, 70.
58. GstAPK: IHA Rep.76 Bl.248. Letter of Roy to an unnamed official at the Education Ministry, 17.3.32.
59. GstAPK: IHA Rep.76 Bl.251.
60. GstAPK: IHA Rep.76 Bl.300. Letter dated 4.2.33.
61. GstAPK: IHA Rep.76 vaSek2 Nr.124 Bd.XIITC. Tarachand Roy's letter to the Education Ministry, 3.12.33.
62. GstPK: IHA Rep.76 vaSek2 Nr.124 Bd.XIITC Bl.152.
63. AHU: Oriental Seminar Band 245. Nr. III. Personalakten Tarachand Roy. Letter dated 30.7.1931.
64. AHU: Oriental Seminar Band 245. Nr. III. Personalakten Tarachand Roy.
65. AHU: Oriental Seminar Band 245. Nr. III. Personalakten Tarachand Roy.

66. AHU: Oriental Seminar Band 245. Nr. III. Personalakten Tarachand Roy.
67. GstAPK: IHA Rep.76 vaSek2 Nr.124 Bd.XII Bl.143–50. Letter from Schaeder to the Education Minister, 2.9.33.
68. GstAPK: IHA Rep.76 vaSek2 Nr.124 Bd.XII Bl.297. Letter dated 23.1.34.
69. GstAPK: IHA Rep.76 Nr.124 Bl.334. Kamffmeyer's note to Schaeder, 25.2.34.
70. GstAPK: IHA Rep.208A Bl.58. Schaeder to the Education Ministry, 27.11.33.
71. GstAPK: IHA Rep.208A Bl.53. Roy to Schaeder, 31.8.33. Also, Bl.51, Roy to Schaeder, 3.9.33.
72. GstAPK: IHA Rep.76 Nr.124 Bl.323–4. Letter dated 15.12.1933.
73. GstAPK: IHA Rep.208A Bl.58. Schaeder to the Education Ministry, 27.11.33.
74. Hanisch, Marc, 2014, 167–91.
75. GstAPK: IHA Rep.76 Nr.124 Bl. 324. Letter dated 15.12.33.
76. GstAPK: IHA Rep.208A Bl.51. Roy to Schaeder, 3.9.33.
77. IOR/L/PJ/12/629. List of pro-Axis Indians in Europe, 1940, 13.
78. IOR/L/PJ/12/659. List of pro-Axis Indians in Europe, 1944, 24.
79. *Mitteilungen des Seminar für Orientalische Sprachen*, 15.10.1933 to 15.10.1934. For the history of the Leipziger Mission in India, see Nehring, Andreas, 2003.
80. GstAPK: IHA Rep.76 vaSek2 Nr.124 Bd.XII Bl.103. Letter from the Lecturers' Association to the Education Ministry, 27.5.1933.
81. BA Berlin: R4901/16571. *Lebenslauf* Hermann Beythan.
82. AHU: Oriental Seminar. *Rektor und Senat* (RS) 234, *Lebenslauf* Hermann Beythan.
83. Nehring, Andreas, 2003.
84. Nehring, Andreas, 2005, 271–83.
85. AHU: R/S 234, *Lebenslauf* Hermann Beythan.
86. BA Berlin: R4901/16571. Hermann Beythan *Lebenslauf*. On the role of protectors, see Geissler, Gert, 2002, 246.
87. BA Berlin R9361/V, Sig.14161. Beythan's letter to the Reich Chamber of Literature (*Reichsschrifttumskammer*), 29.10.1938. In another letter to the Chamber, Beythan admitted joining the NS Teachers' Association, Bl.1098.
88. Franckesche Stiftungen zu Halle, ALMW II, Beythan to Ihmels, 24.9.1936.
89. BA Berlin: Beythan's letter to Reich Chamber for Literature, 29.10.1938.
90. Framke, Maria, 2014, 103.
91. Beythan, Hermann, 1936, chapter 8, 'New Dharma', translation by Dr Thomas Lehmann, SAI, University of Heidelberg. I thank Dr Lehmann and Professor Hans Harder, SAI, University of Heidelberg.
92. Ibid., chapter 15, 'Efforts to Achieve World Peace'.
93. Ibid., chapter 8.
94. Ibid., chapter 8.
95. Ibid., chapter 15.
96. Franckesche Stiftungen zu Halle, ALMW II, 31.1. 10. Beythan to Ihmels, 24.9.1936.
97. Evangelisch-Lutherisches Missionsblatt, March 1937, Nr.3, 74.
98. Franckesche Stiftungen zu Halle, ALMW II, 31.1. 10. Beythan to Ihmels, 24.9.1936 and 12.1.1937.
99. IOR: Library Reference Division: Publications proscribed by the government of India. Edition 1–31, 135. Nr.1328.
100. Franckesche Stiftungen zu Halle, ALMW II, 31.1. 10. Ihmels to Beythan, 15.1.1937.
101. Brückenhaus, Daniel, 2017, 172.
102. GstAPK: IHA Rep.76 vaSek 2 Nr.124 Bd.XII.Bl, 69.
103. On Gansser, see Gossweiler, Kurt, 1982, 346, 558–60.
104. GstAPK: IHA Rep.76 Nr.124 Bl.448.
105. GstAPK: IHA Rep.76 vaSek2 Nr.124 Bd.XII Bl.203, 1933. BA Berlin: R4901/24156. Personalakten Devendra Nath Bannerjea, Bl.2147, 1934.
106. GstAPK: IHA Rep.76 Nr.124 Bl42. Letter of recommendation for Bannerjea from Professor Ludwig Bernhard, Department of Political Science at the University of Berlin, to Ernst Schultze, 22.11.1932 mentions Grobba. On Grobba's career, see Ellinger, Ekkehard, 2006, 484–5.
107. GstAPK: IHA Rep.76 Nr.124 Bl418. Letter dated 10.7.1933.
108. GstAPK: IHA Rep.76 vaSek 2 Nr.124 Bd.XII Bl.242. Certification by Ernst Schultze, 28.11.33.
109. Bannerjea, Devendra Nath, 1934.
110. BA Berlin: R4901/24156, Bl.2141.
111. GstAPK: IHA Rep.76 vaSek2 Nr.124 Bd.XII Bl.206, Bannerjea's letter to the Kultusministerium, 7.10.33. GstAPK: IHA Rep.76 Nr.124 Bl.635, Directive from the Education Ministry, Berlin, to the Ministry of Sachsen, 10.7.33.

112. GstAPK: IHA Rep.76 vaSek2 Nr.124 Bd.XII Bl.119, 20.7.33. On Vahlen, see Grüttner, Michael, 2004, 176–7.
113. GstAPK: IHA Rep.76 Nr.124 Bl.451, 12.2.34.
114. GstAPK: IHA Rep.76 Nr.124. Bannerjea's article about 'Winter Help' was published in *The Advisor* and Hilda Bannerjea's article was published in *The Insurance and Finance Review* sometime in 1934.
115. GstAPK: IHA Rep.76 Nr.124 Bl.400. Schaeder to the Education Minister, 23.1.1934.
116. GstAPK: IHA Rep.76 Nr.124 Bl.403. Nazi Students' Association, University of Berlin to Schaeder, 22.1.1934.
117. GstAPK: IHA Rep.76 Nr.124 Bl.400. Letter dated 23.1.1934.
118. GstAPK: IHA Rep.76 Nr.124 Bl.435.
119. GstAPK: IHA Rep.76 Nr.124 Bl. 353.
120. GstAPK: IHA Rep.76 Nr.124 Bl.350–2.
121. GstAPK: IHA Rep.76 Nr.124 Bl.363. Letter from N.G. Swami, president of the Indian Students' Association to Schaeder, 30.3.1934.
122. GstAPK IHA Rep.76 Nr.124 Bl.641. Kommunismus und indische Ueberlieferung, undated.
123. On the details of M.S. Khanna's allegations, see Framke, Maria, 2013, 72.
124. GstAPK: IHA Rep.76 Nr.124 Bl.644, 645. D.N. Bannerjea, 'The Case for Germany', in *Bombay Chronicle*, 4.9.1934.
125. NAI: Home Political, NA-1925, NA-F272.
126. BA Berlin: R4901/16270. A secret report of the Reichsstudentenführung (an umbrella organization of various Nazi associations of students and teaching staff) to the Education Ministry, 30.5.38.
127. IOR/L/PJ/12/410. Indian associations in Germany.
128. Laursen, Ole Birk, 2023. https://thewire.in/world/hindustan-house-indian-restaurant-weimar-berlin.
129. GstAPK: IHA Rep.76 Nr.124 Bl.408–9.
130. GstAPK: IHA Rep.76 Nr.124 Bl.415. Bannerjea's letter to Vahlen, 10.7.33.
131. Brückenhaus, Daniel, 2017, 176.
132. PA-AA Berlin: RZ207/77416. I thank Professor Suchetana Chattopadhyay and Dr. Ole Birk laursen for sharing this file with me.
133. Bannerjea's letter to Gestapo, GstAPK: IHA Rep.76 vaSek2 Nr.124 Bd.XII Bl.272.
134. GstAPK: IHA Rep.76 Nr.68E Bd.8. Bl.78. Letter dated 22.10.1934.
135. On Eugen Mattiat, see Bozsa, Isabella, 2014.
136. BA Berlin: R4901/24156. Letter dated 29.1.34.
137. GstAPK: IHA Rep.76 vaSek2 Nr.124 Bd.XII Bl.239.
138. BA Berlin: R4901/24156. Ministerial decree dated 5.2.1935.
139. BA Berlin: R4901/24156, Bl.2182. Letter dated 29.7.35.
140. BA Berlin: R901/24156. Letter dated 8.4.1935.
141. BA Berlin: R901/24156, Bl.2202. Letter dated 5.9.35.
142. AHU: NS Dozentenschaft. Letter dated 26.3.1935.
143. BA Berlin: R4901/24156. Letter dated 9.1.1935.
144. BA Berlin: R4901/16270. Letter from Meckelein to Wiedermann.
145. BA Berlin: R4901/16270. Letter dated 9.3.1937.
146. AHU Berlin: R/S 234. Lebenslauf Wagner.
147. BA Berlin: Sig. BDC (for NSLB). NSDAP membership, R 9361-VIII KARTEI/24750011.
148. Jung, Michael, 1989, 772.
149. AHU Berlin: R/S 234.
150. Ortmeyer, Benjamin, 2013.
151. BA Berlin: NSDAP-Gaukartei, R 9361-IX KARTEI/46590498.
152. BA Berlin: Sig. BDC. Wagner joined the RLB on 19.8.33 and the FMSS on 11.4.34.
153. BA Berlin: Sig. BDC NSLB. Wagner joined the NSDB on 3.3.33.
154. Ellinger, Ekkehard, 2006, 170.
155. Leutner, Mechthild, 2001, 436–7.
156. Stoecker, Holger, 2002, 105; Ellinger, Ekkehard, 2006, 124.
157. Mitteilungen der Ausland Hochschule an der Universität Berlin. Chronicle from October 1937 to October 1938.
158. AHU Berlin: Universitätskurator (UK) 1064. NS Dozentenschaft. Letter dated 12.11.1934.
159. IOR/L/PJ/12/659. List of suspected Indians in Germany, 7.
160. BA Berlin: R4901/16270. Letter dated 27.10.37.

161. Mitteilungen der Ausland Hochschule. Chronicle from October 1937 to October 1938 and from October 1938 to October 1939.
162. BA Berlin: R4901/24156, Bl. 2221.
163. BA Berlin: R4901/24156, Bl.2247. Letter dated 24.3.1942.
164. BA Berlin: R4901/24156, Bl.2253. Letter dated 27.1.42.
165. Framke, Maria, 2023.
166. IOR/L/PJ/12/659, 7.
167. BA Berlin: R4901/24156, Bl.2238. Letter from Fels to the Education Ministry, 22.9.39.
168. BA Berlin: R4901/16571. Letter dated 25.11.36.
169. BA Berlin: R4901/16571. Letter dated 11.10.37.
170. Mitteilungen der Auslandshochschule, Sommer Semester, 1937.
171. BA Berlin: R4901/16571, Lebenslauf Beythan. Also, letter from Beythan to the *Reichsschrifttumskammer*, 29.10.1938.
172. Botsch, Gideon, 2006, 42–3.
173. Eisfeld, Rainer, 1991, 178–9.
174. For details on AF and DAWI, see Botsch, Gideon, 2006.
175. Ibid., 184.
176. On Six's engagements for Nazi politics, see Hachmeister, Lutz, 1998.
177. Augustinovic, Werner and Moll, Martin, 2017, 773.
178. Ibid., 774.
179. Schreiber, Carsten, 2019, 38.
180. Hachmeister, Lutz, 1998, 244.
181. Framke, Maria, 2014, 125.
182. BA Berlin: R901/24156. Letter dated 11.3.40.
183. AHU: R/S 163. Lehraufträge AF. June 1940–February 1945.
184. BA Berlin: R4901/24234. Letter from Six to the Education Ministry, 2.3.1940.
185. Framke, Maria, 2014, 112.
186. AHU: R/S 234, Lebenslauf, Wagner, 3.
187. NAUK: KV2/3904/2. Post-war statement of A.C.N. Nambiar, 58.
188. Conze, Eckart et al., 2010, 402.
189. BA Berlin: NS15, Bd.158a, Bl.74. Letter dated 2.2.1939.
190. NAI: EAD, File No. 341 – X. P.137. Weekly report, 22 April–6 May 1940.
191. Roy, Baijayanti, 2017, 737–41.
192. *Ostasiatische Zeitschrift*, 1940, 83.
193. Almgren, Birgitta, Hecker-Stampehl, Jan, and Piper, Ernst, 2008.
194. Der Norden, Band 19, 1942, 351.
195. IOR/L/PJ/12/513. Indians in Germany, 91.
196. Hochschule und Ausland, Band 18, 1940, 293.
197. *News from Germany*, No.30, November 1940, 10–12.
198. IOR/L/PJ/12/506. Survey number 7 of 1939, 12.
199. IOR/L/PJ/7/4538. Pol.2925\41.
200. Kuhlmann, Jan, 2003, 168.
201. NAUK: KV23-907. Statement of Mukund Rai Vyas, Appendix B.9.
202. Tarachand Roy: Subhas Chandra Bose. Das XX Jahrhundert, Band 4, 191–2.
203. Roy, Baijayanti, 2022a, 5.
204. PA-AA: RZ214/100690.
205. IOR/L/PJ/12/513. Indians in Germany, 91.
206. NAUK: KV23/907. Statement of Mukund Rai Vyas, 1945, Appendix C.16.
207. Ibid., Appendix G.6.
208. NAUK: GFM33/565. No. 345762. Rühle to Keppler, 9.2.1942.
209. Boelcke, Willi A., 1974, 247–8.
210. NAUK: KV2/3904/3. Post-war statement of A.C.N. Nambiar, 59.
211. IfZ Munich: MA1190. Letter dated 16. 1.1942.
212. IfZ Munich: MA116/1. Letter dated 11.5.1942.
213. Ibid. Letter from Dr Borger to the headquarters of the NSDAP, 12.6.1942.
214. Framke, Maria, 2014, 112.
215. AHU: Personalakten Alsdorf. H51.Bd.III.
216. *Zeitschrift für Politik*, vol. 32, no. 12 (December 1942), 824.
217. Vorlesungsverzeichnis, AF. Summer semester 1942, 12–13.
218. BA Berlin: R4901/24156, Bl.2297. Letter dated 19.1.1943.

219. Botsch, Gideon, 2006, 298.
220. BA Berlin: R4901/24156, Bl.22591. Letter dated 20.4.1942.
221. BA Berlin: R4901/24156, Bl.2261. Report dated 27.4.1942.
222. BA Berlin: R4901/24156, Bl.2248. Bannerjea to the rector of the University of Berlin, 1.4.1942.
223. BA Berlin: R4901/24156, Bl.2274, Foreign Ministry to Bannerjea, 12.6.42; Bl.2270, Bannerjea to Ribbentrop, 20.4.42.
224. BA Berlin: R4901/24156, Bl.2284. AF to the Education Ministry, 30.9.42.
225. NAUK: GFM33/564–1312. No. 349782–5.
226. NAUK: GFM33/564/13/1312. Letter dated 21.2.1943.
227. Framke, Maria, 2014, 122.
228. BA Berlin: R4901/24156, Bl.2287. Letter from Bannerjea to Von Stechow, 17.10.1942.
229. BA Berlin: R4901/24156, Bl.2286. Letter dated 24.10.1942.
230. Framke, Maria, 2014, 126.
231. Vorlesungsverzeichnis, AF. Summer Semester 1944. 49.
232. Botsch, Gideon, 2006, 299.
233. BA Berlin: R4901/24234. Letter from AF to the Education Ministry, dated 3.1.1944.
234. Vorlesungsverzeichnis, AF. Summer semester 1944, 50.
235. Beythan, Hermann, 1943.
236. AHU: R/S 163, Lehrauftrag, 31.10.1944.
237. AHU: R/S 163, Lebenslauf Albert Wissler.
238. AHU: R/S 163. Letter from the rector of the University of Berlin to the Education Ministry, 31.10.1944.
239. Botsch, Gideon, 2006, 128, 133.
240. Framke, Maria, 2014, 112.
241. Nachrichten des DAWI, November 1941, 265.
242. Pfeffer, Karl Heinz, 1942, 884–96.
243. Alsdorf, Ludwig, 1943 (1).
244. Ibid., 47.
245. Ibid., 142.
246. Alsdorf, Ludwig, 1943 (2), 637–58.
247. Alsdorf, Ludwig, 1944, 674–89.
248. On the ZfP, see Bleek, Wilhelm, 2001, 236.
249. Botsch, Gideon, 2006, 151.
250. ZfP, vol. 32, no. 5 (May 1942), 361–3.
251. ZfP, vol. 33, no. 8/9 (August/September 1943), 422–3. On Ahmed, see Hensel, Michael, http://www.hmhensel.com/hafiz-manzooruddin-ahmad/.
252. BA Berlin: R4901/24156, Bl.2255–6.
253. Botsch, Gideon, 2006, 156, 263.
254. Thierfelder, Franz, 1940, 7.
255. Ibid., 29.
256. Botsch, Gideon, 2006, 188, 269–70.
257. Lehmann, Heinz, 1942, 770–6.
258. Lehmann, Heinz, *Monatshelfte für Auswärtige Politik* (May 1942), 386–401.
259. Lehmann, Heinz, 1965.
260. Haushofer, Karl, 1941.
261. University Archive, Munich: *Karteikarte*, 1938.
262. Motadel, David, 2014, 345.
263. Hauner, Milan, 1981, 230–5; Kuhlmann, Jan, 2003, 179–82, 245–9.
264. Botsch, Gideon, 2006, 88–9.
265. Details of Alsdorf's post-war rehabilitation, unless otherwise stated, are from Roy, Baijayanti, 2023b, 275–306.
266. Schüring, Michael, 2006, 332.
267. Pollock, Sheldon, 1993, 94.
268. BA Berlin: NS15/257. Undated list of lectures for the Volksbildungserk.
269. Bruhn, 1990, 5–13.
270. Stiftung Sächsische Gedenkstätten Dokumentationsstelle, Dresden. StSG-DokStSl-2020\9. The information has been kindly provided by Dr. Bert Pampel, director of the Dresden Document Centre for the History of Resistance and Repression during the Nazi period and the SBZ\DDR. On the NKVD, see Weigelt, Andreas, 2001.

271. Stiftung Sächsische Gedenkstätten Dokumentationssttelle, Dresden. StSG-DokStSl-2020\9. I am grateful to Professor Lorenz Rumpf, Goethe University, Frankfurt am Main, for translating this document from Russian.
272. Leifer, Walter, 1977, 146.
273. Kuhlmann, Jan, 2003, 347.
274. UAB: Tarachand Roy. Personalakt 7606. Letter dated 10.7.1946.
275. UAB: Tarachand Roy. Personalakt 7606. Note dated 21.5.1949.
276. UAB: Tarachand Roy. Personalakt 7606. Letter from Otto Spies to the dean of the Philosophical Faculty, 9.1.1952.
277. UAB: Tarachand Roy. Personalakt 7606. Note from Hacker and Spies to the dean of the Philosophical Faculty, 2.10.1957.
278. Framke, Maria, 2014, 108.
279. Ibid., 122–3.
280. IOR/L/PJ12/2. Unsigned note, 20.11.1946.
281. Framke, Maria, 2023, 307–32.

The Nazi Study of India and Indian Anti-Colonialism: Knowledge Providers and Propagandists in the 'Third Reich'.
Baijayanti Roy, Oxford University Press. © Baijayanti Roy 2024. DOI: 10.1093/9780191981951.003.0004

4

'India Experts' and the Indian Legion

Background: An Indian Legion in Germany

The fourth—and last—case study relates to the deployment of the knowledge of contemporary Indian languages, culture, and history by a number of German scholars who functioned as interpreters with the 'Indian Legion'. The latter, officially known as the 'Indian Infantry Legion 950' of the Wehrmacht or the German Armed Forces was informally known as the 'Tiger Legion' since the soldiers of this Legion wore, in addition to the Wehrmacht uniform, a specially designed badge on the right arm depicting a leaping tiger.

The history and activities of the Legion have been extensively researched.[1] Nevertheless, a synopsis of its genesis and development is in order here.[2] The recruitment and training of the Legion, mostly comprising volunteers from the Indian POWs who had fought the Axis forces in Africa as a part of the British Imperial Army, started in 1941 in Germany. By the beginning of 1943, there were about 3,500 soldiers in the Indian Legion. In May 1943, the Legion was deployed near the North Sea coast in Holland. However, the cold and rainy weather of the North Sea coast appeared to dampen the spirits of the soldiers. Moreover, the German Army Staff began to suspect that the Indian legionaries developed interpersonal and even sexual relationships with the locals. A similar 'problem' had occurred in the training camps in Germany, where the 'exotic' Indian men allegedly exerted magnetic powers of attraction for the local German women. The resulting relationships threatened to disrupt the 'racial purity' of the *Volksgemeinschaft* or national community as envisaged by the Nazi regime.

In September 1943, the Legion was transferred to the south of France. They were given the task of patrolling a part of the coastline, extending about 60 km east of Bordeaux. The headquarters of the regiment was set up at Lacanau. With the exception of some units which were sent to Italy, the Legion remained in France until the Allied invasion of Normandy in June 1944, when they were forced to retreat towards Germany. During the retreat, the Legion became involved in combats with the *Maquisard* or French resistance fighters. Such skirmishes often turned brutal and led to loss of lives on both sides. In September 1944, as the Legion reached Alsace, it received the news that like the other 'foreign legions' of the Wehrmacht, it had been incorporated into the *Waffen* SS. The Indians had little choice but to obey this order, which some of them viewed with reluctance and suspicion.

By the time Christmas arrived, the Legion was stationed in Heuberg in south Germany. Here, they were imparted some training for Panzer warfare. However, in April 1945 they had to give up their weapons to the Wehrmacht as arms became scarce. The end of the Legion came in early May 1945, as most soldiers and officers, along with the interpreters, were imprisoned by the Americans. The Indians were given over to the British and subsequently sent back to India. A number of German officers and soldiers were handed over to the French and put on trial. The rest were tried in Germany under Allied jurisdiction.

While this history of the Legion is quite well known, none of the scholarly or memorial literature on the Legion has sufficiently emphasized its role as a symbol of Nazi politics and propaganda. The different kinds of knowledge pertaining to India, as deployed by the 'India experts' associated with the Legion, formed an important part of Nazi cultural politics, as this chapter intends to demonstrate. This is to be done by focusing on the relevant biographical aspects of these 'India experts'—the German scholars who functioned as interpreters and cultural mediators between the Indian soldiers and the German military personnel, as well as by examining the manifestations of the kinds of knowledge that these 'experts' produced for the Legion.

Archival materials relating to the activities of the interpreters are, however, inadequate. Therefore, we must depend partially on the available post-war reminiscences of the personnel involved with the Indian Legion, while exercising due caution about the unreliability of such memorial narratives. Attempts will be undertaken to check and supplement their accounts as far as possible with other primary and secondary sources.

Indian Legion: Political Context

In order to examine the role of the 'India experts' concerned, it is first necessary to take note of the political context in which the Indian Legion came into existence. The recruiting of *fremdvölkisch* (which can be insufficiently translated as belonging to an alien Volk, a concept that had a pronounced racial connotation) volunteers to serve in the German military began at the time of the German invasion of the Soviet Union, codenamed Operation Barbarossa.[3] During the preparations for this Operation, Hitler ordered the formation of a military Mission (codenamed *Sonderstab F*) under General Helmuth Felmy. This Mission was to be deployed in Iraq to assist the anti-colonial (anti-British) aspirations of the people there. The intervention failed, but the *Sonderstab F* was instructed to encourage anti-British propaganda in the 'Orient'. In 1941, volunteers, mostly comprising Arab students living in Germany, were organized to form the nucleus of a *Deutsch-arabischen Lehrabteilung* (German–Arabic department of instruction). The intention was to train a future Arab Legion of the Wehrmacht.[4]

Around the same time and inspired by the same example, the Nazi regime started to eye as potential recruits the Indian soldiers stationed in Africa as a part of the British Imperial Army. In early 1941, the Information department of the Foreign Ministry, together with the SD and the *Abwehr* (military secret service) started to conduct anti-British propaganda among these soldiers. Flyers in Hindustani and Punjabi, written and printed in Germany, were distributed among the Indian soldiers from Luftwaffe aircraft.[5] The stage was thus already set for the formation of an Indian Legion when Subhas Chandra Bose arrived in Berlin on 2 April 1941.

During his first meeting with the German Foreign Minister Ribbentrop on 1 May 1941, Bose suggested that the Indian POWs held by the Wehrmacht in Africa should be used to form an army which would advance together with the Wehrmacht to the port of Basra, from where the Indians would march into their homeland. This suggestion aligned well with the German strategy. Notably, during his talk with Ribbentrop, Bose emphasized the propagandistic value of the Indian Legion, claiming that the latter would inspire Indian soldiers of the British Army in India to revolt against their colonial masters.[6] This symbolic value of the Indian Legion corresponded to Nazi Germany's wartime attempts to project itself as a well-wisher of the Indian anti-colonial movement. However, Bose laid down one condition: the Legion should be 'kept in the background' in the European theatre of the war and deployed only on the route to India and solely against the British. This condition was accepted by the Foreign Ministry and the Wehrmacht.[7]

According to the post-war statement of Hans Franzen, who served as an officer of the Indian Legion, the latter was a 'political instrument' in Hitler's war of conquest; it was to be a flag-bearer when German military divisions stood before Alexandria and before the Caucasus. But for Bose, claimed Franzen, the Legion was the core of an 'Indian National Army'. It was to conduct a military campaign against the British in India. The two distinct aims were reconciled only through common enmity against the British.[8] The first set of Indian POWs, comprising about 1,200 men, was taken by Field Marshall Rommel's *Afrika Korps* at El Macchili in April 1941.[9] Some of these POWs formed the first group of volunteers for the Indian Legion. The formation of the Legion actually began in December 1941, soon after Germany declared war on the USA.[10]

Though Bose and a few of his Indian associates from the Free India Centre campaigned intensively among the Indian POWs to join the Indian Legion as volunteers, only a small percentage could be convinced to join his cause (Figure 17). This was because most Indian POWs in Germany were ordinary soldiers for whom freedom from colonial rule was an abstract notion. Besides, the situation of the Indian POWs was in some respects better than the prisoners from some other countries and even the average German citizen. One luxury that the Indian POWs enjoyed comprised the Red Cross packets sent twice a month from Canada. These packets contained items like rice, sugar, cigarettes, tea, chocolates,

Figure 17 Subhas Chandra Bose and the Indian Legion, 1942.
Source: Bundesarchiv 1011-823-2704-30/Aschenbroich/CC-BY-SA 3.0.

and tinned meat, which were out of bounds even for most ordinary citizens of wartime Germany.[11] The importance of these packets is underscored by the fact that the Red Cross was not informed of the formation of the Indian Legion since the soldiers who joined the Legion automatically lost their POW status and were no longer entitled to these parcels. Thus, the soldiers joining the Legion continued to be registered as POWs so that they could continue to receive the Red Cross parcels.[12]

Right from the beginning, the Wehrmacht intended to exercise full control over the Indian Legion, as a note written in 1943 by Hans Kutscher, one of the adjutants, indicates. Kutscher hinted that the Wehrmacht could not repose full trust in Bose. Hence, it decided that 'The Legionaries must become accustomed under all circumstances to obey only the orders of their military commanders' (i.e. senior Wehrmacht officials).[13] This could be achieved primarily through political propaganda glorifying the achievements of Nazi Germany and its 'Führer' as well as by indoctrinating the soldiers in the Nazi world view. This was of course, not an isolated instance. Nazi propaganda was conducted by the Wehrmacht among all its soldiers, German and foreign, since ideological indoctrination was supposed to complement the use of physical weapons.[14]

By February 1942, military training of the Indian soldiers was in full swing. Major Kurt Krappe, who joined the Legion in December 1941, had already been appointed commander of the Legion.[15] The reason for Krappe's appointment, according to a post-war British report, was that he had lived in Tanganyika in Africa for a long time and had experience in dealing with 'colonials'. The report also claimed that Krappe was an alcoholic and incompetent military officer who supported the Nazis.[16]

This view was also reiterated by Eugen Rose, an evangelical pastor and Indologist who served as an interpreter with the Legion.[17] The formation of the Indian Legion was thus an undertaking dictated more by the exigencies of German politics rather than military demands.

Interpreters and Cultural Mediators

Training and commanding the Indian soldiers posed some unique challenges for the Germans. In the British Indian Army, every regiment consisted of battalions formed on the basis of religion, region, or ethnicity (Sikh, Pathan, Rajput, Maratha, etc.). The language of command was English. Following his political vision, Bose wanted the soldiers to bridge the chasms of caste, creed, region, and language. He was convinced that bridging the divisions prevailing in the British Army would lead to true comradeship among the soldiers, which would in turn generate a pan-Indian nationalist consciousness.[18] Following Bose's principles, Hindustani, the popular language of north India was to be the language of command. Every unit of the Indian Legion was to incorporate men from diverse religious, linguistic, and regional backgrounds who were expected to intermingle freely on the battlefield as well as in the living quarters.

The result of this 'colourful mixing', in the words of Lieutenant Ulrich von Kritter, one of the officers responsible for training the Indians, was that 'certain inconveniences had to be consciously accepted'.[19] Such 'inconveniences' included the preparation of different meals (vegetarian, halal, prohibitions on certain kinds of meat for certain groups), as well as the different religious practices (prayer times, religious festivals). A list of holidays for religious occasions of the three major faiths represented within the Legion (Sikhism, Hinduism, and Islam) needed to be compiled as well. Such specialized knowledge was to be provided by the 'India experts' who were employed as interpreters with the Legion.

Interpretation (*dolmetschen*) for any official entity in the 'Third Reich' had a political aspect. The Nazi regime considered professional interpretation to be a highly politicized occupation and expected the interpreters to be 'politically reliable' agents who would, along with translating languages, propagate the greatness of the 'Reich' among foreigners. It was therefore in the interest of the Nazi government to indoctrinate the interpreters in Nazi ideology.[20] The training of military interpreters was conducted under the aegis of the Wehrmacht at the *Dolmetscher-Lehr-und-Ausbildungskompanien* (companies for training of interpreters) in Berlin.

Another institute in Meißen in Saxony trained the personnel to gather military news in foreign languages. Persons called upon to teach at these institutes and occasionally to function as interpreters in the battlefields were men who had 'lived experiences' in foreign countries, like professional academics, missionaries, and traders.[21] The books for training military interpreters were provided by a Nazified Council for professional interpreters (*Reichsfachschaft für das Dolmetscherwesen* or RfD). Along with fulfilling the requirements of the Wehrmacht, the textbooks served as 'vehicles for Nazi ideology'.[22] Such ideological infiltration was considered particularly important for the foreign legions since they needed to be made aware of the purpose and aims of the military operations from the Nazi standpoint.[23]

It was a sign of the political importance of the professional interpreters working for the Wehrmacht that they had to take an official oath of loyalty to Hitler.[24] All these factors were reflected in the different undertakings of the interpreters accompanying the Indian Legion.

Linguistic Devices as Propaganda Tools: Ernst Bannerth and Otto Spies

Most of the scholars working as interpreters with the Indian Legion were well equipped to answer the political demands of the NS regime. Some of these scholars were already actively involved in National Socialist politics. In some instances, the connections between the scholars and the Nazi political establishment were more complicated, as in the case of the chief interpreter of the Legion, Dr Ernst Bannerth (1895–1976).

A scion of a well-to-do family from Leipzig, Bannerth had joined the German Army during the First World War.[25] In 1916, he was made a lieutenant in the German Asian Corps which was assisting the Turkish troops in the Persian Gulf. After a year of combat, Bannerth was taken prisoner by the British. During his imprisonment, which lasted till 1920, Bannerth learnt Arabic and started working as an interpreter. For the last two years of his captivity, he was lodged at the POW camp in Ahmednagar in India (the relevant surveillance record erroneously claims that it was Ahmedabad). Here he picked up Urdu, which was spoken widely in north India and was associated predominantly with Indian Muslims.[26]

After returning to Germany in the aftermath of the First World War, Bannerth entered the Church. He completed his studies in theology in Vienna and became a pastor in 1930. Soon thereafter, he shifted permanently to Austria. From 1933, Bannerth worked as a chaplain at Stoob, a town in Burgenland near the Hungarian border. During this time, Bannerth took up the study of *Orientalistik* (Oriental subjects) in Leipzig and Vienna and completed his dissertation from the University of Vienna in 1941. According to a British report, in 1942 Bannerth was called upon as a military interpreter, on account of his knowledge of Hindustani, the 'street language' of north India which was heavily influenced by Urdu. Bannerth was given training in military interpretation at the department of interpretation in Rosslauer Kaserne, Vienna, and sent to the military camp of Frankenberg in Saxony where the soldiers of the Indian Legion were being trained.[27] Bannerth worked as an interpreter with the Indian Legion until 23 August 1944, when he deserted the Legion together with the regiment's attendant physician, Dr Ernst Koch- Grünberg, the adjutant officer Heinrich von Trott, and a few Indian followers. The group joined the *Maquisards* or French resistance fighters who, however, were suspicious of their intentions and gave them over to the British authorities.[28]

In his post-war statement given to the British military authorities, Bannerth claimed that after he was recruited for the Indian Legion, the Gestapo kept an eye on him since they knew about his 'Catholic activities' in Austria.[29] Bannerth also professed that he conducted propaganda among the Indian soldiers of the Legion, urging them to join the Allies.[30] A closer look into Bannerth's past, however, reveals some nuances that he elided from his tale. During his time as a pastor in Burgenland, Bannerth served as a curator of the conservative nationalist group, *Burgenländisch Heimatschütz*. Bannerth's political activities did bring him into conflict with the Nazis soon after Austria was incorporated into the 'Reich' in 1938, leading to his imprisonment which lasted a few months.[31] However, contrary to the image that he tried to project after the war, Bannerth was no progressive anti-Nazi resistance fighter. He belonged to the politicized Catholics who saw themselves as Austrian nationalists. Most of them supported the authoritarian Austrian government, the *Ständestaat*, which was headed by Engelbart Dollfuß, a politician deeply influenced by certain fascist notions. Dollfuß and his followers resented the Nazis because the latter did not possess an Austrian identity, which, for them, was based largely on Catholic faith.[32]

Since Bannerth belonged to this *austrofascist* or Austrian fascist political milieu, it is evident that his opposition to Nazism was not exactly grounded on anti-fascist politics. Some of the British personnel interrogating Bannerth suspected that the latter had deserted the sinking ship since he was 'hopeful of securing some good post in the new German government when it is formed (after the war)'.[33] In his reminiscences, the interpreter Rudolf Hartog claimed that Bannerth played an 'opaque' role after his desertion by incriminating Krappe and other officers and later withdrawing his allegations about some of them.[34] The post-war letter of Eugen Rose, the other pastor associated with the Indian Legion, requesting Bannerth to exonerate Krappe, probably led Bannerth to relent.[35]

Bannerth's initial duty in the Legion was to teach Hindustani to the German officers and military trainers. He began this task in 1942 with the assistance of Otto Spies, then professor for Arabic and Islamic Studies (*Islamkunde*) at the University of Breslau (now Wroclaw in Poland) whom we have encountered briefly.[36] A joint composition of Spies and Bannerth was the *Lehrbuch der Hindustani Sprache* (*Textbook for Hindustani Language*), published in 1945, too late to be of any use to the Legion. The book provides a practical guide to Hindustani through 30 lessons, incorporating written scripts in Arabic (adapted in Urdu) and Devanagari (used in Hindi).[37]

According to Eugen Rose, the textbook was written under the supervision of the department Ic of the Wehrmacht.[38] This department was originally responsible for military intelligence. From 1939, it started to cooperate with the Propaganda Units (PK or *Propaganda Kompanie*) of the Wehrmacht in providing news of the war, conducting propaganda in the occupied areas, and 'caring' for soldiers at the Front. The 'care service for the troops' (*Truppenbetreuung*) included procuring and generating books and magazines including foreign language ones for the soldiers, who were provided spiritual or religious ministration as well.[39] This 'care service' also entailed a thorough indoctrination of the soldiers in Nazi *Weltanschauung*. It was an instrument for bringing about the *gleichschaltung* of the Wehrmacht.[40]

The book by Bannerth and Spies omitted to mention its connections to the Indian Legion. Nor did it reveal that one of the writers, Bannerth, had already deserted. The preface thanked 'our comrade' the Indo-Iranist Karl Hoffmann, who, it was stated, was with the Wehrmacht at the time. Special thanks were offered to Tarachand Roy, 'M.A., Professor in Lahore', who 'kindly proof read and offered many suggestions for improvement'.[41] The final proof of the book allegedly reached the Legion's staff on 16 January 1945. It was read by Otto Spies, his 'Indian comrades' from the *Waffen* SS as well as by Karl Hoffman and 'Cron', the pseudonym that Eugen Rose used for himself in his auto-fictional work which forms an important if imperfect source for this discussion.[42] However, neither Rose nor the unnamed Indians were mentioned in the preface of the published version.

The book did not contain any overtly political lessons, except an article titled 'The National Government in Burma' (*Burma men qaumi hukumat*).[43] This text depicted the puppet regime installed in Burma in 1942 by the Japanese as a quasi-independent entity. However, even a cursory reading of the book reveals that its real purpose was to teach the German personnel to decipher hand-written Hindustani, presumably so that they could censor the posts sent and received by the Indian soldiers. The book emphasized studying cursive handwritings and *shiksata*, the form of Nastaliq script used for writing letters and notes.[44] In following this political objective, this book was not unique. It was preceded by at least two similar texts. One of them was *Hindustani Briefe* (*Hindustani Letters*) written by Ernst Bannerth and published in 1943. It contained 15 Urdu and six Hindi letters, along with their transcription and translation.[45]

Censoring letters was a politically significant function in the totalitarian, paranoia-ridden ambience permeating Nazi Germany. The Wehrmacht was not immune to the climate of perennial suspicion. The personnel censoring letters were required to submit a monthly report on them to the department of Military Intelligence III. The military and political establishments needed to know about the prevailing mood of the soldiers and to guard against all 'negative influences' that incoming and outgoing letters had the potential to transmit.[46]

Apart from these workbooks, a German–Hindustani military dictionary was published in 1943 by the High Command of the Army (*Oberkommando des Heeres* or OKH). It was called *Military Dictionary for the Leaders and Assistant Leaders* (*Militärwörterbuch für den Führer und Unterführer*) and claimed to have been produced through the efforts of the Indian Legion. According to a later statement of the Indologist Wilhelm Rau (1922–1999), who functioned as an interpreter for an Ersatz battalion of Indian soldiers stationed at Naundorf, the function of the dictionary was to find Hindustani equivalents for military commands in German, so that the officers of the Wehrmacht could learn them by rote without having to master the Hindustani language.[47] The military dictionary used the Urdu (Nastaliq) script and Latin transcripts.[48] The authors of the dictionary, which seemed to have enjoyed little popularity among the German soldiers, remain anonymous.[49] These books were also intended to reinforce the propaganda trope of Germany being a friend and benefactor of Indian anti-colonialists. Wilhelm Rau expressed this political purpose decades later, as he claimed that the military dictionary represented 'a remarkable accommodation' on the part of the Germans, since in the British Indian Army the Indian soldiers had to learn the commands, which were in English.[50]

The military dictionary was followed in October 1944 by a shorter version called *Abriß der Hindustani Sprachlehre und deutsch-indisches Wörterverzeichnis*

(*Outline of Hindustani Grammar and German-Indian List of Words*). It used only 'Roman Hindustani', which Bose wanted to be the written language of the Legion. The preface of the book claimed that this work was a contribution to the deepening friendship between the 'Greater German Reich' and the Indian national movement.[51] This dictionary was informally known as '*Kleine Hoffmann*' (Little Hoffmann) after the scholar Karl Hoffmann who contributed the most to it.[52]

The *Hindustani Lehrbuch*, published under the names of Spies and Bannerth, and Eugen Rose's version of its genesis, indicate that Otto Spies was attached to the Indian Legion until the end. This contradicts a British report which claimed that Spies joined the Legion in June 1942 but left soon thereafter since his knowledge of the script was considered to be insufficient.[53]

A similar claim was made by Ulrich von Kritter in his diary.[54] Letters written by the authorities of the University of Breslau in mid-1942, requesting the return of Spies to the University mention that he was posted at the *Arbeitskommando* in Frankenberg where he was devoid of 'any major engagement'. The letters indicate that Spies had been enlisted by the Wehrmacht to teach Islamic subjects (*Islamkunde*) but the course attracted few students.[55]

One of the main tasks of the *Arbeitskommando* at Frankenberg was to win over potential legionaries from the Indian POWs so that they could be trained.[56] The Islamic Studies course offered by Spies was probably a cover for conducting such recruitment propaganda. Ulrich von Kritter's diary also indicates that both Spies and Bannerth functioned as propagandists for recruitments to the Indian Legion.[57] The aforementioned letters hint that in the initial days, the recruitment propaganda had only limited success, an impression confirmed by other sources.[58] Interestingly, the University of Breslau wanted to recall Spies for performing the 'national duties' of teaching about the Near East, a 'politically significant area'. He was asked to occupy the Chair for Turkish Studies, which, according to the University authorities, was a medium for conducting German propaganda among the Turks.[59] This incident demonstrates once more that the employment of scholars, whether with the Army or with the University, was often dependent on their usefulness in terms of Nazi Germany's political, cultural, or military interests, which could align as well as differ substantially.

Commissioning Otto Spies, an expert on Islamic (Arabic, Persian, and Turkish) languages for the Indian Legion was, as with Ludwig Alsdorf, due to his 'living experience' of India. Since Spies had spent several years in India, it was assumed that he had acquaintance with Hindustani. Spies himself would later claim that though he had good theoretical knowledge of Hindustani, Arabic, and Hebrew, he could not speak these languages so well.[60] This was probably what the British record meant when it commented about his insufficient linguistic skills. According to Eugen Rose, after he failed to demonstrate an adequate knowledge of spoken Hindustani, Spies was sent to work with a smaller unit, a *Kompanie* of the Legion, signifying a demotion.[61]

Spies' knowledge of Hindustani and his role in the Indian Legion remain debatable, but his loyalty to Nazism remains beyond doubt. Otto Spies pursued Oriental Studies as well as jurisprudence in Bonn and Tübingen, acquiring a doctorate in the former subject from Tübingen in 1923 and another in the latter from Bonn in 1924. From May 1925, he joined the department of Oriental Studies at the University of Bonn, where he completed his *Habilitation* on Islamic law in 1928. After a stint as a researcher in Istanbul, Spies took up a position as professor of Arabic and Islamic Studies at the Aligarh Muslim University (AMU) in north India in October 1932. [62]

At Aligarh, Spies established himself as a propagandist for the 'new national Germany' which, according to him, was being maligned in India through British influence. He stated this in a letter dated 19 September 1933, to the curator of the University of Bonn, with a copy to the Prussian Minister for Education. Spies cited this political engagement as he pleaded for an extension of the lien from the University of Bonn. He professed that he had joined 'the movement' back in 1930. He also maintained that after joining the AMU, he and Sattar Kheiri, the German lector at the Aligarh Muslim University, had established a 'German Society' which organized lectures and published a journal disseminating the 'true face' of the 'new national Germany'.[63]

The German Society of the AMU did earn the reputation of being a mouthpiece for Hitler and his government in India.[64] Such 'German cultural politics in the Orient', as Spies claimed in a bio-data that he submitted to the rector of the University of Breslau in 1936, probably had a connection in securing him a position with a professorial title at the Arabic and Islamic Studies Department at this University in the same year.[65] In another bio-data submitted to this University, Spies claimed that he had been a part of the Nazi party's 'external section' (*Auslandsorganisation*) in Calcutta, India.[66]

After joining the University of Breslau, Spies functioned as the head of the 'External Section' of the *Dozentenschaft* (the Nazified organization of lecturers), a political function valued by the University authorities, as we saw in the case of Ludwig Alsdorf.[67] Unlike Alsdorf, however, by the time Spies officially joined the NSDAP in 1937, he had established himself as a loyal National Socialist. In 1942, the University successfully applied to the Minister for Education to promote Spies to a full professor on the grounds of his academic works as well as his political role.[68]

Bhaiband: Axis Propaganda, Anti-Colonialism, and 'Expert Knowledge' of India

A tangible testimony to the role of the scholar-interpreters in the Legion is its magazine (*Legionszeitung*) called *Bhaiband* (*Brotherhood*). It was called *Kamerad*

(*Comrade*) in its German translation. Written initially by hand in Devanagari and Nastaliq and from the end of 1944 in Latin script, this pamphlet was edited by successive German scholars. It was published at close but irregular intervals from mid-1943 until the end of April 1945. It is, however, not known how many copies of each issue were published.

Several copies of the *Bhaiband*, held at the German Military Archives in Freiburg, bear the official stamp OKW/Wpr, signifying that these pamphlets were supervised by the department of Wehrmacht propaganda (Wpr). This department, set up in 1939 by the OKW (the High Command of the Armed Forces), was responsible for military propaganda, 'care service for the troops', and military censor.[69] In 1941, it was subordinated to the aforementioned section 1c of the Wehrmacht.[70]

In its structure and contents, *Bhaiband* echoes various magazines issued by the Wehrmacht for 'Troop support', as part of its care service. Such magazines were important since they aimed both to counter enemy propaganda and to influence the soldiers' psychology and political attitudes. The contents of such magazines generally followed the same pattern. They included 'news' of military developments, political articles disseminating National Socialist ideology, texts which were supposedly written by soldiers, and some light-hearted subjects like jokes, short stories, and poems.[71]

In his post-war statement, Bannerth claimed that in the spring of 1943, he was asked by the OKW to edit a news sheet for the soldiers of the Indian Legion, then stationed in Holland. The pamphlet was expected to counter the low spirits and demotivation that prevailed among the soldiers.[72] Bannerth maintained that the texts of this magazine, *Bhaiband*, were written by the soldiers. *Bhaiband* did publish regular calls to the soldiers to contribute and some of the poems or jokes seem indeed to have come from them. But most of the texts conveyed ideological, religious, and military propaganda which evidently followed the prototype provided by the Wehrmacht. Such propaganda was indeed beyond the cognitive horizons of the Indian soldiers.

Moreover, the texts written in Devanagari and Nastaliq appear to have been created by non-native speakers, who almost literally translated their thoughts from another language, presumably German. As a result, the syntax, vocabulary, and grammar in these texts are often erroneous and highly uneven. In any case, *Bhaiband* was deliberately written in rudimentary language, since few if any of its readers had attained a high level of education. Eugen Rose claimed that Bannerth had three Indian 'writing slaves' from the Legion: Hassan Beg for Urdu, Thakur for Hindi, and Jamil Ahmad for illustrations. Bannerth supposedly isolated himself in a 'special apartment' where he 'composed' the *Bhaiband* with the help of his 'writing slaves' who followed him as he deserted the Legion.[73]

In the absence of the voices of the Indians who took part in the creation as well as the perusal of *Bhaiband*, it is not easy to ascertain how it was received by the soldiers. What is fairly certain is that this magazine was regarded as an effective instrument for influencing soldiers by the German military personnel.[74]

Bhaiband was not the only magazine which was designed especially for Indian soldiers in Nazi Germany. An Urdu magazine called *Azad Hind* was published primarily for the Indian POWs in Germany who refused to join the Indian Legion. It was written and edited by Habibur Rahman, the trusted follower of Bose and a valued employee of the German Ministry of Propaganda.[75] What the magazines had in common was their role as an instrument of Axis propaganda, particularly military propaganda which was combined with the promotion of Bose's nationalist agenda. A precedent of the German government creating propagandistic magazines for Indian soldiers with the help of Orientalist scholars had already been set during the First World War with the publication of *Hindostan*, a journal for the Indian POWs. It contained mostly pro-German propaganda and some amount of radical anti-colonialist/anti-British items, a pattern that was repeated to some extent in *Bhaiband*. In fact, the German Foreign Ministry had unsuccessfully attempted to induce South Asian POWs to join the German Army during the First World War.[76]

The title *Bhaiband* hinted at a combat fraternity or community (*Kampfgemeinschaft*), a form of group identity that the Wehrmacht evidently thought was capable of holding the troops together.[77] The cover of every issue of *Bhaiband* contained two sketches—a mountain range and a sea coast—representing the Himalayas and the Kanyakumari, the two geographical end points of India. The idea of this masthead and illustrations supposedly came from Jamil Ahmed.[78]

In his recollections, Eugen Rose claimed to have been involved in the production of *Bhaiband* almost from its inception. He purportedly found a press at Bordeux for printing this hand-written magazine.[79] According to a post-war British report, Delmas in Bordeux printed issues of *Bhaiband* though it is not clear whether Rose had been the one to find it.[80] However, none of the other works dealing with the Indian Legion mentions Rose's connections to *Bhaiband*. Details of his background including his relationship with Nazi politics are also somewhat nebulous.

Eugen Rose (1909–2003) was born in Barmen in Wuppertal.[81] He completed his doctorate in Indology from the University of Bonn in 1933. Simultaneously, he trained to be an Evangelical theologian and a pastor. For a time, Rose was influenced by the *Bekennende Kirche* (Confessional Church) which tried to resist the Nazification of the Protestant Church in Germany. During this time, Rose associated with the anti-Nazi theologian and pastor, Dietrich Bonhoeffer, the founder of the *Bekennende Kirche*. Based on this short-lived association, Rose could later style himself as an anti-Nazi whose name 'stood on the black list of the Gestapo', as a British record claims.[82]

In 1936, Rose attended Bonhoeffer's lectures at the seminary of the *Bekennende Kirche* in Finkenwalde (now in Poland). The seminary was being watched by the

Gestapo. This incident probably formed the basis of Rose's later claim of being in this dreaded Organization's black book. However, by 1937, during a wave of arrests of persons connected to the *Bekennende Kirche*, Rose moved away from this Church or made a successful show of doing so. To all appearances, Rose returned to the mainstream Protestant Church, completing his ordination at Mühlheim in 1937. He started working as an auxiliary priest for a church in Brandenburg in the same year. From 1939 to 1945, he held the position of pastor in this church. This short background indicates that Rose was possibly not very deeply involved with the anti-Nazi activities of the *Bekennende Kirche* and also that he was flexible about public displays of his political orientation.

Early on in 1943, the young pastor was sent to the interpreter training institute in Berlin. He took courses in Hindustani from 15 February to 15 August. At the end of his training, he was certified as being 'supremely able to read difficult Indian handwriting' for which he was employed to censor the posts of the Indian POWs.[83] This indicates, apart from Rose's linguistic proficiency, the authorities' implicit trust in him, since, as we noted, censoring the soldiers' letters was a politically sensitive function.

Rose was posted with the Indian Legion as a *Sonderführer* ('special leader') with limited military command from 9 September 1943.[84] In his memorial narrative, Rose claimed that while he did not get along well with the Jesuit priest Bannerth, he did find an ally in the ethnologist Günther Spannaus, who was a 'silent member of the *Bekennende Kirche*'.[85] Spannaus was both an interpreter with the Regiment Staff as well as an officer in the Wehrmacht division 1b, which was responsible for supplying provisions.

After the war, Spannaus claimed that he was against the Nazis and he tried to resist the Indian Legion's absorption into the SS.[86] This particular narrative is open to doubt. Günther Spannaus (1901–1984) belonged to the Nazi academic-political complex in multiple ways. He was a loyal student of the ethnologist Otto Reche, who was active in several Nazi organizations including the NSDAP.[87] Spannaus endorsed Reche's views on racial hygiene, which provided academic legitimacy to Nazi racial politics.[88] By 1935, Spannaus had joined the SA.[89] He began working for the OKW from 1938 and was sent to the Indian Legion in January 1944.[90] Interestingly, he also received an assignment to teach 'colonial anthropology' at the DAWI.[91] As we have seen in the last chapter, such assignments at the DAWI were frequently handed out to loyalists of the NS regime, either as rewards or sinecures, or as a cover for other 'politically important' functions. These factors indicate that instead of opposing the Nazi regime, Spannaus concurred with different aspects of Nazi politics.

After Bannerth's desertion, Rose alias 'Cron' claimed to have been 'promoted' to the rank of editor of *Bhaiband* along with the Indo-Iranist Karl Hoffman.[92] However, in the near canonical narrative of the Indian Legion provided by Rudolf Hartog, only the scholars Paul Thieme and Karl Hoffmann are mentioned as the editorial successors to Bannerth.[93] In a biographical essay on Paul Thieme, his wife Renate Sohnen-Thieme also claimed that her husband, together with Hoffmann, edited *Bhaiband* 'which was supposed to promote the feeling of solidarity' in the Legion.[94] Notably, Rose's book was published in 1979 when both Thieme and Hoffman were alive. Hartog's reminiscences also appeared during Eugen Rose's lifetime. It is not known whether this discrepancy led to any formal or informal disputes among those 'India experts'. Since historical records are unable to resolve this issue, it is probably not too far-fetched to assume that Rose was involved in the production of *Bhaiband* in an 'unofficial' capacity.

By all accounts, Karl Hoffmann took a leading role in the composition of *Bhaiband*. Hoffmann joined the Legion sometime in 1943. According to the rather dramatic account provided by Eugen Rose, the young scholar landed up unannounced at the Legion's headquarters in Lacanau and introduced himself as 'a real pig from the Front' (*ein richtiges Frontschwein*) who had to wear the same shirt for nine months and whose toes had frozen in the severe Russian winter. After a short spell of recovery, he had been sent to the Indian Legion which, however, had not been informed of his imminent arrival.[95]

How did this extraordinary posting come about? The answer lies in Hoffmann's trajectory. Karl Hoffmann (1915–1996), the son of a railway official in Bavaria, joined the University of Munich in 1934 to study Indology, *Iranistik* and *Indogermanistik* (Iranian and Indo-German studies). The bio-data that he submitted to the University of Munich after the war provides some glimpses of Hoffmann's student life. It claims that he had joined the right-wing paramilitary group, *Stahlhelm* ('steel helmet') in November 1933 while at school, since it had been made obligatory for his batch. Similarly, he had been enlisted as a member of the SA during his university days, but he had resigned from this notorious paramilitary group on 20 May 1938, citing professional reasons. The bio-data also states that during his time at the University of Munich, Hoffmann studied under the professors Otto Mausser, Hanns Oertel, Rudolf Pfeiffer, Albert Rehm, Josef Schnetz, Ferdinand Sommer, and Walther Wüst.[96]

This bio-data is noteworthy for eliding and playing down several aspects of Hoffmann's student life, the most conspicuous of which is the marginalization of his connections with Walther Wüst. The latter's influence on Hoffmann's career and life was enormous. Hoffmann, by all accounts a prodigiously talented linguist, was a prized student of Wüst, who became his research guide when he began his dissertation in 1937. Wüst apparently promised his favourite student a position in an institute that he wished to set up in Munich, as Hoffmann wrote in a letter to the military authorities in 1937, requesting a shortening of his military service.[97] This request was supported in writing by Wüst, then SS *Hauptsturmführer* and dean of the Faculty of Philosophy of the University of Munich. In this letter, Wüst described Hoffmann as an efficient SA man and as an exceptionally talented student, who had chosen to study one of the most important cultural political subjects in the 'Third Reich'. Hoffmann was given a prolonged exemption from military service, because Himmler, who was on amiable terms with Wüst, personally approved of Hoffmann's application.[98]

These details were understandably missing from Hoffmann's post-war curriculum vita, which also left out the fact that in July 1938, soon after his exit from the SA, Wüst facilitated Hoffmann's entry into the more elite and powerful SS.[99] Wüst also promoted Hoffmann's academic career by publishing his article on *Vedische Namen* (Vedic names) in the journal *Wörter und Sachen* (Words and Objects) in 1940.[100] Wüst exerted considerable influence on this academic journal, which he succeeded in bringing 'fully within the orbit of the SS'.[101]

Hoffmann's dissertation, on *Die altindoarischen Wörter mit -nd- besonders in Rgveda* ('The old Indo-Aryan Words with nd, especially in the Rg Veda') was officially passed on 29 January 1940. However, he received his PhD certificate on 5 April 1941 due to the disruption caused by the war.[102] As the president of the *Ahnenerbe*, Wüst managed to include Hoffmann's dissertation in the series published by this organization, which also paid a part of the subvention required to publish the dissertation as a monograph.[103]

In another manifestation of favour, Wüst placed Hoffmann in one of the research projects of *Ahnenerbe*.[104] The project was called '*Wald und Baum in der arisch-germanischen Geistes und Kulturgeschichte*' ('Forest and Tree in Aryan-Germanic Spiritual and Cultural History'). The aim of this project was to provide pseudo-scientific legitimacy to the myth of the Germans being warlike forest dwellers, an idea that had found favour with the *Völkisch* movement and was subsequently taken up by Himmler.[105] Wüst provided a list of ideas for individual projects, to be pursued in 1937 and 1938 within the framework of the research concept. The individual topics were oriented towards 'Aryan-Germanic history'. He also presided over the project committee.[106] For Himmler and his SS, the ideal personnel to be engaged in this project were not traditional bookish academics from the universities, but young dynamic researchers who were imbued with National Socialist ideals, preferably incubated in the *Ahnenerbe* itself.[107]

Hoffmann fitted this description in every respect. Wüst had already engaged him to work for the *Ahnenerbe* from 1 June 1936, in Wüst's own project of compiling a '*Vergleichenden und etymologischen Wörterbuch des Alt-Indoarischen*' (*Comparative and Etymological Dictionary of Ancient Indoaryans*).[108] Hoffmann's research within the *Wald und Baum* project was on the spurious subject of '*Wald und Baum in der arischen Überlieferung*' ('Forest and Tree in the Aryan Tradition'). Notably, Wüst himself made the final selection of the candidates for this project. As part of the selection process, he consulted the dossiers of the SD on each individual candidate to determine whether they ideologically conformed to National Socialism.[109] Presumably, the SD report on Hoffmann confirmed his suitability. Wüst himself informed his 'dear comrade Hoffmann' of the felicitous news of his selection, which could not have come as a surprise for this protégé of Wüst.[110]

Meanwhile, Hoffman had advanced to the position of *Rottenführer* (akin to a squadron leader) within the SS. He requested further exemption from military service while he worked on his individual research project within the conceptual parameters of *Wald und Baum*.[111] Wüst ensured that this wish was also fulfilled by warranting that Hoffmann's research work for the *Ahnenerbe* was to be considered equivalent to rendering a service for the SS.[112] It is not known whether Hoffmann's research for this specious project was ever published or even undertaken.

Hoffmann was therefore well on his way to become an ideal 'Nazi academic', following the footsteps of his mentor, the multi-functionary Wüst. However, despite the best efforts of the powerful Wüst, Hoffmann could not evade military service forever. On 31 August 1939, he was called to military duty. He participated in the invasion of France in 1940. From 22 January 1942, he was posted at the Eastern Front which had by that time become a disastrous killing field. It was again Walther Wüst who saved Hoffmann from a possibly lethal fate at the Eastern Front by managing to recall him on the pretext of engaging him in a secret assignment related to Germany's external politics. Hoffmann was supposed to be deployed in a 'significant propaganda work of an academic nature' ordered by the *Reichsführer SS*.[113]

Wüst probably took Himmler's help in arranging Hoffmann to be sent to the Indian Legion. Hoffmann had to be engaged in a special category in the Legion since all the 'normal' positions were already occupied.[114] Hoffmann did not know Hindustani when he came to the Legion, but he apparently learnt it 'almost with a flick of his hand' (*im Handumdrehen*), a sign of his great linguistic talent. Wüst's protege, who was proficient in Sanskrit, had reportedly developed some early interest in Bengali.[115] He also had a personal meeting with 'a rather haughty' Subhas Chandra Bose, a native speaker of Bengali.[116] It is not known whether they spoke in Bengali but evidently Hoffmann, like many German elites, found the militant Indian leader not as obsequious as expected.

Hoffmann allegedly took near complete charge of *Bhaiband*, dictating the texts in Urdu to Hans Seippel, a corporal from Hamburg whom the British records classified as a 'definite Nazi' (Hoffmann was referred to as 'SS man').[117] According to Rose, Seippel laboriously typed the texts in Roman Urdu as Hoffmann played a hit pop song from the 1920s to him and stroked his carefully combed hair, while Cron was purportedly reduced to a mute spectator of this recurrent drama.[118] Rose claimed further that Hoffmann and Cron were also deployed by the division Ic to censor the letters of all Indian soldiers including the POWs, a task that was performed earlier by Bannerth.[119] Rose and Hoffmann also took turns as interpreters for training Indian paramedics at the military hospital at the coastal town of Biarritz.[120]

In the spring of 1944, the 'Cron Hoffmann duo' was sent to Paris to meet the propaganda section of the Army Group West, to make preparations for starting a special radio channel for the Indian soldiers. This channel, known as Radio *Bhaiband*, began to broadcast from 25 June 1944, under the direction of 'Sergeant Hoffmann'. Three Indian soldiers were engaged as announcers. The programmes included propagandistic items in the garb of 'reports' from the Wehrmacht as well as Indian folklore, fairy tales, and plays which were stolen from the BBC's Hindustani broadcasts. Some 'home-made' entertainment, mainly in the form of patriotic songs, was also broadcast. The channel, which supposedly became quite popular among the soldiers, had to be shut down on 14 August 1944 after the Allied invasion of Normandy.[121]

The role of Paul Thieme, the other editor of *Bhaiband*, is more difficult to reconstruct. Thieme (1905–2001) studied Indology, Indogerman Linguistics, and Iranian Studies at the Universities of Göttingen and Berlin from 1923 to 1932.[122] He completed his dissertation from the University of Berlin in 1929 on *Das Plusquamperfektum im Veda* ('The Past Perfect in Veda'). This work received a prize and set him on the path to become an expert on the Vedas. His *Habilitation*, completed in 1932 from the University of Göttingen, was on 'Pāṇini and the Veda, Studies in the Early History of Linguistic Science in India' (as the English translation was called). It examined the 'Vedic expressions' of Panini, the ancient Indian grammarian.[123]

In 1932, Thieme became Alsdorf's successor as the lecturer for German and French at the University of Allahabad. Here, apart from perfecting his Sanskrit, Thieme also learnt Hindi.

Thieme returned to Germany in 1935. He taught as a private lecturer at Göttingen for six months, before joining the University of Breslau in March 1936 as a successor to 'the Jew Otto Strauß, who fled to Holland in 1935 before the persecutions of the Nazis began', in the words of his wife, Renate Söhnen Thieme, who claimed that Thieme also received offers from the Universities of Göttingen and Leipzig, underscoring his scholarly reputation. Söhnen-Thieme maintained that her husband perceived this period as 'politically difficult'.[124]

A review of the available archival sources, however, does not provide any indication of Thieme's supposed political difficulties. On the contrary, Thieme seems to have conformed quickly to the prevailing political milieu. The University of Göttingen envisaged Thieme as the successor to Emil Sieg, the retired professor of Indology who had earned a reputation as a scholar of Sanskrit grammar. Sieg had signed the 'Declaration of allegiance to Adolf Hitler' (*Bekenntnis zu Adolf Hitler*) in November 1933.[125] Through his demonstration of loyalty to Hitler, Sieg had attuned himself to the political ambience of the University of Göttingen which was no exception among German universities in undergoing a voluntary *gleichschaltung* with National Socialist politics.[126] Sieg, in the words of the dean of the Faculty of Philosophy, 'belonged to those powers which contribute to the reorganisation of our university in the spirit of National Socialism'.[127]

In an official evaluation (*Gutachten*) on Thieme, Sieg expressed his 'special wish' to appoint the young scholar as his professional successor. He claimed that he, along with his colleagues from neighbouring disciplines had 'carefully observed' Thieme, and had concluded that this quiet, unassuming, and decent young man felt the duty to offer himself, with all his strength, to the 'new Germany'. Sieg used the dean's parlance by stating further that Thieme is ready in every way to work for 'a further reorganisation of the National Socialist University'. He concluded this report by stating that Thieme's personal characteristics, ideological directions, and academic achievements rendered him suitable for the professorial chair.[128]

Thus, the purported wish to participate in the 'reorganisation' (*Aufbau*) of the University according to National Socialist principles was at least as important as Thieme's impressive academic record in securing him an employment at the University of Göttingen. Thieme himself was well aware of this criterion. As he wrote in January 1936 to the Indologist Otto Strauss at Breslau, that 'Herr Minister' wanted to appoint him, Thieme, already in the winter semester, but he deferred to the wish of the faculty of the University of Göttingen 'in order to provide me the opportunity to strive towards making commitments to the new conditions'.[129] Thieme, who requested Strauss to keep this information secret, ended his letter with the *deutschem Gruß* or the Nazi salute. He also concluded some of his official letters to the university with 'Heil Hitler!' as a statement of his willingness to adapt to the 'new Germany'.[130] The correspondence between Thieme and Strauß indicates that the latter, who lost his position as professor of Indology at the University of Breslau due to the Nuremberg Race Laws of 1935, also suggested the name of Thieme as his successor.[131] Neither Paul Thieme nor his wife ever mentioned this fact, or that 'the Jew' Strauß as Renate Söhnen Thieme so disparagingly stated, was a victim of Nazi persecution who 'fled to Holland' not before but because of it.

By his own admission, Thieme also attended a course at the Lecturers' Training Academy (*Dozentenlehrgang Akademie*) in Kiel, the Nazi indoctrination centre that Ludwig Alsdorf also attended. Thieme absolved his training at this academy from 24 February to 14 March 1936.[132] Thieme's 'progress report' from this institution is not available. However, since the authorities of the University of Göttingen were satisfied with Thieme's political development, one can presume that his report was not overtly negative.

Also, from 1936 to 1941, Thieme was a member of the Nazi Party's welfare organization, the *Nationalsozialistische Volkswohlfahrt* (NSV).[133] The NSV, as we already noted, organized welfare activities exclusively for 'Aryans' according to the Nazi ideal of *Volksgemeinschaft* or national community.[134] This organization not only excluded those it considered the politically and racially unworthy of receiving welfare, but it also called upon the citizens to fight against 'racial decline' by joining it, as some of its posters demonstrated. This affiliation was not mentioned in the biographical sketch provided by Renate Söhnen-Thieme, who also remained silent on Thieme's voluntary military service with the Infantry Regiment 49 of the Wehrmacht from August to October 1938, after which he was given the military rank of *Unterführeranwärter* (sub-commander aspirant).[135]

Paul Thieme was therefore well invested in fulfilling the NS regime's ideal of serving in 'practical' ways, for which he was adequately rewarded. In 1936, he was given a provisional *Lehrauftrag* (teaching contract) at the University of Breslau, while at the University of Göttingen, the Indologist Ernst Waldschmitt (1897–1985) was given the position of professor. Waldschmitt had studied Indian philosophy under Emil Sieg and Paul Deussen at the University of Kiel before completing his PhD and *Habilitation* in Indology from the University of Berlin.[136] Waldschmitt followed the political footsteps of his erstwhile professor, Emil Sieg and aligned with the political orientation of the University of Göttingen by joining the Nazi party on 1 May 1937 and the National Socialist Lecturers' Association (NSDB) on 1 January 1939.[137]

This did not necessarily mean that Thieme's political commitment was considered inadequate. One of the contenders for the position at Breslau was Erich Frauwallner (1898–1974) whom we have mentioned briefly in the Introduction. A trained Indologist and a teacher of classical languages at a high school (Gymnasium) in Vienna, Frauwallner was a member of the Nazi Party of Austria from 1932 and of the NSDB from 1933. He had earned the reputation of being a Nazi loyalist since he continued to work for the NSDAP, particularly by supplying politically useful information from Vienna, even during the period 1933–8 when the Party was made illegal in Austria.[138] The fact that he was passed over for Thieme probably reflects the latter's convincing demonstration of trustworthiness to the Nazi authorities as well as his brilliant academic record.

In 1939, Thieme was made an *Außerplanmässigen Professor* (akin to an assistant professor) at the University of Breslau due to his impressive academic achievements and his willingness for political cooperation, albeit it was stated that Thieme was a little reserved as far politics was concerned.[139] Available archival records remain practically silent on Thieme's activities in 1940. He applied for and received the post of a non-tenured professor for Comparative Linguistics and Sanskrit at the University of Halle from 1 January 1941.[140] In June 1941, he was made an associate professor with tenure (*außerordentlichen Professor*).[141]

Was Thieme teaching continuously at the University of Breslau throughout 1940? The name of a certain Paul Thieme is mentioned as a reserve guard at Auschwitz from 30 January 1940 to 1 February 1941 as Joydeep Bagchee has written in an online note, a claim which I subsequently took up with the archives of Auschwitz-Birkenau. This Paul Thieme was a member of the SS (Number 215965) who started as a guard in the 'political department' and occupied the position of a

Sturmmann within the SS. He was promoted to an *Unterscharführer* by the time his duty officially ended.[142] Was this Paul Thieme identical with our brilliant, ambitious Indologist? Was he, due to his service at Auschwitz, promoted from an aspiring sub-commander to a fully fledged one and also rewarded with the position at Halle? Due to the absence of any conclusive evidence, one can only speculate.

What is beyond doubt is that Thieme was conscripted for military service from July 1941. He was posted at the Russian Front (*Feldkommandantur 244*).[143] Here, Thieme befriended Karl Hoffmann. Like the latter, Thieme was spared the catastrophic fate shared by many German soldiers at the Eastern Front due to his academic connections. Thieme's 'saviour' was not his guru but his disciple—his student Gustav Roth, then engaged as a teacher of Hindustani at the Wehrmacht's 'News Interpreter training institute' at Meißen near Halle.[144] Through Roth's recommendation, Thieme joined this institute as the head instructor of Hindustani from 1 April 1942. He continued to train interpreters for the Indian Legion here until he was called on to join the Legion from 16 February 1944.[145]

Thieme's student Rudolf Hartog was also conscripted at the same time. Hartog mentions that apart from editing *Bhaiband*, Thieme often functioned as a mediator between different dissenting factions of Indians (e.g. Sikhs and Muslims) as well as between the German officers and the Indian soldiers. Thieme would later reminisce to Hartog that the Indian soldiers often discarded their weapons demonstratively and sat down on the parade ground like 'Arjuna between the armies in Mahabharata'.[146] According to Rose, Thieme decided to live in the 'Indian quarter' to improve his knowledge of Hindustani.[147] It is probable that Thieme 'edited' *Bhaiband* when Hoffmann and Rose were busy with their other duties. After the war, Thieme would describe *Bhaiband* as the 'greatest rag of this century', thereby playing down its political significance.[148]

It is clear from the foregoing discussion that the scholars who produced 'useful' knowledge in various forms for the Indian Legion belonged, with different degrees of engagement, within the political and ideological parameters set by the Nazi political and academic establishments. Editing *Bhaiband* was for them another way to answer the political demands of the 'Third Reich', as was interpretation. None of them seemed to be particularly averse to fulfilling their political assignments. All the more so, since the Indian Legion provided some of them a sanctuary from the terrible human tragedy that was unfolding in other theatres of the war.

It is pertinent to mention here that according to the linguist Professor Tista Bagchi, the Hindustani used in *Bhaiband* was too lucid to be written by either Thieme or Hoffmann. It seems much more plausible that one or more Hindustani-speaking soldiers of the Indian Legion were involved in the writing of the texts for *Bhaiband*, although Thieme and/or Hoffmann may have helped to write down/transcribe the texts through dictation.[149]

In the following section, we will examine certain dominant tropes that appeared repeatedly in the *Bhaiband* which, as mentioned, belonged to the matrix of Nazi military propaganda. Knowledge of India, particularly of its cultural and political nationalism, served as an instrument of this propaganda, to which the perspectives of the 'India experts' added a distinctive character.[150]

'Long live Hitler! Long live Netaji':
Legitimizing German Authority

Bhaiband was used for reinforcing the authority of the Legion's commander Kurt Krappe as well as that of the Nazi ruling elite. Consolidating the authority of the Germans was considered necessary to secure the loyalty of the Indian soldiers to the Nazi regime. The name of Netaji Subhas Chandra Bose was used frequently in association with the German authorities in order to legitimize the latter. For example, one of the earliest issues of *Bhaiband*, dated 14 July 1943, published a short text congratulating the 'Kommander Sahib' Krappe on his 45th birthday. The text claimed that it was Krappe who decided to start a Legion in January 1943. Then it mentioned the 'deep friendship' that supposedly existed between Krappe and 'His Excellency Bose' and ended with the cry of 'Long live Hitler!' preceding 'Long live Netaji!'. This dual salutation reflected the oath of allegiance that the Indian soldiers took, of carrying out their Netaji ('respected leader') Subhas Chandra Bose's fight for the freedom of India by accepting Adolf Hitler, the supreme leader of the German state, as the Commander in Chief (Figure 18).[151]

A message of Subhas Chandra Bose, published in *Bhaiband* in November 1943, proclaimed the Indian Legion in Europe to be a part of the Indian National Army that he was leading in East Asia. Bose claimed that he now officially placed the Indian National Army in Europe under German command. The Indian Legion should now fight the enemy at all places.[152] Bose's missive thus sanctioned German military leadership's complete control over the Indian Legion and overturned his earlier stipulation that the Indian soldiers were to fight only the British.

This principle of dual loyalty of the Indian soldiers to Hitler and Bose was promoted by the representatives of the Wpr, the army propaganda unit, which wrote articles in the German press about the common destiny of the German soldiers of the Wehrmacht and the *jawans* (Indian soldiers) of the Indian National Army in Europe 'as they fight for independence in faithfulness towards their Führer, their Netaji'.[153] An issue of *Bhaiband* (21 January 1944) reiterated this propaganda by stating that a political and cultural friendship between German and Indian Volk could only be possible though common military service.

Bhaiband was used to project Krappe as the ideal successor of Bose, who could unite divergent groups of Indians for the common anti-colonial cause. A message published in *Bhaiband* celebrating the second anniversary of the formation of the

Figure 18 An issue of the Indian Legion's magazine, *Bhaiband*, showing the commander of the Legion, Kurt Krappe (left) with Subhas Chandra Bose.

Source: Bundesarchiv Militärarchiv MSG/230/32.

Legion claimed that under the leadership of Krappe, for the first time in history, Indians have come together voluntarily to take part in the foundation of a Free India Army (Azad Hind Fauj).[154] *Bhaiband* projected an image of Krappe as a hard-working, dutiful leader. The issue celebrating the Legion's second Christmas, for example, mentioned that the 'commander sahib' refrained from visiting his family during Christmas to stay with the Indians at Bordeaux.[155] Speeches given by Krappe, which were replete with calls to fight for 'Bharat Mata' (Mother India) and for 'free Germany' and liberally peppered with Nazi diction like glory in battle and final victory, were regularly reported in *Bhaiband*.

The authority of 'the German Führer Adolf Hitler' was also drawn time and again, most significantly to make the recalcitrant Indian soldiers accept the Indian Legion's incorporation within the *Waffen* SS. The issue of *Bhaiband* published on 4 October 1944, for example, proclaimed that Hitler ordered the Indian Legion and other foreign legions to be incorporated in the *Waffen* SS since he was impressed by their courage and their military significance.[156] The next issue (9 October) featured an essay on the SS. It tried to present the infamous paramilitary organization as a loyal, courageous, and self-sacrificing unit which Hitler wanted to keep around him, much like Bose surrounding himself with Indian followers. The article claimed that the *Waffen* SS was an elite and highly respected part of the veteran German troops, the SS. It attracted foreign volunteers who wanted to fight the Anglo-Americans and the Bolsheviks together with Hitler. The essay ended by recalling that Netaji was impressed with the SS and sent 16 Indians to be part of it.[157]

There was some truth in this claim since Bose, who admired certain kinds of authoritarian and disciplinarian organizations, did entrust Keppler to convey a request to Himmler to train some Indian soldiers on the lines of the SS.[158] As Keppler informed Himmler of this request, the latter replied contemptuously that the Indians were more suitable for being trained as police, though he gave Keppler permission to discuss the issue with Ernst Kaltenbrunner, who became the chief of the SD in January 1943.[159] In the end, only a handful of Indians received the training suitable for German police.[160] Such details were naturally not disclosed in the *Bhaiband*. The image of the murderous *Waffen* SS as a 'military ideological elite troop' was a piece of Nazi propaganda.[161] Several issues of the *Bhaiband* faithfully reproduced this trope, indicating the involvement of the German military's propaganda machine.

From the account provided by M.R. Vyas and the available photos of Himmler's meeting with Bose, in which the most famous genocidal leader in modern history supposedly talked about the classical Sanskrit drama *Shakuntala* and fittingly, Walther Wüst acted as the interpreter, it does seem that Himmler cherished a modicum of interest in the Indian cause (Figure 19).[162] It was probably Himmler's relative solicitude compared to the indifference and instrumental attitude of the other Nazi leaders, that led Bose to write a personal farewell letter to the *Reichsführer* SS in which the Indian politician expressed, 'on behalf of the Indian

Figure 19 Walther Wüst (facing the camera) at a meeting of Subhas Chandra Bose (far right) and Heinrich Himmler (right), summer 1942.
Source: Bundesarchiv, Bild 101III-Alber-064-04/Kurt Alber.

national freedom movement, the spirit of loyal unity in the common struggle for freedom and victory.'[163]

Bhaiband continued to publish promises and fabrications, since many German and Indian officers of the Indian Legion refused to join the *Waffen* SS.[164] It became evident to the Wehrmacht and the SS that concessions had to be made for the sensibilities of the Indians. Thus, the issue of *Bhaiband* published on 17 October assured the Indian soldiers that instead of the SS emblem, they would be allowed to wear the sign of the tiger to symbolize that 'we are fighting only for our country' and also that the soldiers would be allowed to uphold their religious and cultural practices as before.[165] This assertion was not devoid of truth. A letter from Himmler's chief adjutant, the SS officer Werner Grothmann to the Wehrmacht, dated 23 December 1944, stated that the *Reichsführer SS* wished that the officers of the Legion who did not wish join the SS should not be pressurized into doing so.[166]

Another issue of *Bhaiband* from mid-November 1944 claimed that the *Waffen* SS was not the normal SS but 'a chosen army', being a part of which was a matter of pride. The article made the dishonest claim that Hitler was interested in the freedom of India since he had a 'hearty friendship' with Netaji.[167] *Bhaiband* also exalted Himmler as the *ala sardar* (top leader) of the SS and the Home Ministry of Germany who had benevolently bestowed the high rank of *Standartenführer* on 'our commander' Krappe. As late as on 1 January 1945, *Bhaiband* informed the Indian soldiers that Himmler had sent packets to the soldiers for Christmas since he had a great interest in the Indian Legion. The 'report' further claimed that Himmler had also promised 'our commander sahib' to provide all kinds of weapons including new ones to the Legion.[168]

At this point, Himmler and his SS seemed to have achieved a level of control over the propaganda concerning India, as a note written by Franz Alfred Six in October 1944 to Rudolf Brandt, SS *Standartenführer* (akin to unit commander) and Himmler's advisor, demonstrates. In this note dated 23 October 1944, Six claimed that the Indian Legion was included in the *Waffen* SS, and the RSHA (Reich Security Main Office, which was controlled by the SS) and the SS *Hauptamt* (SS Main Office) were responsible for the 'political supervision' of the Free India Centre.[169]

That the propaganda disseminated by *Bhaiband* had some effect is indicated by the fact that the Indian soldiers did not openly rebel against this order. Some of the soldiers, like Gurbachan Singh Mangat, even believed the propaganda in *Bhaiband*, deeming the transfer to the 'crack German troops, the *Waffen* SS', to be 'a token of appreciation of the Indian acts of valor' on the part of *Reichsführer* Himmler.[170]

The *Reichsführer* SS seemed to have used the Legion in different ways. In March 1945, an issue of *Bhaiband* stated that Himmler sent a telegram to Krappe, asking him to 'kindly congratulate all the soldiers of the Indian Legion on my behalf' for the great gift of 31,311 Marks that the Legion supposedly sent to the 'Jarman Red Krass'.[171] The German Red Cross was thoroughly infiltrated by the SS and acted primarily according to the priorities dictated by Nazi politics.[172]

Führer Cult and Anti-Bolshevism

Various elements of Nazi propaganda, including attempts to inculcate the Führer cult among Indian soldiers, were increasingly disseminated through *Bhaiband* as the war situation deteriorated. The issue of *Bhaiband* dated 17 April 1944, for example, proudly proclaimed that celebrating the birthday of Hitler, 'the leader of the German empire' was an event in the Legion since its foundation. The article sought to present Hitler as an inborn military leader who was unafraid of violence by claiming that, in his childhood, Hitler was always given the part of a General in the war games that he played with other boys, 'and when he came to his mother after each game, his clothes were torn and his face was covered in blood' (Figure 20).

Hitler was also eulogized in the guise of informing the Indian soldiers about German history. The issue of 9 November 1944, for example, commemorated Hitler's failed putsch from 1923, stating that, on this date, Hitler made 'valiant

Figure 20 Hitler's birthday was celebrated by the Indian Legion, according to the issue of *Bhaiband* published on 17 April 1944.

Source: Bundesarchiv Militärarchiv RS17/47.

efforts to free the German nation'. The write up claimed in a rather macabre tone that 'from the blood of the sixteen loyal National Socialists who became martyrs trying to defend Hitler, sprouted the plant of freedom of the German nation'. Towards the end of 1944, Nazi paroles of keeping up the fighting spirit as well as *Endsieg* (final victory) were conveyed in almost every issue. Thus, the little effective V2 rocket, the world's first long-range guided ballistic missile, developed by the Nazis, was hyped as Germany's 'new invisible weapon' which, it was untruthfully reported, wreaked havoc on London. *Bhaiband* made attempts to cover up the lack of success of the V2 by claiming that the British were keeping the news and photos of the devastation caused by the V2 under wraps.[173]

Similarly, *Bhaiband* glorified the Nazi cult of violent self-destruction. Glowing references to the *Sturmwikinger* (Storm Vikings), individual sea vessels containing suicide fighters, who torpedoed bigger cargo or passenger ships belonging to the enemy, appeared repeatedly. In reality, this was a desperate and militarily useless operation which sent very young German men without enough military training to their horrific deaths.[174] The issue of *Bhaiband* published on 9 January 1945 claimed that these 'little torpedo boats' were named after magnificent heroes from the past who could sail from one ship to another in the midst of storm. The article celebrated the 'self-sacrifice of the Germans who died such heroic deaths'.[175] These 'torpedo boats' were also compared favourably to the Japanese Kamikaze which *Bhaiband* extolled as Japanese 'live bombs' who attacked the enemy like a powerful storm, sacrificing their own selves in the process. The Indian soldiers were asked to take note of such sacrifices.[176] Death of an individual as part of an aggressive undertaking was seen in the National Socialist worldview as a worthwhile way to die since it was a self-sacrifice for the sake of saving the national community or *Volksgemeinschaft*.[177]

A distinctive trait of Nazi propaganda espoused by *Bhaiband* was anti-Bolshevism, which, apart from the period of the Hitler–Stalin pact, was an ideological mainstay of National Socialist world view. Hitler and his henchmen equated all forms of leftist politics with 'international Jewry' and Bolshevism which needed to be wiped out.[178] However, the construction of a hated 'Judeo-Bolshevism' pervaded the German military community from the time of the First World War. This antipathy could dovetail well with Nazi propaganda and ideological indoctrination that pervaded the Wehrmacht after 1933.[179]

Such anti-Bolshevik rhetoric was expressed in *Bhaiband* through a regular column titled 'What is Bolshevism?'. This column tried to present the ongoing war as a righteous battle against Bolshevism that was being led by Adolf Hitler. The anti-Bolshevik propaganda increased as the Red Army advanced into the 'Reich'. On 20 January 1945, *Bhaiband* reported a 'massive attack by the Bolsheviks' and claimed that due to the harsh winter, which was favourable to Stalin's army, the Bolsheviks have been able to temporarily occupy several outposts of the 'Reich'.

The report assured the soldiers that the *Reichsführer* SS has announced that new German weapons would be deployed against them at a suitable moment.

From March 1945, *Bhaiband* began to spew venom against the 'iron curtain' that the Bolsheviks had set up in front of the 'wretched countries' of Rumania, Serbia, and Bulgaria. An article claimed that the just war that the Soviet Union was claiming to conduct actually suppressed nationalist sentiments of others, like Ukrainians, a statement which possessed a kernel of truth that continues to manifest itself.[180] The atrocities committed by the Nazis themselves in Ukraine were, of course, not even hinted at.

Anti-Bolshevism in Nazi Germany was, in the words of Aristotle Kallis, a 'potent and effective ideological platform for promoting the Volk's most basic form of negative integration.'[181] The Indians were now sought to be psychologically integrated into the warring community under the aegis of the Wehrmacht through the device of anti-Bolshevism. The Ic which overaw the military propaganda during this time thus ignored the directive of the Foreign Ministry, which had realized the appeal that the Soviet Union exerted among ordinary Indians, that German propaganda aimed at India was not to condemn the Soviet Union and its Socialist tenets except by highlighting the (negative) actions of the Red Army.[182] Indeed, at least from the early 1930s, the Communist Party of India propagated, with some amount of success, the idea of a just and equitable 'Communist Raj' among the soldiers.[183] Bannerth also stated in his post-war statement that the Indian soldiers were inclined towards the Soviet Union 'due to an earlier propaganda' to which they were exposed, though most Indians in the Legion did not have a proper idea of what communism meant. Bannerth claimed that the Indian soldiers were not receptive towards the anti-Soviet/anti-Bolshevik propaganda with which they were inundated.[184]

From early 1945, the 'News of war' in *Bhaiband* focused increasingly on *Bolshewiki hamle* (Bolshevik invasions) on different areas of the 'Greater Reich', the supposed success of the German forces in resisting them, and the approaching 'final victory'.[185] The most direct expression of National Socialist propaganda in the *Bhaiband* was a column called 'the German Führer's message'. These 'messages', which did not mention India, started to appear towards the end of the war, indicating the NS regime's desperation. The message on 28 February 1945, for example, celebrated 25 years of Hitler's proclamation of the programme for the National Socialist movement by calling on soldiers to fight according to the directions of the German leadership and with more vigour for the final victory. Most of the messages railed against the 'foreign criminals' and 'hated enemies' of the German nation. The 'message' published on 4 March 1945 told the soldiers to fight on so that 'our cities and towns' can be rebuilt soon, thereby admitting the wreckage caused by the Allied bombardments.[186] According to Rose, the final issue of *Bhaiband* commemorated the birthday of Adolf Hitler soon after 20 April 1945. This number carried Commander Krappe's speech, in which he announced an 'appeal from the Führer' and reiterated the formulaic invocation of Netaji's call to fight for the freedom of India together with the Wehrmacht 'till the final victory'.[187]

Apart from Hitler, the other member of the Nazi ruling coterie to find mention in *Bhaiband* was Goebbels. The issue on 8 March quoted the *Jarman wazir* (German minister) *Daktar* Goebbels as saying that while it was not ignominious to attack the foe repeatedly and unsuccessfully, the greatest pride for a soldier lay in avoiding defeat. Among the military elite, *Bhaiband* repeatedly mentioned the Field Marshal Erwin Rommel, whose name was familiar to most of the Indian soldiers from their time in Africa. Rommel had 'inspected' the Indian Legion after the Allied landing on Normandy in 1944 (Figure 21). The Wehrmacht's propaganda team (PK) had photographed Rommel with the Indian soldiers near the Atlantic Wall in order to reassure the domestic population that they were being protected. Rommel appeared to have charmed the Indian soldiers with his fatherly manners and affable ways.

The news of the death of 'ala Field Marshal Rommel sahib' supposedly spread like wild fire in the Legion, so that the Staff had to write a condolence message on behalf of the soldiers in the *Bhaiband* on 17 October 1944, praising 'the great soldier who was ready to sacrifice his life' for Hitler.[188] The writers and their readers did not know that Rommel had literally sacrificed his life at the command of the

Figure 21 Field Marshal Rommel (right) inspecting the Indian Legion in occupied France in 1944.

Source: Bundesarchiv 183-J16796/Aschenbroich/CC-BY-SA 3.0.

'Führer' by taking a cyanide capsule after his connections with the failed putsch of 20 July 1944 were uncovered.[189]

The 'great impression' that Rommel had on the soldiers was subsequently cited to reconcile the Indians to their inclusion into the *Waffen* SS as well as to proclaim that the necessary task of the Legion, now in retreat from France to Germany, was to fight 'the French rebels' (the *Maquisards*).[190] Castigating the *Maquisards* as 'Communo-terrorists' was a part of the training provided by the Wehrmacht to its interpreters.[191] Presumably, the interpreters of the Indian Legion were already familiar with the idea of criminalizing the French Resistance. There were indeed several skirmishes between the Indian Legion and members of the Resistance which, according to Eugen Rose, were characterized by intense hatred of the Indian soldiers towards the French.[192] The violence involved in the encounters between the Indian soldiers and the French Resistance has been recorded in historical scholarship.[193]

(Fake) News of War

The main feature of *Bhaiband* was the column, 'News from the battlefield' which, according to Bannerth, commanded maximum interest among the soldiers.[194] This 'news' was allegedly sent to the editors of *Bhaiband* as communiques by the Wehrmacht.[195] Such 'news' was based on 'facts', which were being generated by the OKW/Wpr from 1939.[196] As the chances of victory constantly receded, it was necessary to keep the fighting morale up and hold the *Volksgemeinschaft* together through a conscious manipulation of military news. One strategy of the Wpr was to provide 'news' of supposed military successes, contrasted by excessively high figures of enemy losses.[197]

Promotion of Bose's anti-British agenda and of Japan's military advances were integrated within such 'news' in *Bhaiband*. This was done in different ways (e.g. through columns named 'News from East Asia' and 'News of Azad Hind'). *Bhaiband* regularly carried propagandistic messages from Bose. While the victory of the Japanese Army and, with it, the Indian National Army at Arakan in Burma in March 1944 was extolled through a quotation from Bose, the routing of these combined forces at the battle of Kohima at the north-eastern border of India in July 1944 was not mentioned until November 1944, when another message from Bose claimed that the Azad Hind Fauj (Indian National Army) had to retreat due to inclement weather but it was preparing to relaunch the offensive.[198]

Several 'news items' published towards the end of 1944 diverted the focus from actual military news by stating that Bose was in Tokyo to meet the Japanese emperor and to step up the united military efforts. However, in most of the issues of *Bhaiband*, the military 'successes' achieved by Japan were given more jubilant attention than any item on Netaji and his army. Japanese technology, nationalism, and martial qualities were constantly glorified. Bose himself apparently contributed to this line of propaganda. On the second anniversary of Japan's invasion of Singapore, *Bhaiband* published a speech delivered by Bose, who claimed that 8 December 1941 'opened a new chapter in the history of Asia as well as the history of the entire world'.[199]

From the end of 1944, India's anti-colonial concerns were completely eclipsed by the despondency of Germany's military situation. The changing interests were reflected in a special issue of *Bhaiband*, published on 9 December 1944, in which Subhas Chandra Bose's radio speech from Tokyo, urging the German nation to keep fighting, was published. The last radio speech of Bose, delivered at Shonan (now Singapore) and published subsequently in *Bhaiband* in early January 1945, mentioned the readiness of the Indian National Army to reinvade Burma together with the Japanese but it mostly harped on the bravery of the German Army and endorsed the German Führer's confidence in *Endsieg*.[200]

The last published 'news' of Burma from 16 January 1945 did not mention the Indian National Army at all. It merely declared that Japan was engaged in a difficult and desperate war with the Allies.

Specialized Knowledge of India and Orientalist Stereotypes

Distinctive contributions of the 'India experts' can be discerned in the 'news' concerning India's internal developments, which were published regularly in *Bhaiband*. Such 'news' was apparently collected from an agency in Bangkok. The 'India experts' were in a better position to understand the significance of such news and to use them more appropriately than the personnel of the OKW/Wpr. The issue of *Bhaiband* dated 31 May 1944, for example, discussed in detail the military threats posed by the Japanese Army and Bose's Indian National Army to Calcutta and Jamshedpur. Calcutta was then the economic centre of India and Jamshedpur housed an important arms manufacturing unit. Occasionally, under the guise of 'news', *Bhaiband* tried to whitewash the anti-Axis views of the leaders of the Indian National Congress. Thus, the issue of *Bhaiband* on 11 October 1944 quoted Gandhi as stating that if India became independent it would not go to war against Japan.[201]

Using Indian history and culture was a part of *Bhaiband*'s efforts to inspire the Indian soldiers to fight. The 'India experts' were uniquely positioned to answer this demand. A purported contribution of Cron to *Bhaiband* was quoting nationalistic songs and poems, mostly from the Urdu and Hindustani canon. These included the repeated use of a few militant lines attributed to the last Mughal emperor, Bahadur Shah Zafar.[202] These popular lines were also publicly and frequently quoted by Subhas Bose.[203] Lines from the poet Muhammad Iqbal's famous patriotic song '*Sare jahan se achha/Hindustan hamara*' ('The best land in the world/is our India') were also quoted (and occasionally misquoted).[204]

The poet Ahmad Phaphoondvi's lines about 'one does not know how to live/if one does not know how to die' (*use jina nahi aata jise marna nahin aata*) appeared rather ominously and with some fallacies in translation on 25 January 1945. Less well known but equally emotional couplets, for example, about 'garlands on the pyres of the martyrs who died for their country' were also published in connection with the Kamikaze.

Some of the poems published in *Bhaiband* were supposedly original compositions of the soldiers of the Indian Legion. One such poem appeared in the special issue of 21 October 1944, which celebrated the anniversary of the government of Free India. The poem, belligerent in tone, celebrated India's patriotic sons 'Gandhi, Gaffar, Subhas, Jawahar, Azad' and assured the country of their readiness to shed their blood for her. Another 'original' poem, celebrating India's 'Independence Day' (26 January) was dedicated to 'Netaji' Subhas Chandra Bose. The poem, published on 25 January 1945, a day after Bose's birthday, congratulated him for 'showing the day of freedom' and raising an army to free India.[205]

The 'India experts' also deployed their specialized knowledge creatively through articles which dealt with India's history, culture, and different religions. These articles were considered necessary for addressing certain 'problems' that arose with the intermingling of different castes and religions as well as due to the soldiers' exposure to the Western way of life. These texts were almost always influenced by the 'Orientalist gaze' of the experts concerned, and were often predicated on racialized stereotypes about 'Orientals'. The German interpreters as well as the officers associated with the Indian Legion were united in their complaint about a supposed lack of discipline among the Indian soldiers. This view on the part of the Germans was at least partially based on their racialized image of the laid back Oriental, steeped in his superstitious and archaic religious traditions, which collided with the 'efficiency oriented Occidental attitude, bearing the particular Prussian-German imprint', as Hans Franzen, an officer of the Legion whom we have already come across, wrote in a letter decades after the war.[206]

Ernst Bannerth claimed after the war that he tried to deal with the lack of discipline among the Indian soldiers by making the 'more ambitious among the Indians' write moralizing articles on virtues such as obedience, self-sacrifice, and sobriety in *Bhaiband*. However, claimed Bannerth, the writers produced mostly clichés.[207] Efforts to rectify the alleged lack of discipline among the Indian soldiers and instil obedience to the authorities were continued by Bannerth's successors, as several articles in *Bhaiband* demonstrate. A short piece titled 'Who is a volunteer?' posits, among other virtues to be cultivated by the ideal volunteer, the readiness 'to throw himself like a moth on the flame as soon as he sees the gesture of his leader.'[208] Another write up focused on the importance of *Huqum manna* (obeying orders).[209]

Some articles linked up these virtues with India's anti-colonial movement. A write up on courage, published on 2 June 1944 claimed that Gandhi was a 'glowing example of courage'. This was another example of the cynical use of the Mahatma's aura for German propaganda, notwithstanding the Nazi elite's contempt for the Indian leader. Such virtues were also occasionally sought to be invoked for serving Nazi politics. In the issue published on 27 July 1944, an article on 'loyalty' (*wafadari*) mentioned that some evil and disloyal people in Germany have made an attack 'upon the representatives of the German people' but the brave and loyal German soldiers were fighting on, referring to the attempt on Hitler's life on 20 July. These articles, written in a pedantic tone, were evidently considered to be pedagogical tools by the German trainers and their interpreters.

The British colonial racial stereotypes influencing this attitude are best manifested in a handout written for German officers by Ulrich von Kritter. It claimed: 'Indians, despite their intelligence are primitive in certain ways and they are susceptible to pedagogical influence.'[210] Kritter advised the officers to devote great attention to *geistigen Betreuung* ('care of the spirit') of the Indian soldiers, for which he considered *Der Kamerad* to be a proven medium.[211] Such infantilization of the so-called 'peasant-soldiers of the Raj' was also widely prevalent in the British Indian Army, thereby pointing to intersection of racialized tenets in both British colonialism and Nazi politics.[212]

Racial bigotry was also expressed by Eugen Rose. He criticized the wish of Bose to Indianize the Legion by gradually substituting the German officers with Indian ones by comparing this move with the revolution in Haiti, where every Negro soldier (*Negerkrieger*) like Toussant L'Ouverture wanted to be a captain if not immediately General.[213] Such racial prejudices seem to have percolated deep among the German personnel, who referred to the Indians as 'bimbos' and Hindustani as 'Bimbostani' among themselves.[214] Derogatory attitudes towards foreign legions were, however, by no means limited to the Indian Legion. Instances of other non-German volunteers being designated as savages, Bushmen, Hottentotten, and so on were quite widespread.[215]

For the scholars associated with the Indian Legion, certain stereotypes about caste- and religion-based identities of the Indians played a role in defining their attitude towards the soldiers. This was particularly true of both Bannerth and Rose who viewed the Indian soldiers through an additional prism of missionary morals. Both these Orientalists disapproved of Bose's ideal of raising a secular national army. Bannerth felt that Bose's policy and the European surroundings in which it was put into effect, 'led to the disappearance of religion generally'. He also feared that the traditional Indian religions would be superseded by a 'national religion', an Indian version of the Nazi ideal of *Reichskirche* or Reich church controlled by Hitler and the Nazi party. The marginalization of religion in the Indian

Legion, according to Bannerth, resulted in 'moral depravity' of the soldiers. 'Depraved acts' included the consumption of alcohol even by Muslims and visits to brothels—activities which were allegedly encouraged by the German officers.[216]

Bannerth maintained that he tried to counter such 'immoral behaviour' through the *Bhaiband*. One method adopted by Bannerth was to encourage traditional learning and values, not only through the use of Devanagari and Nastaliq scripts instead of the Roman Urdu that Bose wanted, but also by publishing texts and images associated with Indian religious traditions. Religious songs (*bhajan*) on the Hindu gods accompanied by their photos, short biographies of Sikh Gurus along with the photo of the Golden Temple in Amritsar, the holy site of Sikhism, appeared in several issues of *Bhaiband* (Figure 22).

What Bannerth did not disclose was that such articles were also used to conduct pro-German propaganda. An article titled 'Spreading the word of the Vedas', published on 20 August 1943, praised the 'German professor Max Müller' who translated the *Rig* Veda through 30 years of labour, whereas 'no British or French academic tried to do this'. The article conveniently omitted the fact that the said German scholar pursued this task at Oxford with financial support from the English East India Company. This article thus anticipated the appropriation of Max Müller, who used his scholarship to legitimize British colonial rule, as the representative of German Indology in post-colonial India.[217]

Eugene Rose considered Hitler to be primarily responsible for the policy of abolishing a strict separation of soldiers on the basis of religion, ethnicity, and so on. For Rose, the Indian Legion was the manifestation of Nazi propaganda displaying an Indian *Volksgemeinschaft*. The result, according to him, was a loss of soldierly moral and military discipline.[218] Both Rose and Thieme mentioned an incident in France in which a Sikh soldier had to be executed by the military tribunal for killing several of his Muslim comrades who had torn off his turban.[219] Another incident concerned the murder of a Sikh soldier, Balwant Singh, who had done something unthinkable for a Sikh—he had shaved off his beard in accordance with the wishes of his lover, 'a little Schwabisch girl', during the Legion's retreat through Germany. It was evident that one of his co-religionists had killed him in the middle of the night, though no one confessed.[220]

However, such occurrences seemed to have been relatively rare. Neither Bannerth nor Rose had much sympathy for the concept of a pluralistic and secular Indian Army, which was a reflection of what Indian anti-colonialists like Bose wanted an independent India to be. These scholar-missionaries, performing the distinctly 'Orientalist' function of translating the words of colonized 'Orientals' into an European metropolitan language of power, could not think beyond Orientalist stereotypes about India, like religion being the bedrock of Indian society and 'Orientals' leading an unchanging life by clinging on to their religious practices. A non-religious 'Oriental' was, to them, not an authentic Oriental but a caricature of the same.

Figure 22 A sketch of the Golden Temple of Amritsar, which featured in several issues of *Bhaiband.*

Both Bannerth and Rose were disgusted by what they considered to be a dis-proportionately high sexual drive and lust among the Indians. There were at least three recorded instances of Indians being accused of raping French women. The details of each case vary, as did the sentencing, which ranged from execution to acquittal. The sexual crimes committed by a few Indian soldiers apparently com-promised the reputation of the entire Legion.[221] The attitude of Bannerth and Rose was another expression of Orientalist imaginary combined with prevalent racist stereotypes of 'uncontrolled sexual appetites' of non-Germans, particularly non-whites. Such stereotypes were also firmly established among the military elite of Nazi Germany. In order to 'channelize' such 'carnal cravings' of non-Germans, brothels were set up exclusively for foreign soldiers in both Eastern and Western sectors.[222]

Rose described in detail the establishment of a separate military brothel for the Indian soldiers in France since the German officers were not ready to share such pleasures with 'racially inferior' Indians. The brothel, for which a number of non-German and non-French white women were procured, was known as *Phulvari* (flower garden) among Indians.[223] R.L. Fischer, a self-styled Hindu convert who accompanied the Legion as a soldier, who would later become the monk Agehananda Bharati, wrote in his autobiography that the 'flower garden' was no different than a German military brothel as far as 'revolting coarseness and vulgarity' were concerned.[224]

The Guru, the Prophet, and the Gods

As the war situation deteriorated, religion was used to improve the fighting spirit of the soldiers. The German military authorities believed that a soldier who believed God to be on his side and who believed in an eternal afterlife could remain steadfast in battle, fight valiantly, and die courageously.[225] The emphasis on religion played out in different ways in the Indian Legion. The Sikhs, who were regarded as a martial race by the British, seem to have domi-nated the Indian Legion in number as well as influence. Nazi propaganda units like the PK also found the turbaned Sikhs with their tall and well-built bodies particularly exotic and photographed them most as representatives of the Indian Legion.[226]

Both Bannerth and Rose found the Sikhs overbearing and arrogant. In other words, the Sikhs were the least submissive among the different groups of Indian soldiers. Both the scholars claimed that the Sikhs were also most susceptible to 'moral corruption'. Different issues of the *Bhaiband* reflected some of these concerns. There were special issues published on the occasions of the birth of Sikh gurus, in which their lives were extolled along with appeals to return to the moral virtues taught by them. For example, the article on Guru Nanak, published on

31 October 1944, was followed by an entreaty to the Sikh fraternity to be tolerant of other religions as preached by this fifteenth-century messiah, reflecting the purported hostility of the Sikhs towards their Muslim compatriots.

The life of another Sikh guru, Tegh Bahadur, was celebrated on 2 November 1944. An accompanying write up, ostensibly from a Sikh soldier called Nahar Singh, called upon his fellow soldiers not to besmirch the reputation of India through their immoral actions. Another special issue dedicated to Guru Govind Singh was published on 19 December 1944. The long tribute to the Guru mentioned the religious significance of keeping long hair and beard. The article exhorted the Sikhs to follow the Guru's example and not dispense with long hair and beard due to the 'banal desires' which they had incurred after coming to Europe.

Another lengthy article, published in the special issue of *Bhaiband* on 23 December 1944 commemorating the martyrdom of the sons of Guru Govind Singh, also included an emotional appeal, supposedly from a soldier called Randhir Singh to his 'Sikh brothers'. In a beseeching tone, the writer entreated the Sikh fraternity not to forget the virtues taught by the Guru and the sacrifices that he made. The article included quotes from an English book, *The Religion of the Sikhs*, which indicates that it was written not by any soldier but by the German scholars in charge of *Bhaiband*.

Writing about Sikh religion was not easy for the German 'India experts' since, unlike Hindu and Muslim religious works, the Sikh *Granth* (religious texts) were written in Punjabi language and in Gurmukhi script. The use of this language and the script were limited to Punjab, an area about which the scholars who worked for the Legion had little or no direct knowledge.[227] Rose claimed that the scholars had to learn the script with a lot of difficulty. The primary concern in learning the language was, according to Rose, the desire to prevent any enemy propaganda written in Gurmukhi from reaching the soldiers along with the parcels sent by the Red Cross from Canada.[228]

Hinduism was honoured in *Bhaiband* through articles and poems on the two major annual festivals, Holi in spring and Diwali in autumn/winter. The festivals were also used by the German 'India-experts' for propaganda as well as pedagogy. On 26 February 1945, *Bhaiband* commemorated Holi, the spring festival of exchanging colours, by publishing a poem which, along with exalting the beauty of spring, commented somewhat morbidly that Gandhi and Bose helped to bring about the blossoms of freedom 'which were in the colours of blood'. An accompanying article carried echoes of Bollywood melodramas by declaring that 'we have to play Holi with the blood of our enemies...'. Another issue of *Bhaiband* recounted the main storyline of the Hindu epic Ramayana, claiming that it was 'our duty' to remember the holy books of 'Mother India'.[229] The epic was thus used as a pedagogical tool to 'bring back' the supposedly prodigal Hindus to their authentic way of life.

Mother India and her Children

The specialized knowledge of the 'India experts' was also called upon to write on India's history as well as contemporary politics as part of the anti-British/anti-colonial propaganda in *Bhaiband*. In commenting on the internal developments of the Indian subcontinent, the focus was mostly on the INC, which was presented as uncompromising in its demand for independence. Incidents of militant protests against colonial rule and the latter's repression were highlighted. For example, the issue of *Bhaiband* published on 18 October 1943 reported on the spread of violent anti-colonial protests in Ahmedabad, the resultant curfew, and deaths of some of the protesters. The texts engaged not only with prominent leaders like Gandhi and Nehru but occasionally highlighted lesser known figures like Sarojini Naidu, Aruna Asaf Ali, and Abul Kalam Azad.

Following the guidelines of Germany's propaganda concerning India, *Bhaiband* eulogized Gandhi as 'India's guru' and castigated the 'repressive English government' for incarcerating him. On 1 October 1943, *Bhaiband* reported that the government of Azad Hind and the Indian nation were deeply saddened that Mahatma Gandhi will be forced to spend his birthday, which was on the next day, in prison. Ignoring Gandhi's disapproval of Bose's militant politics and his collaboration with the Axis, the write up claimed that Gandhi's 'intention is to fight along with all the powers which will combat British imperialism.'[230]

The issue of 11 October 1944 mentioned *sarhadd ka Gandhi* (Frontier Gandhi) Khan Abdul Gaffar Khan, a political leader from India's North-West Frontier Province (NWFP), who followed Gandhi's ideals of non-violent resistance and Hindu–Muslim unity.[231] Surprisingly, though Bose's speeches and activities were reported regularly, a detailed sketch of his life appeared only on 28 January 1945, a few days after his birthday. *Bhaiband* also regularly reported on the famine that devastated Bengal in 1943. The famine, as we noted, provided Germany with a particularly useful instrument of propaganda against the British. Details of the plight of the starving and dying population of Bengal were regularly published, along with the indictment that the relief measures adopted by the colonial administration were hopelessly inadequate.

Appeals to the soldiers to free *Bharat Mata* (Mother India) from the yoke of foreign rule often took recourse to India's history. They were reminded that even in 1914, the blood of many Indian soldiers were shed for the British Empire, the 'reward' for which was 'the slaughter of Amritsar' orchestrated by the colonial powers, referring to the massacre of unarmed civilians at Jallianwala Bagh in Punjab at the orders of General Dyer on 13 April 1919. The text also remembered the war of independence of 1857 and the historical figures who fought in it—Ranjit Singh, the Sikh king of Punjab and Bahadur Shah Zafar, the last Mughal emperor. The name of Bal Gangadhar Tilak, the early twentieth-century nationalist leader from Maharashtra was also invoked in a separate article on Indian nationalism. Tilak was termed a reincarnation of Shivaji, the iconic seventeenth-century Hindu king from the same region.[232]

Bhaiband followed Bose's politics of commemorating particular historical events which he deemed to be important landmarks in India's anti-colonial movement, as we have noted in earlier chapters. On 13 April 1944, for example, *Bhaiband* commemorated the Indians who perished at Jallianwala Bagh. In the dramatic tone that *Bhaiband* often reserved for its readers, the article claimed that the souls of those who died at Jallianwala Bagh are wandering in vain and they cry out for vengeance, which the soldiers of the Legion must now provide to propitiate them. This write up bore the name of a soldier—Ranjit Singh Rawat.[233]

Epilogue

After the disbandment of the Indian Legion, the fates of the 'interpreters' took divergent turns but all of them could work their ways into the professional and social establishment in West Germany by erasing their links to Nazi politics.

Despite his attempts to present himself as 'anti-Nazi', Bannerth was interned by the British until 1947. After his release, he returned to his ecclesiastic duties. He also took up his academic pursuits, focusing on Arabic dialects and Islamic mysticism. Apart from performing his duties as a pastor, Bannerth became a guest lecturer at the University of Vienna, from where he completed his *Habilitation* in 1956. In 1961, Bannerth immigrated to Cairo. He joined a Dominican convent there and continued his scholarly pursuits at the Oriental Institute affiliated to it. He died in Cairo in 1976.[234]

In his post-war statement to the Allied authorities, Otto Spies claimed that he was living in the town of Meiningen in Thuringia when the war officially came to an end. Subsequently, he returned to Bonn and registered himself as a displaced person, since a return to Breslau, now under Soviet occupation, was out of the question.[235] In a statement to the Allied authorities, Spies claimed that he had always remained aloof from political activities and that his only connection to the war had been the compulsory military duty that he had to perform in 1940–1.[236] He did not mention the Indian Legion at all. His statement described instead his supposed opposition to the Nazi regime, as a punishment for which he was sent to work near the Polish border along with some other 'politically unreliable' persons and 'half-Jews'.[237]

As in the case of Ludwig Alsdorf, this dubious narrative was endorsed by various influential academics, which culminated in Spies' complete exoneration. Due to the sympathy of his peers and colleagues, the University of Bonn offered him the position of a guest lecturer in 1946. In 1951, Spies was made a professor for Semitic Philology and Islamic Studies at the same university. He remained in this position until his retirement in 1969 (Figure 23).[238]

Figure 23 Otto Spies. *General Anzeiger*, 1 April 1966.
Source: University Archives, Bonn, UAB 1033/PFPA. Nachlass Otto Spies.

After the war, Karl Hoffmann could conceal his political engagements perfectly. On 19 April 1947, the *Spruchkammer* (the judicial chamber deciding on
individual culpability connected to Nazism) of Munich officially declared
Hoffmann not guilty of any Nazi association or war crimes.[239] Equipped with this
exculpating statement, Hoffmann could join the University of Munich as a part-
time lecturer of Sanskrit in 1948. Simultaneously, he worked on his *Habilitation*.
Professor Ferdinand Sommer, who knew Hoffmann since his student days,
supported him and vouched for his political blamelessness to the University
authorities.[240]

Hoffmann completed his *Habilitation* on *Der Injunktiv im Veda* ('Injunctive in
the Veda') in 1951 from the same University.[241] After a short stint as a private lecturer (*privatdozent*) at the University of Munich, Hoffmann joined the newly
founded University of Saarbrucken as tenured faculty in 1952. From there, he
moved on to become a professor of Comparative Indo-European linguistics and
Indo-Iranian at the University of Erlangen in 1955. He remained there until his
retirement, commanding immense respect and affection from his students. He
also earned a formidable reputation as a scholar of Indo-Iranian linguistics.
Notably, Hoffmann's obituary mentions that he always praised Walther Wüst for

the latter's 'methodological rigor' though he was 'less forthcoming' about Wüst's 'other works'.[242] The obituary also claims that Hoffmann was 'critical about Wüst's naïve political escapades'. The obituary of course did not mention that Hoffmann continued to correspond with Wüst after 1945, referring to the latter as *'hoch-verehrter lieber guru'* ('highly respected, beloved guru').[243] This pattern of *guru–shishya* relationship, it should be recalled, was seen in the case of another duo who offered their knowledge of Indian subjects for Nazi politics—Hauer and Bhatta. Following the guru's political orientation along with his academic direction seemed to have been an important requirement for professional advancement for some 'India experts' in Nazi Germany.

The obituary of Hoffmann stated further that the latter 'was clever enough to escape the usual fate of becoming a member of the party's youth organization'. It also jokingly mentioned that Hoffmann privately renamed Lacanau, the head-quarters of the Indian Legion in France, as Lucknow after the north Indian city. He supposedly spent his time reading scholarly books under the table while preparing the Legion's newspaper and Hindustani programmes for its short-lived radio.[244] This was the way in which Hoffmann trivialized and depoliticized his role as a Nazi academic and propagandist. His refashioned narrative was perpetuated by his students.

As in the case of Hoffmann, this trivialization of *Bhaiband* as well as his own role as interpreter was a part of Paul Thieme's retrospective elimination of all Nazi connections from his trajectory, a venture that he undertook soon after his surrender to the US forces in South Germany.[245]

The success of his efforts is proved by a post-war British report which claimed that Thieme was 'anti-Nazi'.[246] Nevertheless, Thieme was imprisoned for a year by the Americans who were apparently suspicious about his claims. However, no incriminating evidence of Thieme's Nazi connections was found and he could return to his former position in Halle. He was made a full professor in 1946. In 1953, Thieme fled to West Germany to take up a professorial post at Frankfurt am Main for a short time. Thereafter, he received professorial posts at Yale University (1954–60) and Tübingen, where he worked until his retirement in 1973. By then, he had established himself as a scholar with 'monumental achievements'.[247]

Eugen Rose could return to his priestly duties in Wüppertal in 1946, from where he shifted to Boppard in 1963.[248] He remained there until his retirement in 1970. His book on the 'Indian fairy tale' that he called the days of the Legion survives as an exculpating narrative that smoothly glosses over all associations with Nazi politics behind the veil of exoticization and obfuscations.

Among the more peripheral 'India experts' attached to the Legion, Günther Spannaus landed in French imprisonment. By 1946, he had regained both his personal freedom as well as his academic reputation. After working as an anthropologist for more than a decade, he was made a full professor of Anthropology at the University of Göttingen in 1959.[249]

Notes

1. Harbich, Walter, 1970. 46–57. Rose, Eugen, 1979. Franzen, Hans,1981. Mangat, Gurbachan Singh, 1986. Hartog, Rudolf, 1991. Weidemann, Diethelm, Günther, Lothar, 2000. 199–208. Günther, Lothar, 2003. Goel, Urmila. 2003. 27–30. Günther, Lothar, 2013. Oesterheld, Joachim, 2015. 120–143. Kuhlmann, Jan, 2015. 91–119.
2. Kuhlmann, Jan, 2003. 234–238, 294–300. 328–345. Kuhlmann, Jan, 2015. 91–119.
3. Müller, Rolf-Dieter, 2007.
4. Seidt, Hans Ulrich, 2002. 317.
5. NAUK: GFM33-2109. E233365. Subject: Anti English propaganda among Indian troops. 7.4.1941.
6. Kuhlmann, Jan, 2003, 234–35.
7. NAUK: WO208/823. Purpose of the Legion. 2.
8. BA MA (Bundesarchiv Militärarchiv or the Federal Military Archives) Freiburg: MSG/230/32. Letter from Franzen, 2.4.1984.
9. Mangat, Gurbachan Singh, 1986. 29.
10. Hartog, Rudolf, 1991. 59.
11. BA-MA Freiburg: MSG230/32. Diary of the officer Ulrich von Kritter. 6. 25.11.1942.
12. Kuhlmann, Jan, 2015. 95.
13. NAUK: WO208/823. Purpose of the Legion. 2.
14. Vossler, Frank, 2005. 386.
15. Hartog, Rudolf, 1991. 60. Kuhlmann, Jan, 2015. 100.
16. NAUK: WO106/5881. German officers of the Indian Legion. Appendix 4.
17. Archiv der Evangelischen Kirche in Rheinland (EKIR): Nachlass Eugen Rose: 7NL/145/18/9/17. Letter from Rose to Ernst Bannerth, dated 25.1.49.
18. Hartog. Rudolf, 1991. 71–72.
19. BA MA Freiburg: MSG230/32. Ulrich von Kritter, Diary entry: 10.2.43.
20. On the Nazification of official interpreters, see Kieslich, Charlotte P., 2018.
21. Winter, Miriam, 2012. 25–28.
22. Ibid. 58.
23. Petke, Stefan, 2021. 12.
24. Ibid: P.101.
25. Biographical details of Ernst Bannerth, unless otherwise noted, are from www.atlasburgenland.at.
26. NAUK: WO208/5659. Interrogations of POW. German officers of the Indian Legion. 12.10.1944.
27. NAUK: KV23/907. Indian Infantry Legion 950: Preamble.
28. Hartog, Rudolf, 1991. 140.
29. NAI: INA 242. 2. I thank Jan Kuhlmann for sharing these files with me.
30. NAUK: KV23/907. Report of the preliminary and joint interrogation of Bannerth and Koch. 2.
31. www.atlasburgenland.at
32. Hanisch, Ernst, 2014. 67–87.
33. NAUK: WO 106/588. Report no. G/85. 25.1.1945.
34. Hartog, Rudolf, 1991. 190–191.
35. EKIR: Nachlass Eugen Rose: 7NL/145/18/9/17. Letter dated 25.1.49.
36. Hartog, Rudolf, 1991. 121.
37. Spies, Otto, Bannerth, Ernst, 1945.
38. Rose, Eugen, 1979. 89.
39. Petke, Stefan, 2021. 211–212.
40. Ibid.18. On 'care service' (*Truppenbetreuung*): Vossler, Frank, 2005.
41. Spies, Otto, Bannerth, Ernst, 1945. Vorwort, VI.
42. Rose, Eugen, 1979. 89.
43. Spies, Otto, Bannerth, Ernst, 1945. 94.
44. Spies, Otto, Bannerth, Ernst, 1945. 155.
45. Bannerth, Ernst, 1943. Heft 49.
46. Vossler, Frank, 2005. 196–197.
47. BA-MA Freiburg: Msg/230/32. 10.7.83.
48. Hartog, Rudolf, 1991. 123.
49. Rose, Eugen, 1991. 40.
50. BA-MA: MSG/230/23. Statement of the Indologist Wilhelm Rau. 10.7.83.32.
51. Hartog, Rudolf, 1991.125.
52. Rose, Eugen, 1979. 89–90.

53. NAUK: WO106/5881. Sheet 16: Former German members of the Unit.
54. BA MA Freiburg: MSG230/32. Ulrich von Kritter, 20.11.1942. 3.
55. Archive of the University of Wroclaw (AUW): S220/472: Spies Otto. Letter from the curator dated 25.7.1942 and letter from the Rector, dated 3.8.1942.
56. Hartog, Rudolf, 1991. 59–63.
57. BA MA Freiburg: MSG230/32. 20.11.1942. 3.
58. Günther, Lothar, 2003.106–110. Kuhlmann, Jan, 2003. 94–95.
59. AUW: S220/472: Spies Otto. Letter from the curator dated 25.7.1942.
60. Universitätsarchiv Bonn (UAB): 1033\PFPA: Otto Spies. Questionnaire from the Military Government, 1946.
61. Rose, Eugen, 1979. 93.
62. UAB: 1033\PFPA: Nachlass Spies. Lebenslauf.
63. UAB: 1033\PFPA. Nachlass Spies.
64. D'Souza, Eugen, 2000. 79.
65. AUW: S220/472: Spies Otto. 'Für die Kartei des Rektors.' UAB: 1033\PFPA: Spies Lebenslauf.
66. AUW.S220/472: Spies Otto. 6.
67. Ibid.
68. Ibid. Letter dated 9.2.1942.
69. Kallis, Aristotle, 2005. 57.
70. Vossler, Frank, 2005. 108.
71. Ibid. 190.
72. NAI: INA 242.
73. Rose, Eugen, 1979. 45.
74. BA MA Freiburg: MSG 230/32. Ulrich von Kritter: Führungsgrundsätze (Guidelines for leadership). 4.
75. NAUK: Report No. G/85, 25 January1945, WO105/5881. 15.
76. Ahuja, Ravi, 2010. 149–150; Liebau, Heike, 2014b; 2014c.
77. Messerschmidt, Manfred, 1969. 206.
78. Rose, Eugen, 1979. 79.
79. Ibid.
80. NAUK: KV3/907. Indian Infantry Legion 950. P.9.
81. This bio-data is taken from: https://www.dietrich-bonhoeffer.net/bonhoeffer-umfeld/eugen-rose/
82. NAUK: KV23/907. Appendix 4.
83. EKIR: 7NL 145. Assessment report, 1.8.1943.
84. Ibid. Certificate issued by the OKW, 17.9.43.
85. Rose, Eugen, 1979. 45.
86. Hartog, Rudolf, 1991. 132. Rose, Eugen, 1979. 44.
87. Geisenhainer, Katja, 2017. 616–620.
88. Geisenhainer, Katja, 2000. 169.
89. Ibid, 2000. 486.
90. Ibid. 486–487.
91. Botsch, Gideon, 2005. 257.
92. Rose, Eugen, 1979.79.
93. Hartog, Rudolf, 1991. 133.
94. Söhnen-Thieme, Renate, 2003. 261.
95. Rose, Eugen, 1979. 92–93.
96. Universitätsarchiv München: o-vII-138. Hoffmann, Karl. Lebenslauf, 10.1.1951.
97. BA Berlin: NS 21/566. Akt Karl Hoffmann. Letter dated 23.4.1937.
98. BA Berlin: NS 21/566. Letter from the Ahnenerbe to SS Sturmbannführer Galke. 8.5.37.
99. BA Berlin: NS 21/566. Letter from Walther Wüst to the Reichsführer SS, persönlicher Stab. 19.7.1938.
100. Hoffmann, Karl, 1940. 139–161.
101. Hutton, Christopher, 1999. 38–39.
102. Universitätsarchiv München: o-vII-138. Hoffmann, Karl. Lebenslauf, 10.1.1951.
103. BA Berlin: NS 21/566. Wüst`s letter to Karl Hoffmann, 3.3.1941.
104. BA Berlin: NS21/336. Verzeichnis der Mitarbeiter Wald und Baum.
105. Fugger, Ulrich, 2017, 1297–304.
106. Ibid. 1299–1300.
107. Rusinek, Bernd A. 2000. 296.
108. BA Berlin: NS21/566. Undated bio-data written and signed by Hoffmann.

109. Rusinek, Bernd A., 2000. 297.
110. BA Berlin: NS21/566. Wüst to Hoffmann, 21.10.1938.
111. BA Berlin: NS21/566. Hoffmann to Ahnenerbe, 15.10.1938.
112. BA Berlin: NS21/566. Copy of a notice from Wüst, then SS Obersturmbannführer, dated 5.12.1938.
113. BA Berlin: NS21/566. Letter from the Ahnenerbe to SS Obersturmbrandführer Dr. Brandt. 6.11.1942.
114. Rose, Eugen, 1979. 92–93.
115. Ibid. 93.
116. Witzel, Michael, 1997. 246.
117. NAUK: KV23907. Indian Infantry Regiment 950. Appendix 4. P.1.
118. Rose, Eugen, 1979. 96.
119. Ibid.
120. Ibid. 53–54.
121. Ibid. 70–71.
122. Söhnen-Thieme, Renate, 2003. 251–280.
123. Heimann, Betty, 1938. 300–1.
124. Söhnen-Thieme, Renate, 2003. 258–59.
125. Pollock, Sheldon, 1993. 94.
126. https://www.uni-goettingen.de/de/die+universit%C3%A4t+im+nationalsozialismus/30772.html
127. Universitätsarchiv Göttingen: Phil. Pers. 516. Letter from the Dean to the 'Reich Education Minister', 1.6.1935.
128. Universitätsarchiv Göttingen: Phil. Pers. 516. Sieg`s report, dated 6.1.1936.
129. AUW: PL 372 1-0-1-S_220-503. Letter 6.1.1936.
130. Universitätsarchiv, Göttingen: Phil. Pers. 516. Thieme`s letter to Strauß, 6.1.1936.
131. For biographical information on Otto Strauß, see Pax, Elpidius, 1950. 42.
132. AUW: PL 372 1-0-1-S_220-503. Thieme, *Lebenslauf.*
133. Universitätsarchiv Halle-Wittemberg: UAHW, Rep. 11, PA 15956. Undated questionnaire, 1946.
134. Hansen, Eckhard, 1991. 36.
135. AUW: PL 372 1-0-1-S_220-503. Thieme, *Lebenslauf.* Thieme trained with the IR 49 from 18.8.38 to 10.8.38.
136. Bechert, Heinz, 1986. 147.
137. Szabo, Aniko, 2000. 132.
138. Stuchlik, Jakob, 2009. 193–195.
139. AUW: PL 372 1-0-1-S_220-503. Letter from the dean to the Ministry of Education, 5.7.1939.
140. Ibid. Letter from the Ministry of Education to Thieme, 8.1.1941.
141. UAHW: Rep.`11, PA 15956. Letter from the Ministry of Education to Thieme, 19.6.1941.
142. Bagchee, Joydeep, undated. https://www.academia.edu/42749714/Paul_Thieme. The details of a certain Paul Thieme at the archives of Auschwitz-Birkenau: Archiwum Państwowego Muzeum Auschwitz-Birkenau w Oświęcimiu (APMA-B), Planstellenbesetzung, D-AuI-1/1, inventory number: 156990.
143. UAHW, Rep. 11, PA 15956. Undated questionnaire, 1946. Also, BA Berlin: B 563/31514.
144. Söhnen-Thieme, Renate, 2003. 260.
145. UAHW, Rep. 11, PA 15956. Undated questionnaire, 1946.
146. Hartog, Rudolf, 1991. 74, 76.
147. Rose, Eugen, 1979, 40.
148. Hartog, Rudolf, 1991. 133.
149. Personal communication with the author. 24.10.2020.
150. I am indebted to Aalia Shaik and Mohammed Irfan for translating the Urdu texts and to Anup Roy for translating the Hindi texts from *Bhaiband.*
151. BA-MA Freiburg: MSG/230/32.
152. BA-MA Freiburg: MSG 230/22. "Der Kamerad." 26.11.1943.
153. Rose, Eugen, 1979. 50.
154. BA-MA Freiburg: MSG 230/22. "Der Kamerad" No.66. 22.12.43.
155. BA-MA Freiburg: MSG 230/22. *Bhaiband,* 22.12.1943.
156. BA-MA Freiburg: RS17/47. *Bhaiband,* 4.10.1944.
157. BA-MA Freiburg: RS17/47. *Bhaiband,* 9.10.1944.
158. BA Berlin: NS 19/3769. Letter from Keppler to Himmler, 16.2.1943.
159. Ibid. Himmler's reply, 24.2.43.
160. Kuhlmann, Jan, 2003. 262.

161. Lehnhardt, Jochen, 2017.18.
162. Vyas, M.R., 1982. 379–380.
163. BA Berlin: NS19/3760. Letter from December 1942.
164. Hartog, Rudolf, 1991. 163–164.
165. BA-MA Freiburg: Rs17/47. *Bhaiband*, 17.10.1944.
166. BA Berlin: NS 34\47. Betreff: Angelegenheit Indische Legion. Anruf SS Ostubaf. Grothmann.
167. BA-MA Freiburg: Rs17/47. *Bhaiband*, 17.11.1944.
168. BA-MA Freiburg: Rs17/47. *Bhaiband*, 3.12.1944. Also, *Bhaiband*, 1.1.1945.
169. BA Berlin: NS19/2453. Propaganda nach Indien. 3.
170. Kuhlmann, Jan, 2003. 333.
171. BA-MA Freiburg: Rs17/47. *Bhaiband*, 6.3.1945.
172. On the German Red Cross during the NS rule: Morgenbrod, Birgit, Merkenich, Stephanie, 2008.
173. BA-MA Freiburg: Rs17/47. *Bhaiband*, 17.4.1944 and *Bhaiband*, 12.11.1944.
174. Rahn, Werner, 2005. 519.
175. BA-MA Freiburg: Rs17/47. *Bhaiband*, 4.3.1945.
176. BA-MA Freiburg: Rs17/47. *Bhaiband*, 4.11.1944.
177. Behrenbeck, Sabine, 1996, 521.
178. On Nazi anti-Bolshevism, see Waddington, Lorna Louise, 2007.
179. Crim, Brian, E., 2011, 624–41.
180. BA MA Freiburg: RS17/47. *Bhaiband*, 20.1.1945 and *Bhaiband*, 8.3.1945.
181. Kallis, Aristotle, 2005, 76.
182. BA Berlin: NS19/2453, 3. Undated report Indien-Berichterstattung, Anti-Bolschewistische Information.
183. Singh, Gajendra, 2006, 2–45.
184. NAUK: WO106/5881. Appendix 5, sheet 2.
185. BA MA Freiburg: RS17/47. *Bhaiband*, 4.1.1945.
186. BA MA Freiburg: RS17/47. *Bhaiband*, 4.3.1945.
187. Rose, Eugen, 1979, 202–3.
188. Ibid., 50–2.
189. Arnold, Klaus Jochen, Rommel unterstützte das Attentat auf Hitler, 2014. https://www.kas.de/de/veranstaltungsberichte/detail/-/content/rommel-unterstuetzte-das-attentat-auf-hitler.
190. BA MA Freiburg: RS17/47. *Bhaiband*, 24.10.1944.
191. Werner, Kirstin 2014, 110.
192. Rose, Eugen, 1979, 159.
193. Oesterheld, Joachim, 2015, 120–43.
194. NAUK: WO106/5881. Appendix 5, sheet 2.
195. Rose, Eugen, 1979, 201.
196. Kallis, Aristotle, 2005, 46.
197. Ibid., 118.
198. BA MA Freiburg: RS17/47. *Bhaiband*, 9.11.1944.
199. BA MA Freiburg: MSG/230/22. *Bhaiband*, 22.10.1943.
200. BA MA Freiburg: RS17/47. *Bhaiband*, 4.1.1945.
201. BA MA Freiburg: RS17/47. *Bhaiband*, 11.10.1944.
202. BA MA Freiburg: RS17/47. *Bhaiband*, 21.10.1944.
203. Bose, Sisir Kumar and Bose, Sugata, 2007, 253.
204. BA MA Freiburg: RS17/47. *Bhaiband*, 31.10.1944, 2.3.1945.
205. BA MA Freiburg: RS17/47. *Bhaiband*, 4.11.1944, 2. *Bhaiband*, 21.10.1944, *Bhaiband*, 25.1.1945.
206. BA MA Freiburg: MSG/230/32. Letter dated 2.4.1984.
207. NAUK: WO106/5881. Appendix 5, sheet 2.
208. BA MA Freiburg: MSG/230/32. *Bhaiband*, 13.10.1943.
209. BA MA Freiburg: RS17/47. *Bhaiband*, 17.10.1944.
210. BA MA Freiburg: MSG/230/32. Ulrich von Kritter: Führungsgrundsätze, 5.
211. Ibid., 8.
212. Ahuja, Ravi, 2010, 139.
213. Rose, Eugen, 1979, 38.
214. Hartog, Rudolf, 1991, 21.
215. Petke, Stefan, 2021, 11.
216. NAUK: WO106/5881. Appendix 5.
217. Roy, Baijayanti, 2016, 217–28.
218. Rose, Eugen, 1979, 10.

219. Rose, Eugen, 1979, 63–4; Hartog, Rudolf, 1991, 74.
220. Rose, Eugen, 1979, 198.
221. Oesterheld, Joachim, 2015, 131.
222. Petke, Stefan, 2021, 275.
223. Rose, Eugen, 1979, 103–6.
224. Bharati, Agehanananda, 1970, 61.
225. Petke, Stefan, 2021, 219.
226. Rose, Eugen, 1979, 113.
227. Ibid., 77.
228. Ibid., 78.
229. BA MA Freiburg: RS17/47. *Bhaiband*, 26.2.1945. *Bhaiband*, 18.10.1944.
230. BA-MA Freiburg. RS17/45. *Bhaiband*, 1.10.1943.
231. BA MA Freiburg: RS17/47. *Bhaiband*, 11.10.1944.
232. BA MA Freiburg: MSG/230/32. *Bhaiband*, 13.9.1943.
233. BA MA Freiburg: RS17/44. *Bhaiband*, 134.1944.
234. See http://www.atlas-burgenland.at
235. UAB: 1033/PFPA. Meldebogen.
236. UAB: 1033/PFPA. Otto Spies, chronological record of full time employment and military service.
237. UAB: 1033/PFPA. Otto Spies, Appendix 3.
238. UAB: 1033/PFPA. Otto Spies, Lebenslauf, 1981.
239. Universitätsarchiv München, o-vII-138. Hoffmann's bio-data, 10.1.1951.
240. Universitätsarchiv München, o-xIV-137. Letter dated 5.4.1948.
241. Universitätsarchiv München, o-vII-138. Letter from the dean of the Faculty of Philosophy, University of Munich to the Minister for Education and Culture in Bavaria, 6.3.1951.
242. Witzel, Michael, 1997, 246.
243. Schreiber, Maximilian, 2008, 133.
244. Witzel, Michael, 1997, 246.
245. Hartog, Rudolf, 1991, 178.
246. NAUK: KV/2/3907. Indian Infantry Regiment 950. Appendix 4, 13.
247. Narten, Johanna, 2002. https://web.archive.org/web/20071213034922/http://www.badw.de/publikationen/sonstige/nachrufe/2002/Thieme.pdf.
248. See https://www.dietrich-bonhoeffer.net/bonhoeffer-umfeld/eugen-rose/.
249. See http://www.germananthropology.com/short-portrait/gunther-spannaus/269.

The Nazi Study of India and Indian Anti-Colonialism: Knowledge Providers and Propagandists in the 'Third Reich'.
Baijayanti Roy, Oxford University Press. © Baijayanti Roy 2024. DOI: 10.1093/9780191981951.003.0005

Conclusion

This monograph set out to examine, through four different case studies, the relationship between a number of knowledge providers comprising German academics, some non-academic 'India experts', and a few Indian anti-colonialist intellectuals on the one hand, and various organs of the Nazi state, on the other. The research questions that this book has tried to answer include those that are commonly raised by historians probing the connections between scholars of humanities and Nazi politics, as well as some additional ones generated by the particular context of this study.

Continuity and Discontinuity

The first and inevitable question that arises in any study of organizations in the 'Third Reich' is that of continuity/discontinuity of the personnel involved, after 1933. As far as Indian studies in German universities are concerned, this pivotal and sensitive issue has not been dealt with in any detail by historians, though a list of names of victimized scholars has been provided by Sheldon Pollock in his path-breaking essay which provided a vital impetus to this book.[1] The persecution and the subsequent fates of the 'racially and politically undesirable' scholars of Indology deserve a full-length study. The present writer has tried to contribute to this subject through an article on the Indologist Heinrich Zimmer, pointing to the problems of viewing his situation which defied the usual binary of oppressors and oppressed.[2]

The issue of transformations that occurred after 1933, as far as the four case studies are concerned, has exhibited multiple dimensions, a crucial one among them being the racially motivated expulsion of the scholars Lucian Scherman and Otto Strauß from their academic positions as well as from the India Institute of the DA. Concomitant with the dismissals is the aspect of usurpation and appropriation, as demonstrated by the shamelessness and unscrupulousness with which Walther Wüst tried to assume the position of Lucian Schermann, or the bitter irony of Otto Strauß having to nominate his possible successor at the University of Breslau, a contingency from which the young Indologist Paul Thieme profited without ever acknowledging it.

Another significant facet of this study is to locate the occasional 'grey zone' which complicates the Manichean narrative of perpetrators and victims. A case in point is Hans Heinrich Schaeder, known for his complicity with the Nazi regime. Schaeder was nevertheless instrumental in the appointment of the 'half-Jewish' scholar Hugo Figulla at the Seminar for Oriental Studies in Berlin in 1934, though he could not or did not prevent Figulla's dismissal in 1937, as we saw.

The admittedly limited perspectives offered by this monograph seem to suggest that it was the iniquitous mix of anti-Semitism, over investment in Germany's 'Aryan past' and hope for career advancement that led most of the scholars to react to the removal of their colleagues with responses ranging from indifference to active endorsement.

Self-Mobilization and Knowledge Discourses

An associated theme that is central to this study, as it is in all discussions on academia in Nazi Germany, pertains to the *Selbstgleichschaltung* ('self-co-ordination') of the scholars with Nazi politics, a subject which Alan Steinweis, in his recently published chapter on the humanities in Nazi Germany, has fittingly described as the ways in which academics 'accommodated themselves to the ideological and political priorities of the Nazi regime'.[3] Such 'accommodations', as the case studies have sought to establish, entailed political engagements in the form of membership of the NSDAP and/or its various affiliations as well as cultivation and conversion of aspects of India's past and present into usable knowledge for different Nazi organizations.

For the India Institute, Hindu revivalism based on Aryanism was transformed into an instrument of Nazi propaganda by Walther Wüst and Jakob Wilhelm Hauer, between 1933 and 1938. Knowledge pertaining to India's colonization and anti-colonialist movement as well as other aspects of contemporary India became the most sought after intellectual resource as the war approached and particularly after the appearance of Subhas Chandra Bose in Berlin in April 1941. Hence, knowledge of India's anti-colonial movement is a leitmotif for all the four case studies. The individual chapters highlight the diverse ways in which this valued intellectual capital was invested by knowledge providers for the cynical projection of Nazi Germany's purported support for India's independence.

The SRI, as the second case study shows, mostly generated knowledge relating to India's colonization and its contemporary situation, for the benefit of the German government as well as ordinary Germans. While the fortnightly reports were written specifically for the foreign minister, Joachim von Ribbentrop, the book series provided background information to the relevant Nazi authorities and the German press. The book series also tried to convince the wider German society of Nazi Germany's sympathy for the downtrodden Indians and the need to 'rescue' them from their colonial oppressors. The books also represented an effort to reassure the Germans that they could trust their Indian partners, repeating the tenor of German propaganda, particularly those concerning the 'Islamic oriental partners' during the First World War.[4]

Propaganda aimed directly at India required knowledge of the country's 'living' languages and material culture (*Realien*), which formed another exchangeable resource for various German and Indian intellectuals, as the third case study establishes. The dissemination of such knowledge in the classrooms, as this chapter shows, progressively became a formal and routine affair, while the inducement to use this cognitive device outside the academic arena to serve certain objectives of the Nazi state assumed greater political relevance. The most conspicuous example of such linguistic and cultural propaganda was Hermann Beythan's book on Hitler in Tamil.

The fourth case study presents further manifestations of propagandistic amalgamation of linguistic and cultural tropes in the Indian Legion's magazine, *Bhaiband*. Invocation of Indian religious traditions and precepts in combination with various disparate and sometimes contradictory elements—the glorification of Gandhi, Bose's militant messages, fabricated news of the military situation, and extolling Hitler—were all combined into a propaganda pastiche by a number of scholars of India and their Indian henchmen in these pamphlets written in Hindustani and Urdu.

Rewards

An equally, if not more significant issue which this study has set out to explore is that of the resources or rewards that the knowledge providers received in exchange for the capital that they supplied to different power centres. This work has tried to ascertain whether providing intellectual capital yielded more 'valuable' remunerations to the knowledge providers in the form of increased career prospects, financial gains, or accumulation of power and influence than more direct involvement in Nazi politics in the form of working for the Nazi party and its various affiliates.

The four case studies provide, not unexpectedly, variegated answers to this question. The first case study shows that Walther Wüst, who had become a part of the Nazi political and academic elite not long after 1933, used his knowledge of ancient and contemporary India to propagate Nazism among Indians as another way of demonstrating his service to the Nazi regime and thereby furthering his power and prestige within the India Institute. Among all the knowledge providers discussed in this book, Ludwig Alsdorf profited the most in terms of career opportunities. As we noted, Alsdorf's *Selbstgleichschaltung* through his membership of the Nazi Party and its various associations did not fetch him the career prospects that he hoped for. However, providing usable knowledge of India's colonialization through his book *Indien* established him as the ideal expert on modern India for the Nazi regime and ultimately paved the way to a 'tenure track position' at the AF for him.

Utilization of the knowledge of modern Indian languages and culture for propaganda and other services (censorship, listening to enemy broadcasts) provided both prestige and emoluments to Hermann Beythan and Reinhard Wagner, who were not professional Indologists following university careers. The case studies also point to the different levels of 'self-co-ordination' of the three Indian knowledge providers—Koodavuru Anantrama Bhatta, Tarachand Roy, and Devendra Nath Bannerjea—and the 'rewards' that they received in return. In the case of Bannerjea, the most important knowledge that he provided, as perceived by the Nazi regime, pertained to his fellow Indian immigrants in Berlin whom he denounced as communists, for which he was provided with the sinecure of teaching 'practical' subjects related to India. In his case, this reward was an existential lifeline saving him from starvation, as this book as well as Maria Framke's recently published essay on him shows.[5] Among the Indians, Bhatta advanced to become a valued knowledge provider for different Nazi organizations as well as a prominent functionary of the Free India Centre that Subhas Bose was allowed to form in Berlin.

This equation of interchanging knowledge for material and other benefits seems to have been reversed in the cases of Paul Thieme and Karl Hoffmann, whose involvement in Nazi politics in the mid-1930s was remunerated through academic positions in teaching and research, respectively. It is doubtful whether Wüst would have offered Hoffmann the opportunities that he did if this talented student had failed to correspond to the ideal of a 'scholar-soldier' as envisaged by the Nazi regime. Thieme, as we have seen, could convince the authorities at the University of Göttingen of the sincerity of his political commitment. For Thieme, Hoffmann, and others working for the Indian Legion, using their knowledge of modern India to disseminate Nazi (and Axis) propaganda and to 'rein in' the 'unruly Oriental' soldiers carried the life-saving prize of evading the carnage that was unfolding on the Eastern Front.

Navigating Knowledge and Power

The organizations under review functioned to fulfil the (sometimes competing) interests of various Nazi entities including the Foreign Ministry, the SS, Alfred Rosenberg's office (*Amt Rosenberg*), and the Education Ministry. This resulted in the formation of intricate webs comprising the representatives of these organs of the Nazi state and the knowledge providers. The case studies show that despite the importance attached to them as providers of utilizable knowledge, the space for manoeuvre of the scholars and 'India experts' was dependent primarily on their ability to draw support from the centres of power. Hence, Alsdorf could not have his way against Franz Alfred Six who had the backing of Heinrich Himmler. On the other hand, Walther Wüst could undertake several significant measures on his own authority due to his well-entrenched position within academia as well as his cordial relationship with Himmler. Devendra Nath Bannerjea could get away with his insolence and squabbles, which would have normally led to punitive reactions from the totalitarian and racist Nazi state, due to his contact with influential functionaries in the Foreign Ministry and the Gestapo.

This work has also made it clear that despite the palpable limits of their power, most of the academics and experts involved in these networks and constellations were not helpless victims of circumstances, as some of them would claim later. Nor did they view themselves as such. The majority of them, including the Indians, perceived themselves as self-assured members of the intellectual elite, negotiating their own terms with the different representatives of state power. The expectations of the regime from the scholarly experts on India, as we saw in the Introduction, were clearly articulated by established Indologists like Walther Wüst who made it obvious that the academics were supposed to serve the 'Volk' (in other words, the Nazi state) through their knowledge.

Though knowledge production was the most valued aspect of an ideal scholar's profile, one must not lose sight of the military-political dimension, as epitomized by the Lecturers' Academy at Kiel, which aimed to train 'scholar-soldiers' who would be no less effective in defending the Nazi state on the battlefield than in the classroom. This physical and ideological training was absorbed by the younger generation of academics pursuing careers in university, like Alsdorf and Thieme. For the older scholars, making financial contributions to the Nazi cause (regular donations to the SS by Reinhard Wagner, for example) apart from acting as informants for the SD (as Wüst and Hauer did), were integral to the scholarly archetype contemplated by the Nazi regime. Though memberships of some affiliates of the Nazi Party like the NSV (Nazi Party's welfare organization), or the NSDB (Nazi Lecturers' Association) were virtually compulsory, the case studies make it manifest that none of the protagonists joined such organizations unwillingly or were reluctant to use their memberships for professional advancement. It is also unambiguously apparent that the academics concerned were aware of the political implications of their knowledge production.

Interventions of the SS

A special feature shared by the organizations under review is the influence of the SS. The India Institute (as part of the DA) came under the Cultural Political Department of the Foreign Ministry, over which the SS began to wield increasing influence from 1943 onwards through the appointment of Franz Alfred Six. Around the same time, the SRI became integrated into the Information Department of the Foreign Ministry which also came under the authority of Six. The latter, backed by the SS-controlled RSHA (Reich Security Main Office) was instrumental in the establishment of the chair for Indian Studies at the AF.

It is pertinent to recollect here the note written by Six on 23 October 1944 (quoted in Chapter 4), which claimed that the RSHA as well as the SS *Hauptamt* (Main Office) was responsible for the 'political supervision' of the Free India Centre. Chapter 4 also provides details of the incorporation of the Indian Legion into the *Waffen* SS, though this was the fate of all 'foreign' legions of the Wehrmacht. Future research must investigate the nature of the connection between the SS, different kinds of knowledge of India deployed by the Nazi regime, and the diasporic Indian anti-colonialism conducted under Subhas Bose in Berlin. To my knowledge, there is only one article written by Lothar Günther that indirectly touches on the subject while focusing on Himmler's interest in Bose and the Indians.[6]

Coping with the Nazi Past

The fortunes of politically compromised scholars after the war form an indispensable part of this study, as the epilogues to each chapter have indicated. The case studies demonstrate that Wüst and Hauer, the scholars whose proximity with the Nazi political establishment was much too prominent to be ignored were not reintegrated into the professional community after the war.

The blatant culpability of these two mandarins could obscure the less visible political involvements of scholars like Thieme and Hoffmann. Alsdorf, whose complicity with the Nazi regime fell somewhere between the conspicuous and the concealed, could find his way back to West German academia with the help of some of his academic peers who assisted him to refashion his trajectory by eviscerating the darker aspects of his past, which in turn helped them to expunge their own political liabilities.

This pattern of 'group exoneration' was intrinsic to West Germany's coming to terms with the Nazi past, as various historians including this writer have pointed out.[7] More detailed and critical examinations of the post-war trajectories of the academics specializing in India who 'adjusted' with the NS system must be undertaken in future, whereby researchers should be motivated by a spirit of genuine inquiry and not by the desire to settle personal scores or to suppress incriminating truths.

The present monograph has attempted to locate its Indian protagonists within the intertwined hierarchy of knowledge and power that all the four organizations incorporated. It is evident that despite the pragmatism with which the different representatives of the Nazi regime treated the Indians, the inherently racist core of the Nazi state led to their relative marginalization within the organizations. Also, 'the hierarchies and inequalities that marked even the most advanced and enlightened forms of Orientalist scholarship' were manifested in the humiliation faced by Faroqhi, Vyas, Bhatta, and Hassan in the episode concerning the book series published under the aegis of Alsdorf and Furtwängler.[8]

The peripheral position of the Indians was to help them in minimizing their association with Nazism after the war, as the case studies show. The collusion of Indian anti-colonial intellectuals with the Nazi state, beyond the instances of the prominent knowledge providers we encountered in this book, remains an under-researched field, which is completely overshadowed by the larger than life figure of Subhas Chandra Bose. The few contributions to the subject include my article on the Indians involved in the publication of the magazine *Azad Hind* and Maria Framke's essay on Devendra Nath Bannerjea.[9]

Three Questions

Three prescient questions raised by Alan Steinweis in his aforementioned article on the humanities in Nazi Germany are particularly relevant for this monograph. The three questions are: 'What strategies did the regime use to steer scholarship in the desired ideological and political direction? What was the relationship between the established universities and the many external institutes set up by the regime? What role did the scholars play, as consultants or as experts in the employ of the government and the party, in the formulation and implementation of policy?'[10]

The case studies have furnished us with some pointers and indicators in lieu of conclusive answers to these questions. The India Institute represents a model case of an institution 'working towards the Führer', even before the Nazi regime discovered its value as an instrument of propaganda. As far as the SRI and the AF are concerned, the appointment of Ludwig Alsdorf, an expert on Jainism, as its most important provider and arbiter of strategic knowledge of modern India signifies the Nazi regime's manoeuver to 'steer' this scholar and his scholarship towards its preferred direction. Incentives and rewards, mostly in the form of financial compensation, led Hermann Beythan and Reinhard Wagner to channel their knowledge of modern Indian languages to serve Nazi politics. In the case of the interpreters of the Indian Legion, the imperative was 'war duty' together with the urge to escape the horrors of the Eastern Front.

The organizations under review were connected to different universities, either through administrative apparatuses or through personal affiliations. The organizations drew their authority from the cultural prestige that the university and academics associated with it traditionally enjoyed in Germany, as we mentioned in the Introduction. This factor contributed to the influence amassed by Ludwig Alsdorf at the SRI, despite lacking a power base within the Nazi political ecosystem (unlike Wüst and Hauer, for example). Alsdorf's training as an academic Indologist was certainly one of the determinants in his receiving the only 'tenure track' position for Indian Studies at the AF. Similarly, if one is to accept Eugene Rose's auto-fictional account, Karl Hoffmann's pursuit of an academic career set him apart from his colleagues in the Indian Legion and rendered this young scholar enough import to take over the editorship of the Legion's magazine, *Bhaiband*, soon after his arrival at the Legion, even though he possessed neither any prior knowledge of the required languages—Hindustani and Urdu—nor any 'living experience' of India.

The third question raised by Steinweis, about the role of scholars within the different structures of power, has been addressed in the sections above. Nevertheless, a few additional dimensions need to be enumerated. It is irrefutable that the knowledge that was required from and provided by the 'India experts' comprised mostly propagandistic texts dictated by Nazi cultural politics, or information needed to produce such propaganda. We have also noted that the power and space for negotiation enjoyed by the 'experts and consultants' was circumscribed by the political authorities in charge of the organizations concerned. The 'formulation and implementation of policy' was decided through the dialectics of competition and collaboration between the different organs of the Nazi state like the Foreign Ministry, the SS and, as in the last case study, the Wehrmacht.

Nevertheless, the knowledge providers could occasionally interject their perspectives and biases in the texts they composed, provided these did not hinder the political goals of the regime. Such subjective interventions mostly reflected the Orientalist stereotypes and racist notions which extended across academic Indology, popular views of India and disciplines like Ethnology and/or *Rassenkunde* (Race Science). Therefore, Ludwig Alsdorf could articulate his anti-Islamic prejudices in his book *Indien*, but he had to refrain from doing so after Bose and the Foreign Ministry decided on an inclusive and tolerant tone. The pastors Bannerth and Rose could express their visions of Muslim, Sikh, and Hindu religiosities in moralistic overtones in *Bhaiband* since such perspectives did not run counter to the strategic aims of the Nazi regime.

Utility Issues

A singular concern of this book has been to examine the scholars' projections of the 'usefulness' of Indology (and Indologists) to the Nazi authorities. Justifying the existence of 'non-utilitarian' subjects like Indology which belonged to the corpus of *Orientalistik* in German universities was of course not specific to the Nazi era. Traditionally, Orientalists had to convince the state of the necessity to teach and cultivate their subjects in terms of 'scientific progress' since they attracted few students.[11]

However, the situation became critical for the Orientalists after 1933, since, as we discussed in the Introduction, Nazi authorities expected the universities and academics to further the regime's ideology and politics through their teachings and research. The obvious political capital that the Indologists could offer to the NS regime was Aryanism. This study has shown that various scholars took recourse not only to the Aryan discourse but also managed to invent various other reasons for the continued state sponsorship of Indology. Such rationalizations included Heinrich Lüders' claim of Indology attracting respect from Indians and Alsdorf's effusions about the contribution of Indologists to the nationalist project of enhancing the prestige of German academia in the world, concepts that survived the war and even helped Alsdorf's restitution in West German academia.

A more pragmatic rationale for modern Indian studies, relating to the necessity of maintaining diplomatic connections with an independent India, was provided by Franz Alfred Six to 'win' Alsdorf for the AF. As we saw, his arguments prevailed over Alfred Rosenberg's polemic about the ideological significance of 'Aryan India'. Six's futuristic reasoning also outlived the NS state.

This book posits that by defending their academic existence and generating knowledge discourses on India with the aim of legitimizing and propagating Nazi cultural politics, the knowledge providers belonged to the discursive system of 'power-knowledge' that Edward Said had referred to in his 'Orientalism', borrowing the concept advanced by Michel Foucault. While using the Saidian premise to situate our 'India experts' in the knowledge–power equation, one can simultaneously challenge Said's contention that the 'German Orient' was a scholarly one. Ironically, this refutation can be premised on another of Said's assertions, that Orientalism was a discourse of collecting knowledge which could be used to justify colonization, conquest, and humanitarian intervention.[12] Knowledge of India was cultivated and deployed by the 'India specialists' for promoting Nazi propaganda and aggressive politico-military goals. The Indic Orient invoked by them was thus a strategic topos and not an area of disinterested scholarship.

To return to a point mentioned in the Introduction, Said viewed Orientalism as a form of 'intellectual authority over the Orient', which he divided into 'historical authority' signifying an autonomous discursive formation and 'the personal authorities' of individual writers.[13] A number of the academic knowledge providers discussed in this book drew their 'personal authorities' from their status as university-trained Indologists. Such authority, which validated the knowledge discourses provided by them, was also deeply interlaced with their affiliations in the Nazi party and/or its various subsidiaries as well as their compliance (or at least lack of confrontation) with the dominant ideological discourse of the Nazi state.

Impact

A natural postscript to the discussions this book has engaged in relates to the possible impact of the knowledge generated by the 'experts'. The most wide-reaching echo of German propaganda concerning India was Bose's (and his team's) radio broadcasts, which were a part of the German radio propaganda. However, the determinant in this success was, above all, the personal aura of Bose, who, in his provocative broadcasts tapped 'the mood of public defiance' accompanying the 'Quit India' movement from 1942 to at least 1944.[14] The 'India experts' we encountered in the present study, with the possible exception of Abdul Rauf Malik, Habibur Rahman, and Abdul Quddus Faroqhi, played only a marginal part in the radio propaganda programme.

Press reports within the 'Reich' and the areas controlled by it followed certain predetermined propaganda tropes decided upon by the Foreign Ministry (particularly its 'Orient' section) and the SRI. Within these parameters, Ludwig Alsdorf seems to have exercised considerable influence by writing many of the reports on which German media's coverage of India was based. He also exerted some authority as a gatekeeper of what was considered suitable for publication on modern India in Germany. However, anti-British reports and books in German were hardly likely to reach ordinary readers in India; they were intended more for the audience at home, as we have already noted.

It is also evident that from 1933 to about 1938, German propaganda aimed at Indians was more concerned with spreading Nazi influence. Among the organizations we reviewed, the India Institute was particularly successful in reaching out to diverse religious and secular groups who were susceptible to the propaganda of Germany's revitalization under Hitler, which they deemed to be an aspirational model for the colonized Indians.

Propagandistic texts composed in regional language and in English by Hermann Beythan, Tarachand Roy, and Koodavuru Anantrama Bhatta reached India through various channels. However, it is difficult, in the near total absence of records of indigenous responses, to gauge how such propaganda was received by the Indians themselves. On the other hand, the palpable apprehensions of the colonial government in India which tried to track such propaganda and occasionally prohibit them (as with Beythan's book on Hitler) shows that the colonial authorities were worried about the possible ramifications of German propaganda. It is also hard to assess the impact of the magazine *Bhaiband*, written in modern Indian languages, on the Indian soldiers who remain practically voiceless.

Generally, propaganda concerning the superiority of Nazism and Hitler remained confined to a relatively small section of Indians, usually belonging to the right-wing religious and/or political fringe, as I have explored elsewhere.[15] By the time the propaganda trope of expressing sympathy for Indian nationalism assumed political significance, most Indians under the leadership of Gandhi, Nehru, and the Indian National Congress had publicly rejected Fascism and Nazism, a rebuff that Nazi propaganda resolutely ignored. The clumsy attempts undertaken by propagandists like Alsdorf to promote Gandhi and Subhas Bose in the same breath, ironing out their fundamental differences, represent the refusal or obtuseness of the Nazi policymakers and their knowledge providers in acknowledging the strength of the conviction underlying the anti-colonial messages articulated by the INC, condemning fascism and imperialism alike.[16]

A few long-term effects of the knowledge discourses generated in the organizations discussed can probably be discerned in both Indian and German contexts. In the Indian perspective, this legacy is mostly present in the ideological realm. If European Orientalism left its imprint in the nineteenth- and early twentieth-century conceptions of Hinduism infused with Aryanism, the Nazi overtures, particularly to Hindu revivalists and Hindu nationalists (whose ideological paths often intersect), has contributed to a tradition of ahistorical and ignorant admiration of Hitler. Admittedly, this potentially dangerous fetishization of Hitler and Nazism among some Indians is a complex phenomenon involving a plethora of reasons and historical circumstances including the feeling of inferiority generated by centuries of colonial rule. Nevertheless, Nazi propaganda seems to have has left its mark in the Indian federal states where Hindu nationalism traditionally finds resonance as well as those in which authoritarian and militaristic ethos are prioritized. In these states, Hitler is still invoked as an epitome of patriotic leadership, as their government-approved school textbooks demonstrate.[17]

In the German context, a possible impact concerns contemporary Germany's relationship with India, some of the rationale for which can be located in Franz Alfred Six's pleas for establishing a chair for modern Indian Studies at the AF. Six predicated the establishment of such a chair upon the confident vision of a victorious Nazi Germany entering into diplomatic relationship with an independent India, for which knowledge of contemporary Indian languages and *Realien* would be essential. One could probably detect an element of this vision in the establishment of present-oriented departments of Indian (and South Asian) Studies in different German universities in the decades after the war, though this is not to deny vital factors like the influence of the emergence of interdisciplinary 'area studies' in the USA after the Second World War.

The Way Ahead

In the Introduction to this book, I mentioned two recently published texts—a forum on the historiography of Indian Studies and an introduction to the special issue of the journal NTM, in which a few of us had pointed to the various questions that remain open three decades after the publication of Pollock's groundbreaking article.[18] This book has attempted, on the basis of the case studies, to provide answers to some of them. A multitude of queries remain, pertaining, for example, to the crucial issue of whether and to what extent career advancement was possible for scholars of India without serving the Nazi regime in overt and covert ways.

I have briefly traced in the Introduction the long and difficult journey, strewn with different roadblocks, which researchers trying to study the complex interactions between various knowledge discourses on India, their purveyors, and Nazi politics were fated to encounter. I hope that through my attempt to navigate this contested field, other researchers will feel motivated and emboldened enough to explore further aspects of this theme which wait to be illuminated. It is time that we moved on from *ex oriente nox* as referred to by Sheldon Pollock, to *Tamaso ma Jyotirgamaya* (from darkness to light) as the Sanskrit prayer in the Upanishad says.[19]

Notes

1. Pollock, Sheldon, 1993, 95.
2. Roy, Baijayanti, 2022b, 11–29.
3. Steinweis, Alan, 2022, 45.
4. Marchand, Suzanne, 2022, 73.
5. Framke, Maria, 2023, 307–32.
6. Günther, Lothar, 2012, 29–32.
7. Roy, Baijayanti, 2016a.
8. Schatz, Adam, 2019.
9. Roy, Baijayanti, 2022a, 537–53; Framke, Maria, 2023, 307–32.
10. Steinweis, Alan, 2022, 45.
11. Marchand, Suzanne, 2022, 72.
12. Schatz, Adam, 2019.
13. Said, Edward, 1978, 19.
14. Gupta, Diya, 2019, 8–9.
15. See Roy, 2023, The Bengali Society of German Culture at https://www.projekt-mida.de/reflexicon/bengali-society-of-german-culture/; Roy, 2024.
16. Framke, Maria and Tschurenev, Jana, 2018, 74.
17. Roy, Baijayanti, 2019, 209, 213.
18. See https://link.springer.com/journal/48/volumes-and-issues/31-3.
19. Pollock, Sheldon, 2002, 335–71.

The Nazi Study of India and Indian Anti-Colonialism: Knowledge Providers and Propagandists in the 'Third Reich'.
Baijayanti Roy, Oxford University Press. © Baijayanti Roy 2024. DOI: 10.1093/9780191981951.003.0006

Bibliography

1. Primary Source Archives

Archives of the Auschwitz-Birkenau State Museum in Oświęcim Auschwitz-Birkenau State Museum in Oświęcim (Archiwum Państwowego Muzeum Auschwitz-Birkenau w Oświęcimiu), Poland: APMA-B

Archives of the Evangelical Church of Rhineland (Archiv der Evangelischen Kirche in Rheinland): EKIR

Archive of Humboldt University in Berlin: AHU

Archive of the University of Göttingen

Archive of the University of Tübingen

Archive of the University of Wroclaw, Poland: AUW

Bayerisches Hauptstaatsarchiv (Bavarian Main State Archives), Munich: BayHstA

Bundesarchiv (Federal Archives), Berlin: BA Berlin

Bundesarchiv (Federal Archives), Koblenz: BA Koblenz

Bundesarchiv Militärarchiv (Federal Military Archives), Freiburg: BA MA

Franckesche Stiftungen zu Halle (Francke Foundations in Halle): ALMW Halle

Geheimesstaatsarchiv Preußischer Kulturbesitz (Secret State Archives Prussian Cultural Heritage Foundation), Berlin: GstAPK

India Office Records, British Library, London: IOR

Leibnitz Institut für Zeitgeschichte (Leibnitz Institute for Contemporary History), Munich: IfZ Munich

National Archives of India, New Delhi: NAI

National Archives United Kingdom, Kew: NAUK

Politisches Archiv Auswärtigen Amtes (Political Archive of the German Foreign Ministry), Berlin: PA-AA

Sächsisches Hauptstaatsarchiv (The Main State Archives of Saxony), Dresden: SaHStA

Stiftung Sächsische Gedenkstätten, Dokumentationsstelle Dresden (Saxony Memorial Foundation, Document Center, Dresden): StSG-DokStSl

University Archive, Bonn: UAB

University Archive, Halle-Wittemberg: UAHW

University Archive, Munich ((Universitätsarchiv München)

University Archive, Münster: UAM

West Bengal State Archives, Kolkata: WBSA

2. Secondary Sources

Adluri, Vishwa, Bagchee, Joydeep, 2019, The Banality of Indology: Franco, Pollock and the Friedrich Weller Prize, https://www.academia.edu/41372157/The_Banality_of_Indology_Franco_Pollock_and_the_Friedrich_Weller_Prize.

Adluri, Vishwa P., 2011, Pride and Prejudice: Orientalism and German Indology, *International Journal of Hindu Studies*, 15, 3, 253–92.

Ahuja, Ravi, 2010, The Corrosiveness of Comparison: Reverberations of Indian Wartime Experiences in German Prison Camps (1915–1919). In Heike Liebau, Katrin Bromber, Kathariana Lange, Dyala Humza, Ravi Ahuja (eds), *The World in World Wars: Experiences, Perceptions and Perspectives from Africa and Asia*, Leiden: Brill, 131–66.

Ahuja, Ravi, 2020, Asian Industrialism, Labour Movements and Cultural Nationalism: Interwar Contexts of German Trade-Union Writings on "Working India". In Ravi Ahuja, Marcel van der Linder, Anna Sailer (eds), '*The Distress is Impossible to Convey*'. *British and German Trade Union Reports on Labour in India (1926–1928)*, Berlin: De Gruyter Oldenbourg, 246–72.

Aijaz, Ahmed, 2016, Liberal Democracy and the Extreme Right, https://indianculturalforum. in/2016/09/07/india-liberal-democracy-and-the-extreme-right/?fbclid=IwAR0FcmJOrFaRI Bf0oDIMilLKIhZC3FQ4u9SInpAqpgrHFBh3ze335NOB9mA.

Alcade, Angel, 2020, The Transnational Consensus: Fascism and Nazism in Current Research, *Contemporary European History*, 29, 243–52.

Almgren, Birgitta, Hecker-Stampehl, Jan, Piper, Ernst, 2008, Alfred Rosenberg und die Nordische Gesellschaft Der 'nordische Gedanke' in Theorie und Praxis, *NORDEUROPA forum*, 2, https://edoc.hu-berlin.de/bitstream/handle/18452/8624/3.pdf?sequence=1.

Alsdorf, Ludwig, 1940, *Indien*, Berlin: Deutscher Verlag.

Alsdorf, Ludwig, 1942, *Deutsch-indische Geistesbeziehungen*, Heidelberg: Kurt Vowinckel.

Alsdorf, Ludwig, 1943, *Indien und Ceylon*, Berlin: Junker & Dünnhaupt.

Alsdorf, Ludwig, 1943, Indien, *Jahrbuch der Weltpolitik*, 637–58.

Alsdorf, Ludwig, 1944, Indien, *Jahrbuch der Weltpolitik*, 674–89.

Arnold, Klaus Jochen, 2014, Rommel unterstützte das Attentat auf Hitler, https://www.kas.de/ de/veranstaltungsberichte/detail/-/content/rommel-unterstuetzte-das-attentat-auf-hitler.

Ash, Mitchell G., 2002, Wissenschaft und Politik als Ressourcen für einander. In Rudiger Bruch, Brigitte Kaderas (eds), *Wissenschaften und Wissenschaftspolitik. Bestandsaufnahme zu Formationen, Brüchen und Kontinuitäten im Deutschland des. 20. Jahrhunderts*, Stuttgart: Steiner, 32–51.

Augustinovic, Werner, Moll, Martin, 2017, Franz Alfred Six. In Michael Fahlbusch, Ingo Haar, Alexander Pinwinkler (eds), *Handbuch der Völkischer Wissenschaften*, Vol. 1, Berlin: De Gruyter, 773–8.

Bagchee, Joydeep, Paul Thieme (1905–2001), https://www.academia.edu/42749714/Paul_Thieme

Bannerjea, Devendra Nath, 1934, *Das indische Bauerntum unter britischer Herrschaft*, Berlin: Verlag Dr. Emil Ebering.

Bannerth, Ernst, 1943, *Hindustani Briefe*. Arbeitshefte für den Sprachermittler. Heft 49, Leipzig: Harrassowitz.

Barooah, Elizabeth, Barooah, Nirode K., 2015, *Franz Josef Fürtwangler and India: A German Trade Union Internationalist's Extraordinary Engagement with India*, Norderstedt: Books on Demand.

Barooah, Nirode Kumar, 2004, *Chatto: The life and Times of an Anti-Imperialist in Europe*, New Delhi: Oxford University Press.

Barooah, Nirode Kumar, 2018, *Germany and the Indians*, Norderstedt: Books on Demand.

Basu, Anustup, 2020, *Hindutva as Political Monotheism*, Durham, NC: Duke University Press.

Bates, Crispin, 1995, *Race, Caste and Tribe in Central India: The Early Origins in Indian Anthropometry*, Edinburgh: University of Edinburgh Press.

Baumann, Schaul, 2005, *Die Deutsche Glaubensbewegung und ihr Gründer Jakob Wilhelm Hauer (1821–1962)*, Marburg: Diagonal.

Bautz, Friedrich Wilhelm, 1990, Hauer, Jakob Wilhelm. In *Biographisch- Bibliographisches Kirchenlexicon*, Vol. 2, Hamm: Verlag Traugott Bautz, 593–4.

Bayley, Christopher, Harper, Tim, 2005, *Forgotten Armies: Britain's Asian Empire and the War with Japan*, London: Penguin UK.

Bechert, Heinz, 1986, Obituary Enst Waldschmidt (1897–1985), *Journal of the International Association of Buddhist Studies*, 9, 1, 147–9.

Behrenbeck, Sabine, 1996, *Der Kult um die Toten Helden. Nationalsozialistische Mythen, Riten und Symbole 1923 bis 1945*, Vierow bei Greifswald: SH Verlag.

Benz, Wolfgang, 2013, Unis in der NS Zeit: Hitlers willige Professoren, https://www.tagesspie-gel.de/wissen/hitlers-willige-professoren-6651781.html.

Beythan, Hermann, 1936, *Atolp Hitlar allatu Tiramaiyin verri*, Cennai: Tēcīya Vittiya Cankam.

Beythan, Hermann, 1942, *Was ist Indien?*, Heidelberg: Kurt Vowinckel.

Beythan, Hermann, 1943, *Praktische Grammatik der Tamilsprache in Umschrift*, Leipzig: Otto Harrassowitz.

Bharati, Agehananda, 1970, *The Ochre Robe: An Autobiography*, New York: Doubleday & Company.

Bhatt, Chetan, 2001, *Hindu Nationalism: Origins, Ideologies and Modern Myths*, Oxford: Berg.

Bhatta, K.A., 1943, *Indien im Britischen Reich*, Heidelberg: Kurt Vowinckel (second edition).

Bialas, Wolfgang, Rabinbach, Anson (eds), 2007, *Nazi Germany and the Humanities*, Oxford: Oneworld.

Bleek, Wilhelm, 2001, *Geschichte der Politikwissenschaft in Deutschland*, München: CH Beck.

Boelcke, Willi A., 1974, Das 'Seehaus' in Berlin-Wannsee. Zur Geschichte des deutschen Monitoring Service während des Zweiten Weltkrieges. In Klaus Neitmann (ed.), *Jahrbuch für die Geschichte Mittel-und Ostdeutschlands*, Berlin: De Gruyter, 231–69.

Bose, Mihir, 1982, *The Lost Hero: A Biography of Subhas Bose*, London: Quartet.

Bose, Mihir, 2017, This Indian was probably the Most Extraordinary Spy of World War II, https://scroll.in/article/833360/this-indian-was-probably-the-most-extraordinary-spy-of-world-war-ii.

Bose, Neilesh, 2020a, Taraknath Das: A Global Biography. In Neilesh Bose (ed), *South Asian Migrations in Global History: Labour, Law, and Wayward Lives*, London: Bloomsbury, 157–77.

Bose, Neilesh, 2020b, Taraknath Das (1884–1958), British Columbia, and the Anti-Colonial Borderlands, *BC Studies*, 204, 67–88.

Bose, Sugata, 2011, *His Majesty's Opponent: Subhas Chandra Bose and India's Struggle against Empire*, Cambridge, MA: Harvard University Press.

Botsch, Gideon, 2006, *Politische Wissenschaft im Zweiten Weltkrieg: die 'Deutschen Auslandswissenschaften' im Einsatz 1940–1945*, Paderborn: Schöningh.

Bourdieu, Pierre, 1990, Die biographische Illusion, *BIOS*, 3, 1, 75–81.

Bozsa, Isabella, 2014, *Eugen Mattiat (1901–1976). Vom 'Deutschen Christen' zum Volkskundeprofessor und wieder zurück ins Pastorat. Fallstudie einer Karriere im Nationalsozialismus*, Göttingen: Schmerse Media.

Breloer, Bernhard, 1927, *Kautaliya Studien. Vol. 1, Das Grundeigentum in Indien*, Bonn: Schroeder.

Bremm, Klaus-Jürgen, 2013, *Propaganda im Ersten Weltkrieg*, Darmstadt: wbg Theiss.

Brückenhaus, Daniel, 2017, *Policing Transnational Protest: Liberal Imperialism and the Surveillance of Anticolonialists in Europe, 1905–1945*, New York: Oxford University Press.

Bruhn, Klaus, 1990, Obituary. In Klaus Bruhn, Magdalene Duckwitz, Albrecht Wezle (eds), *Ludwig Alsdorf and Indian Studies*, Delhi: Motilal Banarssidas.

Buschak, Willy A., 2010, *Franz Josef Furtwängler. Gewerkschafter, Indienreisender, Widerstandskämpfer. Eine politische Biografie*, Essen: Klartext.

Casolari, Marzia, 2000, Hindutva's Foreign Tie-Ups in the 1930s: Archival Evidence, *Economic and Political Weekly*, 35, 4, 222–5.

Conze, Eckart, Frei, Norbert, Hayes, Peter, Zimmermann, Moshe, 2010, *Das Amt und die Vergangenheit. Deutsche Diplomaten im Dritten Reich und in der Bundesrepublik*, Munich: Blessing.

Crim, Brian E., 2011, 'Our most serious enemy': The Specter of Judeo-Bolshevism in the German Military community, 1914–1923, *Central European History*, 44, 4, 624–41.

Dainat, Holgar, Danneberg, Lutz (eds), 2003, *Literaturwissenschaft und Nationalsozialismus*, Berlin: De Gruyter.

Delf, Tobias, 2008, *Hindunationalismus und europäischer Faschismus: Vergleich, Transfer-und Beziehungsgeschichte*, Hamburg: Schenefeld.

Deussen, Paul, 1922, *Erinnerungen an Indien*, Saarbrücken: VDM Verlag Dr Müller.

Dierks, Margarete, 1986, *Jakob Wilhelm Hauer 1881–1962. Leben, Werk, Wirkung*, Heidelberg: Lambert Schneider.

D'Souza, Eugene, 2000, Nazi Propaganda in India, *Social Scientist*, 28, 5/6, 77–90.

Egorova, Yulia, 2006, *Jews and India: Perceptions and Image*, London: Routledge.

Eisfeld, Rainer, 1991, *Ausgebürgert und doch angebräunt. Deutsche Politikwissenschaft 1920–45*, Baden Baden: Nomos.

Ellinger, Ekkehard, 2006, *Deutsche Orientalistik zur Zeit des Nationalsozialismus 1933–45*, Edingen-Neckarhausen: Deux mondes.

Figueira, Dorothy M., 1994, The Authority of an Absent Text: The Veda, Upangas, Upavedas and Upnekhata in European Thought. In Laurie L. Patton (ed.), *Authority, Anxiety and Canon: Essays in Vedic Interpretation*, Albany, NY: State University of New York Press, 201–34.

Figueira, Dorothy M., 2002, *Aryans, Jews Brahmins: Theorising Authority Through Myths of Identity*, Albany, NY: State University of New York Press.

Fischer-Tiné, Harald, 2013, Arya Samaj. In J. Bronkhorst, A. Malinar (eds), *Handbook of Oriental Studies. Section Two: India*, volume 22/5, Leiden: Brill, 389–96.

Flora, Giuseppe, 1994, *Benoy Kumar Sarkar and Italy: Culture, Politics and Economic Ideology*, Delhi: Italian Embassy Cultural Centre.

Framke, Maria, 2013, *Delhi Rom Berlin. Die indische Wahrnehmung von Faschismus und Nationalsozialismus 1922–1939*, Darmstadt: WBG (Wissenschaftliche Buchgesellschaft).

Framke, Maria, 2014, Die Rolle der Berliner Indologie und Indienkunde im „Dritten Reich. In Maria Framke, Hannelore Lötzke, Ingo Strauch (eds), *Indologie und Südasienstudien in Berlin: Geschichte und Positionsbestimmung*, Berlin: Trafo, 89–128.

Framke, Maria, 2016, Shopping Ideologies for Independent India? Taraknath Das's Engagement with Italian Fascism and German National Socialism, *Itinerario*, 40, 1, 55–81.

Framke, Maria, 2023, Manoeuvring Across Academia in National Socialist Germany: The Life and Work of Devendra Nath Bannerjea, *NTM Zeitschrift für Geschichte der Wissenschaften, Technik und Medizin*, 31, 3, 307–32.

Framke, Maria, Tschurenev, Jana, 2018, Umstrittene Geschichte. (Anti-)Faschismus und (Anti-) Kolonialismus in Indien, *PROKLA Zeitschrift für Kritische Sozialwissenschaft*, 40, 158, 67–83.

Franco, Eli, 2023, There Is No Reliable Evidence to Pass Moral Judgement on Frauwallner. Erich Frauwallner, Jakob Stuchlik, Walter Slaje and the Whitewashing of Austrian Indology During the Time of National Socialism, *NTM Zeitschrift für Geschichte der Wissenschaften, Technik und Medizin*, 31, 245–74.

Franzen, Hans, 1981, *Aus meinem Leben und meiner Zeit*, Wiesbaden: Carl Ritter.

Fugger, Ulrich, 2017, Wald und Baum. In Michael Fahlbusch, Ingo Haar, Alexander Pinwinkler (eds), *Handbuch der völkischen Wissenschaften. Akteure, Netzwerke, Forschungsprogramme*, Vol. II, Berlin: De Gruyter, 1297–304.

Furtwängler, Franz Joseph, 1951, *Männer die ich sah und kannte*, Hamburg: Auerdruck.

Furtwängler, Franz Joseph, Schrader, Karl, 1928, *Das Werktätige Indien. Sein Werden und Sein Kampf*, Berlin: Deutscher Textilarbeiter-Verband.

Geisenhainer, Katja, 2000, *'Rasse ist Schicksal!' Otto Reche (1879–1966)—ein Leben als Anthropologe und Völkerkunder*, Leipzig: Evangelische Verlagsanstalt.

Geisenhainer, Katja, 2017, Otto Reche. In Michael Fahlbusch, Ingo Haar, Alexander Pinwinkler (eds), *Handbuch der völkischen Wissenschaften. Akteure, Netzwerke, Forschungsprogramme*, Vol. 1, Berlin: De Gruyter Oldenbourg, 616–20.

Geissler, Gert, 2002, Die Schulgruppen des 'Vereins für das deutschtum ins Ausland.' Das Beispiel Groß-Berlin in den Jahren 1920 bis 1940. In Peter Dudek, Hanno Schmitt, Heinz-Elmar Tenorth (eds), *Jahrbuch für Historische Bildungsforschung*, Vol. 8, Bad Heilbrunn: Obb, 229–58.

Gesche, Katja, 2006, *Kultur als Instrument der Außenpolitik totalitärer Staaten: das Deutsche Ausland-Institut 1933–1945*, Köln: Bohlau.

Ghoshal, Sayori, 2021, Race in South Asia: Colonialism, Nationalism and Modern Science, *History Compass*, 19, 2, http://dx.doi.org/10.1111/hic3.12647.

Goebbel, Michael, 2015, *Anti-Imperial Metropolis: Interwar Paris and the Seeds of Third World Nationalism*, Cambridge: Cambridge University Press.

Goel, Urmila, 2003, Indische Legion. Ein Stück deutsche Geschichte. *Südasien*, 4, 3, 27–30.

Göllnitz, Martin, 2016, Wissenschaftspolitik im Spannungsfeld von akademische Tradition und Ideologie. Die nationalsozialistische Dozentenakademie der Universität Kiel (1934–36), *Zeitschrift für Geschichtswissenschaft*, 50–72, https://www.academia.edu/35384526/ Wissenschaftspolitik_im_Spannungsfeld_von_akademischer_Tradition_und_Ideologie_ Die_nationalsozialistische_Dozentenakademie_der_Universit%C3%A4t_Kiel_1934_1936_ ?hb-sb-sw=38230359.

Gondhalekar, Nandini, Bhattacharya, Sanjoy, 1999, The All India Hindu Mahasabha and the End of British Rule in India 1939–1947, *Social Scientist*, 27, 7/8, 48–74.

Gordon, Leonard A., 1990, *Brothers against the Raj: A Biography of Indian Nationalists Sarat and Subhas Bose*, New York: Columbia University Press.

Gossweiler, Kurt, 1982, *Kapital, Reichswehr und NSDAP 1912–1924*, Köln: Pahl-Rugenstein.

Gould, William, 2009, *Hindu Nationalism and the Language of Politics in Late Colonial India*, Cambridge: Cambridge University Press.

Grünendahl, Reinhold, 2006, Von der Indologie zum Völkermord: Die Kontinuitätskonstrukte Sheldon Pollocks und seiner Epigonen im Lichte ihrer Beweisführung. In Ute Hüsken et al. (eds), *Jaina-Itihāsa-Ratna: Festschrift für Gustav Roth zum 90. Geburtstag*, Marburg: Indica et Tibetica, 209–36.

Grünendahl, Reinhold, 2008, Wissenschaftsgeschichte im Schatten post-orientalischer De/ Konstruktion. Orientalische Literaturzeitung, 103, 457–78.

Grünendahl, Reinhold, 2012a, *Archives des artifices, or the Reinvention of "German Indology" in Terms of a Mythical Quest for National Origins*, Studia Indologica Universitatis Halensis, Vol. 5, Halle an der Saale: Universitätsverlag Halle-Wittenberg.

Grünendahl, Reinhold, 2012b, History in the Making: On Sheldon Pollock's "NS Indology" and Vishwa Adluri's "Pride and Prejudice", *International Journal of Hindu Studies*, 16, 2, 189–257.

Grünendahl, Reinhold, 2019, *Pseudodoxia Postorientalis: Erkundungen eines amerikanischen Diskurses über die Indienrezeption in der Wilhelminischen Kaiserzeit (1871–1918)*, Studia Indologica Universitatis Halensis, Vol. 12, Halle an der Saale: Universitätsverlag Halle-Wittenberg.

Grüttner, Michael, 2004, *Biographisches Lexikon zur nationalsozialistischen Wissenschaftspolitik* (Studien zur Wissenschafts- und Universitätsgeschichte Vol. 6), Heidelberg: Synchron.

Grüttner, Michael, Rüdiger, Hachtmann, Jarausch, Konrad H., John, Jürgen, Middell, Matthias (eds), 2010, *Gebrochene Wissenschaftskulturen. Universität und Politik in 20. Jahrhundert*, Göttingen: Vandenhoeck & Ruprecht.

Günther, Lothar, 1996, *Taraknath Das: Ein Lebensbild des indischen Revolutionärs, Freiheitskämpfer und Gelehrten*, Berlin: Taraknath Das Stiftung.

Günther, Lothar, 2003, *Von Indien nach Annaburg*, Berlin: Verlag am Park.

Günther, Lothar, 2012, Die wahren Handlanger von Subhas Chandra Bose. Meine Welt. *Zeitschrift des Deutsch-Indischen Dialogs*, 2, 29, 29–32.

Günther, Lothar, 2013, *Die Indische Legion und das Dritte Reich: Das zentrale Kriegsgefangenenlager der Inder in Annaburg und der Kampf um Indiens Unabhängigkeit*, Berlin: Verlag am Park.

Günther, Lothar, Rehmer, Hans-Joachim, 1990, *Inder Indien und Berlin. 100 Jahre Begegnung Berlin und Indien*, Berlin: Lotos Verlag Roland Beer.

Gupta, Diya, 2019, The Raj in Radio Wars: BBC Monitoring Reports on Broadcasts for Indian Audiences During the Second World War, *Media History*, 25, 4, 414–29.

Hachmeister, Lutz, 1998, *Der Gegnerforscher: die Karriere des SS-Führers Franz Alfred Six*, München: C.H. Beck.

Hanisch, Ernst, 2014, Der politische Katholizismus als ideologischer Träger des 'Austrofaschismus'. In Emmerich Talos, Wolfgang Neugebaur (eds), *Austrofaschismus. Politik—Ökonomie— Kultur 1933–1938*, Wien: LIT Verlag, 67–87.

Hanisch, Marc, 2014, Curt Prüfer—Orientalist, Dragoman und Oppenheims 'man on the spot'. In Wilfried Loth, Marc Hanisch (eds), *Erster Weltkrieg und Dschihad. Die Deutschen und die Revolutionierung des Orients*, München: Oldenbourg, 167–91.

Hannedar, Jürgen, 2013, 'Zukunftsphilologie' oder nächste M(eth)ode, *Zeitschrift der Deutschen Morgenländischen Gesellschaft*, 163, 1, 159–72.

Hansen, Eckhard, 1991, *Wohlfahrtspolitik im NS-Staat: Motivationen, Konflikte und Machtstrukturen im 'Sozialismus der Tat' des Dritten Reiches*, Augsburg: Maro-Verlag.

Harbich, Walter, 1970, A Report on the Organisation and Training of the Free India Army in Europe 1941–1942. In Alexander Werth, Walter Harbich, *Netaji in Germany: An Eyewitness Account of Indian Freedom Struggle in Europe during World War II*, Calcutta: Netaji Research Bureau, 46–57.

Hartog, Rudolf, 1991, *Im Zeichen des Tigers. Die indische Legion auf deutscher Seite 1941–1945*, Herford: Busse & Seewald.

Harvolk, Edgar, 1990, *Eichenzweig und Hakenkreuz. Die Deutsche Akademie in München (1924–1962) und ihre volkskundliche Sektion*, München: Münchner Vereinigung für Volkskunde.

Hassan, Abid, 1943, *Der Islam in Indien. Indien in Weltislam*, Heidelberg: Kurt Vowinckel.

Hauer, Jakob Wilhelm, 1937, *Der Religiöse Artbild der indogermanen und die Grundtypen der Indoarischen Religion*, Stuttgart: Kohlhammer.

Hauner, Milan, 1981, *India in Axis Strategy: Germany, Japan, and Indian Nationalists in the Second World War*, Stuttgart: Klett-Cotta.

Haushofer, Karl, 1941, *Wehr-geopolitik. Geographische Grundlagen einer Wehrkunde*, Berlin: Junker & Dünnhaupt.

Hayes, Romain, 2011, *Subhas Chandra Bose in Nazi Germany: Politics, Intelligence and Propaganda*, London: Hurst & Company.

Heimann, Betty, 1938, Review: Panini and the Veda (Studies in the Early History of Linguistic Science in India), *Journal of the Royal Asiatic Society*, 70, 2, 300–301.

Hensel, Hans Michael, 2019, Hafiz Manzooruddin Ahmad. Der Asien- und Indienerklärer der Nationalsozialisten, http://www.hmhensel.com/hafiz-manzooruddin-ahmad/ (published 8.4.2019).

Herf, Jeffrey, 2009, *Nazi Propaganda for the Arab World*, New Haven, CT: Yale University Press.

Herren, Madeleine, 2013, Between Territoriality, Performance, and Transcultural Entanglement (1920–1939): A Typology of Transboundary Lives, *Comparativ: Zeitschrift für Globalgeschichte und vergleichende Gesellschaftsforschung*, 23, 6, 100–24.

Hochstretter, Dorothee, 2005, *Motorisierung und volksgemeinschaft. Das NS Kraftfahrkorps (NSKK) 1931–45*, München: R. Oldenbourg.

Hoffmann, Karl, 1940, Vedischen Namen. *Wörter und Sachen*, 21, 139–61.

Hoßfeld, Uwe, Simunek, Michal V., 2017, Rassenbiologie. In Michael Fahlbusch, Ingo Haar, Alexander Pinwinkler (eds), *Handbuch der Völkischen Wissenschaften*, Berlin: De Gruyter Oldenbourg, 1114–22.

Hufnagel, Ulrich, 2003, Religionswissenschaft und indische Religionsgeschichte in den Arbeiten Jakob Wilhelm Hauers: Wissenschaftskonzept und politische Orientierung. In Heidrun Brückner, Klaus Butzenberger, Angelika Malinar, Gabrielle Zeller (eds), *Indienforschung im Zeitenwandel. Analysen und Dokumente zur indologie und Religionswissenschaft in Tübingen*, Tübingen: Attempto Verlag, 145–74.

Hutton, Christopher, 1999, *Linguistics and the Third Reich: Mother-Tongue Fascism, Race and the Science of Language*, New York: Routledge.

Impekoven, Holger, 2013, *Die Alexander von Humboldt-Stiftung und das Ausländerstudium in Deutschland 1925–1945*, Bonn: Bonn University Press.

Jenkins, Jennifer, Liebau, Heike, Schmid, Larissa, 2020, Transnationalism and Insurrection: Independence Committees, Anti-Colonial Networks, and Germany's Global War, *Journal of Global History*, 15, 1, 61–79.

Jha, Ganganath, 1920 (1999 edition), *Manusmriti with the Commentary of Medhatithi*, Delhi: Motilal Banarasidas.

Jung, Michael, 1989, *Liederbücher im Nationalsozialismus: Dokumente*, Frankfurt am Main: Johann Wolfgang Goethe Universität zu Frankfurt am Main.

Junginger, Horst, 1999, *Von der philologischen zur völkischen Religionswissenschaft*, Stuttgart: Steiner.

Junginger, Horst, 2003, Das 'Arische Seminar' an der Universität Tübingen 1940–1945. In Heidrun Brückner, Klaus Butzenberger, Angelika Malinar, Gabrielle Zeller (eds), *Indienforschung im Zeitenwandel. Analysen und Dokumente zur indologie und Religionswissenschaft in Tübingen*, Tübingen: Attempto Verlag, 177–207.

Junginger, Horst, 2008, From Buddha to Adolf Hitler: Walther Wüst and the Aryan Tradition. In Horst Junginger (ed.), *The Study of Religion under the Impact of Fascism*, Leiden: Brill, 107–78.

Junginger, Horst, 2017a, Jakob Wilhelm Hauer. In Michael Fahlbusch, Ingo Haar, Alexander Pinwinkler (eds), Handbuch der Völkischen Wissenschaften, Berlin: De Gruyter Oldenbourg, 274–9.

Junginger, Horst, 2017b, Walther Wüst. In Michael Fahlbusch, Ingo Haar, Alexander Pinwinkler (eds), Handbuch der Völkischen Wissenschaften, Berlin: De Gruyter Oldenbourg, 925–33.

Kaider, Gerhard, 2006, Grenzverwirrungen: Literaturwissenschaft im Nationalsozialismus, Berlin: Akademie Verlag.

Kallis, Aristotle, 2005, Nazi Propaganda and the Second World War, Basingstoke: Palgrave Macmillan.

Kannan, K.S (ed.), 2017, Western Indology and Its Quest for Power, Chennai: Infinity Foundation India.

Kater, Michael H., 2006, Das 'Ahnenerbe' der SS 1935–1945. Ein Beitrag zur Kulturpolitik des Dritten Reiches, München: Oldenbourg (fourth edition).

Kathe, Steffen R., 2005, Kulturpolitik um jeden Preis, München: Meidenbauer.

Kieslich, Charlotte P., 2018, Dolmetscher Seminar der Reichsfachschaft für das Dolmetscherwesen (RfD), Berlin: Frank & Timme.

Klee, Ernst, 2005, Das Personenlexikon zum Dritten Reich. Wer war was vor und nach 1945, Frankfurt am Main: Fischer Taschenbuch Verlag, 415 (second edition).

Koop, Volker, 2009, Hitler's Fünfte Kolonne. Die Auslands-Organisation der NSDAP, Berlin: be.bra.

Koops, Tilman, 2017, Karl Haushofer. In Michael Fahlbusch, Ingo Haar, Alexander Pinwinkler (eds), Handbuch der Völkischen Wissenschaften, Berlin: De Gruyter Oldenbourg, 281–2.

Krekeler, Norbert, 1973, Revisionsanspruch und geheime Ostpolitik der Weimarer Republik, München: DVA.

Krug, Samuel, 2020, Die 'Nachrichtenstelle für den Orient' im Kontext globaler Verflechtungen (1914–1921) Strukturen—Akteure—Diskurse, Bielefeld: Transcript.

Kruse, Wilhelm, 1942, Denkmäler indischer Kunst, Heidelberg: Kurt Vowinckel.

Kuhlmann, Jan, 2003, Subhas Chandra Bose und die Indienpolitik der Achsenmächte, Berlin: Hans Schiler.

Kuhlmann, Jan, 2015, Die indische Legion im Zweiten Weltkrieg: Interkulturelle Menschenführung zwischen Atlantikwall und Wehrmacht Gefängnis, Südasien-chronik—South Asia Chronicle, 5, 91–119.

Laursen, Ole Birk, 2023, Hindustan House: The Forgotten Indian Restaurant in Weimar Era Berlin, The Wire, 7 February.

Lehmann, Heinz, 1942, Indien, Jahrbuch der Weltpolitik, 770–6.

Lehmann, Heinz, 1942, Cripps' Mission in Indien. Monatshefte für Auswärtige Politik, 5, 386–401.

Lehmann, Heinz, 1965, Nehru: Baumeister des Neuen Indien, Zürich: Musterschmidt-Verlag.

Lehnhardt, Jochen, 2017, Die Waffen SS: Geburt einer Legende. Himmlers Krieger in der Propaganda, Paderborn: Schöningh.

Leifer, Walter, 1977, India and the Germans: 500 years of Indo-German Contacts, Bombay: Shakuntala.

Leutner, Mechthild, 2001, Vom Spracheninstitut zur nationalsozialistischen Auslandswissenschaftlichen Fakultät: Das Seminar für Orientalische Sprachen 1933–1945 unter besonderer Berücksichtigung der Chinesisch-Abteilung. In Christine Neder, Heiner Roetz, Ines-Susanne-Schilling (eds), China in seinen biographischen Dimensionen. Gedenkschrift für Helmut Martin, Wiesbaden: Harrassowitz, 427–50.

Levinson, Bernard M., Erickson, Robert, P., 2022, The Betrayal of the Humanities: The University during the Third Reich, Bloomington, IN: Indiana University Press.

Liebau, Heike, 2014a, Berlin Indian Independence Committee. In Ute Daniel, Peter Gatrell, Oliver Janz (eds), International Encyclopedia of the First World War, https://encyclopedia.1914-1918online.net/article/berlin_indian_independence_committee?version=1.0.

Liebau, Heike, 2014b, Das Deutsche Auswärtige Amt, Indische Emigranten und propagandistische Bestrebungen unter den südasiatischen Kriegsgefangenen im „Halbmondlager. In

Franziska Roy, Heike Liebau (eds), *Soldat Ram Singh und der Kaiser: indische Kriegsgefangene in deutschen Propagandalagern 1914–1918*, Heidelberg: Draupadi, 109–44.

Liebau, Heike, 2014c, Hindostan. Eine Zeitung für südasiatische Kriegsgefangene in Deutschland 1915–1918. In Franziska Roy, Heike Liebau (eds), *Soldat Ram Singh und der Kaiser: indische Kriegsgefangene in deutschen Propagandalagern 1914–1918*, Heidelberg: Draupadi, 261–85.

Liebau, Heike, 2019a, 'Unternehmungen und Aufwiegelungen': Das Berliner Indische Unabhängigkeitskomitee in den Akten des Politischen Archivs des Auswärtigen Amts (1914–1920), https://perspectivia.net/servlets/MCRFileNodeServlet/pnet_derivate_00005699/liebau_aufwiegelungen.pdf.

Liebau, Heike, 2019b, Navigating Knowledge, Negotiating Positions: The Kheiri Brothers on Nation and Islam, *Geschichte und Gesellschaft*, 45, 3, 341–61.

Liebau, Heike, 2020, South Asian Muslims and German Scholars in Berlin 1915–1930, *Comparative Studies of South Asia, Africa and the Middle East*, 40, 2, 309–21.

Liebau, Heike, 2022, 'Undertakings and Instigations': The Berlin Indian Independence Committee in the Files of the Political Archive of the Federal Foreign Office (1914–1920), https://www.projekt-mida.de/reflexicon/undertakings-and-instigations/.

Lubinski, Christina, 2014, Liability of Foreigners in Historical Context: German Business in Preindependence India (1880–1940), *Enterprise and Society*, 15, 4, 722–58.

Lüders, Heinrich, 1935, Indien. In Hans Heinrich Schaeder (ed.), *Der Orient und Wir. Sechs Vorträge des Deutschen Orient Vereins, Berlin Oktober 1934 bis Februar 1935*, Berlin: De Gruyter (reprint 2020), 68–92.

Ludwig, Botho, 1942, *Indiens Weg zur Freiheit*, Berlin: Walter Titz Verlag.

Lufft, Hermann, 1936, *Das Empire in Verteidigung und Angriff*, Reichenau i. Sa.: Schneider.

Lufft, Hermann, 1940, *Das Empire gegen Europa*, Berlin: Junker & Dunnhaupt.

Lufft, Hermann, 1942, *Die Wirtschaft Indiens*, Heidelberg: Kurt Vowinckel.

McGetchin, Douglas T., 2009, *Indology, Indomania and Orientalism: Ancient India's Rebirth in Modern Germany*, Madison, NJ: Fairleigh Dickinson University Press.

McGetchin, Douglas T., 2010, Indo-German Connections, Critical and Hermeneutical, in the First World War, *The Comparatist*, 34, 1, 95–126.

Mangat, Gurbachan Singh, 1986, *The Tiger Strikes: An Unwritten Chapter of Netaji's Life History*, Ludhiana: Gagan.

Manjapra, Kris, 2014, *Age of Entanglement: German and Indian Intellectuals across Empire*, Cambridge, MA: Harvard University Press.

Marchand, Suzanne, 2007, Nazism, "Orientalism" and Humanism. In Wolfgang Bialas, Anson Rabinbach (eds), *Nazi Germany and the Humanities*, Oxford: Oneworld, 267–305.

Marchand, Suzanne, 2009, *German Orientalism in the Age of Empire: Religion, Race and Scholarship*, Cambridge: Cambridge University Press.

Marchand, Suzanne, 2022, The "Orient" and "Us": Making Ancient Oriental Studies Relevant during the Nazi Regime. In Bernard M. Levinson, Robert P. Erickson (eds), *The Betrayal of the Humanities: The University during the Third Reich*, Bloomington, IN: Indiana University Press, 64–113.

Mehrtens, Herbert, 1980, Das 'Dritte Reich' in der Naturwissenschaftsgeschichte: Literaturbericht und Problemskizze. In Herbert Mehrtens, Steffen Richter (eds), *Naturwissenschaft, Technik und NS Ideologie. Beiträge zur Wissenschaftsgeschichte des Dritten Reiches*, Frankfurt am Main: Suhrkamp, 15–87.

Mehrtens, Herbert, 1994, Kollaborationsverhältnisse. Natur und Technikwissenschaften im NS-Staat und ihre Historie. In Christoph Meinel, Peter Voswinckel (eds), *Medizin, Naturwissenschaft, Technik und Nationalsozialismus. Kontinuitäten und Diskontinuitäten*, Stuttgart: GNT, 13–32.

Messerschmidt, Manfred, 1969, *Die Wehrmacht im NS-Staat. Zeit der Indoktrination*, Hamburg: Deckers Verlag.

Michaels, Axel, 2022, Sheldon Pollock and German Indology. In Hans Harder, Dhruv Raina (eds), *Disciplines and Movements: Conversations between India and the German-Speaking World*, Hyderabad: Orient Blackswan, 85–104.

Michels, Eckard, 2005, *Von der Deutschen Akademie zum Goethe Institut. Sprach und auswärtige Kulturpolitik 1923–60*, München: R. Oldenbourg.

Morgenbrod, Birgit, Merkenich, Stephanie, 2008, *Das Deutsche Rote Kreuz unter der NS-Diktatur, 1933–1945*, Paderborn: Schöningh.

Motadel, David, 2014, *Islam and Nazi Germany's War*, Cambridge, MA: The Belknap Press of Harvard University Press.

Motadel, David, 2019, Global Authoritarian Moment and the Revolt against Empire. *American Historical Review*, June, 843–77.

Mukharji, Projit Bihari, 2022, *Brown Skins, White Coats: Race Science in India 1920–1966*, Chicago, IL: University of Chicago Press.

Mukherjee, Haridas, 1953, *Benoy Kumar Sarkar: A Study*, Calcutta: National Council of Education, Bengal.

Mukherjee, Tapan, 1998, *Taraknath Das: Life and Letters of a Revolutionary in Exile*, Calcutta: National Council of Education, Bengal.

Müller, Rolf-Dieter, 2007, *An der Seite der Wehrmacht. Hitlers ausländische Helfer beim 'Kreuzzug gegen den Bolschewismus, 1941–1945*, München: C.H. Links.

Narten, Johanna, 2002, Paul Thieme (18.3.2005–24.4.2001). *Jahrbuch der Bayerischen Akademie der Wissenschaften*, 311–17, https://web.archive.org/web/20071213034922/http://www.badw. de/publikationen/sonstige/nachrufe/2002/Thieme.pdf.

Nehring, Andreas, 2003, *Orientalismus und Mission: die Repräsentation der tamilischen Gesellschaft und Religion durch Leipziger Missionare 1840–1940*, Wiesbaden: Harrassowitz.

Oesterheld, Joachim, 2000, Die Indische Legion in Frankreich. In Gerhard Höpp, Brigitte Reinwald (eds), *Fremdeinsätze. Afrikaner und Asiaten in europäischen Kriegen, 1914–1945*, Berlin: Das Arabische Buch, 209–26.

Oesterheld, Joachim, 2005, British Policy towards German-Speaking Emigrants in India 1939–1945. In Anil Bhatti, Johannes H. Voigt (eds), *Jewish Exile in India 1933–1945*, Delhi: Manohar, 25–44.

Oesterheld, Joachim, 2010, Lohia as a Doctoral Student in Berlin, *Economic and Political Weekly*, 45, 40, 85–91.

Oesterheld, Joachim, 2015, The Last Chapter of the Indian Legion, *Südasien-Chronik—South Asia Chronicle*, 5, 120–43.

Olivelle, Patrick, 2013, *King, Governance and Law in Ancient India: Kautilya's Arthasastra*, New York: Oxford University Press.

Ortmeyer, Benjamin, 2013, *Indoktrination. Rassismus und Antisemitismus in der Nazi-Schülerzeitschrift 'Hilf mit!' (1933–1944). Analyse und Dokumente*, Weinheim: Beltz Juventa.

Padfield, Peter, 1991, *Himmler: Reichsführer SS*. New York: Henry Holt & Company.

Paletschek, Sylvia, 2010, Was heißt 'Weltgeltung deutscher Wissenschaft?' Modernisierungsleistungen und -defizite der Universitäten im Kaiserreich. In Michael Grüttner, Rüdiger Hachtmann, Konrad H. Jarausch, Jürgen John, Matthias Middell (eds), *Gebrochene Wissenschaftskulturen. Universität und Politik im 20. Jahrhundert*, Göttingen: Vandenhoeck and Ruprecht, 29–54.

Parzer, Robert, 2015, Krankenmord im besetzten Polen, https://kmibp.hypotheses.org/ author/kmibp.

Pax, Elpidius, 1950, Otto Strauß, *Zeitschrift der Deutschen Morgenländischen Gesellschaft*, 100, 1, 42–8.

Petke, Stefan, 2021, *Muslime in der Wehrmacht und Waffen SS. Rekrutierung-Ausbildung-Einsatz*, Berlin: Metropol.

Pfeffer, Karl Heinz, 1942, Begriff und Methode der Auslandswissenschaften, *Jahrbuch der Weltpolitik*, 884–96.

Poewe, Karla O., 2006, *New Religion and the Nazis*, New York: Routledge.

Poewe, Karla O., Hexham, Irving, 2005, Jakob Wilhelm Hauer's New Religion and National Socialism. *Journal of Contemporary Religion*, 20, 195–215.

Pollock, Sheldon, 1993, Deep Orientalism? Notes on Sanskrit and Power beyond the Raj. In Carol A. Breckenridge, Peter van der Veer (eds), *Orientalism and the Post-Colonial*

Predicament: Perspectives on South Asia, Philadelphia, PA: University of Pennsylvania Press, 76–133.

Pollock, Sheldon, 2002, Ex Oriente Nox: Indologie im nationalsozialistischen Staat. In Sebastian Conrad, Shalini Randeria (eds), *Jenseits des Eurozentrismus: Postkolonialen Perspektiven in den Geschichts- und Kulturwissenschaften*, Frankfurt am Main: Campus, 335–71.

Rahn, Werner, 2005, Wikelriede, Opferkämper oder Sturmwikinger? Zu besonderen Einsatzformen der Deutsche Kriegsmarine 1944/45. In Werner Rahn (ed.), *Deutsche Marinen im Wandel: Vom Symbol nationaler Einheit zum Instrument Internationaler Sicherheit*, München: Oldenbourg, 503–24.

Raina, Dhruv, 2022, Late Colonial India and Weimar Germany. In Hans Harder, Dhruv Raina (eds), *Disciplines and Movements: Conversations between India and the German-Speaking World*, Hyderabad: Orient Blackswan, 61–84.

Rennstich, Karl, 1992, *Der Deutsche Glaube. Jakob Wilhelm Hauer (1881–1962): ein Ideologe des Nationalsozialismus*, Stuttgart: Evangelische Zentralstelle für Weltanschauungsfragen Information Nr. 121.

Rose, Eugen, 1979, *Azad Hind, ein europäisches Indermärchen oder die 1299 Tage der Indischen Legion in Europa*, Wuppertal: Bhaiband Verlag.

Rosenberg, Alfred, 1934, Der Mythus des 20. Jahrhunderts. Eine Wertung der seelisch-geistigen Gestaltenkämpfe unserer Zeit. 33–34 Auflage, München: Hoheneichen.

Roy, Baijayanti, 2016a, *The Making of a Gentleman Nazi: Albert Speer's Politics of History in the Federal Republic of Germany*, Frankfurt am Main: Peter Lang.

Roy, Baijayanti, 2016b, Friedrich Max Müller and the Emergence of Identity Politics in India and Germany, *Publications of the English Goethe Society*, 85, 217–28.

Roy, Baijayanti, 2017a, Völkisch Indology. In Michael Fahlbusch, Ingo Haar, Alexander Pinwinkler (eds), *Handbuch der Völkischen Wissenschaften*, Berlin: De Gruyter Oldenbourg, 1190–7.

Roy, Baijayanti, 2017b, Leopold von Schroeder. In Michael Fahlbusch, Ingo Haar, Alexander Pinwinkler (eds), *Handbuch der Völkischen Wissenschaften*, Berlin: De Gruyter Oldenbourg, 737–41.

Roy, Baijayanti, 2019, The Past Is Indeed a Different Country: Perception of Holocaust in India. In Anja Ballis, Markus Gloe (eds), Holocaust Education Revisited: Wahrnehmung und Vermittlung. Fiktion und Fakten. Medialität und Digitalität, Wiesbaden: Springer VS, 209–17.

Roy, Baijayanti, 2021, India Institute of the Deutsche Akademie (1928–45), https://www.projekt-mida.de/wp-content/uploads/2021/02/Roy-Baijayanti-India-Institute-of-the-Deutsche-Akademie-1928-45.pdf.

Roy, Baijayanti, 2022a, At the Crossroads of Anti-Colonialism, Axis Propaganda and International Communism: The Periodical *Azad Hind* in Nazi Germany, *Media History*, 29, 4, 537–53.

Roy, Baijayanti, 2022b, Pragmatism Paves the Way? A Scholar's Adventurous Exit from Nazi Germany, *Jahrbuch für Universitätsgeschichte*, 22, 11–29.

Roy, Baijayanti, 2023a, The Bengali Society of German Culture (Bangiya Jarman Vidya Samsad) in German Archives, https://perspectivia.net/receive/pnet_mods_00005840.

Roy, Baijayanti, 2023b, Knowledge of India as an Instrument of Nazi Politics: Ludwig Alsdorf, German Indology and Indian Anti-Colonialism, *NTM Zeitschrift für Geschichte der Wissenschaften, Tchnik und Medizin*, 31, 275–306.

Roy, Baijayanti, 2024, Hakenkreuz, Swastika and Crescent: The Religious Factor in Nazi Cultural Politics Regarding India. In Isabella Schwaderer, Gerdien Jonker (eds), *Religious Entanglements between Germans and Indians, 1800–1945*, Cham: Palgrave Macmillan, 253–82.

Rudiger, Karlheinz, 1941, Die "Weltpolitische Bücherei", *Nationalsozialistische Monatshefte*, 12, 2, 74–5.

Rusinek, Bernd A., 2000, 'Wald und Baum in der arisch-germanischen Geistes und Kulturgeschichte'—Ein Forschungsprojekt des 'Ahnenerbe' der SS 1937–1945. In Albrecht Lehmann, Klaus Schriewer (eds), *Der Wald—Ein deutscher Mythos? Perspektiven eines Kulturthemas*, Berlin: Dietrich Reimer Verlag, 267–353.

Said, Edward, 1978, *Orientalism*, London: Penguin Books (2003 edition).

Sardella, Ferdinando, 2013, *Modern Hindu Personalism: The History, Life and Thought of Bhaktisiddhanta Saraswati*, New York: Oxford University Press.

Sardella, Ferdinando, 2019, Bhaktisiddhanta Sarasvati and ISCKON. In Torkel Brekke (ed.), *Modern Hinduism*, Oxford: Oxford University Press, 72–92.

Sareen, Tilak Raj, 1999, Indian Responses to Holocaust. In Anil Bhatti, Johannes H. Voight (eds), *Jewish Exile in India 1933–1945*, New Delhi: Manohar in association with Max Mueller Bhavan, 55–63.

Sartori, Andrew, 2010, Beyond Culture-Contact and Colonial Discourse: Germanism in Colonial Bengal. In Shruti Kapila (ed.), *An Intellectual History for India*, Cambridge: Cambridge University Press, 68–84.

Schatz, Adam, 2019, Orientalism Then and Now, https://www.nybooks.com/online/2019/05/20/orientalism-then-and-now/.

Schmul, Hans-Walter, 2005, *Grenzüberschreitungen. Kaiser Wilhelm Institut für Anthropologie, menschliche Erblehre und Eugenik 1927–1945*, Göttingen: Wallstein.

Schnabel, Reimund, 1968, *Tiger und Schakal: Deutsche Indienpolitik 1941–1943*, Vienna: Europa Verlag.

Scholten, Dirk, 2001, *Sprachverbreitungspolitik des nationalsozialistischen Deutschlands*, Frankfurt am Main: Peter Lang.

Schöttler, Peter (ed.), 1997, *Geschichtsschreibung als Legitimationswissenschaft, 1918–1945*, Frankfurt am Main: Suhrkamp.

Schreiber, Carsten, 2019, Lebensgebiets-Nachrichtendienst. Das Amt III des Reichssicherheitshauptamtes. In Michael Wildt (ed.), *Das Reichssicherheitshauptamt. NS-Terror-Zentrale im Zweiten Weltkrieg*, Berlin: Hentrich & Hentrich, 29–52.

Schreiber, Maximillian, 2008, *Walther Wüst, Dekan und Rektor der Universität München 1935–1945*, München: Herbert Utz Verlag.

Schüring, Michael, 2006, *Minervas verstoßene Kinder. Vertriebene Wissenschaftler und die Vergangenheitspolitik der Max-Planck-Gesellschaft*, Göttingen: Wallstein.

Sebastian, Luna, 2018, Spaces on the Temporal Move: Weimar Geopolitik and the Vision of an Indian Science of the State, 1924–1945, *Global Intellectual History*, 3, 2, 231–53.

Seidt, Hans Ulrich, 2002, *Berlin Kabul Moskau. Oskar Ritter von Niedermayer und Deutschlands Geopolitik*, München. Universitas.

Sen, Satadru, 2015, *Benoy Kumar Sarkar: Restoring the Nation to the World*, New Delhi: Routledge.

Sengupta, Indra, 2005, *From Salon to Discipline: State, University and Indology in Germany, 1821–1914*, Heidelberg: Ergon Verlag.

Sharma, Jyotirmay, 2007, History as Revenge and Retaliation: Rereading Savarkar's "The War of Independence of 1857", *Economic and Political Weekly*, 42, 19, 1717–19.

Sharma, Jyotirmaya, 2013, A Restatement of Religion: Swami Vivekananda and the Making of Hindu Nationalism, New Haven, CT: Yale University Press.

Singh, Gajendra, 2006, The Anatomy of Dissent in the Military of Colonial India during the First and the Second World Wars, *Edinburgh Papers in South Asian Studies*, 20, 2–45.

Sinha, D.P., Coon, Carleton S., 1963, Biraja Sankar Guha, 1894–1961, *American Anthropologist*, 65, 2, 382–7. https://www.academia.edu/9847012/Obituary_of_B_S_Guha.

Slaje, Walter, 2010, Review of Stuchlik 2009. *Asiatische Studien/Études Asiatiques*, 64, 447–62.

Söhnen-Thieme, Renate, 2003, Paul Thieme (1905–2001): Ordinarius für Indologie und Vergleichende Religionswissenschaft an der Universität Tübingen 1960–1973. In Heidrun Brückner et al. (eds), *Indienforschung im Zeitenwandel. Analyse und Dokumente zur Indologie und Religionswissenschaft in Tübingen*, Tübingen: Attempto Verlag, 251–80.

Spang, Christian W., 2013, *Karl Haushofer und Japan. Die Rezeption seiner geopolitischen Theorien in der deutschen und japanischen Politik*, Munich: Iudicium.

Spies Otto, Bannerth, Ernst, 1945, *Lehrbuch der Hindustani Sprache*, Leipzig: Harrassowitz.

Steinweis, Alan, 2022, The History of the Humanities in the Third Reich. In Bernard M. Levinson, Robert P. Erickson (eds), *The Betrayal of the Humanities: The University during the Third Reich*, Bloomington, IN: Indiana University Press, 41–63.

Stier, Antje, 2015, Die Reichsschrifttumskammer, https://www.dhm.de/lemo/kapitel/ns-regime/kunst-und-kultur/reichsschrifttumskammer.html.

Stoecker, Holger, 2002, Das Seminar für Orientalische Sprachen. In Ulrich van der Heyden, Joachim Zeller (eds), *Kolonialmetropole Berlin. Eine Spurensuche*, Berlin: BeBra.

Strehle, Stephen, 2011, The Nazis and the German Metaphysical Tradition of Voluntarism, *The Review of Metaphysics*, 65, 1, 113–37.

Stuchlik, Jakob, 2009, Der arische Ansatz. Erich Frauwallner und der Nationalsozialismus, Wien: Verlag der Österreichischen Akademie der Wissenschaften.

Stuchlik, Jakob, 2011, Rejoinder to Slaje 2010, *Asiatische Studien/Études Asiatiques*, 65, 287–308.

Szabo, Aniko, 2000, *Vertreibung, Rückkehr, Wiedergutmachung. Göttinger Hochschullehrer im Schatten des Nationalsozialismus*, Göttingen: Wallstein.

Tenorth, Elmar H., 1993, Bildung und Wissenschaft im 'Dritten Reich'. In Karl Dietrich Bracher, Hans-Adolf Jacobsen, Manfred Funke (eds), *Deutschland 1933-1945. Neue Studien zur nationalsozialistischen Herrschaft, 2. Auflage*, Bonn: Bundeszentrale für Politische Bildung, 240–55.

Thamer, Hans-Ulrich, Daniel Droste, Sabine Happ (eds), 2012, *Die Universitat Munster im Nationalsozialismus. Kontinuitaten und Bruche zwischen 1920 und 1960*, Munster: Aschendorff.

Thapar, Romila, 2019, Multiple Theories about the 'Aryan'. In Romila Thapar, Michael Witzel, Jaya Menon, Kai Friese, Razib Khan (eds), *Which of Us Are Aryans?*, New Delhi: Aleph, 30–93.

Thierfelder, Franz, 1937, *India Institute of the Deutsche Akademie 1928-1937*, Munich: India Institute.

Thierfelder, Franz, 1940a, *Englischer Kulturimperialismus*, Berlin: Junker und Dünnhaupt.

Thierfelder, Franz, 1940b, *Das Freiheitsringen der Indier. Das Britische Reich in Weltpolitik*, Berlin: Junker und Dünnhaupt.

Thierfelder, Franz, 1959, 30 Jahre India Institut München, 1928-58, *Mitteilungen des Instituts für Auslandsbeziehungen 2, Stuttgart 9*.

Toye, Hugh, 1991, *Subhas Chandra Bose: The Springing Tiger*, Mumbai: Jaico.

Trautmann, Thomas R., 1997, Aryans and British India, Berkeley, CA: University of California Press.

Voigt, Johannes H., 1971, Hitler und Indien, *Vierteljahrshefte für Zeitgeschichte*, 19, 1, 33–63.

Vossler, Frank, 2005, *Propaganda in die eigene Truppe. Die Truppenbetreuung in der Wehrmacht 1939-1945*, Paderborn: Schöningh.

Vyas, Mukund Rai, 1942, *Männer und Mächte in Indien*, Heidelberg: Kurt Vowinckel Verlag.

Vyas, Mukund Rai, 1982, *Passage through a Turbulent Era: Historical Reminiscences of the Fateful Years 1937-47*, Bombay: Indo-Foreign Publications & Publicity.

Waddington, Lorna Louise, 2007, *Hitler's Crusade: Bolshevism and the Myth of the International Jewish Conspiracy*, London: I.B. Tauris.

Wagner, Reinhard, 1926, *Bengalische Erzähler. Der Sieg der Seele*, Berlin: Weltgeist-Bücher.

Wagner, Reinhard, 1930, *Bengalische Texte in Urschrift und Umschrift* (= Lehrbücher des Seminars für Orientalische Sprachen zu Berlin, Band 33), Berlin: De Gruyter.

Wagner, Reinhard, 1933, *Bengalische Texte in der Aussprache des Standard Colloquial*, Berlin: De Gruyter.

Wassiltschikow, Marie ['Missie'], 1991, *Die Berliner Tagebücher 1940-1945*, trans. Elke Jesset, Munich: Der Goldman Verlag (second edition).

Weidemann Diethelm, Günther, Lothar, 2000, Das Indische-Infanterie Regiment 900. Historische Realitäten und subjektive Wahrnehmungen. In Gerhard Höpp, Brigitte Reinwald (eds), *Fremdeinsätze. Afrikaner und Asiaten in europäischen Kriegen, 1914-1945*, Berlin: Verlag Das Arabische Buch, 199–208.

Weigelt, Andreas, 2001, *'Umschulungslager existieren nicht!' Zur Geschichte der Sovietische Speziallagers Nr. 6 in Jamlitz 1945-47*, Potsdam: Brandenburgische Landeszentrale für politische Bildung.

Werner, Kirstin, 2014, *Zwischen Neutralität und Propaganda. Französisch Dolmetscher im Nationalsozialismus*, Berlin: Frank & Timme.

Werth, Alexander, 1971, *Der Tiger Indiens. Subhas Chandra Bose. Ein Leben für die Freiheit des Subkontinents*, München/Esslingen: Bechtle.

Wijeyeratne, Roshan de Silva, 2014, Nation, Constitutionalism and Buddhism in Sri Lanka, Routledge Contemporary South Asia Series, Vol. 72, New York: Routledge.

Wildt, Michael (ed.), 2016, *Nachrichtendienst, politische Elite und Mordeinheit: Der Sicherheitsdienst des Reichsführers SS*, Hamburg: Hamburger Edition HIS.

Wildt, Michael, 2019, *Das Reichssicherheitshauptamt: NS-Terror-Zentrale im Zweiten Weltkrieg*, Berlin: Hentrich & Hentrich.

Winter, Miriam, 2012, *Das Dolmetscherwesen im Dritten Reich. Gleichschaltung und Indoktrinierung*, Frankfurt am Main: Peter Lang.

Witzel, Michael, 1997, Obituary Karl Hoffmann (1915–1996), *Indo Iranian Journal*, 40, 3, 245–53.

Wüst, Walter, 1939, Die Deutsche Aufgabe der Indologie, *Deutsche Kultur im Leben der Völker. Mitteilungen der deutschen Akademie*, 3, 339–48.

Wüst, Walter, 1940, Überlieferung als Völkische Kraftquelle, *Die Wissenschaft im Lebenskampf des deutschen Volkes. Festschrift zum fünfzehnjährigen Bestehen der Deutschen Akademie*, 5, 5, 13–30.

Wüst, Walter, 1941, *Indogermanisches Bekenntnis. Rede gehalten am 5. Juli 1941 zur feierlichen Übernahme des Rektorates der Ludwig Maximilians Universität München*, München: Universitäts Buchdruckerei Dr C. Wolf & Sohn.

Zachariah, Benjamin, 2014, A Voluntary *Gleischschaltung*? Perspectives from India towards a Non-Eurocentric Understanding of Fascism, *Transcultural Studies*, December, 63–100.

Zachariah, Benjamin, 2015, At the Fuzzy Edges of Fascism: Framing the Volk in India, *South Asia: Journal of South Asian Studies*, 38, 4, 639–55.

Zachariah, Benjamin, 2022, Falling into a Brown Study: Völkisch Nationalism, Indo-Nazism, and Historical Translations. In Hans Harder, Dhruv Raina (eds), *Disciplines and Movements: Conversations between India and the German-Speaking World*, Hyderabad: Orient Blackswan, 105–28.

Zöllner, Hans-Bernd, 2000, '*Der Feind meines Feindes ist mein Freund'. Subhas Chandra Bose und das zeitgenössische Deutschland unter dem Nationalsozialismus 1933–1943*, Münster: LIT Verlag.

Index

Since the index has been created to work across multiple formats, indexed terms for which a page range is given (e.g., 52–53, 66–70, etc.) may occasionally appear only on some, but not all of the pages within the range.